Michel Foucault, acknowledged as the preeminent philosopher of France in the seventies and eighties, continues to have enormous impact throughout the world in many disciplines.

Arnold I. Davidson is a professor at the University of Chicago and at the University of Pisa. He is the author of *The Emergence of Sexuality: Historical Epistemology and the Formation of Concepts* and coeditor of the anthology *Michel Foucault: Philosophie.*

Translator Graham Burchell has written essays on Michel Foucault and was an editor of *The Foucault Effect.*

Psychiatric Power

MICHEL FOUCAULT

Psychiatric Power

LECTURES AT THE COLLÈGE DE FRANCE, 1973–1974

Edited by Jacques Lagrange
General Editors: François Ewald and Alessandro Fontana
English Series Editor: Arnold I. Davidson

Translated by Graham Burchell

PICADOR
NEW YORK

 Printed in the United States of America. For information, address Picador, 175 Fifth Avenue, New York, N.Y. 10010.

www.picadorusa.com

For information on Picador Reading Group Guides, please contact Picador.
E-mail: readinggroupguides@picadorusa.com

Library of Congress Cataloging-in-Publication Data

Foucault, Michel, 1926–1984.
Psychiatric power : lectures at the Collège de France, 1973–1974 / Michel Foucault ; edited by Jacques Lagrange ; translated by Graham Burchell.
p. cm.
Includes bibliographical references and indexes.
ISBN-13: 978-0-312-20331-3
ISBN-10: 0-312-20331-4
1. Psychiatry—Philosophy. I. Title.

RC437.5 .F6813 2006
616.890092—dc22

2006281876

Originally published in France by Éditions du Seuil/Gallimard

First published in the United States by Palgrave Macmillan

D 10 9 8 7 6 5 4 3

CONTENTS

FOREWORD

MICHEL FOUCAULT TAUGHT AT the Collège de France from January 1971 until his death in June 1984 (with the exception of 1977 when he took a sabbatical year). The title of his chair was "The History of Systems of Thought."

On the proposal of Jules Vuillemin, the chair was created on 30 November 1969 by the general assembly of the professors of the Collège de France and replaced that of "The History of Philosophical Thought" held by Jean Hyppolite until his death. The same assembly elected Michel Foucault to the new chair on 12 April 1970.[1] He was 43 years old.

Michel Foucault's inaugural lecture was delivered on 2 December 1970.[2] Teaching at the Collège de France is governed by particular rules. Professors must provide 26 hours of teaching a year (with the possibility of a maximum of half this total being given in the form of seminars[3]). Each year they must present their original research and this obliges them to change the content of their teaching for each course. Courses and seminars are completely open; no enrolment or qualification is required and the professors do not award any qualifications.[4] In the terminology of the Collège de France, the professors do not have students but only auditors.

Michel Foucault's courses were held every Wednesday from January to March. The huge audience made up of students, teachers, researchers and the curious, including many who came from outside France, required two amphitheaters of the Collège de France. Foucault often complained about the distance between himself and his "public" and of how few exchanges the course made possible.[5] He would have liked a seminar in which real collective work could take place and made a number of attempts to bring this about. In the final years he devoted a long period to answering his auditors' questions at the end of each course.

This is how Gérard Petitjean, a journalist from *Le Nouvel Observateur*, described the atmosphere at Foucault's lectures in 1975:

> When Foucault enters the amphitheater, brisk and dynamic like someone who plunges into the water, he steps over bodies to reach his chair, pushes away the cassette recorders so he can put down his papers, removes his jacket, lights a lamp and sets off at full speed. His voice is strong and effective, amplified by loudspeakers that are the only concession to modernism in a hall that is barely lit by light spread from stucco bowls. The hall has three hundred places and there are five hundred people packed together, filling the smallest free space . . . There is no oratorical effect. It is clear and terribly effective. There is absolutely no concession to improvisation. Foucault has twelve hours each year to explain in a public course the direction taken by his research in the year just ended. So everything is concentrated and he fills the margins like correspondents who have too much to say for the space available to them. At 19.15 Foucault stops. The students rush towards his desk; not to speak to him, but to stop their cassette recorders. There are no questions. In the pushing and shoving Foucault is alone. Foucault remarks: "It should be possible to discuss what I have put forward. Sometimes, when it has not been a good lecture, it would need very little, just one question, to put everything straight. However, this question never comes. The group effect in France makes any genuine discussion impossible. And as there is no feedback, the course is theatricalized. My relationship with the people there is like that of an actor or an acrobat. And when I have finished speaking, a sensation of total solitude . . ."[6]

Foucault approached his teaching as a researcher: explorations for a future book as well as the opening up of fields of problematization were formulated as an invitation to possible future researchers. This is why the courses at the Collège de France do not duplicate the published books. They are not sketches for the books even though both books and courses share certain themes. They have their own status. They arise from a specific discursive regime within the set of Foucault's "philosophical activities." In particular they set out the programme for a genealogy of knowledge/power relations, which are the terms in which he thinks of his work from the beginning of the 1970s, as opposed to the programme of an archeology of discursive formations that previously orientated his work.[7]

The courses also performed a role in contemporary reality. Those who followed his courses were not only held in thrall by the narrative that unfolded week by week and seduced by the rigorous exposition, they also found a perspective on contemporary reality. Michel Foucault's art consisted in using history to cut diagonally through contemporary reality. He could speak of Nietzsche or Aristotle, of expert psychiatric opinion or the Christian pastoral, but those who attended his lectures always took from what he said a perspective on the present and contemporary events. Foucault's specific strength in his courses was the subtle interplay between learned erudition, personal commitment, and work on the event.

With their development and refinement in the 1970s, Foucault's desk was quickly invaded by cassette recorders. The courses—and some seminars—have thus been preserved.

This edition is based on the words delivered in public by Foucault. It gives a transcription of these words that is as literal as possible.[8] We would have liked to present it as such. However, the transition from an oral to a written presentation calls for editorial intervention: At the very least it requires the introduction of punctuation and division into paragraphs. Our principle has been always to remain as close as possible to the course actually delivered.

Summaries and repetitions have been removed whenever it seemed to be absolutely necessary. Interrupted sentences have been restored and faulty constructions corrected. Suspension points indicate that the recording is inaudible. When a sentence is obscure there is a conjectural integration or an addition between square brackets. An asterisk directing the reader to the bottom of the page indicates a significant divergence between the notes used by Foucault and the words actually uttered. Quotations have been checked and references to the texts used are indicated. The critical apparatus is limited to the elucidation of obscure points, the explanation of some allusions and the clarification of critical points. To make the lectures easier to read, each lecture is preceded by a brief summary that indicates its principal articulations.[9]

The text of the course is followed by the summary published by the *Annuaire du Collège de France*. Foucault usually wrote these in June, some time after the end of the course. It was an opportunity for him to pick out retrospectively the intention and objectives of the course. It constitutes the best introduction to the course.

Each volume ends with a "context" for which the course editors are responsible. It seeks to provide the reader with elements of the biographical, ideological, and political context, situating the course within the published work and providing indications concerning its place within the corpus used in order to facilitate understanding and to avoid misinterpretations that might arise from a neglect of the circumstances in which each course was developed and delivered.

Psychiatric Power, the course delivered in 1973 and 1974, is edited by Jacques Lagrange.

A new aspect of Michel Foucault's "œuvre" is published with this edition of the Collège de France courses.

Strictly speaking it is not a matter of unpublished work, since this edition reproduces words uttered publicly by Foucault, excluding the often highly developed written material he used to support his lectures. Daniel Defert possesses Michel Foucault's notes and he is to be warmly thanked for allowing the editors to consult them.

This edition of the Collège de France courses was authorized by Michel Foucault's heirs who wanted to be able to satisfy the strong demand for their publication, in France as elsewhere, and to do this under indisputably responsible conditions. The editors have tried to be equal to the degree of confidence placed in them.

FRANÇOIS EWALD AND ALESSANDRO FONTANA

---

1. Michel Foucault concluded a short document drawn up in support of his candidacy with these words: "We should undertake the history of systems of thought." "Titres et travaux," in *Dits et Écrits, 1954-1988*, four volumes, ed. Daniel Defert and François Ewald (Paris: Gallimard, 1994) vol. 1, p. 846; English translation, "Candidacy Presentation: Collège de France," in *The Essential Works of Michel Foucault, 1954-1984, vol. 1: Ethics: Subjectivity and Truth*, ed. Paul Rabinow, trans. Robert Hurley and others (New York: The New Press, 1997) p. 9.
2. It was published by Gallimard in May 1971 with the title *L'Ordre du discours* (Paris). English translation: "The Order of Discourse," trans. Rupert Swyer, appendix to M. Foucault, *The Archeology of Knowledge* (New York: Pantheon, 1972).
3. This was Foucault's practice until the start of the 1980s.
4. Within the framework of the Collège de France.
5. In 1976, in the vain hope of reducing the size of the audience, Michel Foucault changed the time of his course from 17.45 to 9.00. See the beginning of the first lecture (7 January 1976) of *"Il faut défendre la société". Cours au Collège de France, 1976* (Paris: Gallimard/Seuil, 1997); English translation, *"Society Must be Defended". Lectures at the Collège de France 1975-1976*, trans. David Macey (New York: Picador, 2003).
6. Gérard Petitjean, "Les Grands Prêtres de l'université française," *Le Nouvel Observateur*, 7 April 1975.
7. See especially, "Nietzsche, la généalogie, l'histoire," in *Dits et Écrits*, vol. 2, p. 137. English translation, "Nietzsche, Genealogy, History," trans. Donald F. Brouchard and Sherry Simon in, *The Essential Works of Michel Foucault 1954-1984, vol. 2: Aesthetics, Method, and Epistemology*, ed. James Faubion, trans. Robert Hurley and others (New York: The New Press, 1998), pp. 369-92.
8. We have made use of the recordings made by Gilbert Burlet and Jacques Lagrange in particular. These are deposited in the Collège de France and the Institut Mémoires de l'Édition Contemporaine.
9. At the end of the book, the criteria and solutions adopted by the editors of this year's course are set out in the "Course context."

INTRODUCTION

Arnold I. Davidson

MICHEL FOUCAULT'S CENTRAL CONTRIBUTION to political philosophy was his progressive development and refinement of a new conception of power, one that put into question the two reigning conceptions of power, the juridical conception found in classical liberal theories and the Marxist conception organized around the notions of State apparatus, dominant class, mechanisms of conservation, and juridical superstructure. If the first volume of his history of sexuality, *La Volonté de savoir* (1976), is a culminating point of this dimension of Foucault's work, his courses throughout the 1970s return again and again to the problem of how to analyze power, continually adding historical and philosophical details that help us to see the full import and implications of his analytics of power. At the beginning of the chapter "Méthode" in *La Volonté de savoir* Foucault warns his readers against several misunderstandings that may be occasioned by the use of the word "power," misunderstandings concerning the identity, the form, and the unity of power. Power should not be identified, according to Foucault, with the set of institutions and apparatuses in the State; it does not have the form of rules or law; finally, it does not have the global unity of a general system of domination whose effects would pass through the entire social body. Neither state institutions, nor law, nor general effects of domination constitute the basic elements of an adequate analysis of how power works in modern societies.[1] Without having yet developed all of the tools of his own analysis, *Psychiatric Power* already exhibits Foucault's awareness of the shortcomings of available conceptions of power, and nowhere more clearly than in his own critique of notions implicit or explicit in his *Histoire de la folie*. Foucault's dissatisfaction with his previous analysis of asylum power centers around two basic features of the analysis in *Histoire de la folie*: first, the privileged role he gave to the "perception of madness" instead of starting, as he does in *Psychiatric Power*, from an apparatus of power itself; second, the use of notions that now seem to him to be "rusty locks with which we cannot get very far" and that therefore compromise his analysis of power as it is articulated in *Histoire de la folie*.[2]

As regards this second point, Foucault's critique of his own use of the notions of violence, of institution, and of the family can be seen in retrospect to be an important part of his development of that alternative model of power that will be at the center of *Surveiller et punir* and *La Volonté de savoir*. In effect, Foucault's criticisms here take aim precisely at assumptions concerning the identity, the form, and the unity of power. Rather than thinking of power as the exercise of unbridled violence, one should think of it as the "physical exercise of an unbalanced force" (in the sense of an unequal, non-symmetrical force), but a force that acts within "a rational, calculated, and controlled game of the exercise of power."[3] Instead of conceptualizing psychiatric power in terms of institutions, with their regularities and rules, one has to understand psychiatric practice in terms of "imbalances of power" with the tactical uses of "networks, currents, relays, points of support, differences of potential" that characterize a form of power.[4] Finally, in order to understand the functioning of asylum power, one cannot invoke the paradigm of the family, as if psychiatric power "does no more than reproduce the family to the advantage of, or on the demand of, a form of State control organized by a State apparatus"; there is no foundational model that can be projected onto all levels of society, but rather different strategies that allow relations of power to take on a certain coherence.[5] In *La Volonté de savoir*, with more conceptual precision, Foucault explicitly understands power in terms of a multiplicity of relations of force, of incessant tactical struggles and confrontations that affect the distribution and arrangement of these relations of force, and of the strategies in which these relations of force take effect, with their more general lines of integration, their patterns and crystallizations.[6] And the nominalism advocated in *La Volonté de savoir* is present in practice in *Psychiatric*

Power: power is "the name that one gives to a complex strategic situation in a given society."[7]

The stakes of this nominalism are evident in one of the first theoretical claims about power that Foucault makes in *Psychiatric Power*, a claim that, despite its apparent simplicity, already requires an entire reelaboration of our conception of power:

> ... power is never something that someone possesses, any more than it is something that emanates from someone. Power does not belong to anyone or even to a group; there is only power because there is dispersion, relays, networks, reciprocal supports, differences of potential, discrepancies, etcetera. It is in this system of differences, which have to be analyzed, that power can begin to function.[8]

This claim is the basis of Foucault's later insistence on "the strictly relational character of relationships of power" (and of relationships of resistance), the fact that power "is produced at every moment, in every point, or rather in every relation from one point to another."[9] Foucault was never interested in providing a metaphysics of Power; his aim was an analysis of the techniques and technologies of power, where power is understood as relational, multiple, heterogeneous, and, of course, productive.[10] Foucault went so far as once to proclaim, "power, it does not exist" so as to emphasize that, from his perspective, it is always bundles of relations, modifiable relations of force, never power in itself, that is to be studied—that is to say, to render the exercise of power intelligible, one should take up the point of view of "the moving base of relations of force that, by their inequality, continually lead to states of power, but always local and unstable."[11] As late as 1984, when the focus of his interests had already shifted, he stressed this point yet again: "I hardly employ the word power, and if I occasionally do, it is always as a shorthand with respect to the expression that I always use: relations of power."[12]

I believe that it is precisely this relational conception of power, with all of its accompanying instruments of analysis, that allows Foucault to give his extraordinary historical reinterpretation of the problem of hysteria at the conclusion of *Psychiatric Power.* When in the final part of his lecture of 6 February Foucault takes up Charcot's treatment of hysterics and what he names "the great maneuvers of hysteria," he announces the angle of analysis he will adopt: "I will not try to analyze this in terms of the history of hysterics any more than in terms of psychiatric knowledge of hysterics, but rather in terms of battle, confrontation, reciprocal encirclement, of the laying of mirror traps [by which Foucault means traps that reflect one another], of investment and counter-investment, of struggle for control between doctors and hysterics."[13] All of the terms in this description answer to his new analytics of power, with its "pseudo-military vocabulary," that will provide the framework for his examination of a wide variety of historical phenomena during the 1970s.[14] And when he sets aside the idea of an epidemic of hysteria (a scientific-epistemological notion) in favor of an analysis focused on "the maelstrom of this battle" (*le tourbillon de cette bataille*) that surrounds hysterical symptoms, one cannot help but hear an anticipation of the last line of *Surveiller et punir* where Foucault tells us that in those apparatuses of normalization that are intended "to provide relief, to cure, to help" one should hear "the rumbling of battle" (*le grondement de la bataille*).[15] It is this rumbling, this maelstrom of battle that Foucault's perspective renders visible, a struggle that is effaced in a purely epistemological analysis and that is left out of sight within a theory of power built on a juridical and negative vocabulary. (Hence the way in which the "repressive hypothesis" renders imperceptible the multiplicity of possible points of resistance.) To take just one example, Foucault's analytics restores this relational dimension of battle to the great problem of simulation that was so crucial to the history of psychiatry; it enables him to treat simulation not as a theoretical problem, but as a process by which the mad actually responded to psychiatric power, a kind of "anti-power," that is a modification of the relations of force, in the face of the mechanisms of psychiatric power—thus the appearance of simulation not as a pathological phenomenon, but as a phenomenon of struggle.[16] As a result, from this point of view, hysterical simulation becomes "the militant underside [the militant reverse side] of psychiatric power" and hysterics can be seen as "the true militants of antipsychiatry."[17] Moreover, the elaboration of this microphysics of power does not require

Foucault to ignore the epistemological dimensions of the history of psychiatry, the discursive practices of psychiatric knowledge. On the contrary, it allows him to place these practices within a political history of truth, to reconnect these practices to the functioning of an apparatus of power, to link them to a level "that would allow discursive practice to be grasped at precisely the point where it is formed."[18] *Psychiatric Power* can be read as a kind of experiment in method, one that responds in historical detail to a set of questions that permeated the genealogical period of Foucault's work:

> . . . to what extent can an apparatus of power produce statements, discourses and, consequently, all the forms of representation that may then [. . .] derive from it . . . How can this deployment of power, these tactics and strategies of power, give rise to assertions, negations, experiments (*expériences*), and theories, in short to a game of truth?[19]

At the very end of his course, when Foucault returns to the relations of power between hysteric and doctor, to hysterical resistance to medical power, the scene of sexuality is center stage. But the introduction of sexuality into this scenario does not derive from the "power" of the doctors, but rather from the hysterics themselves, as their putting into play of a point of resistance within the strategic field of existing relations of power. As a counter-attack to the medical need to find an etiology for hysteria that will give its symptoms a pathological status, and more specifically (given the distributions of power-knowledge that surround the hysterical body) to find a trauma that will function as a "kind of invisible and pathological lesion which makes all of this a well and truly morbid whole," the hysteric will respond with the counter-maneuver of a recounting of her sexual life, with all of its possible traumatism, thereby effecting a redistribution of force relations and a new configuration of power.

> . . . what will the patients do with this injunction to find the trauma that persists in the symptoms? Into the breach opened by this injunction they will push their life, their real, everyday life,

> that is to say their sexual life. It is precisely this sexual life that they will recount, that they will connect up with the hospital and endlessly reactualize in the hospital.[20]

And Foucault draws the following remarkable conclusion, which needs to be underlined and related, after the fact, to the context of his later history of sexuality:

> It seems to me that this kind of bacchanal, this sexual pantomime, is not the as yet undeciphered residue of the hysterical syndrome. My impression is that this sexual bacchanal should be taken as the counter-maneuver by which the hysterics responded to the ascription of trauma: You want to find the cause of my symptoms, the cause that will enable you to pathologize them and enable you to function as a doctor; you want this trauma, well, you will get all my life, and you won't be able to avoid hearing me recount my life and, at the same time, seeing me mime my life anew and endlessly reactualize it in my attacks!
>
> So this sexuality is not an indecipherable remainder but the hysteric's victory cry, the last maneuver by which they finally get the better of the neurologists and silence them: If you want symptoms too, something functional; if you want to make your hypnosis natural and each of your injunctions to cause the kind of symptoms you can take as natural; if you want to use me to denounce the simulators, well then, you really will have to hear what I want to say and see what I want to do![21]

This victory cry of the hysteric, although a genuine cry of victory, is not a definitive cry. Like all triumphs within the field of mobile and reversible power relations, one can be sure that it will be met by further tactical interventions, actions intended to modify the new disposition of force relations, rearranging yet again the existing relations of power. If it is the hysteric herself who, from within the field of power relations, imposes the sexual body on the neurologists and doctors, these latter, according to Foucault, could respond with one of two possible attitudes. They could either make use of these sexual connotations to discredit hysteria as a genuine illness, as did Babinski, or they could attempt to circumvent this new hysterical maneuver by surrounding it once more medically—"this new investment will be the medical, psychiatric, and psychoanalytic take over of sexuality."[22] History has taught us that the second response would be the triumphant one. And the first volume of Foucault's history of sexuality picks up the battle where *Psychiatric Power* left off, with the codification of *scientia sexualis* and the solidification of the apparatus of sexuality, with a new medical victory cry in favor of sexuality. Indeed, the "hysterisation" of women's bodies is one of the four great strategic ensembles with respect to sex that Foucault singles out as having attained an historically noteworthy "efficacity" in the order of power and "productivity" in the order of knowledge.[23] The effects of an initially disruptive recounting of her sexual life by the hysteric will be reorganized by means of the constitution of a scientific modality of confession; the traumas of sexuality will become integrated into those procedures of individualization that produce our subjection.[24] If Charcot could not see or speak of this sexuality, the later history of psychiatry would find it everywhere, would insist on putting sex into discourse, would enjoin its patients to speak of their sexuality. When the science of the subject began to revolve around the question of sex, the hysteric's victory was effectively countered by new tactics and strategies of power, and the reactualization of one's sexual life was divested of its potential of resistance and became a practice now crucial to the functioning of psychiatric power. That is why Foucault's historico-political project will be "to define the strategies of power which are immanent to this will to know" that continues to encircle sexuality.[25]

It is in this light that we should read the last sentence of *Psychiatric Power*, a phrase that might have seemed enigmatic when pronounced by Foucault on 6 February 1974, but whose force is quite clear in the context of *La Volonté de savoir*:

> By breaking down the door of the asylum, by ceasing to be mad so as to become patients, by finally getting through to a true doctor, that is to say the neurologist, and by providing him with genuine functional symptoms, *the hysterics, to their greater pleasure, but doubtless to our greater misfortune, gave rise to a medicine of sexuality.*[26]

This final diagnosis, namely that the great pleasure of the hysteric's victory became the great misfortune of our subjection to the apparatus of sexuality, focuses our attention on that moving stratum of force relations that underlies the instability, the transformability, of relations of power/resistance. If today the sexual body is no longer primarily the hysterical body, but rather, let us say, the perverse body, it remains up to us to learn to hear anew the rumbling of the current battle. Only in this way will we be able "to determine what is the principal danger" and "to render problematic everything that is habitual"—thus we will be able to put into movement the points of support for *our* counter-attack against the apparatus of sexuality.[27]

---

1. Michel Foucault, *Histore de la sexualité*, vol. 1, *La Volonté de savoir* (Paris: Gallimard, 1976), p. 121.
2. This volume, pp. 13-14.
3. This volume, p. 14.
4. This volume, p. 15.
5. This volume, p. 16.
6. Michel Foucault, *La Volonté de savoir*, pp. 121-122.
7. Ibid., p. 123.
8. This volume, p. 4.
9. Michel Foucault, *La Volonté de savoir*, pp. 126, 122. It is this relational conception of power that makes it possible for Foucault to argue that "where there is power, there is resistance...", Ibid., pp. 125-127. For a more detailed discussion, see my introduction to the second part of *Michel Foucault. Philosophie. Anthologie établie et presentée par Arnold I. Davidson et Frédéric Gros*. (Paris: Gallimard, 2004).
10. Michel Foucault, "Précisions sur le pouvoir. Réponses à certaines critiques" in *Dits et écrits II, 1976-1988* (Paris: Gallimard, 2001), p. 630 and "Les mailles du pouvoir" in *Dits et écrits II*, pp. 1005-1008.
11. Michel Foucault, "Le jeu de Michel Foucault" in *Dits et écrits II*, p. 302 and *La Volonté de savoir*, p. 122.
12. Michel Foucault, "L'éthique du souci de soi comme pratique de la liberté" in *Dits et écrits II*, p. 1538.
13. This volume, p. 308.
14. This volume, p. 16.
15. This volume, p. 309 and Michel Foucault, *Surveiller et punir. Naissance de la prison* (Paris: Gallimard, 1975), pp. 359-360.
16. This volume, pp. 136-137.
17. This volume, p. 138 and p. 254.
18. This volume, p. 13.
19. This volume, p. 13.
20. This volume, p. 318.
21. This volume, pp. 322-323.
22. This volume, p. 323.
23. Michel Foucault, *La Volonté de savoir*, p. 137.
24. Ibid., Part III.
25. Ibid., p. 98.
26. This volume, p. 323, my emphasis.
27. Michel Foucault, "À propos de la généalogie de l'éthique: un aperçu du travail en cours" in *Dits et écrits II*, p. 1205 and "À propos de la généalogie de l'éthique: un aperçu du travail en cours" in *Dits et écrits II*, p. 1431. Not many English speaking readers are aware of the fact that there are two versions of this long conversation. The first version was published in English as an appendix to the second edition of H. Dreyfus and P. Rabinow, *Michel Foucault: Beyond Structuralism and Hermeneutics*; when that book was translated into French, Foucault made a number of modifications to this interview. Although the two versions overlap significantly, Foucault's reformulations are of great interest.

TRANSLATOR'S NOTE

IN HIS DESCRIPTION OF the historical figure of "psychiatric power" Foucault frequently uses the term *dispositif*, referring to "disciplinary *dispositifs*" and the "asylum *dispositif*" etcetera. There does not seem to be a satisfactory English equivalent for the particular way in which Foucault uses this term to designate a configuration or arrangement of elements and forces, practices and discourses, power and knowledge, that is both *strategic* and *technical*. On the one hand, in relation to "psychiatric power" the term picks out a sort of strategic game plan for the staging of real "battles" and "confrontations" that involve specific "tactics," "manipulations," "maneuvers," and the overall "tactical disposition" or "deployment" of elements and forces in an organized "battlefield" space. On the other hand, it also refers to a more or less stable "system" of "techniques," "mechanisms," and "devices"; "a sort of apparatus or machinery." I am not entirely happy with some of the existing translations—"deployment," "set up," and even, in the case of Louis Althusser's use of the same term, "dispositive"—and have chosen to translate the word throughout as "apparatus." This has its own drawbacks, the major one being that the same word translates "*appareil*" and perhaps risks confusion with, for example, the notion of "State apparatuses" (*appareils d'État*), from which Foucault clearly wants to distinguish his own analysis. However, it should be said that on occasions Foucault himself uses *appareil* in a way that is difficult to distinguish from his use of *dispositif*. Wherever both words are used in close proximity to each other, or where it seems important to distinguish which word Foucault is using, the English is followed by the French word in brackets. Hopefully, the analyses in which it is embedded will make Foucault's use of the term sufficiently clear.

I have not used existing English translations of authors quoted by Foucault in the lectures, but references to such translations can be found in the notes.

Psychiatric Power

one

7 November 1973

The space of the asylum and disciplinary order. ~ Therapeutic process and "moral treatment." ~ Scenes of curing. ~ Changes made by the course from the approach of Histoire de la folie: *1. From an analysis of "representations" to an "analytics of power"; 2. From "violence" to the "microphysics of power"; 3. From "institutional regularities" to the "arrangements" of power.*

THE TOPIC I PROPOSE to present this year, psychiatric power, is slightly, but not completely, different from the topics I have spoken to you about over the last two years.

I will begin by trying to describe a kind of fictional scene in the following familiar, recognizable setting:

"I would like these homes to be built in sacred forests, in steep and isolated spots, in the midst of great disorder, like at the Grande-Chartreuse, etcetera. Also, before the newcomer arrives at his destination, it would be a good idea if he were to be brought down by machines, be taken through ever new and more amazing places, and if the officials of these places were to wear distinctive costumes. The romantic is suitable here, and I have often said to myself that we could make use of those old castles built over caverns that pass through a hill and open out onto a pleasant little valley ... Phantasmagoria and other resources of physics, music, water, flashes of lightning, thunder, etcetera would be used in turn and, very likely, not without some success on the common man."[1]

This is not the castle of *Cent vingt Journées*.[2] It is a castle in which many more, an almost infinite number of days will be passed; it is Fodéré's description, in 1817, of an ideal asylum. What will take place in this setting? Well, of course, order reigns, the law, and power reigns. Here, in this castle protected by this romantic, alpine setting, which is only accessible by means of complicated machines, and whose very appearance must amaze the common man, an order reigns in the simple sense of a never ending, permanent regulation of time, activities, and actions; an order which surrounds, penetrates, and works on bodies, applies itself to their surfaces, but which equally imprints itself on the nerves and what someone called "the soft fibers of the brain."[3] An order, therefore, for which bodies are only surfaces to be penetrated and volumes to be worked on, an order which is like a great nervure of prescriptions, such that bodies are invaded and run through by order.

"One should not be greatly surprised," Pinel writes, "at the great importance I attach to maintaining calm and order in a home for the insane, and to the physical and moral qualities that such supervision requires, since this is one of the fundamental bases of the treatment of mania, and without it we will obtain neither exact observations nor a permanent cure, however we insist on the most highly praised medicaments."[4]

That is to say, you can see that a certain degree of order, a degree discipline, and regularity, reaching inside the body, are necessary for two things.

On the one hand, they are necessary for the very constitution of medical knowledge, since exact observation is not possible without this discipline, without this order, without this prescriptive schema of regularities. The condition of the medical gaze (*regard médicale*), of its neutrality, and the possibility of it gaining access to the object, in short, the effective condition of possibility of the relationship of objectivity, which is constitutive of medical knowledge and the criterion of its validity, is a relationship of order, a distribution of time, space, and individuals. In actual fact, and I will come back to this elsewhere, we cannot even say of "individuals"; let's just say a certain distribution of bodies, actions, behavior, and of discourses. It is in this well-ordered dispersion that we find the field on the basis of which something like the relationship of the medical gaze to its object, the relationship of objectivity, is possible—a relationship which appears as the effect of the first dispersion constituted by the disciplinary order. Secondly, this disciplinary order, which appears in Pinel's text as the condition for exact observation, is at the same time the condition for permanent cure. That is to say, the therapeutic process itself, the transformation on the basis of which someone who is considered to be ill ceases to be so, can only be produced within this regulated distribution of power. The condition, therefore, of the relationship to the object and of the objectivity of medical knowledge, and the condition of the therapeutic process, are the same: disciplinary order. But this kind of immanent order, which covers the entire space of the asylum, is in reality thoroughly permeated and entirely sustained by a dissymmetry that attaches it imperiously to a single authority which is both internal to the asylum and the point from which the disciplinary distribution and dispersion of time, bodies, actions, and behavior, is determined. This authority within the asylum is, at the same time, endowed with unlimited power, which nothing must or can resist. This inaccessible authority without symmetry or reciprocity, which thus functions as the source of power, as the factor of the order's essential dissymmetry, and which determines that this order always derives from a non reciprocal relationship of power, is obviously medical authority, which, as you will see, functions as power well before it functions as knowledge.

Because, what is the doctor? Well, there he is, the one who appears when the patient has been brought to the asylum by these surprising machines I was just talking about. I know that this is all a fictional description, in the sense that I have not constructed it on the basis of texts coming from a single psychiatrist; if I had used only the texts of a single psychiatrist, the demonstration would not be valid. I have used Fodéré's *Traité du délire*, Pinel's *Traité médico-philosophique* on mania, Esquirol's collected articles in *Des maladies mentales*,[5] and Haslam.[6]

So, how then does this authority without symmetry or limit, which permeates and drives the universal order of the asylum, appear? This is how it appears in Fodéré's text, *Traité du délire* from 1817, that is at that great, prolific moment in the proto-history of eighteenth century psychiatry—Esquirol's great text appears in 1818[7]—the moment when psychiatric knowledge is both inserted within the medical field and assumes its autonomy as a specialty. "Generally speaking, perhaps one of the first conditions of success in our profession is a fine, that is to say noble and manly physique; it is especially indispensable for impressing the mad. Dark hair, or hair whitened by age, lively eyes, a proud bearing, limbs and chest announcing strength and health, prominent features, and a strong and expressive voice are the forms that generally have a great effect on individuals who think they are superior to everyone else. The mind undoubtedly regulates the body, but this is not apparent to begin with and external forms are needed to lead the multitude."[8]

So, as you can see, the figure himself must function at first sight. But, in this first sight, which is the basis on which the psychiatric relationship is built, the doctor is essentially a body, and more exactly he is a quite particular physique, a characterization, a morphology, in which there are the full muscles, the broad chest, the color of the hair, and so on. And this physical presence, with these qualities, which functions as the clause of absolute dissymmetry in the regular order of the asylum, is what determines that the asylum is not, as the psycho-sociologists would say, a rule governed institution; in reality it is a field polarized in terms of an essential dissymmetry of power, which thus assumes its form, its figure, and its physical inscription in the doctor's body itself.

But, of course, the doctor's power is not the only power exercised, for in the asylum, as everywhere else, power is never something that someone possesses, any more than it is something that emanates from someone. Power does not belong to anyone or even to a group; there is only power because there is dispersion, relays, networks, reciprocal supports, differences of potential, discrepancies, etcetera. It is in this system of differences, which have to be analyzed, that power can start to function.

There is, then, a whole series of relays around the doctor, the main ones being the following. First of all there are the supervisors, to whom Fodéré reserves the task of informing on the patients, of being the unarmed, inexpert gaze, the kind of optical canal through which the learned gaze, that is to say the objective gaze of the psychiatrist himself, will be exercised. This relayed gaze, ensured by the supervisors, must also take in the servants, that is to say those who hold the last link in the chain of authority. The supervisor, therefore, is both the master of the last masters and the one whose discourse, gaze, observations and reports must make possible the constitution of medical knowledge. What are supervisors? What must they be? "In a supervisor of the insane it is necessary to look for a well proportioned physical stature, strong and vigorous muscles, a proud and intrepid bearing for certain occasions, a voice with a striking tone when needed. In addition, he must have the strictest integrity, pure moral standards, and a firmness compatible with gentle and persuasive forms (...) and he must be absolutely obedient to the doctor's orders."[9]

The final stage—I skip some of the relays—is constituted by the servants, who hold a very odd power. Actually, the servant is the last relay of the network, of this difference in potential that permeates the asylum on the basis of the doctor's power; he is therefore the power below. But he is not just below because he is at the bottom of the hierarchy; he is also below because he must be below the patient. It is not so much the supervisors above him that he must serve, but the patients themselves; but in this position he must really only pretend to serve them. The servants apparently obey the patients' orders and give them material assistance, but they do so in such a way that, on the one hand, the patients' behavior can be observed from behind, underhand, at the level of the orders they may give, instead of being observed from above, as by the supervisors and the doctor. In a way, the servants will thus set up the patients, and observe them at the level of their daily life and from the side of their exercise of will and their desires; and they will report anything worth noting to the supervisor, who will report it to the doctor. At the same time, when the patient gives orders that must not be carried out, the servant's task—while feigning to be at the patient's service, to obey him and so seeming not to have an autonomous will—must be to not do what the patient requests, and to appeal to the great anonymous authority of the rules or to the doctor's particular will. As a result, the patient who is set up by the servant's observation will find himself outflanked by the doctor's will that he rediscovers when he gives the servant orders, and the patient's encirclement by the doctor's will or by the general regulation of the asylum will be ensured through this pretence of service.

Here is the description of the servants in this scenario:

"§ 398. The servants or warders selected must be big, strong, honest, intelligent, and clean, both personally and in their habits. In order to handle the extreme sensitivity of some of the insane, especially on points of honor, it would almost always be better for the servants to seem to them to be their domestic servants rather than their warders (...). However, since they must not obey the mad, and often are even forced to suppress them, to reconcile the idea of being a servant with a refusal to obey, and to avoid any discord, the supervisor's task will be to insinuate cleverly to the patients that those serving them have been given certain instructions and orders by the doctor, which they cannot exceed without being given direct permission."[10]

So, you have this system of power functioning within the asylum and distorting the general regulative system, a system of power which is secured by a multiplicity, a dispersion, a system of differences and hierarchies, but even more precisely by what could be called a tactical arrangement in which different individuals occupy a definite place and ensure a number of precise functions. You have therefore a tactical functioning of power or, rather, it is this tactical arrangement that enables power to be exercised.

If you go back to what Pinel himself said about the possibility of observation in an asylum, you can see that this observation, which ensures the objectivity and truth of psychiatric discourse, is only possible through a relatively complex tactical arrangement; I say "relatively complex," because what I have just said is still very schematic. But, in fact, if there really is this tactical deployment and so many precautions have to be taken to arrive at something that is, after all, as simple as observation, it is probably because within the asylums field of regulations there is something, a force, that is dangerous. For power to be deployed with all this cunning, or rather, for the asylum's regulated universe to be so obsessed with these kind of relays of power, which falsify and distort this universe, then it is highly likely that at the very heart of this space there is a threatening power to be mastered or defeated.

In other words, if we end up with this kind of tactical arrangement, it is because before the problem being one of knowledge, or rather, for the problem to be able to be one of knowledge, of the truth of the illness, and of its cure, it must first of all be one of victory. So what is organized in the asylum is actually a battlefield.

Obviously it is the mad person who is to be brought under control. I have just quoted the odd definition of the mad person given by Fodéré, who said that he is someone who thinks he is "superior to everyone else."[11] In actual fact, this really is how the madman makes his appearance in psychiatric discourse and practice at the start of the nineteenth century, and it is there that we find the great turning point, the great division that I have already spoken about, which is the disappearance of the criterion of error in the definition of madness or in the ascription of madness.

Broadly speaking, until the end of the eighteenth century—and even in police reports, *lettres de cachet*, interrogations, etcetera, concerning individuals in places like Bicêtre and Charenton—to say that someone was mad, to ascribe madness to him, was always to say that he was mistaken, and to say in what respect, on what point, in what way, and within what limits he was mistaken; madness was basically characterized by its system of belief. Now, very suddenly, at the beginning of the nineteenth century, a criterion appears for recognizing and ascribing madness which is absolutely different and which is—I was going to say, the will, but that is not exactly right—in fact, at the start of the nineteenth century, we can say that what characterizes the madman, that by which one ascribes madness to him, is the insurrection of a force, of a furiously raging, uncontrolled and possibly uncontrollable force within him, which takes four major forms according to the domain it affects and the field in which it wreaks its devastation.

There is the pure force of the individual who traditionally is said to be "raving" (*furieux*).

There is the force inasmuch as it affects the instincts and passions, the force of unbridled instincts and unlimited passions. This will characterize a madness that, precisely, is not one of error, which does not include illusion of the senses, false belief, or hallucination, and which is called mania without delirium.

Third, there is a sort of madness that affects ideas themselves, disrupts them, makes them incoherent, and brings them into conflict with each other. This is called mania.

Finally, there is the force of madness that no longer affects the general domain of ideas, disrupting them all and bringing them into conflict with each other, but which affects one particular idea that is thus indefinitely strengthened and stubbornly lodged in the patient's behavior, discourse, and mind. This is called either melancholy or monomania.

And the first major distribution of this asylum practice at the beginning of the nineteenth century exactly retranscribes what is taking place within the asylum itself, that is to say, the fact that it is no longer a question of recognizing the madman's error, but of situating very precisely the point where the wild force of the madness unleashes its insurrection: What is the point, what is the domain, with regard to which the force will explode and make its appearance, completely disrupting the individual's behavior?

Consequently, the tactic of the asylum in general and, more particularly, the individual tactic applied by the doctor to this or that patient within the general framework of this system of power, will and must be adjusted to the characterization, to the localization, to the domain of application of this explosion and raging outburst of force. So that if the great, unbridled force of madness really is the target of the asylum tactics, if it really is the adversary of these tactics, what else can cure be but the submission of this force? And so we find in Pinel this very simple but, I think, fundamental definition of psychiatric therapeutics, a definition that, notwithstanding its crudity and barbaric character, is not found prior to this period. The therapeutics of madness is "the art of, as it were, subjugating and taming the lunatic by making him strictly dependent on a man who, by his physical and moral qualities, is able to exercise an irresistible influence on him and alter the vicious chain of his ideas."[12]

I have the impression that this definition given by Pinel of the therapeutic process cuts across all that I have been saying to you. First of all, with regard to the principle of the patient's strict dependence in relation to a certain power: This power can be embodied in one and only one man who exercises it not so much in terms of and on the basis of a knowledge, as in terms of the physical and moral qualities that enable him to exercise an influence that can have no limit, an irresistible influence. And it is starting from this that it becomes possible to change the vicious chain of ideas; it is on the basis of this moral orthopedics, if you like, that cure is possible. And finally, that is why, in this proto-psychiatric practice, the basic therapeutic action takes the form of scenes and a battle.

Two types of intervention are very clearly distinguished in the psychiatry of this period. During the first third of the nineteenth century, one of these is regularly and continually discredited: specifically medical, or medicinal, practice. The other, first defined by the English, by Haslam in particular, and then very quickly taken up in France, is the development of the practice called "moral treatment."[13]

This moral treatment is not at all, as one might think, a sort of long-term process whose first and last function would be to bring to light the truth of the madness, to be able to observe it, describe it, diagnose it, and, on that basis, to define the therapy. The therapeutic process formulated between 1810 and 1830 is a scene, a scene of confrontation. This scene of confrontation may present two aspects. The first is, if you like, incomplete, and is like a process of wearing down, of testing, which is not carried out by the doctor—for the doctor himself must obviously be sovereign—but by the supervisor.

Here is an example of this first outline of the great scene, given by Pinel in his *Traité médico-philosophique.*

Faced with a raving lunatic, the supervisor "advances towards the lunatic with an intrepid air, but slowly and gradually, and to avoid exasperating him he does not carry any kind of weapon. As he advances he speaks to him in the firmest, most threatening tone and, with calm warnings, continues to fix the lunatic's attention on himself so as to hide what is going on around him. He gives precise and imperious orders to obey and to surrender. Somewhat disconcerted by the supervisor's overbearing manner, the lunatic loses every other object from view and, at a signal, is suddenly surrounded by assistants, whom he had not noticed slowly advancing on him. Each grabs hold of one of the lunatic's limbs, one an arm, the other a thigh or a leg."[14]

Pinel gives further advice on the use of certain instruments, like the "semicircular piece of iron" fixed to the end of a pole, for example. When the lunatic's attention is captured by the supervisor's haughty demeanor and is fixed on him so that he is unaware of anyone else approaching him, this kind of lance with a semicircular end is used to pin him to the wall and overpower him. This is, if you like, the imperfect scene, the one reserved for the supervisor, and which consists in breaking the wild force of the lunatic with this kind of cunning and sudden violence.

However, it is obvious that this is not the major scene of the cure. The cure scene is complex. Here is a famous example from Pinel's *Traité médico-philosophique*. It involves a young man "dominated by religious prejudices" who thought that for his salvation he had "to imitate the abstinence and mortifications of the old anchorites," that is to say, to refuse not only all the pleasures of the flesh, of course, but also all food. And then one day, with more than his usual firmness, he refuses a soup he is served. "In the evening, citizen Pussin appears at the door of his chamber in a frightening get up [in the sense of classical theater, of course; M.F.], with fiery eyes and a striking voice, and accompanied by a group of assistants close by who are armed with strong chains that they shake noisily. The soup is placed by the lunatic who is given the most precise instruction to take it during the night if he does not wish to incur the most cruel treatment. They withdraw and leave him in the most painful state, wavering between the idea of the threatened punishment and the terrifying perspective of the other life. After an inner struggle of several hours, the first idea wins out and he decides to take his food. He is then subjected to a suitable diet for his recovery; sleep and strength return by degrees, as also the use of reason, and in this way he avoids a certain death. During his convalescence he often confessed to me the cruel agitation and confusion he suffered during the night of his ordeal."[15] We have here, I think, a scene that is very important in its general morphology.

First, you can see that the therapeutic operation does not take place by way of the doctor's recognition of the causes of the illness. The doctor does not require any work of diagnosis or nosography, any discourse of truth, for the success of his operation.

Second, it is an important operation because in this and similar cases, as you see, there is no application of a technical medical formula to something seen as a pathological process of behavior. What is involved is the confrontation of two wills, that of the doctor and those who represent him on the one hand, and then that of the patient. What is established, therefore, is a battle, a relationship of force.

Third, the primary effect of this relationship of force is to provoke a second relationship of force, within the patient as it were, since it involves provoking a conflict between the fixed idea to which the patient is attached and the fear of punishment: one struggle provokes another. And, when the scene succeeds, there must be a victory in both struggles, the victory of one idea over another, which must be at the same time the victory of the doctor's will over the patient's will.

Fourth, what is important in this scene is that there is indeed a moment when the truth comes out. This is when the patient recognizes that his belief in the necessity of fasting to ensure his salvation was erroneous and delirious, when he recognizes what has taken place, when he confesses his experience of wavering, hesitations, and torments, etcetera. In short, in this scene in which, hitherto, the truth was not involved, it is the patient's own account that constitutes the moment when the truth blazes forth.

Finally, the process of the cure is effectuated, accomplished, and sealed when truth has been acquired through confession in this way, in the effective moment of confession, and not by piecing together a medical knowledge.

So there is a distribution of force, power, the event, and truth here, which is unlike anything in what could be called the medical model being constructed in clinical medicine in the same period. We can say that the clinical medicine of this time put together an epistemological model of medical truth, observation, and objectivity that will make possible the real insertion of medicine within a domain of scientific discourse where, with its own modalities, it will join physiology and biology, etcetera. In the period 1800 to 1830 I think something takes place that is quite different from what is usually thought to have occurred. It seems to me that what happened in these thirty years is usually interpreted as the moment when psychiatry was finally inserted within a medical practice and knowledge to which previously it had been relatively foreign. It is usually thought that at that moment psychiatry appeared for the first time as a specialty within the medical domain.

Leaving aside for the moment the problem of why in fact such a practice could be seen as a medical practice, and why the people who carried out these operations had to be doctors, it seems to me that, in its morphology, in its general deployment, the medical operation of the cure performed by those whom we think of as the founders of psychiatry has practically nothing to do with what was then becoming the experience, observation, diagnostic activity, and therapeutic process of medicine. At this level of the cure, of this event, the psychiatric scene and procedure are, I believe, from that moment, absolutely irreducible to what was taking place in medicine in the same period.

It is this heterogeneity then that will mark the history of psychiatry at the very moment at which it is founded within a system of institutions that nevertheless connect it to medicine. For all of this, this staging, the organization of the asylum space, the activating and unfolding of these scenes, are only possible, accepted and institutionalized within establishments that are being given a medical status at this time, and by people who are medically qualified.

⚜

We have here, if you like, a first set of problems. This is the point of departure for what I would like to study a little this year. Actually, it is roughly the point reached by my earlier work, *Histoire de la folie*, or, at any rate, the point where it broke off.[16] I would like to take things up again at this point, except with some differences. It seems to me that in that work, which I take as a reference point because it is a kind of "background"* for me, for the work I am doing now, there were a number of things that were entirely open to criticism, especially in the final chapter in which I ended up precisely at asylum power.

First of all, I think it was still an analysis of representations. It seems to me that, above all, I was trying to study the image of madness produced in the seventeenth and eighteenth centuries, the fear it aroused, and the knowledge formed with reference to it, either traditionally, or according to botanical, naturalistic, and medical models, etcetera. It was this core of representations, of both traditional and non-traditional images, fantasies, and knowledge, this kind of core of representations

* English in original; G.B.

that I situated as the point of departure, as the site of origin of the practices concerning madness that managed to establish themselves in the seventeenth and eighteenth centuries. In short, I accorded a privileged role to what could be called the perception of madness.[17]

Here, in this second volume, I would like to see if it is possible to make a radically different analysis and if, instead of starting from the analysis of this kind of representational core, which inevitably refers to a history of mentalities, of thought, we could start from an apparatus (*dispositif*) of power. That is to say, to what extent can an apparatus of power produce statements, discourses and, consequently, all the forms of representation that may then [. . .]* derive from it.

The apparatus of power as a productive instance of discursive practice. In this respect, in comparison with what I call archeology, the discursive analysis of power would operate at a level—I am not very happy with the word "fundamental"—let's say at a level that would enable discursive practice to be grasped at precisely the point where it is formed. To what should we refer this formation of discursive practice, where should we look for it?

If we look for the relationship between discursive practice and, let's say, economic structures, relations of production, I do not think we can avoid recourse to something like representation, the subject, and so on, appealing to a ready made psychology and philosophy. The problem for me is this: Basically, are not apparatuses of power, with all that remains enigmatic and still to be explored in this word "power," precisely the point from which it should be possible to locate the formation of discursive practices. How can this deployment of power, these tactics and strategies of power, give rise to assertions, negations, experiments, and theories, in short to a game of truth? Apparatus of power and game of truth, apparatus of power and discourse of truth: This is what I would like to examine a little this year, starting from the point I have referred to, that is to say, psychiatry and madness.

The second criticism I have of that final chapter is that I appealed—but, after all, I cannot say I did so very consciously, because I was very ignorant of antipsychiatry and especially of the psycho-sociology of the

---

* (Recording:) be formed from it and

time—I appealed, implicitly or explicitly, to three notions that seem to me to be rusty locks with which we cannot get very far.

First, the notion of violence.[18] What actually struck me when I was reading Pinel, Esquirol, and others, is that contrary to what the hagiographies say, Pinel, Esquirol, and the others appealed strongly to physical force, and consequently it seemed to me that one could not ascribe Pinel's reform to a humanism, because his entire practice was still permeated by something like violence.

Now, if it is true that we cannot in fact ascribe Pinel's reform to humanism, I do not think this is because he resorted to violence. When in fact we speak of violence, and this is what bothers me about the notion, we always have in mind a kind of connotation of physical power, of an unregulated, passionate power, an unbridled power, if I can put it like that. This notion seems to me to be dangerous because, on the one hand, picking out a power that is physical, unregulated, etcetera, allows one to think that good power, or just simply power, power not permeated by violence, is not physical power. It seems to me rather that what is essential in all power is that ultimately its point of application is always the body. All power is physical, and there is a direct connection between the body and political power.

Then again, violence does not seem to me to be a very satisfactory notion, because it allows one to think that the physical exercise of an unbalanced force is not part of a rational, calculated, and controlled game of the exercise of power. Now the examples I have just given clearly prove that power as it is exercised in the asylum is a meticulous, calculated power, the tactics and strategies of which are absolutely definite; and, at the very heart of these strategies, we see quite precisely the place and role of violence, if we call violence the physical exercise of a completely unbalanced force. Taken in its final ramifications, at its capillary level, where it affects the individual himself, this power is physical and, thereby, it is violent, in the sense that it is absolutely irregular, not in the sense that it is unbridled, but in the sense, rather, that it is commanded by all the dispositions of a kind of microphysics of bodies.

The second notion to which I referred, and, I think, not very satisfactorily, is that of the institution.[19] It seemed to me that we could say that from the beginning of the nineteenth century psychiatric knowledge took the forms and dimensions we know in close connection with what could be called the institutionalization of psychiatry; even more precisely, it took these forms and dimensions in connection with a number of institutions of which the asylum was the most important. Now I no longer think that the institution is very satisfactory notion. It seems to me that it harbors a number of dangers, because as soon as we talk about institutions we are basically talking about both individuals and the group, we take the individual, the group, and the rules which govern them as given, and as a result we can throw in all the psychological or sociological discourses.*

In actual fact, we should show, rather, that what is essential is not the institution with its regularity, with its rules, but precisely the imbalances of power that I have tried to show both distort the asylum's regularity and, at the same time, make it function. What is important therefore is not institutional regularities, but much more the practical dispositions of power, the characteristic networks, currents, relays, points of support, and differences of potential that characterize a form of power, which are, I think, constitutive of, precisely, both the individual and the group.

It seems to me that that insofar as power is a procedure of individualization, the individual is only the effect of power. And it is on the basis of this network of power, functioning in its differences of potential, in its discrepancies, that something like the individual, the group, the community, and the institution appear. In other words, before tackling institutions, we have to deal with the relations of force in these tactical arrangements that permeate institutions.

Finally, the third notion I referred to in order to explain the functioning of the asylum at the start of nineteenth century is the family, and I tried to show roughly how the violence of Pinel [or] Esquirol was their introduction of the family model into the asylum institution.[20] Now I do not think that "violence" is the right word, or that we should situate our analysis at the level of the "institution," and I do not think that we should talk of the family. At any rate, re-reading Pinel, Esquirol, Fodéré, and others, in the end I found very little use of this family model. It is not true that the doctor tries to reactivate the image or

---

* The manuscript adds: "The institution neutralizes relations of force, or it only makes them function within the space it defines."

figure of the father within the space of the asylum; I think this takes place much later, even at the end of what could be called the psychiatric episode in the history of medicine, that is to say only in the twentieth century.

It is not the family, neither is it the State apparatus, and I think it would be equally false to say, as it often is, that asylum practice, psychiatric power, does no more than reproduce the family to the advantage of, or on the demand of, a form of State control organized by a State apparatus.[21] The State apparatus cannot serve as the basis,* and the family cannot serve as the model, [...†] for the relations of power that we can identify within psychiatric practice.

In doing without these notions and these models, that is to say, the family model, the norm, if you like, of the State apparatus, the notion of the institution, and the notion of violence, I think the problem that arises is that of analyzing these relations of power peculiar to psychiatric practice insofar as—and this will be the object of the course—they produce statements that are given as valid, justified statements. Rather, therefore, than speak of violence, I would prefer to speak of a microphysics of power; rather than speak of the institution, I would much prefer to try to see what tactics are put to work in these forces which confront each other; rather than speak of the family model or "State apparatus," I would like to try to see the strategy of these relations of power and confrontations which unfold within psychiatric practice.

You will say that it is all very well to have substituted a microphysics of power for violence, tactics for institution, strategy for the model of the family, but have I really made an advance? I have avoided terms that would allow the introduction of a psycho-sociological vocabulary into all these analyses, and now I am faced with a pseudo-military vocabulary which is not much better. Nevertheless, we will try to see what we can do with it.‡

---

* The manuscript specifies: "We cannot use the notion of State apparatus because it is much too broad, much too abstract to designate these immediate, tiny, capillary powers that are exerted on the body, behavior, actions, and time of individuals. The State apparatus does not take this microphysics of power into account."

† (Recording:) for what takes place

‡ The manuscript (pages 11-23) continues on the question of defining the current problem of psychiatry and puts forward an analysis of antipsychiatry.

---

1. François Emmanuel Fodéré (1764-1835), *Traité du délire, appliqué à la médecine, à la morale et à la législation* (Paris: Croullebois, 1817), Vol. 2, section VI, ch. 2: "Plan et distribution d'un hospice pour la guérison des aliénés," p. 215.
2. Donatien Alphonse François de Sade (1740-1814), *Les Cent vingt Journées de Sodome, ou l'École du libertinage* (1785), in *Œuvres complètes* (Paris: Jean-Jacques Pauvert, 1967), vol. 26; English translation in Marquis de Sade, *The 120 days of Sodom and other writings*, trans. Austryn Wainhouse and Richard Seaver (New York: Grove Press, 1966).
3. Joseph Michel Antoine Servan (1737-1807), *Discours sur l'administration de la justice criminelle*, delivered by Monsieur Servan (Geneva: 1767), p. 35: "The unshakeable basis of the most solid empires is founded on the soft fibers of the brain." (Republished in C. Beccaria, *Traité des délits et des peines*, trans. P.J. Dufey [Paris: Dulibon, 1821]).
4. Philippe Pinel (1745-1826), *Traité médico-philosophique sur l'aliénation mentale, ou la Manie* (Paris: Richard, Caille and Ravier, Year 9/1801), section II, "Traitement moral des aliénés," § xxiii: "Nécessité d'entretenir un ordre constant dans les hospices des aliénés," pp. 95-96; abridged English translation of original, 1801 edition [omitting Pinel's introduction and material added in longer French 1809 edition; G.B.], *A Treatise on Insanity*, trans. B.B. Davis (New York: Hafner, 1962), section II: "The Moral Treatment of Insanity"; "The necessity of maintaining constant order in lunatic asylums, and of studying the varieties of character exhibited by the patients," p. 99.
5. Jean Étienne Dominique Esquirol (1772-1807), *Des maladies mentales considérées sous les rapports médical, hygiénique et médico-légal*, 2 volumes (Paris: J.-B. Baillière, 1838). Abridged English translation and with additions by the translator, *Mental Maladies. A Treatise on Insanity*, trans. E.K. Hunt (Philadelphia: Lea and Blanchard, 1845) [Hunt says, p. vi: "All that portion of this Treatise, relating properly to insanity, has been published entire; the remainder, referring, for the most part, to the statistics and hygiène of establishments for the insane, together with the medico-legal relations of the subject, have been omitted"; G.B.].
6. John Haslam (1764-1844), *Observations on Insanity, with Practical Remarks on the Disease, and an Account of the Morbid Appearances of Dissection* (London: Rivington, 1798), republished in an expanded edition under the title, *Madness and Melancholy* (London: J. Callow, 1809); and, *Considerations on the Moral Management of Insane Persons* (London: R. Hunter, 1817).
7. J.E.D. Esquirol, *Des établissements consacrés aux aliénés en France, et des moyens d'améliorer le sort de ces infortunés* (Report to the Minister of the Interior, September 1818), printed by Mme. Huzard, 1819. Reprinted in *Des maladies mentales*, vol. 2, pp. 399-431.
8. F.E. Fodéré, *Traité du délire*, vol. 2, section 6, ch. 3, "Du choix des administrateurs, des médicins, des employés et des servants," pp. 230-231.
9. Ibid. p. 237.
10. Ibid. pp. 241-242.
11. Ibid. p. 230.
12. P. Pinel, *Traité médico-philosophique*, section II, § vi: "Avantages de l'art de diriger les aliénés pour seconder les effets des médicaments," p. 58; *A Treatise on Insanity*, pp. 59-60.
13. "Moral treatment," which develops at the end of the eighteenth century, brings together all the means of acting on the patient's psyche, as opposed to "physical treatment," which acts on the body through remedies and means of constraint. Following the death in 1791 of the wife of a Quaker, in suspicious circumstances at the York asylum, William Tuke (1732-1822) proposed the creation of an establishment for members of the Society of Friends affected by mental disorders. The Retreat opened on 11 May 1796 (see below, lecture of 5 December 1973, note 18). John Haslam, the apothecary at Bethlehem hospital, before becoming a medical doctor in 1816, developed principles of moral treatment in his works (see above, this lecture, note 6). In France, Pinel took up the principle in his "Observations sur le régime moral que est le plus propre à rétablir, dans certains cas, la raison égarée des maniaques," *Gazette de santé*, no. 4, 1789, pp. 13-15, and in his report, "Recherches et observations sur le traitement moral des aliénés," *Mémoires de la Société médicale d'émulation. Section Médicine*, no. 2, 1798, pp. 215-255, republished with some changes in *Traité médico-philosophique*, section II, pp. 46-105. Étienne Jean Georget (1795-1828) systematized the principles in *De la folie. Considérations sur cette maladie: son siège et ses*

symptômes, la nature et la mode d'action de ses causes; sa marche et ses terminaisons; les différences qui la distinguent du délire aigu; les moyens du traitement qui lui conviennent; suivies de recherches cadavériques (Paris: Crevot, 1820). François Leuret emphasizes the doctor-patient relationship; see, *Du traitement moral de la folie* (Paris: J.-B. Baillière, 1840). See the pages devoted to moral treatment in M. Foucault, *Histoire de la folie à l'âge classique* (Paris: Gallimard, 1972), Part 3, ch. 4: "Naissance de l'asile" pp. 484-487, 492-496, 501-511, 523-527; Abridged English translation, *Madness and Civilization. A History of Insanity in the Age of Reason*, trans. R. Howard (New York: Random House, 1965 and London: Tavistock, 1967) pp. 243-255, 269-274 (pages 484-500 of the French edition are omitted from the English translation). See also, R. Castel, "Le traitement moral. Thérapeutique mentale et contrôle sociale au XIXe siècle," *Topique*, no. 2, February 1970, pp. 109-129.

14. P. Pinel, *Traité médico-philosophique*, Section II, § xxi: "Caractère des aliénés les plus violents et dangereux, et expédiens à prendre pour les réprimer" pp. 90-91; *A Treatise on Insanity*, "The most violent and dangerous maniacs described, with expedients for their repression" pp. 93-94.
15. Ibid. Section II, § viii: "Avantage d'ébranler fortement l'imagination d'un aliéné dans certains cas" pp. 60-61; English, ibid. "The advantages of restraint upon the imagination of maniacs illustrated" pp. 61-63.
16. M. Foucault, *Folie et Déraison. Histoire de la folie à l'âge classique* (Paris: Plon, 1961); *Madness and Civilization.* [Apart from in this note, the French editor always refers to the 1972, Gallimard edition, *Histoire de la folie*, as above in note 13; G.B.]
17. For example, *Histoire de la folie*, Part 1, ch. 5, "Les insensés" p. 169 and p. 172; Part 2, ch. 1, "Le fou au jardin des espèces" p. 223; and Part 3, ch. 2, "Le nouveau partage" p. 407 and p. 415; *Madness and Civilization*, ch. 3, "The insane" p. 77 and pp. 80-81 (pages 223, 407, and 415 of French edition are omitted from the English translation). The point of departure for this criticism of the notion of "perception" or "experience" is *L'Archéologie du savoir* (Paris: Gallimard, 1969), ch. 3, "La formation des objets" and ch. 4, "La formation des modalités enonciatives" pp. 55-74; English translation, *The Archeology of Knowledge*, trans. A. Sheridan (London: Tavistock and New York: Pantheon, 1972), Part II, ch. 3, "The formation of objects" and ch. 4, "The formation of enunciative modalities" pp. 40-55.
18. The notion of violence underlies the analysis of the mode of treatment in *Histoire de la folie*, Part 2, ch. 4, "Médecins et malades" pp. 327-328 and p. 358, and Part 3, ch. 4, "Naissance de l'asile" p. 497, pp. 502-503, p. 508, and p. 520; *Madness and Civilization*, ch. 6, "Doctors and Patients" pp. 159-160 and p. 196, and ch. 9, "The Birth of the Asylum" pp. 243-245, p. 251, and p. 266 (page 497 of the French edition is omitted from the English translation). See below, "Course context" pp. 354-355.
19. The analyses devoted to the "Naissance de l'asile," ibid. pp. 483-530; "Birth of the asylum" ibid. pp. 241-278.
20. On the role of the family model in the reorganization of relations between madness and reason and the constitution of the asylum, see ibid. pp. 509-511; ibid. pp. 253-255.
21. Foucault is alluding here to the analyses of Louis Althusser who introduced the concept of "State apparatus" in his article "Idéologie et appareils idéologiques d'État. Notes pour une recherche," *La Pensée. Revue du rationalisme moderne*, no. 51, June 1970, pp. 3-38; reprinted in *Positions (1964-1975)* (Paris: Éditions Sociales, 1976) pp. 65-125; English translation, "Ideology and Ideological State Apparatusses" in L. Althusser, *Lenin and Philosophy*, trans. (London: New Left Books, 1971).

two

14 NOVEMBER 1973

[*Scene of a cure: George III. From the "macrophysics of sovereignty" to the "microphysics of disciplinary power." ~ The new figure of the madman. ~ Little encyclopedia of scenes of cures. ~ The practice of hypnosis and hysteria. ~ The psychoanalytic scene; the antipsychiatric scene. ~ Mary Barnes at Kingsley Hall. ~ Manipulation of madness and stratagem of truth: Mason Cox.*]

OBVIOUSLY YOU KNOW WHAT passes for the great founding scene of modern psychiatry, or of psychiatry period, which got under way at the beginning of the nineteenth century. It is the famous scene at Bicêtre, which was not yet a hospital exactly, in which Pinel removes the chains binding the raving lunatics to the floor of their dungeon, and these lunatics, who were restrained out of fear that they would give vent to their frenzy if released, express their gratitude to Pinel as soon as they are freed from their bonds and thereby embark on the path of cure. This then is what passes for the initial, founding scene of psychiatry.[1]

Now there is another scene that did not have the same destiny, although it had considerable repercussions in the same period, for reasons that are easy to understand. It is a scene which did not take place in France, but in England—and was reported in some detail by Pinel, moreover, in his *Traité médico-philosophique* of Year IX (1800)—and which, as you will see straightaway, was not without a kind of force, a malleable presence, inasmuch as in the period, not in which it took place, which was in 1788, but in which it became known in France, and finally in the whole of Europe, it had become, let's say, a certain custom for kings to lose their heads. It is an important scene because it stages precisely what psychiatric practice could be in that period as a regulated and concerted manipulation of relations of power.

Here is Pinel's text, which circulated in France and made the affair known:

"A monarch [George III of England; M.F.] falls into a mania, and in order to make his cure more speedy and secure, no restrictions are placed on the prudence of the person who is to direct it [note the word: this is the doctor; M.F.]; from then on, all trappings of royalty having disappeared, the madman, separated from his family and his usual surroundings, is consigned to an isolated palace, and he is confined alone in a room whose tiled floor and walls are covered with matting so that he cannot harm himself. The person directing the treatment tells him that he is no longer sovereign, but that he must henceforth be obedient and submissive. Two of his old pages, of Herculean stature, are charged with looking after his needs and providing him with all the services his condition requires, but also with convincing him that he is entirely subordinate to them and must now obey them. They keep watch over him in calm silence, but take every opportunity to make him aware of how much stronger than him they are. One day, in fiery delirium, the madman harshly greets his old doctor who is making his visit, and daubs him with filth and excrement. One of the pages immediately enters the room without saying a word, grasps by his belt the delirious madman, who is himself in a disgustingly filthy state, forcibly throws him down on a pile of mattresses, strips him, washes him with a sponge, changes his clothes, and, looking at him haughtily, immediately leaves to take up his post again. Such lessons, repeated at intervals over some months and backed up by other means of treatment, have produced a sound cure without relapse."[2]

I would like to analyze the elements of this scene. First of all, there is something quite striking in Pinel's text, which he took from Willis, the king's doctor.[3] It seems to me that what appears first of all is, basically, a ceremony, a ceremony of deposition, a sort of reverse coronation in which it is quite clearly shown that it involves placing the king in a situation of complete subordination; you remember the words: "all trappings of royalty having disappeared," and the doctor, who is, as it were, the effective agent of this dethronement, of this deconsecration, explicitly telling him that "he is no longer sovereign."

A decree, consequently, of deposition: the king is reduced to impotence. And it seems to me that the "matting," which surrounds him and plays [such a big] role* both in the setting and the final scene, are important. The matting is both what isolates the king from the outside world, and, as well as preventing him from hearing and seeing the outside world, prevents him from communicating his orders to it; that is to say, all the essential functions of the monarchy are, in the strict sense, bracketed off by the matting. In place of the scepter, crown, and sword, which should make the universal power of the king reigning over his kingdom visible and perceptible to all the spectators, in place of these signs, there is no more than the "matting" which confines him and reduces him, there where he is, to what he is, that is to say, to his body.

Deposition and therefore the king's fall; but my impression is that it is not the same type of fall as we find in, say, a Shakespearian drama: this is not Richard III[4] threatened with falling under the power of another sovereign, nor King Lear[5] stripped of his sovereignty and roaming the world in solitude, poverty, and madness. In fact, the king's [George III] madness, unlike that of King Lear, condemned to roam the world, fixes him at a precise point and, especially, brings him under, not another sovereign power, but a completely different type of power which differs term by term, I think, from the power of sovereignty. It is an anonymous, nameless and faceless power that is distributed between different persons. Above all, it is a power that is expressed through an implacable regulation that is not even formulated, since, basically, nothing is said, and the text actually says that all the agents of this power remain silent. The silence of regulation takes over, as it were, the empty place left by the king's dethronement.

So this is not a case of one sovereign power falling under another sovereign power, but the transition from a sovereign power—decapitated by the madness that has seized hold of the king's head, and dethroned by the ceremony that shows the king that he is no longer sovereign—to

* (Recording:) such an important role

a different power. In place of this beheaded and dethroned power, an anonymous, multiple, pale, colorless power is installed, which is basically what I will call disciplinary power. One type of power, that of sovereignty, is replaced by what could be called disciplinary power, and the effect of which is not at all to consecrate someone's power, to concentrate power in a visible and named individual, but only to produce effects on its target, on the body and very person of the dethroned king, who must be rendered "docile and submissive"[6] by this new power.

Whereas sovereign power is expressed through the symbols of the dazzling force of the individual who holds it, disciplinary power is a discreet, distributed power; it is a power which functions through networks and the visibility of which is only found in the obedience and submission of those on whom it is silently exercised. I think this is what is essential in this scene: the confrontation, the submission, and the connecting up of a sovereign power to a disciplinary power.

Who are the agents of this disciplinary power? Curiously, the doctor, the person who organizes everything and really is in fact, up to a certain point, the focal element, the core of this disciplinary system, does not himself appear: Willis is never there. And when we have the scene of the doctor, it is precisely an old doctor and not Willis himself. Who then are the agents of this power? We are told that they are two old pages of Herculean stature.

I think we should stop here for a moment, for they too are very important in the scene. As a hypothesis, and subject to correction, I will say that this relationship of the Herculean pages to the mad king stripped bare should be compared with some iconographic themes. I think the plastic force of this history is due in part precisely to the fact that it contains elements [...*] of the traditional iconography for representing sovereigns. Now it seems to me that the king and his servants are traditionally represented in two forms.

There is the representation of the warrior king in breastplate and arms deploying and displaying his omnipotence—the Hercules king, if you like—and beside him, beneath him, subject to this kind of overwhelming power, are figures representing submission, weakness, defeat,

* (Recording:) which are part

slavery, or possibly beauty. This, more or less, is one of the primary oppositions found in the iconography of royal power.

Then there is another possibility, but with a different play of oppositions. This is not the Herculean king, but the king of human stature who is, rather, stripped of all the visible and immediate signs of physical force and clothed only in the symbols of his power; the king in his ermine, with his scepter, his globe, and then, beneath him, or accompanying him, the visible representation of a force subject to him: soldiers, pages, and servants who are the representation of a force, but of a force which is, as it were, silently commanded by the intermediary of these symbolic elements of power, by scepter, ermine, crown, and so forth. Broadly speaking, it seems to me that the relationship of king to servants is represented in this way in the iconography: always in terms of opposition, but in the form of these two kinds of opposition.

Now, here, in this scene taken from Willis that is recounted by Pinel, you find these same elements, but completely shifted and transformed. On the one hand, you have the wild force of the king who has become the human beast again and who is in exactly the same position as those submissive and enchained slaves we found in the first of the iconographic versions I spoke about. Opposite this, there is the restrained, disciplined, and serene force of the servants. In this opposition of the king who has become wild force and servants who are the visible representation of a force, but of a disciplined force, I think you have in fact the point at which a sovereignty that is disappearing is caught up in a disciplinary power that is being constituted and whose face, it seems to me, can be seen in these silent, muscular, and magnificent pages who are both obedient and all-powerful.

How do these Herculean servants exercise their functions? Here again I think we should examine the text in some detail. The text says that these Herculean servants are present in order to serve the king; it even says very precisely that their purpose is to serve his "needs" and his "condition." Now it seems to me that in what could be called the power of sovereignty, in actual fact the servant really does serve the sovereign's needs and really must satisfy the requirements and needs of his condition: he is in fact the person who dresses and undresses the king, who ensures the provision of services for his body and his property, and so on.

However, when the servant ministers to the sovereign's needs and condition, it is essentially because this is the sovereign's will. That is to say, the sovereign's will binds the servant, and it binds him individually, as this or that servant, to that function which consists in ensuring that he serves the sovereign's needs and condition. The king's will, his status as king, is what fixes the servant to his needs and condition.

Now, in the disciplinary relationship that we see appearing here, the servant is not at all in the service of the king's will, or it is not because it is the king's will that he serves the king's needs. He is in the service of the king's needs and condition without either the king's will or his status being involved. It is only the mechanical requirements of the body, as it were, which fix and determine what the servant's service must be. Consequently will and need, status and condition are disconnected. What's more, the servant will only act as a repressive force, he will leave off serving only in order to curb the king's will, when the latter is expressed over and above his needs and his condition.

This, more or less, is roughly the scene's setting. I would now like to move on to the important episode of this scene set in this context, that is to say the episode of the confrontation with the doctor: "One day, in fiery delirium, the madman harshly greets his old doctor who is making his visit, and daubs him with filth and excrement. One of the pages immediately enters the room without saying a word, grasps by his belt the delirious madman . . ."[7]

After the deposition scene, or dethronement if you like, there is the scene of rubbish, excrement, and filth. This is no longer just the king who is dethroned, this is not just dispossession of the attributes of sovereignty; it is the total inversion of sovereignty. The only force the king has left is his body reduced to its wild state, and the only weapons he has left are his bodily evacuations, which is precisely what he uses against his doctor. Now in doing this I think the king really inverts his sovereignty, not just because his waste matter has replaced his scepter and sword, but also because in this action he takes up, quite exactly, a gesture with a historical meaning. The act of throwing mud and refuse over someone is the centuries old gesture of insurrection against the powerful.

There is an entire tradition that would have it that we only speak of excrement and waste matter as the symbol of money. Still, a very serious political history could be done of excrement and waste matter, both a political and a medical history of the way in which excrement and waste matter could be a problem in themselves, and without any kind of symbolization: they could be an economic problem, and a medical problem, of course, but they could also be the stake of a political struggle, which is very clear in the seventeenth century and especially the eighteenth century. And this profaning gesture of throwing mud, refuse, and excrement over the carriages, silk, and ermine of the great, well, King George III, having been its victim, knew full well what it meant.

So there is a total reversal of the sovereign function here, since the king takes up the insurrectional gesture not just of the poor, but even of the poorest of the poor. When the peasants revolted, they used the tools available to them as weapons: scythes, staves, and suchlike. Artisans also made use of the tools of their trade. It was only the poorest, those who had nothing, who picked up stones and excrement in the street to throw at the powerful. This is the role that the king is taking up in his confrontation with the medical power entering the room in which he finds himself: sovereignty, both driven wild and inverted, against pale discipline.

It is at this point that the silent, muscular, invincible page enters, who seizes the king around the waist, throws him on the bed, strips him naked, washes him with a sponge, and withdraws, as the text says, "looking at him haughtily."[8] And once again you find here the displacement of the elements of a scene of power, which this time is no longer of the coronation, of the iconographic representation; it is, as you can see clearly, the scaffold, the scene of public torture. But here as well there is inversion and displacement: whereas the person who violates sovereignty, who throws stones and excrement over the king, would have been killed, hung and quartered according to English law, here instead, discipline, making its entrance in the form of the page, will control, bring down, strip naked, scrub, and make the body clean and true.

That is what I wanted to say about this scene, which, much more than the scene of Pinel freeing the mad, appears to me typical of what is put to work in what I call proto-psychiatric practice, that is to say, roughly, the practice which develops in the last years of the eighteenth century and in the first twenty or thirty years of the nineteenth century, before the appearance of the great institutional edifice of the psychiatric asylum in the years between 1830 and 1840, say 1838 in France, with the law on confinement and the organization of the major psychiatric hospitals.[9]

This scene seems to me to be important. First of all because it means I can correct an error I made in *Histoire de la folie*. You can see that there is no question here of the imposition of anything like a family model in psychiatric practice; it is not true that the father and mother, or the typical relationships of the family structure, are borrowed by psychiatric practice and pinned on madness and the direction of the insane. The relationship to the family will appear in the history of psychiatry, but this will be later, and, as far as I can see at present, we should identify hysteria as the point at which the family model is grafted on to psychiatric practice.

You can see also that the treatment, which, with an optimism subsequently contradicted by the facts, Pinel said would produce "a sound cure without relapse,"[10] takes place without anything like a valid description, analysis, diagnosis, or true knowledge of the king's illness. Here again, just as the family model only enters later, so too the moment of truth only enters psychiatric practice later.

Finally, I would like to emphasize that one can see very clearly here an interplay of elements, elements of power in a strict sense, which are put to work, shifted, turned around, and so on, outside of any institution. Here again, my impression is that the moment of the institution is not prior to these relationships of power. That is to say, the institution does not determine these relationships of power, any more than a discourse of truth prescribes them, or a family model suggests them. In actual fact, in this kind of scene you see these relationships of power functioning, I was going to say nakedly. In this it seems to me to pick out quite well the basis of relationships of power that constitute the core element of psychiatric practice, on the basis of which, in fact, we will later see the construction of institutional structures, the emergence of discourses of truth, and also the grafting or importation of a number of models.

However, for the moment, we are witnessing the emergence of a disciplinary power, the specific figure of which seems to me to appear here with remarkable clarity precisely to the extent that, in this case, disciplinary power is confronted by another form of political power that I will call the power of sovereignty. That is to say, if the first hypotheses now guiding me are correct, it will not be enough to say that right from the start we find something like political power in psychiatric practice; it seems to me that it is more complicated, and what's more will become increasingly complicated. For the moment I would like to schematize. We are not dealing with just any kind of political power; there are two absolutely distinct types of power corresponding to two systems, two different ways of functioning: the macrophysics of sovereignty, the power that could be put to work in a post-feudal, pre-industrial government, and then the microphysics of disciplinary power, whose functioning we find in the different components I am presenting to you and which makes its appearance here leaning on, as it were, the disconnected, broken down, unmasked components of sovereign power.

There is a transformation, therefore, of the relationship of sovereignty into disciplinary power. And you see at the heart of all this, at bottom, a kind of general proposition which is: "You may well be the king, but if you are mad you will cease to be so," or again: "You may well be mad, but this won't make you king." The king, George III in this case, could only be cured in Willis's scene, in Pinel's fable if you like, to the extent that he was not treated as king, and to the extent that he was subjected to a force that was not the force of royal power. "You are not king" seems to me to be the proposition at the heart of this kind of proto-psychiatry I am trying to analyze. If you refer then to the texts of Descartes, where it is a question of madmen who take themselves for kings, you notice that the two examples Descartes gives of madness are "taking oneself for a king" or believing one "has a body made of glass."[11] In truth, for Descartes and generally [...*] for all those who spoke about madness up until the end of the eighteenth century, "taking oneself for a king," or believing one has "a body made of glass," was exactly the same thing, that it to say they were two absolutely identical types of error, which immediately contradicted the most elementary facts of sensation. "Taking oneself for a king," "believing that one has a body of glass," was, quite simply, typical of madness as error.

Henceforth, it seems to me that in this proto-psychiatric practice, and so for all the discourses of truth that get going on the basis of this practice, "believing oneself to be a king" is the true secret of madness.

---

* (Recording:) we can say

If you look at how a delirium, an illusion, or a hallucination was analyzed in this period, you see that it doesn't much matter whether someone believes himself to be a king, that is to say, whether the content of his delirium is supposing that he exercises royal power, or, to the contrary, believes himself to be ruined, persecuted, and rejected by the whole of humanity. For the psychiatrists of this period, the fact of imposing this belief, of asserting it against every proof to the contrary, even putting it forward against medical knowledge, wanting to impose it on the doctor and, ultimately, on the whole asylum, thus asserting it against every other form of certainty or knowledge, constitutes a way of believing that one is a king. Whether you believe yourself to be a king or believe that you are wretched, wanting to impose this certainty as a kind of tyranny on all those around you basically amounts to "believing one is a king"; it is this that makes all madness a kind of belief rooted in the fact that one is king of the world. Psychiatrists at the start of the nineteenth century could have said that to be mad was to seize power in one's head. Moreover, for Georget, in a text from 1820, the treatise *De la folie*, the major problem for the psychiatrist is basically "how to persuade otherwise" someone who believes that he is a king.[12]

There are a number of reasons why I have stressed this scene of the king. First of all, it seems to me that it enables us to have a better understanding of that other founding scene of psychiatry, the scene of Pinel I spoke about at the start, the scene of liberation. Pinel, at Bicêtre in 1792, entering the dungeons, removing the chains from this or that patient who has been chained up for weeks or months, would seem to be the exact opposite of the history of the king who is dispossessed, the exact opposite of the history of the king who is confined, seized around the waist, and supervised by muscular pages. Actually, when we look closely, we can see the continuity between the two scenes.

When Pinel liberates the patients confined in the dungeons, the person who is liberated incurs a debt to his liberator that will and must be settled in two ways. First, the person liberated will settle his debt continually and voluntarily by obedience; the wild violence of a body, which was only restrained by the violence of chains, will be replaced by the constant submission of one will to another. In other words, removing the chains ensures something like subjection through grateful obedience.

Then the patient will wipe out the debt in a second way, this time involuntarily. From the moment he is subjected in this way, where the continual and voluntary repayment of the debt of gratitude will have made him submit to the discipline of medical power, the working of this discipline and its own force will itself bring about the patient's cure. As a result, the cure will become involuntarily the second payment in kind for his liberation, the way in which the patient, or rather, the patient's illness, will pay the doctor for the gratitude he owes him.

You see that, in fact, this scene of liberation is not exactly a scene of humanism, and of course everyone knows this. But I think we can analyze it as a relationship of power, or as the transformation of a certain relationship of power that was one of violence—the prison, dungeon, chains, and here again, all this belongs to the old form of the power of sovereignty—into a relationship of subjection that is a relationship of discipline.

This is the first reason for recounting the history of George III, since it seems to me to inaugurate a psychiatric practice for which Pinel is generally given credit.

The other reason for quoting this case is that it seems to me that the scene of George III is one in a whole series of other scenes. First of all, it is part of a series of scenes, which, in the first twenty-five or thirty years of the nineteenth century, constitute this proto-psychiatric practice. We could say that in the first quarter of the nineteenth century there was a kind of little encyclopedia of canonical cures constituted on the basis of the cases published by Haslam,[13] Pinel,[14] Esquirol,[15] Fodéré,[16] Georget,[17] and Guislain.[18] And this little encyclopedia includes around fifty cases which circulate in all the psychiatric treatises of the time and all of which more or less conform to a similar model. Here, if you like, are one or two examples which show very clearly, I think, how all these scenes of cure resemble that major scene of the cure of George III.

Here, for example, is an example from Pinel's *Traité médico-philosophique*: "A soldier, still in a state of insanity (. . .) is suddenly dominated by the single idea of leaving for the army." He refuses to return to his room in the evening when he is ordered to do so. When he is in his room, he sets about tearing everything apart and making a mess; then he is tied to the bed. "For eight days he is in this violent state, and he finally appears to realize that in continuing with his tantrums he is not the master. In the morning, during the head doctor's round, he adopts the most submissive tone and, kissing his hand, says to him, 'You promised to give me my freedom within the home if I was peaceful. Well! I implore you to keep your word.' Smiling, the other tells him of the pleasure he experiences at this happy return to himself; he speaks gently, and instantly removes all constraint."[19]

Another example: a man was occupied with the single idea of "his omnipotence." Only one consideration held him back, the "fear of destroying the Condé army (...) which, according to him, was destined to fulfill the designs of the Eternal." How to overcome this belief? The doctor watched out for "a misdemeanor that would put him in the wrong and authorize severe treatment." And then, by chance, when "one day the supervisor complained to him about the filth and excrement he had left in his room, the lunatic flared up against him violently and threatened to destroy him. This was a favorable opportunity to punish him and convince him that his power was chimerical."[20]

Yet another example: "A madman at the Bicêtre asylum, who has no other delirium than that of believing himself to be a victim of the Revolution, repeating day and night that he was ready to suffer his fate." Since he is to be guillotined, he thinks it no longer necessary to take care of himself; he "refuses to sleep in his bed," and lays stretched out on the floor. The supervisor is obliged to resort to constraint: "The madman is tied to his bed, but he seeks revenge by refusing any kind of food with the most invincible stubbornness. Exhortations, promises, and threats are all in vain." However, after a time the patient is thirsty; he drinks some water but "firmly rejects even the broth, or any other kind of nourishment, liquid or solid, which is offered to him." Towards the twelfth day, "the supervisor tells him that, since he is so disobedient, he will henceforth be deprived of his drink of cold water and will be given fatty broth instead." Finally, thirst wins out and "he greedily takes the broth." On the following days he takes some solid food and "thus gradually reacquires the qualities of a sound and robust health."[21]*

---

* The manuscript also refers to a case set out in paragraph ix: "Exemple propre à faire voir avec quelle attention le caractère de l'aliéné doit être étudié pour le ramener à la raison" pp. 196-197; "An instance illustrative of the advantage of obtaining an intimate acquaintance with the character of the patient" pp. 191-193.

I will come back to the detailed morphology of these scenes, but I would like to show you that at the beginning of nineteenth century psychiatry, even before and, I think, quite independently of any theoretical formulation and institutional organization, a tactic of the manipulation of madness was defined which in a way sketched out the framework of power relationships needed for the mental orthopedics that had to lead to the cure. The scene of George III is basically one of these scenes, one of the first.

I think we could then trace the future development, and transformation of these scenes, and find again how, and under what conditions, these proto-psychiatric scenes are developed in a first phase, between 1840 and 1870, of what could be called moral treatment, of which Leuret was the hero.[22]

Later, this same proto-psychiatric scene, transformed by moral treatment, is further greatly transformed by a fundamental episode in the history of psychiatry, by both the discovery and practice of hypnosis and the analysis of hysterical phenomena.

Then there is, of course, the psychoanalytic scene.

And finally, there is, if you like, the anti-psychiatric scene. Even so, it is strange to see how close this first scene of proto-psychiatry, the scene of George III, is to the scene described in the book by Mary Barnes and Berke. You are familiar with the story of Mary Barnes at Kingsley Hall, in which the elements are more or less the same as those found in the story of George III:

"One day Mary presented me with the ultimate test of my love for her. She covered herself in shit and waited to see what my reaction would be. Her account of this incident amuses her because of her blind confidence that her shit could not put me off. I can assure you the reverse was true. When I, unsuspectingly, walked into the games room and was accosted by foul smelling Mary Barnes looking far worse than the creature from the black lagoon, I was terrified and nauseated. My first reaction was to escape and I stalked away as fast as I could. Fortunately she didn't try to follow me. I would have belted her.

"I remember my first thoughts very well: 'This is too much, too bloody much. She can damn well take care of herself from now on. I want nothing more to do with her'."

Then Berke reflects and says to himself that, after all, if he does not do it, it will be all up for her, and he does not want this. This final argument brooks no reply. He follows Mary Barnes, not without considerable reluctance on his part. "Mary was still in the games room, her head bowed, sobbing. I muttered something like, 'Now, now, it's all right. Let's go upstairs and get you a nice warm bath.' It took at least an hour to get Mary cleaned up. She was a right mess. Shit was everywhere, in her hair, under her arms, in between her toes. I had visions of the principal character in an oldie terror movie, *The Mummy's Ghost*."[23]

In reality he had failed to recognize the proto-scene of the history of psychiatry, that is to say the history of George III: it was precisely that.

What I would like to do this year is basically a history of these psychiatric scenes, taking into account what is for me perhaps a postulate, or at any rate a hypothesis, that this psychiatric scene and what is going on in this scene, the game of power which is sketched out in it, should be analyzed before any institutional organization, or discourse of truth, or importation of models. And I would like to study these scenes emphasizing one thing, which is that the scene involving George III that I have been talking about is not only the first in a long series of psychiatric scenes, but is historically part of another, different series of scenes. In the proto-psychiatric scene you find again everything that could be called the ceremony of sovereignty: coronation, dispossession, submission, allegiance, surrender, restoration, and so forth. But there is also the series of rituals of service imposed by some on others: giving orders, obeying, observing rules, punishing, rewarding, answering, remaining silent. There is the series of judicial procedures: proclaiming the law, watching out for infractions, obtaining a confession, establishing a fault, making a judgment, imposing a penalty. Finally, you find a whole series of medical practices, and crucially the major medical practice of the crisis: looking out for the moment at which the crisis intervenes, encouraging its unfolding and its completion, ensuring that the healthy forces prevail over the others.

It seems to me that if we want to produce a true history of psychiatry, at any rate of the psychiatric scene, it will be by situating it in this series of scenes—scenes of the ceremony of sovereignty, of rituals of service, of judicial procedures, and of medical practices—and not by making analysis of the institution the essential point and our point of departure.* Let's be really anti-institutionalist. What I propose to bring to light this year is, before analysis of the institution, the microphysics of power.

I would like now to look more closely at this proto-psychiatric scene of which I have given you a first idea. It seems to me that the scene of George III marks a very important break insofar as it clearly departs from a number of scenes that had been the regulated and canonical way of treating madness until then. It seems to me that until the end of the eighteenth century, and we still find some examples of this right at the start of the nineteenth century, the manipulation of madness by doctors was part of the stratagem of truth. It involved constituting around the illness, in the extension of the illness as it were, by letting it unfold and by following it, a sort of both fictional and real world in which madness will be caught in the trap of a reality that has been insidiously induced. I will give you an example of this; it is a case of Mason Cox, which was published in England in 1804 and in France in 1806, in his book *Practical Observations on Insanity*.

"Mr . . . . . aged 36, of full habit, melancholic temperament, extremely attached to literary pursuits, and subject to depression of spirits without any obvious cause. His lucubrations were sometimes extended through whole days and nights in succession, and at these periods he was very abstemious, drank only water, and avoided animal food; his friends remonstrated with him on the hazard of such proceedings; and his house-keeper being urgent for his adopting some plan that had his health for the immediate object, the idea struck him of her having some sinister design and that she intended to destroy him by means of a succession of poisoned shirts, under the baneful influence of which he believed himself then suffering. No arguments availed, and all reasoning was ineffectual, the hallucination therefore was humoured, a suspected shirt was exposed to some simple chemical experiments, continued, repeated, and varied with much ceremony, and the results so contrived as to prove the truth of the patient's suspicions; the house-keeper, notwithstanding all her protestations of innocence was served with a pretended warrant, and in the presence of the patient, hurried out of the house by the proper officers, and

* The manuscript clarifies the notion of scene: "Understanding by scene, not a theatrical episode, but a ritual, a strategy, a battle."

secluded from his observation for a time, while he supposed she was in gaol expecting an ignominious death ... After this preface, a formal consultation was held, certain antidotes prescribed, and after a few weeks he perfectly recovered; a new plan of life and regimen were adopted, and he has ever since continued to enjoy mens sana in corpore sano."[24]

In a case history like this, you see finally how a psychiatric practice functioned. Basically, starting from the delirious idea, it involved developing a sort of labyrinth exactly patterned on the delirium itself, homogeneous with the erroneous idea, through which the patient is taken. The patient believes, for example, that his servant gives him shirts poisoned with sulfur which irritate his skin. Okay, we pursue the delirium. His shirts are examined by an expert, which naturally produces a positive result. Since we have a positive result, the case is submitted to a court: the proofs are submitted and a judgment, a condemnation, is pronounced, and we pretend to send the servant to prison.

There is, then, the organization of a labyrinth homogeneous with the delirious idea, and a sort of forked outcome is placed at the end of this labyrinth, an outcome at two levels, which, precisely, will bring about the cure. On the one hand, there will be an event produced within the delirium. That is to say, at the level of the patient's delirium, the imprisonment of the guilty party confirms the truth of the delirium, but, at the same time, assures the patient that he has been freed from what, within his delirium, was the cause of his illness. There is then this first result, at the level of the delirium itself, authenticating the delirium and getting rid of what it is that functions as cause within the delirium.

Now, at a different level, that is to say at the level of the doctors, of those around the patient, something very different happens. By pretending to imprison the servant, she is put out of play, she is separated from the patient, and the patient thus finds himself sheltered from what, in reality, was the cause of his illness, that is to say his mistrust and hatred of her. So that which is the cause within, and the cause of, his delirium are short-circuited in one and the same operation.

This operation had to be one and the same; that is to say, it had to take place at the end of the labyrinth of the delirium, because for the doctors it was quite clear that if the servant was purely and simply dismissed, without being dismissed as the cause within the delirium, then the delirium could have begun again. The patient would imagine that she was still pursuing him, that she had found a way of getting round them, or he would redirect mistrust of his servant on to someone else. From the moment that one effectuates the delirium, that one accords it reality, authenticates it and, at the same time, suppresses the cause within it, one has the conditions for the liquidation of the delirium itself.* And if the conditions for liquidating the delirium are at the same time the suppression of what caused the delirium itself, then the cure is assured as a result. So, if you like, there is both suppression of the cause of delirium, and suppression of the cause within the delirium. And it is this kind of fork, arrived at through the labyrinth of fictional verification, that assures the very principle of the cure.

Now—and this is the third moment—when the patient really believes that his delirium was the truth, when the patient believes that what, within his delirium, was the cause of his illness has been suppressed, then he discovers as a result the possibility of accepting medical intervention. On the pretext of curing him of the illness inflicted on him by the servant, one slips into this kind of opening a medication that is medication within the delirium, a medication that within the delirium will enable him to escape the illness caused by the servant, and which is a medication for the delirium since he is actually given medicine that, by calming his humors, by calming his blood, by discharging all the congestions of his blood system, etcetera, ensures the cure. And again you can see that an element of reality, the medicine, functions at two levels: as medication within the delirium and as therapy for the delirium. It is this kind of organized game around the fictional verification of the delirium that effectively ensures the cure.

Okay, this game of truth, within delirium and of delirium, will be completely suppressed in the psychiatric practice that commences at the start of the nineteenth century. It seems to me that the emergence of what we can call a disciplinary practice, this new microphysics of power, will sweep all this away and establish the core elements of all the psychiatric scenes that develop subsequently, and on the basis of which psychiatric theory and the psychiatric institution will be built.

* The manuscript adds: "One really suppresses that which functions as the cause within the delirium, but it is suppressed in a form that the delirium can accept."

1. "Philippe Pinel freeing the mad from their chains at Bicêtre"—where, appointed on 6 August 1793, he took up his post as "infirmary doctor" on 11 September 1793—is the version given by his eldest son, Scipion Pinel (1795-1859), referring the event to 1792, in an apocryphal article attributed to his father: "Sur l'abolition des chaînes des aliénés, par Philippe Pinel, membre d l'Institut. Note extraite de ses cahiers, communiqués par M. Pinel fils" *Archives de médicine*, 1st year, vol. 2, May 1823, pp. 15-17; and communication to the Academy of Medicine: "Bicêtre en 1792. De l'abolition des chaînes" *Mémoires de l'Académie de médecine*, no. 5, 1856, pp. 32-40. In 1849 the painter Charles Müller immortalized him in a painting entitled *Pinel removes the chains from the mad of Bicêtre*. Foucault refers to this in *Histoire de la folie*, Part 3, ch. 4, pp. 483-484 and 496-501; *Madness and Civilization*, ch. 9, pp. 241-243 (pages 484-501 of the French edition are omitted from the English translation).
2. P. Pinel, *Traité médico-philosophique sur l'aliénation mentale, ou la Manie*, section V: "Police intérieure et surveillance à établir dans les hospices d'aliénation: § vii, Les maniaques, durant leurs accès doivent-ils être condamnés à une réclusion étroite?" pp. 192-193; *A Treatise on Insanity*, "The importance of an enlightened system of police for the internal management of lunatic asylums: Is close confinement requisite in all cases and throughout the whole term of acute mania?" pp. 187-188. George III (1738-1820), King of Great Britain and Ireland, had several episodes of mental disturbance in 1765, 1788-1789, from February to July 1810, and from October 1810 until his death on 29 January 1820. See I. Macalpine and R. Hunter, *George III and the Mad-Business* (New York: Pantheon Books, 1969).
3. Sir Francis Willis (1718-1807), the proprietor of an establishment in Lincolnshire for people suffering from mental disorders, was called to London on 5 December 1788 within the framework of a commission created by Parliament in order to pronounce on the King's condition. Willis looked after George III until the remission of his disorder in March 1789. The episode referred to by Pinel is in "Observations sur le régime moral que est le plus propre à rétablir, dans certains cas, la raison égarée des monarques" pp. 13-15, reproduced in J. Postel, *Genése de la psychiatrie. Les premiers écrits de Philippe Pinel* (Le Plessis-Robinson, Institut Synthélabo, 1998) pp. 194-197, and *Traité médico-philosophique*, pp. 192-193; *A Treatise on Insanity*, pp. 187-188, and pp. 286-290 in which Pinel quotes the *Report from the Committee Appointed to Examine the Physicians who Have Attended His Majesty during his Illness, touching the Present State of His Majesty's Health* (London: 1789) [This latter section, entitled "Exemple mémorable d'une discussion sur la manie, devenue une affaire d'état," is omitted from the English translation; G.B.]
4. William Shakespeare, *The Tragedy of King Richard the Third*, written at the end of 1592 and the beginning of 1593, describes the accession to the throne, by usurpation, of Richard, Duke of Gloucester, the brother of King Edward IV, and then his death at the Battle of Bosworth.
5. *The Tragedy of King Lear* (performed at Court on 26 December 1606, first published in 1608, and then in a revised version in 1623). Foucault refers to King Lear in *Histoire de la folie*, p. 49; *Madness and Civilization*, p. 31, and also refers to the work of A. Adnès, *Shakespeare et la folie. Étude médico-psychologique* (Paris: Maloine, 1935) [the reference to Adnès is omitted from the English translation; G.B.]. He returns to it in the Course at the Collège de France of 1983-1984, "Le Gouvernement de soi et des autres. Le courage de la vérité," lecture of 21 March 1984.
6. P. Pinel, *Traité médico-philosophique*, p. 192; *A Treatise on Insanity*, p. 188.
7. Ibid. p. 193; ibid. p. 188.
8. Ibid.; ibid.
9. On 6 January 1838, the Minister of the Interior, Adrien de Gasparin, presented to the Chamber of Deputies a draft law on the insane, which was voted on by the Chamber of Peers on 22 March, and on 14 June by the Chamber of Deputies. It was promulgated on 30 June 1838. See, R. Castel, *L'Ordre psychiatrique. L'âge d'or de l'aliénisme* (Paris: Éd. de Minuit, 1976) pp. 316-324; English translation, *The Regulation of Madness, the origins of incarceration in France*, trans. W. D. Halls (Berkeley and Los Angeles: University of California Press, 1988) pp. 243-253.

10. P. Pinel, *Traité médico-philosophique*, p. 193; *A Treatise on Insanity*, p. 188.
11. Foucault is alluding here to Descartes evoking those "madmen, whose brains are so damaged by the persistent vapours of melancholia that they firmly maintain they are kings when they are paupers, or say they are (...) made of glass" *Méditations touchant la première philosophie* (1641), trans. duc de Luynes, 1647, "First meditation: Some things that one can put in doubt" in *Œuvres et Lettres*, A. Bridoux (Paris: Gallimard, 1952) p. 268; English translation, "Meditations on First Philosophy" trans. John Cottingham, in *The Philosophical Writings of Descartes*, trans. John Cottingham, Robert Stoothoff, and Dugald Murdoch (Cambridge: Cambridge University Press, 1984) vol. 2, p. 13. See M. Foucault, "Mon corps, ce papier, ce feu" in *Dits et Écrits, 1954-1988*, four volumes, ed. D. Defert and F. Ewald, with the collaboration of J. Lagrange (Paris: Gallimard, 1994), vol. 2, pp. 245-268; English translation, "My Body, This Paper, This Fire" trans. Geoff Bennington, in M. Foucault, *The Essential Works of Michel Foucault 1954-1984, Volume 2: Aesthetics, Method, and Epistemology*, ed. James Faubion, trans. Robert Hurley and others (New York: New Press, 1998) [hereafter, *Essential Works of Foucault*, 2].
12. E. J. Georget, *De la folie. Considérations sur cette maladie*, p. 282: "Nothing in the world can persuade them otherwise. You tell (...) a supposed king that he is not a king and he will reply with insults."
13. J. Haslam, *Observations on Insanity*, *Observations on Madness and Melancholy*, and *Considerations on the Moral Management of Insane Persons.*
14. P. Pinel, *Traité médico-philosophique*. The manuscript refers to cases that figure in section II, § vii, pp. 58-59; § xxiii, pp. 96-97; and section V, § 3, pp. 181-183, and § 9, pp. 196-197; A *Treatise on Insanity*, pp. 60-61; pp. 103-106; pp. 178-179; pp. 191-193.
15. J. E. D. Esquirol, *Des maladies mentales; Mental Maladies.*
16. F. E. Fodéré, *Traité du délire*, and, *Essai médico-légal sur les diverses espèces de folie vraie, simulée et raisonnée, sur les causes et les moyens de les distinguer, sur leurs effets excusant ou atténuant devant les tribunaux, et sur leur association avec les penchants au crime et plusieurs maladies physiques et morales* (Strasbourg: Le Roux, 1832).
17. E. J. Georget, *De la folie*, and, *De la physiologie du système nerveux et spécialement du cerveau. Recherches sur les maladies nerveuses en général, et en particulier sur le siège, la nature et le traitement de l'hystérie, de l'hypocondrie, de l'épilepsie et de l'asthme convulsif*, 2 volumes (Paris: J.-B. Baillière, 1821).
18. Joseph Guislain (1797-1860), *Traité sur l'aliénation mentale et sur les hospices des aliénes*, 2 volumes (Amsterdam: Van der Hey and Gartman, 1826), and, *Traité sur les phrénopathies ou Doctrine naturelle nouvelle des maladies mentales, basée sur des observations pratiques et statistiques, et l'étude des causes, de la nature des symptômes, du pronostic, du diagnostic et du traitement de ces affections* (Brussels: Établissement Encyclographique, 1833).
19. P. Pinel, *Traité médico-philosophique*, section II, § vii, pp. 58-59; A *Treatise on Insanity*, pp. 60-61.
20. Ibid. § xxiii, pp. 96-97n; ibid. p. 100n.
21. Ibid. section V, § iii, pp. 181-183; ibid. pp. 178-179.
22. François Leuret develops his conceptions in "Mémoire sur le traitement moral de la folie" in *Mémoires de l'Académie royale de médecine*, vol. 7 (Paris: 1838) pp. 552-276; *Du traitement moral de la folie*; "Mémoire sur la révulsion morale dans la traitement de la folie" in *Mémoires de l'Académie royale de médecine*, vol. 9 (Paris: 1841) pp. 655-671; and *Des indications à suivre dans le traitement moral de la folie* (Paris: Le Normant, 1846).
23. When she was 42 years old, Mary Barnes, a nurse, entered the reception center of Kingsley Hall, which opened in 1965 for staff suffering from mental problems, before closing on 31 May 1970. She spent five years there and her history is known to us through the work she wrote with her therapist: M. Barnes and J. Berke, *Mary Barnes. Two Accounts of a Journey through Madness* (London: McGibbon and Kee, 1971) pp. 248-249; French translation, *Mary Barnes. Un voyage autour de la folie*, trans. M. Davidovici (Paris: Le Seuil, 1973) pp. 287-288.
24. Joseph Mason Cox (1763-1818), *Practical Observations on Insanity* (London: Baldwin and Murray, 1806), Case IV, pp. 53-5; French translation, *Observations sur la démence*, trans. L. Odier (Geneva: Bibliothèque Britannique, 1806) pp. 80-81. [It has not been possible to consult a copy of the 1st 1804 edition of Mason Cox on which the 1806 French translation is based. English page references are to the 2nd, 1806 edition; G.B.]

three

21 November 1973

[*Genealogy of "disciplinary power." The "power of sovereignty." The subject-function in disciplinary power and in the power of sovereignty. ~ Forms of disciplinary power: army, police, apprenticeship, workshop, school. ~ Disciplinary power as "normalizing agency." ~ Technology of disciplinary power and constitution of the "individual." ~ Emergence of the human sciences.*]

WE CAN SAY THAT between 1850 and 1930 classical psychiatry reigned and functioned without too many external problems on the basis of what it considered to be, and put to work as, a true discourse. At any rate, from this discourse it deduced the need for the asylum institution as well as the need to deploy a medical power as an internal and effective law within this institution. In short, it deduced the need for an institution and a power from a supposedly true discourse.

It seems to me that we can say that criticism of the institution—I hesitate to say "antipsychiatry"—let's say a certain form of criticism which developed from around 1930 to 1940,[1] did not start from a supposedly true psychiatric discourse in order to deduce the need for an institution and a medical power, but rather from the fact of the institution and its functioning, and from criticism of the institution that sought to bring to light, on the one hand, the violence of the medical power exercised within it, and, on the other, the effects of incomprehension that right from the start distorted the supposed truth of this medical discourse. So, if you like, this form of analysis started from the institution in order to denounce power and analyse effects of incomprehension.

What I would like to do instead is try to bring this problem of power to the fore, which is why I have begun the lectures in the way I have. I will leave the relationships between this analysis of power and the problem of the truth of a discourse on madness until a bit later.[2]

I started then with this scene of George III confronted by his servants who were, at the same time, agents of medical power, because it seemed to me a fine example of the confrontation between a power, which, in the person of the king himself, is sovereign power embodied in this mad king, and another type of power, which is instead anonymous and silent, and which, paradoxically, gets support from the servants' strength, from a muscular, obedient force not articulated in discourse. So, on the one hand, there is the king's furious outburst and, facing this, the controlled force of the servants. And the therapeutic process presupposed by Willis and, after him, Pinel, consisted in getting madness to migrate from a sovereignty it drove wild and within which it exploded, to a discipline supposed to subjugate it. What appears in this capture of madness, prior to any institution and outside any discourse of truth, was therefore a power that I call "disciplinary power."

What is this power? I would like to advance the hypothesis that something like disciplinary power exists in our society. By this I mean no more than a particular, as it were, terminal, capillary form of power; a final relay, a particular modality by which political power, power in general, finally reaches the level of bodies and gets a hold on them, taking actions, behavior, habits, and words into account; the way in which power converges below to affect individual bodies themselves, to work on, modify, and direct what Servan called "the soft fibers of the brain."[3] In other words, I think that in our society disciplinary power is a quite specific modality of what could be called the synaptic contact of bodies-power.*

The second hypothesis is that disciplinary power, in its specificity, has a history; it is not born suddenly, has not always existed, and is formed and follows a diagonal trajectory, as it were, through Western society. If we take only the history going from the Middle Ages until our own time, I think we can say that the formation of this power, in its

* The manuscript adds: "Methodologically this entails leaving the problem of the State, of the State apparatus, to one side and dispensing with the psycho-sociological notion of authority."

specific characteristics, was not completely marginal to medieval society, but it was certainly not central either. It was formed within religious communities from where, being transformed in the process, it was taken into the lay communities that developed and multiplied in the pre-Reformation period, let's say in the fourteenth and fifteenth centuries. We can see this transfer to communities like the famous "Brothers of the Common Life," which are not exactly monastic but which, on the basis of techniques taken from monastic life, as well as ascetic exercises taken from a whole tradition of religious exercises, defined disciplinary methods for daily life and pedagogy.[4] This is just one example of the spread of monastic or ascetic disciplines before the Reformation. We then see these techniques gradually spreading far afield, penetrating sixteenth, and especially seventeenth and eighteenth century society, and, in the nineteenth century, becoming the major general form of this synaptic contact: political power-individual body.

To take a somewhat symbolic reference point, I think this evolution, which goes from the Brethren of the Common Life, that is to say from the fourteenth century, to its point of explosion, that is to say, when disciplinary power becomes an absolutely generalized social form, ends up, in 1791, with Bentham's *Panopticon*, which provides the most general political and technical formula of disciplinary power.[5] I think the confrontation between George III and his servants—which is more or less contemporaneous with the *Panopticon*—this confrontation of the king's madness and medical discipline is one of the historical and symbolic points of the emergence and definitive installation of disciplinary power in society. Now I do not think that we can analyze how psychiatry functions by restricting ourselves to the workings of the asylum institution. Obviously there's no question of analyzing how psychiatry functions starting from its supposedly true discourse; but nor do I think we can understand how it functions by analyzing the institution. The mechanism of psychiatry should be understood starting from the way in which disciplinary power works.

So, what is this disciplinary power? This is what I would like to talk about this evening.

It is not very easy to study it. First of all, because I will take a fairly broad time-scale; I will take examples from disciplinary forms that appear in the sixteenth century and develop up until the eighteenth century. It is not easy because, in order to study this disciplinary power, this meeting point of the body and power, it must be analyzed in contrast with another type of power, which preceded it and which will be juxtaposed to it. This is what I will begin to do, without being very certain, moreover, of what I will say.

It seems to me that we could oppose disciplinary power to a power that preceded it historically and with which it was entangled for a long time before finally prevailing in turn. I will call this earlier form of power, in opposition then to disciplinary power, the power of sovereignty, but without being exactly happy with this word for reasons you will soon see.

⚜

What is the power of sovereignty? It seems to me to be a power relationship that links sovereign and subject according to a couple of asymmetrical relationships: a levy or deduction one side, and expenditure on the other. In the relationship of sovereignty, the sovereign imposes a levy on products, harvests, manufactured objects, arms, the labor force, and courage. In a symmetrical reverse process, at the same time as he imposes a levy on services, there will be, not repayment for what he has deducted, for the sovereign does not have to pay back, but the sovereign's expenditure, which may take the form of the gift, which may be made during ritual ceremonies, such as gifts for happy events, like a birth, or gifts of service, such as the service of protection or the religious service ensured by the Church, for example, very different from the kind of service he has levied. It may also be the outlay of expenditure when, for festivals, for the organization of a war, the lord makes those around him work in return for payment. So this system of levy-expenditure seems to me to be typical of this sovereign type of power. Of course, deductions always largely exceed expenditure, and the dissymmetry is so great that, behind this relationship of sovereignty and this dissymmetrical coupling of levy-expenditure, we can see quite clearly the emergence of plunder, pillage, and war.

Second, I think the relationship of sovereignty always bears the mark of a founding precedence. For there to be a relationship of sovereignty there must be something like divine right, or conquest, a victory, an act of submission, an oath of loyalty, an act passed between the sovereign who grants privileges, aid, protection, and so forth, and someone who, in return, pledges himself; or there must be something like birth, the rights of blood. In short, we can say that the relationship of sovereignty always looks back to something that constituted its definitive foundation. But this does not mean that this relationship of sovereignty does not have to be regularly or irregularly reactualized; a characteristic feature of the relationship of sovereignty is that is always reactualized by things like ceremonies and rituals, by narratives also, and by gestures, distinguishing signs, required forms of greeting, marks of respect, insignia, coats of arms, and suchlike. That the relationship of sovereignty is thus founded on precedence and reactualized by a number of more or less ritual actions stems from the fact that the relationship is, in a sense, intangible, that it is given once and for all but, at the same time, is fragile and always liable to disuse or breakdown. For the relationship of sovereignty to really hold, outside of the rite of recommencement and reactualization, outside of the game of ritual signs, there is always the need for a certain supplement or threat of violence, which is there behind the relationship of sovereignty, and which sustains it and ensures that it holds. The other side of sovereignty is violence, it is war.

The third feature of relationships of sovereignty is that they are not isotopic. By this I mean that they are intertwined and tangled up with each other in such a way that we cannot establish a system of exhaustive and planned hierarchy between them. In other words, relationships of sovereignty are indeed perpetual relationships of differentiation, but they are not relationships of classification; they do not constitute a unitary hierarchical table with subordinate and superordinate elements. Not being isotopic means first of all that they are heterogeneous and have no common measure. There is, for example, the relationship of sovereignty between serf and lord, and a different relationship of sovereignty, which absolutely cannot be superimposed on this, between the holder of a fief and a suzerain, and there is the relationship of sovereignty exercised by the priest with regard to the laity, and all these relationships cannot be integrated within a genuinely single system. Furthermore—this again marks the non-isotopic nature of the relationship of sovereignty—the elements it involves, that it puts into play, are not equivalents: a relationship of sovereignty may perfectly well concern the relationship between a sovereign or a suzerain—I do not distinguish them in an analysis as schematic as this—and a family, a community, or the inhabitants of a parish or a region; but sovereignty may also bear on something other than these human multiplicities. Sovereignty may bear on land, a road, an instrument of production—a mill, for example—and on users: those who pass through a tollgate, along a road, fall under the relationship of sovereignty.

So you can see that the relationship of sovereignty is a relationship in which the subject-element is not so much, and we can even say it is almost never, an individual, an individual body. The relationship of sovereignty applies not to a somatic singularity but to multiplicities—like families, users—which in a way are situated above physical individuality, or, on the contrary, it applies to fragments or aspects of individuality, of somatic singularity. It is insofar as one is the son of X, a bourgeois of this town, etcetera, that one will be held in a relationship of sovereignty, that one will be sovereign or, alternatively, subject, and one may be both subject and sovereign in different aspects, so that these relationships can never be wholly plotted and laid out according to the terms of a single table.

In other words, in a relationship of sovereignty, what I call the subject-function moves around and circulates above and below somatic singularities, and, conversely, bodies circulate, move around, rest on something here, and take flight. In these relationships of sovereignty there is therefore a never ending game of movements and disputes in which subject-functions and somatic singularities, let's say—with a word I am not very happy with for reasons you will soon see—individuals, are moved around in relation to each other. The pinning of the subject-function to a definite body can only take place at times in a discontinuous, incidental fashion, in ceremonies for example. It takes place when the individual's body is marked by an insignia, by the gesture he makes: in homage, for example, when a somatic singularity is effectively marked with the seal of the sovereignty that accepts it. Or it takes place in the violence with which sovereignty asserts its rights and forcibly imposes them on someone it subjects. So, at the actual level at which the relationship of sovereignty is applied, at the lower extremity of the relationship, if you like, you never find a perfect fit between sovereignty and corporeal singularities.

On the other hand, if you look towards the summit you will see there the individualization absent at the base; you begin to see it sketched out towards the top. There is a sort of underlying individualization of the relationship of sovereignty towards the top, that is to say, towards the sovereign. The power of sovereignty necessarily entails a sort of monarchical spiral. That is to say, precisely insofar as the power of sovereignty is not isotopic but entails never ending disputes and movements, to the extent that plunder, pillage, and war still rumble behind these sovereign relationships, and the individual as such is never caught in the relationship, then, at a given moment and coming from above, there must be something that ensures arbitration: there must be a single, individual point which is the summit of this set of heterotopic relationships that absolutely cannot be plotted on one and the same table.

The sovereign's individuality is entailed by the non-individualization of the elements on which the relationship of sovereignty is applied. Consequently there is the need for something like a sovereign who, in his own body, is the point on which all these multiple, different, and irreconcilable relationships converge. Thus, at the summit of this type of power, there is necessarily something like the king in his individuality, with his king's body. But straightaway you see a very odd phenomenon, which has been studied by Kantorowicz in his book *The King's Two Bodies*:[6] in order to ensure his sovereignty, the king really must be an individual with a body, but this body must not die along with the king's somatic singularity. The monarchy must remain when the monarch no longer exists; the king's body, which holds together all these relationships of sovereignty, must not disappear with the death of this individual X or Y. The king's body, therefore, must have a kind of permanence; more than just his somatic singularity, it must be the solidity of his realm, of his crown. So that the individualization we see outlined at the summit of the relationship of sovereignty entails the multiplication of the king's body. The king's body is at least double according to Kantorowicz, and on closer examination, starting from a certain period at least, it is probably an absolutely multiple body.

So I think we can say that the relationship of sovereignty does put something like political power in contact with the body, applies it to the body, but that it never reveals individuality.* It is a form of power without an individualizing function, or which only outlines individuality on the sovereign's side, and again, at the cost of this curious, paradoxical, and mythological multiplication of bodies. We have bodies without any individuality on one side, and individuality but a multiplicity of bodies on the other.

Okay, now for disciplinary power, since this is what I particularly want to talk about.

I think we could contrast it almost term for term with sovereignty. First of all, disciplinary power does not make use of this mechanism, this asymmetrical coupling of levy-expenditure. In a disciplinary apparatus there is no dualism, no asymmetry; there is not this kind of fragmented hold. It seems to me that disciplinary power can be characterized first of all by the fact that it does not involve imposing a levy on the product or on a part of time, or on this or that category of service, but that it is a total hold, or, at any rate, tends to be an exhaustive capture of the individual's body, actions, time, and behavior. It is a seizure of the body, and not of the product; it is a seizure of time in its totality, and not of the time of service.

We have a very clear example of this in the appearance of military discipline at the end of the seventeenth century and throughout the course of the eighteenth century. Until the beginning of the seventeenth century, roughly until the Thirty Years War, military discipline did not exist; what existed was a never-ending transition from vagabondage to the army. That is to say, the army was always constituted by a group of people recruited for a finite time for the needs of the cause, and to whom food and lodging were assured through pillage and the occupation of any premises found on the spot. In other words, in this system, which was still part of the order of sovereignty, a certain amount of time was deducted from people's lives, some of their resources were deducted by the requirement that they bring their arms, and they were promised something like the reward of pillage.

---

* The manuscript clarifies: "The subject pole never coincides continually with the somatic singularity, except in the ritual of branding."

From the middle of the seventeenth century you see something like the disciplinary system appearing in the army; that is to say an army lodged in barracks and in which the soldiers are engaged. That is to say, they are engaged for the whole day for the duration of the campaign, and, apart from demobilizations, they are equally engaged during peacetime, because, from 1750 or 1760, when his life of soldiering comes to an end, the soldier receives a pension and becomes a retired soldier. Military discipline begins to be the general confiscation of the body, time, and life; it is no longer a levy on the individual's activity but an occupation of his body, life, and time. Every disciplinary system tends, I think, to be an occupation of the individual's time, life, and body.[7]

Second, the disciplinary system does not need this discontinuous, ritual, more or less cyclical game of ceremonies and marks in order to function. Disciplinary power is not discontinuous but involves a procedure of continuous control instead. In the disciplinary system, one is not available for someone's possible use, one is perpetually under someone's gaze, or, at any rate, in the situation of being observed. One is not then marked by an action made once and for all, or by a situation given from the start, but visible and always in the situation of being under constant observation. More precisely, we can say that there is no reference to an act, an event, or an original right in the relationship of disciplinary power. Disciplinary power refers instead to a final or optimum state. It looks forward to the future, towards the moment when it will keep going by itself and only a virtual supervision will be required, when discipline, consequently, will have become habit. There is a genetic polarization, a temporal gradient in discipline, exactly the opposite of the reference to precedence that is necessarily involved in relationships of sovereignty. All discipline entails this kind of genetic course by which, from a point, which is not given as the inescapable situation, but as the zero point of the start of discipline, something must develop such that discipline will keep going by itself. What is it, then, that ensures this permanent functioning of discipline, this kind of genetic continuity typical of disciplinary power? It is obviously not the ritual or cyclical ceremony, but exercise; progressive, graduated exercise will mark out the growth and improvement of discipline on a temporal scale.

Here again we can take the army as our example. In the army as it existed in the form I call the power of sovereignty, there was certainly something that could be called exercises, but actually its function was not at all that of disciplinary exercise: there were things like jousts and games. That is to say, warriors, those at least who were warriors by status—nobles and knights—regularly practiced jousting and suchlike. We could interpret this as a sort exercise, as a training of the body, in a sense, but I think it was essentially a kind of repetition of bravery, a test by which the individual displayed that he was in a permanent state of readiness to assert his status as a knight and so do honor to the situation in which he exercised certain rights and obtained certain privileges. The joust was perhaps a kind of exercise, but I think it was above all the cyclical repetition of the great test by which a knight became a knight.

On the other hand, from the eighteenth century, especially with Frederick II and the Prussian army, you see the appearance of physical exercise in the army, something that hardly existed before. In the army of Frederick II, and in western armies at the end of eighteenth century, this physical exercise does not consist in things like jousting, that is to say, the repetition and reproduction of the actions of war. Physical exercise is a training of the body; it is the training of skill, marching, resistance, and elementary movements in accordance with a graduated scale, completely different from the cyclical repetition of jousts and games. So what I think is typical of discipline is not ceremony, but exercise as the means for assuring this [sort] of genetic continuity.[8]

I think discipline necessarily resorts to writing as an instrument of this control, of the permanent and overall taking charge of the individual's body. That is to say, whereas the relation of sovereignty entails the actualization of the distinctive mark, I think we could say that discipline, with its requirement of complete visibility, its constitution of genetic paths, this kind of typical hierarchical continuum, necessarily calls on writing. This is first of all to ensure that everything that happens, everything the individual does and says, is graded and recorded, and then to transmit this information from below up through the hierarchical levels, and then, finally, to make this information accessible and thereby assure the principle of omnivisibility, which is, I think, the second major characteristic of discipline.

It seems to me that the use of writing is absolutely necessary for disciplinary power to be total and continuous, and I think we could study the way in which, from the seventeenth and eighteenth centuries, in the army as in schools, in centers of apprenticeship as in the police or judicial system, people's bodies, behavior, and discourse are gradually besieged by a tissue of writing, by a sort of graphic plasma which records them, codifies them, and passes them up through the hierarchy to a centralized point.* I think this direct and continuous relationship of writing to the body is new. The visibility of the body and the permanence of writing go together, and obviously their effect is what could be called schematic and centralized individualization.

I will take just two examples of this game of writing in discipline. The first is in the schools of apprenticeship that are formed in the second half of the seventeenth century and multiply during the eighteenth century. Consider corporative apprenticeship in the Middle Ages, in the sixteenth and still in the seventeenth centuries. For a fee, an apprentice joined a master whose only obligation, in return for this sum of money, was to pass on the whole of his learning to the apprentice. In return the apprentice had to provide the master with any services the latter demanded. There was an exchange, then, of daily service for the major service of the transmission of knowledge. At the end of the apprenticeship, there was only a form of checking, the masterpiece, which was submitted to the *jurande*, that is to say a jury of the responsible individuals of the town's corporation or professional body.

Now a completely new type of institution appears in the second half of the seventeenth century. As an example of this, I will take the Gobelins' professional school of design and tapestry, which was organized in 1667 and gradually improved up until an important regulation of 1737.[9] Apprenticeship takes place here in a completely different way. That is to say, the students are first of all divided up according to age, and a certain type of work is given to each age block. This work must be done in the presence either of teachers or supervisors, and it must be assessed at the same time and together with assessment of the student's behavior, assiduity, and zeal while performing his work. These assessments are entered on registers which are kept and passed on up the hierarchy to the director of the Gobelins' manufacture himself, and, on this

* The manuscripts says: "Bodies, actions, behaviors, and discourses are gradually besieged by a tissue of writing, a graphic plasma, which records them, codifies them, and schematizes them."

basis, a succinct report is sent to the minister of the King's Household concerning the quality of the work, the student's abilities, and whether he can now be considered a master. A whole network of writing is constituted around the apprentice's behavior, and this will first codify all his behavior in terms of a number of assessments determined in advance, then schematize it, and finally convey it to a point of centralization which will define his ability or inability. There is, then, an investment by writing, codification, transfer, and centralization, in short, the constitution of a schematic and centralized individuality.

We could say the same thing about the police discipline established in most European countries, and especially in France, in the second half of the eighteenth century. Police practice in the area of writing was still very simple in the second half of the seventeenth century: when an infraction was committed that was not a court matter, the lieutenant of the police (or his deputies) took charge and made a decision, which was simply notified. And then, in the course of the eighteenth century, gradually you see the individual beginning to be completely besieged by writing. That is to say, you see the appearance of visits to *maisons d'internement* to check up on the individual: why was he arrested, when was he arrested, how has he conducted himself since, has he made progress, and so on? The system is refined and in the second half of the eighteenth century you see the constitution of files for those who have simply come to the notice of the police, or whom the police suspect of something. Around the 1760s, I think, the police are required to make two copies of reports on those they suspect—reports which must be kept up to date, of course—one remaining on the spot, enabling a check to be made on the individual where he lives, and a copy sent to Paris, which is centralized at the ministry and redistributed to the other regions falling under different lieutenants of police, so that the individual can be immediately identified if he moves. Biographies are constituted in this way, or, in actual fact, police individualities based on the techniques of what I will call perpetual investment by writing. This administrative and centralized individuality is constituted in 1826 when a way is found to apply the cataloguing techniques already in use in libraries and botanical gardens.[10]

Finally, the continuous and endless visibility assured by writing has an important effect: the extreme promptness of the reaction of disciplinary power that this perpetual visibility in the disciplinary system made possible. Unlike sovereign power—which only intervenes violently, from time to time, and in the form of war, exemplary punishment, or ceremony—disciplinary power will be able to intervene without halt from the first moment, the first action, the first hint. Disciplinary power has an inherent tendency to intervene at the same level as what is happening, at the point when the virtual is becoming real; disciplinary power always tends to intervene beforehand, before the act itself if possible, and by means of an infra-judicial interplay of supervision, rewards, punishments, and pressure.

If we can say that the other side of sovereignty was war, I think we can say that the other side of the disciplinary relationship is punishment, both miniscule and continuous punitive pressure.

Here again, we could take an example of this from work discipline, from discipline in the workshop. In workers' contracts which were signed, and this was sometimes the case very early on, in the fifteenth and sixteenth centuries, the worker typically had to end his work before a given time, or he had to give so many days work to his patron. If he did not finish the work or provide the full number of days, then he had to give either the equivalent of what was lacking, or add on a certain quantity of work or money as amends. So there was, if you like, a punitive system that hung on, worked on and starting from what had actually been done, as either damage or fault.

On the other hand, from the eighteenth century you see the birth of a subtle system of workshop discipline that focuses on potential behavior. In the workshop regulations distributed at this time you see a comparative supervision of workers, their lateness and absences noted down to the last minute; you also see the punishment of anything that might involve distraction. For example, a Gobelins regulation of 1680 notes that even hymns sung while working must be sung quietly so as not to disturb one's fellow workers.[11] There are regulations against telling bawdy stories when returning from lunch or dinner, because this distracts the workers who will then lack the calmness of mind required for work. So, there is a continuous pressure of this disciplinary power, which is not brought to bear on an offense or damage but on potential behavior. One must be able to spot an action even before it has been performed, and disciplinary power must intervene somehow before the actual manifestation of the behavior, before the body, the action, or the discourse, at the level of what is potential, disposition, will, at the level of the soul. In this way something, the soul, is projected behind disciplinary power, but it is a very different soul from the one defined by Christian practice and theory.

To summarize this second aspect of disciplinary power, which we could call the panoptic character of disciplinary power, the absolute and constant visibility surrounding the bodies of individuals, I think we could say the following: the panoptic principle—seeing everything, everyone, all the time—organizes a genetic polarity of time; it proceeds towards a centralized individualization the support and instrument of which is writing; and finally, it involves a punitive and continuous action on potential behavior that, behind the body itself, projects something like a psyche.

Finally, the third characteristic distinguishing disciplinary power from the apparatus of sovereignty is that a disciplinary apparatus is isotopic or, at least, tends towards isotopy. This means a number of things.

First of all, every element in a disciplinary apparatus has its well-defined place; it has its subordinate elements and its superordinate elements. Grades in the army, or again in the school, the clear distinction between classes of different age groups, between different ranks within age groups, all of this, which was established in the eighteenth century, is a superb example of this isotopy. To show how far this went, we should not forget that in classes that were disciplinarized according to the Jesuit model,[12] and above all in the model of the school of the Brethren of the Common Life, the individual's place in the class was determined by where he was ranked in his school results.[13] So what was called the individual's *locus* was both his place in the class and his rank in the hierarchy of values and success. This is a fine example of the isotopy of the disciplinary system.

Consequently, movement in this system cannot be produced through discontinuity, dispute, favor, etcetera; it cannot be produced as the result of a breach, as was the case for the power of sovereignty, but is produced by a regular movement of examination, competition, seniority, and suchlike.

But isotopic also means that there is no conflict or incompatibility between these different systems; different disciplinary apparatuses must be able to connect up with each other. Precisely because of this codification, this schematization, because of the formal properties of the disciplinary apparatus, it must always be possible to pass from one to the other. Thus, school classifications are projected, with some modification, but without too much difficulty, into the social-technical hierarchies of the adult world. The hierarchism in the disciplinary and military system takes up, while transforming them, the disciplinary hierarchies found in the civil system. In short, there is an almost absolute isotopy of these different systems.

Finally, in the disciplinary system, isotopic means above all that the principle of distribution and classification of all the elements necessarily entails something like a residue. That is to say, there is always something like "the unclassifiable." The wall one came up against in relations of sovereignty was the wall between the different systems of sovereignty; disputes and conflicts, the kind of permanent war between different systems, was the stumbling block for the system of sovereignty. Disciplinary systems, on the other hand, which classify, hierarchize, supervise, and so on, come up against those who cannot be classified, those who escape supervision, those who cannot enter the system of distribution, in short, the residual, the irreducible, the unclassifiable, the inassimilable. This will be the stumbling block in the physics of disciplinary power. That is to say, all disciplinary power has its margins. For example, the deserter did not exist prior to disciplined armies, for the deserter was quite simply the future soldier, someone who left the army so that he could rejoin it if necessary, when he wanted to, or when he was taken by force. However, as soon as you have a disciplined army, that is to say people who join the army, make a career of it, follow a certain track, and are supervised from end to end, then the deserter is someone who escapes this system and is irreducible to it.

In the same way, you see the appearance of something like the feeble-minded or mentally defective when there is school discipline.[14] The individual who cannot be reached by school discipline can only exist in relation to this discipline; someone who does not learn to read and write can only appear as a problem, as a limit, when the school adopts the disciplinary schema. In the same way, when does the category of delinquent appear? Delinquents are not law-breakers. It is true that the correlate of every law is the existence of offenders who break the law, but the delinquents as an inassimilable, irreducible group can only appear when it is picked out in relation to a police discipline. As for the mentally ill, they are no doubt the residue of all residues, the residue of all the disciplines, those who are inassimilable to all of a society's educational, military, and police disciplines.

So the necessary existence of residues is, I think, a specific characteristic of this isotopy of disciplinary systems, and it will entail, of course, the appearance of supplementary disciplinary systems in order to retrieve these individuals, and so on to infinity. Since there are the feeble-minded, that is to say, individuals inaccessible to school discipline, schools for the feeble-minded will be created, and then schools for those who are inaccessible to schools for the feeble-minded. It is the same with respect to delinquents; in a way, the organization of the "underworld" was formed partly by the police and partly by the hard core themselves. The underworld is a way of making the delinquent collaborate in the work of the police. We can say that the underworld is the discipline of those who are inaccessible to police discipline.

In short, disciplinary power has this double property of being "anomizing," that is to say, always discarding certain individuals, bringing anomie, the irreducible, to light, and of always being normalizing, that is to say, inventing ever new recovery systems, always reestablishing the rule. What characterizes disciplinary systems is the never-ending work of the norm in the anomic.

I think all this can be summarized by saying that the major effect of disciplinary power is what could be called the reorganization in depth of the relations between somatic singularity, the subject, and the individual. In the power of sovereignty, in that form of exercising power, I tried to show you how procedures of individualization take shape at the summit, that there was an underlying individualization on the side of the sovereign, with that game of multiple bodies that determines that individuality is lost at the very moment it appears. On the other hand, it seems to me that the individual function disappears at the summit of disciplinary systems, on the side of those who exercise this power and make these systems work.

A disciplinary system is made so that it works by itself, and the person who is in charge of it, or is its director, is not so much an individual as a function that is exercised by this and that person and that could equally be exercised by someone else, which is never the case in the individualization of sovereignty. Moreover, even the person in charge of a disciplinary system is caught up within a broader system in which he is supervised in turn, and at the heart of which he is himself subject to discipline. There is then, I think, an elimination of individualization at the top. On the other hand, the disciplinary system entails, and I think this is essential, a very strong underlying individualization at the base.

I tried to show you that the subject-function in the power of sovereignty is never fastened to a somatic singularity, except in incidental cases like the ceremony, branding, violence, and so on, but that most of the time, and outside of these rituals, the subject-function moves around above and below somatic singularities. In disciplinary power, on the other hand, the subject-function is fitted exactly on the somatic singularity: the subject-function of disciplinary power is applied and brought to bear on the body, on its actions, place, movements, strength, the moments of its life, and its discourses, on all of this. Discipline is that technique of power by which the subject-function is exactly superimposed and fastened on the somatic singularity.

In a word, we can say that disciplinary power, and this is no doubt its fundamental property, fabricates subjected bodies; it pins the subject-function exactly to the body. It fabricates and distributes subjected bodies; it is individualizing [only in that] the individual is nothing other than the subjected body. And all this mechanics of discipline can be summarized by saying this: Disciplinary power is individualizing because it fastens the subject-function to the somatic singularity by means of a system of supervision-writing, or by a system of pangraphic panopticism, which behind the somatic singularity projects, as its extension or as its beginning, a core of virtualities, a psyche, and which further establishes the norm as the principle of division and normalization, as the universal prescription for all individuals constituted in this way.

There is a series in disciplinary power, therefore, that brings together the subject-function, somatic singularity, perpetual observation, writing, the mechanism of infinitesimal punishment, projection of the psyche, and, finally, the division between normal and abnormal. All this constitutes the disciplinary individual and finally fits somatic singularity together with political power. What we may call the individual is not what political power latches on to; what we should call the individual is the effect produced on the somatic singularity, the result of this pinning, by the techniques of political power I have indicated. In no way am I saying that disciplinary power is the only procedure of individualization that has existed in our civilization, and I will try to come back to this next week, but I wanted to say that discipline is this terminal, capillary form of power that constitutes the individual as target, partner, and vis-à-vis in the relationship of power.

To that extent, and if what I have been saying is true, you can see that we cannot say that the individual pre-exists the subject-function, the projection of a psyche, or the normalizing agency. On the contrary, it is insofar as the somatic singularity became the bearer of the subject-function through disciplinary mechanisms that the individual appeared within a political system. The individual was constituted insofar as uninterrupted supervision, continual writing, and potential punishment enframed this subjected body and extracted a psyche from it. It has been possible to distinguish the individual only insofar as the normalizing agency has distributed, excluded, and constantly taken up again this body-psyche.

There is no point then in wanting to dismantle hierarchies, constraints, and prohibitions so that the individual can appear, as if the individual was something existing beneath all relationships of power, preexisting relationships of power, and unduly weighed down by them. In fact, the individual is the result of something that is prior to it: this mechanism, these procedures, which pin political power on the body. It is because the body has been "subjectified," that is to say, that the subject-function has been fixed on it, because it has been psychologized and normalized, it is because of all this that something like the individual appeared, about which one can speak, hold discourses, and attempt to found sciences.

The sciences of man, considered at any rate as sciences of the individual, are only the effect of this series of procedures. And it seems to me that you can see that it would be absolutely false historically, and so politically, to appeal to the original rights of the individual against something like the subject, the norm, or psychology. Actually, right from the start, and in virtue of these mechanisms, the individual is a normal subject, a psychologically normal subject; and consequently desubjectification, denormalization, and depsychologization necessarily entail the destruction of the individual as such. Deindividualization goes hand in hand with these three other operations I have mentioned.

I would like to add just one last word. We are used to seeing the emergence of the individual in European political thought and reality as the effect of a process of both the development of the capitalist economy and the demand for political power by the bourgeoisie. The philosophico-juridical theory of individuality, which develops, more or less, from Hobbes up to the French Revolution, would arise from this.[15] However, although it is true that there is a way of thinking about the individual at this level, I think we should equally see the real constitution of the individual on the basis of a certain technology of power. Discipline seems to me to be this technology, specific to the power that is born and develops from the classical age, and which, on the basis of this game of bodies, isolates and cuts out what I think is an historically new element that we call the individual.

We could say, if you like, that there is a kind of juridico-disciplinary pincers of individualism. There is the juridical individual as he appears in these philosophical or juridical theories: the individual as abstract subject, defined by individual rights that no power can limit unless agreed by contract. And then, beneath this, alongside it, there was the development of a whole disciplinary technology that produced the individual as an historical reality, as an element of the productive forces, and as an element also of political forces. This individual is a subjected body held in a system of supervision and subjected to procedures of normalization.

The function of the discourse of the human sciences is precisely to twin, to couple this juridical individual and disciplinary individual, to make us believe that the real, natural, and concrete content of the juridical individual is the disciplinary individual cut out and constituted by political technology. Scratch the juridical individual, say the (psychological, sociological, and other) human sciences, and you will find a particular kind of man; and what in actual fact they give as man is the disciplinary individual. Conjointly, there is the humanist discourse that is the converse of the discourse of the human sciences, taking the opposite direction, and which says: the disciplinary individual is an alienated, enslaved individual, he is not an authentic individual; scratch him, or rather, restore to him the fullness of his rights, and you will find, as his original, living, and perennial form, the philosophico-juridical individual. This game between the juridical individual and the disciplinary individual underlies, I believe, both the discourse of the human sciences and humanist discourse.

What I call Man, in the nineteenth and twentieth centuries, is nothing other than the kind of after-image of this oscillation between the juridical individual, which really was the instrument by which, in its discourse, the bourgeoisie claimed power, and the disciplinary individual, which is the result of the technology employed by this same bourgeoisie to constitute the individual in the field of productive and political forces. From this oscillation between the juridical individual—ideological instrument of the demand for power—and the disciplinary individual—real instrument of the physical exercise of power—from this oscillation between the power claimed and the power exercised, were born the illusion and the reality of what we call Man.[16]

1. In reality, two forms of the criticism of the asylum institution should be distinguished:
   (a) In the thirties a critical current emerged tending towards a progressive distancing from the asylum space instituted by the 1838 law as the almost exclusive site of psychiatric intervention and the role of which was reduced, as Édouard Toulouse (1865-1947) said, to that of a "supervised assistance" ("L'Évolution de la psychiatrie" Commemoration of the foundation of the Henri Roussel hospital, 30 July 1937, p. 4). Wanting to dissociate the notion of "mental illness" from that of confinement in an asylum subject to particular legal and administrative conditions, this current undertook "to study by what changes in the organization of asylums a wider role could be given to moral and individual treatment" (J. Raynier and H. Beaudouin, *L'Aliéné et les Asiles d'aliénés au point de vue administratif et juridique* [Paris: Le Français, (1922) 1930, 2nd revised and enlarged edition]). In this perspective the traditional hospital centered approach was undermined by new approaches: diversification of ways of taking into care, projects for post-cure supervision, and, especially, the appearance of free services illustrated by the installation, at the heart of the fortress of asylum psychiatry at Sainte-Anne, of an "open service" the management of which was entrusted to Édouard Toulouse - and which became the Henri Roussel hospital in 1926 (see, E. Toulouse, "L'hôpital Henri Roussel" in *La Prophylaxie mentale*, no. 43, January-July 1937, pp. 1-69). This movement became official on 13 October 1937 with the circular of the Minister of Public Health, Marc Rucart, concerning the organization of services for the mentally ill within the departmental framework. On this point see, E. Toulouse, *Réorganisation de l'hospitalisation des aliénés dans les asiles de la Seine* (Paris: Imprimerie Nouvelle, 1920); J. Raynier and J. Lauzier, *La Construction et l'Aménagement de l'hôpital psychiatrique et des asiles d'aliénés* (Paris: Pyronnet, 1935); and G. Daumezon, *La Situation du personnel infirmier dans les asiles d'aliénés* (Paris: Doin, 1935) an account of the lack of means available to psychiatric institutions in the nineteen thirties.
   (b) In the forties criticism took another direction, initiated by the communication of Paul Belvet, at that time director of the hospital of Saint-Alban (Lozère) which became a reference point for all those driven by the desire for a radical change of asylum structures: "Asile et hôpital psychiatrique. L'expérience d'un établissment rural" in *XLIIIe congrès des Médecins aliénistes et neurologistes de France et des pays de langue française. Montpelier, 28-30 octobre 1942* (Paris: Masson, 1942). At this time a small militant fraction of the professional body became aware that the psychiatric hospital is not only a hospital for the insane (*aliénés*), but that it is itself "alienated (*aliéné*)," since it is constituted "into an order that conforms to the principles and practice of a social order that excludes what disturbs it." See, L. Bonnafé, "Sources du désaliénisme" in *Désaliéner? Folie(s) et société(s)* (Toulouse: Presses universitaires du Mirail/Privat, 1991) p. 221. Proposing to reexamine how the psychiatric hospital works in order to turn it into a genuinely therapeutic organization, this current began to question the nature of the psychiatrist's relationships with patients. See G. Daumezon and L. Bonnafé, "Perspectives de réforme psychiatrique en France depuis la Libération" in *XLIVe congrés des Médecins aliénistes et neurologistes de France et des pays de langue franaise. Genève, 22-27 juillet 1946* (Paris: Masson, 1946) pp. 584-590. See also below, "Course context" pp. 355-360.
2. See the lectures of 12 and 19 December 1973, and 23 January 1974.
3. J.M.A. Servan, *Discours sur l'administration de la justice criminelle*, p. 35.
4. Founded by Gérard Groote (1340-1384) at Deventer in Holland in 1383, the community of the "Brethren of the Common Life," inspired by the principles of the Flemish theologian Jan (Johannes) Van Ruysbroek and the Rhenish mysticism of the fourteenth century (see below, lecture of 28 November 1973, note 9), aimed to lay the bases for the reform of teaching by partly transposing spiritual exercises to education. Numerous houses were opened until the end of the fifteenth century at Zwolle, Delft, Amersfoort, Liège, Utrecht, and elsewhere. See, M. Foucault, *Surveiller et Punir. Naissance de la prison* (Paris: Gallimard, 1975) pp. 163-164; English translation, *Discipline and Punish. Birth of the Prison*, trans. A. Sheridan (London: Allen Lane and New York: Pantheon, 1977) pp. 161-162; A. Hyma, *The Brethren of the Common Life* (Grand Rapids: W.B. Erdmans, 1950); Selected texts of G.

Groote in M. Michelet, ed., *Le Rhin mystique. De Maître Eckhart à Thomas a Kempis* (Paris: Fayard, 1957); L. Cognet, *Introduction aux mystiques rhéno-famands* (Paris: Desclée de Brouwer, 1968); and, W. Lourdaux, "Frères de la Vie commune" in, Cardinal A. Baudrillard, ed., *Dictionnaire d'histoire et de géographie ecclésiastiques* (Paris: Letouzey and Ané, 1977).

5. Written in 1787, in the form of letters to an anonymous correspondent, the work was published in 1791 with the title: *"Panopticon": or, the Inspection-House; containing the idea of a new principle of construction applicable to any sort of establishment, in which persons of any description are to be kept under inspection; and in particular to Penitentiary-houses, Prisons, Houses of industry, Workhouses, Poor Houses, Manufacturies, Madhouses, Lazarettos, Hospitals, and Schools; with a plan of management adapted to the principle; in a series of letters, written in 1787, from Crechoff in White Russia, to a friend in England* (in one volume, Dublin: Thomas Byrne, 1791; and in two volumes, London: T. Payne, 1791), included in Jeremy Bentham, *Works*, ed. John Bowring (Edinburgh: W. Tait, 1838-1843). The most recent, and readily available, edition of the Panopticon Letters is Jeremy Bentham, *The Panopticon Writings*, ed. M. Božovič (New York and London: Verso, 1995), and future references will be to this edition (hereafter *The Panopticon*). The twenty-one letters, making up the first part, have been translated into French by Maud Sissung in *Le Panoptique* (Paris: P. Belfond, 1977), preceded by "L'œil du pouvoir. Entretien avec Michel Foucault" (reprinted in *Dits et Écrits*, vol. 3; English translation, "The Eye of Power" trans. Colin Gordon, in Michel Foucault, *Power/Knowledge. Selected Interviews and Other Writings 1972-1977*, ed. Colin Gordon, trans. Colin Gordon and others [Brighton: The Harvester Press, and New York: Pantheon Books, 1980]). The first French version of Bentham's *Panopticon* was, *Panoptique. Mémoire sur un nouveau principe pour construire des maisons d'inspection, et nommément des maisons de force* (Paris: Imprimerie nationale, 1791), republished in *Œuvres de Jérémy Bentham. Le Panoptique*, Dumont, ed. (Brussels: Louis Hauptman and Co., 1829) vol. 1, pp. 245-262.
6. E. Kantorowicz, *The King's Two Bodies: A Study in Medieval Political Theology* (Princeton, NJ: Princeton University Press, 1957); French translation, *Les Deux Corps du Roi. Essai sur la théologie politique du Moyen-Âge*, trans. J.-P. Genet and N. Genet (Paris: Gallimard, 1989).
7. This point will be developed in *Surveiller et Punir*, Part 3, "Discipline" ch.1, "Les corps dociles" pp. 137-171; *Discipline and Punish*, Part 3, "Discipline" ch. 1, "Docile Bodies" pp. 135-169.
8. On the regulations of the Prussian infantry, see, ibid. pp. 159-161; ibid. pp. 158-159.
9. The 1667 edict for the establishment of a manufacture of furniture for the crown at the Gobelins fixed the recruitment and conditions of the apprentices, organized a corporative apprenticeship, and founded a school of design. A new regulation was established in 1737. See E. Gerspach, ed., *La Manufacture nationale des Gobelins* (Paris: Delagrave, 1892). See, *Surveillir et Punir*, pp. 158-159; *Discipline and Punish*, pp. 156-157.
10. *Surveillir et Punir*, pp. 215-219; *Discipline and Punish*, pp. 213-217. On police records in the eighteenth century, see M. Chassaigne, *La Lieutenance générale de police de Paris* (Paris: A. Rousseau, 1906).
11. E. Gerspach, ed., *La Manufacture nationale des Gobelins*, pp.156-160: "Règlement de 1680 imposant de chanter à voix basse des cantiques dans l'atelier."
12. Imposed on Jesuit houses by a circular of 8 January 1599, the *Ratio Studiorum*, drafted in 1586, organized the division of studies by classes split into two camps, and the latter into decuries, at the head of which was a decurion responsible for supervision. See, C. de Rochemonteix, *Un collège de jésuites aux XVII*[e] *et XVIII*[e] *siècles: le collège Henri IV de La Flèche* (Le Mans: Leguicheux, 1889) vol. 1, pp. 6-7 and pp. 51-12. See *Surveillir et Punir*, pp. 147-148; *Discipline and Punish*, pp. 146-147.
13. Foucault is alluding to the innovation introduced by Jean Cele (1375-1417), director of the Zwolle school, distributing students into classes each having its own program, person in charge, and place within the school, students being placed in a particular class on the basis of their results. See, G. Mir, *Aux sources de la pédagogie des jésuites. Le "Modus Parisiensis"* (Rome: Bibliotheca Instituti Historici, 1968) vol. XXVIII, pp. 172-173; M. J. Gaufrès, "Histoire du plan d'études protestant" in *Bulletin de l'histoire du protestantisme*

français, vol. XXV, 1889. See *Surveillir et Punir*, pp. 162-163; *Discipline and Punish*, pp. 159-161.

14. Thus, in 1904 the Minister of Public Education created a commission to "study the means to be used to ensure primary education . . . for all 'abnormal and backward children'." It was within this framework that in 1905 Alfred Binet (1857-1911) was given responsibility for defining the means for screening retarded children. With Théodore Simon (1873-1961), director of the children's colony of Perray-Vaucluse, he conducted inquiries by means of questionnaires in the schools of the first and second *arondissements* of Paris, and, together with Simon, perfected a "metrical scale of intelligence for the purpose of evaluating development retardation." See, A. Binet and T. Simon, "Applications des méthodes nouvelles au diagnostic du niveau intellectuel chez les enfants normaux et anormax d'hospice et d'école" in *L'Année pschologique*, vol. XI, 1905, pp. 245-336. The feeble minded (*débiles mentaux*) [the English translator uses the term "mentally defective"; G.B.] are then defined by a common "negative" characteristic: "by their physical and intellectual organization these children are rendered incapable of benefiting from the ordinary methods of instruction in use in the public schools" A. Binet and T. Simon, *Les Enfants anormaux. Guide pour l'admission des enfants anormaux dans les classes de perfectionnement*, with a preface by Léon Bourgeois (Paris: A. Colin, 1907) p. 7; English translation, *Mentally Defective Children*, trans. W.B. Drummond (London: Edward Arnold, 1914) p. 3. See, G. Nechine, "Idiots, débiles et savants au XIXe siècle" in R. Zazzo, *Les Débilités mentales* (Paris: A. Colin, 1969) pp. 70-107; and, F. Muel, "L'école obligatoire et l'invention de l'enfance anormale" in *Actes de la recherche en sciences socials*, no. 1, January 1975, pp. 60-74.
15. See C. B. MacPherson, *The Political Theory of Possessive Individualism* (Oxford: Oxford University Press, 1961); French translation, *La Théorie politique de l'individualisme possessif, de Hobbes à Locke*, trans. M. Fuchs (Paris: Gallimard, 1971).
16. See, M. Foucault, "Mon corps, ce papier, ce feu"; "My body, this paper, this fire."

four

28 November 1973

[*Elements for a history of disciplinary apparatuses: religious communities in the Middle Ages; pedagogical colonization of youth; the Jesuit missions to Paraguay; the army; workshops; workers' cities.* ~ *The formalization of these apparatuses in Jeremy Bentham's model of the Panopticon.* ~ *The family institution and emergence of the Psy-function.*]

I WILL BEGIN WITH some remarks on the history of these disciplinary apparatuses (*dispositifs*). Last week tried to describe them rather abstractly, without any diachronic dimension and apart from any system of causes that may have led to their establishment and generalization. What I described is a sort of apparatus (*appareil*) or machinery, the major forms of which are clearly apparent in the seventeenth century, let's say especially in the eighteenth century. Actually, the disciplinary apparatuses (*dispositifs*) were not formed in the seventeenth and eighteenth centuries, far from it, and they certainly did not replace overnight those apparatuses of sovereignty with which I tried to compare them. Disciplinary apparatuses come from far back; for a long time they were anchored and functioned in the midst of apparatuses of sovereignty; they were formed like islands where a type of power was exercised which was very different from what could be called the period's general morphology of sovereignty.

Where did these disciplinary apparatuses exist? It is not difficult to find them and follow their history. They are found basically in religious communities, either regular communities, by which I mean statutory communities, recognized by the Church, or spontaneous communities. Now what I think is important is that throughout the Middle Ages, up to and including the sixteenth century, the disciplinary apparatuses we see in religious communities basically played a double role.

These disciplinary apparatuses were, of course, integrated within the general schema of feudal and monarchical sovereignty, and it is true that they functioned positively within this more general apparatus that enframed them, supported them, and at any rate absolutely tolerated them. But they also played a critical role of opposition and innovation. Very schematically, I think we can say that not only religious orders in the Church, but also religious practices, hierarchies, and ideology are transformed through the elaboration or reactivation of disciplinary apparatuses. I will take just one example.

The kind of reform, or rather series of reforms, that took place within the Benedictine order in the eleventh and twelfth centuries, basically represents an attempt to extract religious practice, or to extract the entire order, from the system of feudal sovereignty within which it was held and embedded.[1] Broadly speaking, we can say that the Cluniac form of monasticism had at that time been surrounded or even invaded by the feudal system, and the Cluny order, in its existence, economy, and internal hierarchies, was entirely an apparatus of sovereignty.[2] In what did the Citeaux reform consist?[3] The Cistercian reform restored a certain discipline to the order by reconstituting a disciplinary apparatus which was seen as referring back to a more original and forgotten rule; a disciplinary system in which we find the rule of poverty, the obligation of manual labor and the full use of time, the disappearance of personal possessions and extravagant expenditure, the regulation of eating and clothing, the rule of internal obedience, and the tightening up of the hierarchy. In short, you see all the characteristics of the disciplinary system appearing here as an effort to disengage the monastic order from the apparatus of sovereignty that had permeated it and eaten into it. Furthermore, it was precisely as a result of this reform, as a result of the rule of poverty, the hierarchical systems, the rules of obedience and work, and also the whole system of assessment and accounting linked to disciplinary practice, that the Citeaux order was able to make a number of economic innovations.

It could be said that in the Middle Ages disciplinary systems played a critical and innovative role not only in the economic, but also in the political realm. For example, the new political powers trying to emerge through feudalism and on the basis of apparatuses of sovereignty, the new centralized powers of the monarchy on the one hand and the papacy on the other, try to provide themselves with instruments that are new with regard to the mechanisms of sovereignty, instruments of a disciplinary kind. In this way, the Dominican order, for example, with its discipline that is completely new with regard to the other regular monastic orders,[4] and the Benedictine order, were instruments in the hands of the papacy, and of the French monarchy, for breaking up certain elements of the feudal system, certain apparatuses of sovereignty, which existed, for example, in the Midi, in Occitanie, and elsewhere.[5] Later, in the sixteenth century, the Jesuits were used in the same way, as an instrument for breaking up certain residues of feudal society.[6] So, there was both economic and political innovation.

We can also say that these disciplinary investigations, these kinds of disciplinary islands we see emerging in medieval society, also made social innovations possible; at any rate, they made possible certain forms of social opposition to the hierarchies, to the system of differentiation of the apparatuses of sovereignty. In the Middle Ages, and much more on the eve of the Reformation, we see the constitution of relatively egalitarian communal groups which are not governed by the apparatus of sovereignty but by the apparatus of discipline: a single rule imposed on everyone in the same way, there being no differences between those on whom it is applied other than those indicated by the internal hierarchy of the apparatus. Thus, very early on you see the appearance of phenomena like the mendicant monks, who already represent a kind of social opposition through a new disciplinary schema.[7] You also see religious communities constituted by the laity, like the Brethren of the Common Life, who appear in Holland in the fourteenth century;[8] and then, finally, all the working class or bourgeois communities that immediately preceded the Reformation and which, in new forms, continue up to the seventeenth century, in England for example, with their well-known political and social role; and equally in the eighteenth century. We could also say that freemasonry was able to function in eighteenth century French and European society as a sort of disciplinary innovation intended to work on the networks of systems of sovereignty from within, short circuit them, and, to a certain extent, break them up.

Very schematically, all of this amounts to saying that for a long time disciplinary apparatuses existed like islands in the general plasma of relations of sovereignty. Throughout the Middle Ages, in the sixteenth century, and still in the eighteenth century, these disciplinary systems remained marginal, whatever the uses to which they may have been put or the general effects they may have entailed. They remained on the side, but nevertheless it was through them that a series of innovations were sketched out which will gradually spread over the whole of society. And it is precisely in the seventeenth and eighteenth centuries, through a sort of progressive extension, a sort of general parasitic interference with society, that we see the constitution of what we could call, but very roughly and schematically, a "disciplinary society" replacing a society of sovereignty.

How did this extension of disciplinary apparatuses take place? In what stages? And, finally, what mechanism served as their support? I think we can say, again very schematically, that from the sixteenth to the seventeenth centuries, the historical extension, the overall parasitic invasion carried out by disciplinary apparatuses had a number of points of support.

First, there was a parasitic invasion of young students who, until the end of the fifteenth and beginning of the sixteenth centuries, had maintained their autonomy, their rules of movement and vagabondage, their unruliness, and also their links with popular unrest. Whether this was in the form of the Italian or the French system, whether in the form of a community of students and teachers together, or of an autonomous community of students distinct from that of the teachers, is not important; there was anyway, within the general system of social functioning, a sort of group in movement, coming and going in a kind of emulsive state, a state of unrest. The disciplinarization of this student youth, this colonization of youth, was one of the first points of application and extension of the disciplinary system.

What is interesting is that the point of departure for the colonization of this unruly and mobile youth by the disciplinary system was the community of the Brethren of the Common Life, that is to say, a religious community whose objective, whose ascetic ideal, was very clear, since its founder, someone called Groote, was closely linked to Ruysbroek the Admirable, and therefore well-informed about the fourteenth century movement of German and Rhenish mysticism.[9] We find the mould, the first model of the pedagogical colonization of youth, in this practice of the individual's exercise on himself, this attempt to transform the individual, this search for a progressive development of the individual up to the point of salvation, in this ascetic work of the individual on himself for his own salvation. On the basis of this, and in the collective form of this asceticism in the Brethren of the Common Life, we see the great schemas of pedagogy taking shape, that is to say, the idea that one can only learn things by passing through a number of obligatory and necessary stages, that these stages follow each other in time, and, in the same movement that distributes them in time, each stage represents progress. The twinning of time and progress is typical of ascetic exercise, and it will be equally typical of pedagogical practice.

As a result, in the schools founded by the Brethren of the Common Life, first at Deventer, then at Liège and Strasbourg, for the first time there are divisions according to age and level, with programs of progressive exercises. Second, something very new appears in this new pedagogy with regard to the rule of life for young people in the Middle Ages, that is to say, the rule of seclusion. Pedagogical exercise, just like ascetic exercise, will have to take place within a closed space, in an environment closed in on itself and with minimal relations with the outside world. Ascetic exercise required a special place; in the same way, pedagogical exercise will now demand its own place. Here again, what is new and essential is that the mixing and intrication of the university and the surrounding milieu, and in particular the link between university youth and the popular classes, which was so fundamental throughout the Middle Ages, will be severed by the transfer of this ascetic principle of cloistered life to pedagogy.

Third, one of the principles of ascetic exercise is that although it is an exercise of the individual on himself, it always takes place under the constant direction of someone who is the guide or the protector, at any rate, someone who takes responsibility for the steps of the person setting out on his own ascetic path. Ascetic progress requires a constant guide who keeps his eye on the progress, or setbacks and faults, of the person beginning the exercise. In the same way, and once again this is a complete innovation with regard to the university pedagogy of the Middle Ages, there is the idea that the teacher must follow the individual throughout his career, or, at least, that he must lead him from one stage to the other before passing him on to another, more learned guide, someone more advanced, who will be able to take the student further. The ascetic guide becomes the class teacher to whom the student is attached either for a course of studies, or for a year, or possibly for the whole of his school life.

Finally, and I am not at all sure if the model for this is an ascetic one, but in any case, in the schools of the Brethren of the Common Life we find a very strange paramilitary type of organization. It is quite possible that this schema has a monastic origin. In fact, in monasteries, especially those of the ancient period, we find divisions into "decuries," each comprising ten individuals under the direction of someone who is responsible for them, and which are, at the same time, groupings for work, for meditation, and also for intellectual and spiritual training.[10] This schema, clearly inspired by the Roman army, may have been transposed into the monastic life of the first Christian centuries; in any case, we find it again in the schools of the Brethren of the Common Life that follow a rhythm based on this military schema of the decury. Maybe the organization of bourgeois militias in Flanders could have relayed this model in some way. Anyway, there is this very interesting schema, both monastic and military, which will be an instrument of the colonization of youth within pedagogical forms.

I think we can see all this as one of the first moments of the colonization of an entire society by means of disciplinary apparatuses.

We find another application of these disciplinary apparatuses in a different type of colonization; no longer that of youth, but quite simply of colonized peoples. And there is quite a strange history here. How disciplinary schemas were both applied and refined in the colonial populations should be examined in some detail. It seems that disciplinarization took place fairly unobtrusively and marginally to start with, and, interestingly, as a counterpoint to slavery.

In fact, it was the Jesuits in South America who opposed slavery for theological and religious reasons, as well as for economic reasons, and who countered the use of this probably immediate, brutal and, in terms of the consumption of human lives, extremely costly and poorly organized practice of slavery, with a different type of distribution, control and [...*] exploitation by a disciplinary system. The famous, so-called "communist" Guarani republics in Paraguay were really disciplinary microcosms in which there was a hierarchical system to which the Jesuits held the keys; Guarani individuals and communities received an absolutely statutory schema of behavior indicating their working hours, mealtimes, time allowed for rest, and the fixed time when they were woken up to make love and produce children.[11] It therefore involved the full employment of time.

Permanent supervision: everyone had their own dwelling in the villages of these Guarani republics, however, there was a sort of walkway alongside these dwellings from which it was possible to look through the windows, which naturally had no shutters, so that what anyone was doing during the night could be supervised at any time. Above all, there was also a kind of individualization, at least at the level of the family micro-cell, since each one received a dwelling, which broke up the old Guarani community moreover, and it was precisely on this dwelling that the supervising eye was focused.

In short, it was a kind of permanent penal system, which was very lenient in comparison with the European penal system at the same time—that is to say, there was no death penalty, public execution or torture—but which was an absolutely permanent system of punishment that followed the individual throughout his life and which, at every moment, in each of his actions or his attitudes, was liable to pick out something indicating a bad tendency or inclination, and that consequently entailed a punishment which, on the one hand, could be lighter because it was constant, and, on the other, was only ever brought to bear on potential actions or the beginnings of action.

---

* (Recording:) human

The third type of colonization you see taking shape, after that of student youth and colonized peoples, was the internal colonization and confinement of vagrants, beggars, nomads, delinquents, prostitutes, etcetera, in the classical age. I will not return to this, because it has been studied a thousand times. Disciplinary apparatuses are installed in more or less all of these cases, and we can see quite clearly that they derive directly from religious institutions. In a way, it was religious institutions, like the "Brethren of the Christian Doctrine," then followed by the big teaching orders, like the Jesuits, which extended, by pseudopodia as it were, their own discipline over young people able to attend school.[12]

It was also the religious orders, in this case the Jesuits again, who transposed and transformed their own discipline in colonial countries. As for the system of confinement and the methods for colonizing vagrants and nomads, etcetera, the forms were again very close to those of religion, since in most cases it was the religious orders who had, if not the initiative for creating, at least the responsibility for managing these establishments. It is therefore the external version of religious disciplines that we see being progressively applied in ever less marginal and ever more central sectors of the social system.

Then, at the end of the seventeenth century, and during the eighteenth century, disciplinary apparatuses appear and are established which no longer have a religious basis, which are the transformation of this, but out in the open as it were, without any regular support from the religious side. You see the appearance of disciplinary systems. There is, of course, the army, with quartering to start with, which dates from the second half of the eighteenth century, the struggle against deserters, that is to say, the use of files and all the techniques of individual identification to prevent people from leaving the army as they entered it, and, finally, in the second half of the eighteenth century, physical exercises and the full use of time.[13]

After the army, it was quite simply the working class that began to receive disciplinary apparatuses. With the appearance of the big workshops in the eighteenth century, of the mining towns or big centers of metallurgy, to which a rural population had to be transported and was employed for the first time using completely new techniques, with the metallurgy of the Loire basin and the coalmines of the Massif Central and northern France, you see the appearance of disciplinary forms imposed on workers, with the first workers' cities, like that of Creusot. Then, in the same period, the great instrument of worker discipline, the employment document, the *livret*, is imposed on every worker. No worker can or has the right to move without a *livret* recording the name of his previous employer and the conditions under which and reasons why he left him; when he wants a new job or wants to live in a new town, he has to present his *livret* to his new boss and the municipality, the local authorities; it is the token, as it were, of all the disciplinary systems that bear down on him.[14]

So, once again very schematically, these isolated, local, marginal disciplinary systems, which took shape in the Middle Ages, begin to cover all society through a sort of process that we could call external and internal colonization, in which you find again all the elements of the disciplinary systems I have been talking about. That is to say: fixing in space, optimum extraction of time, application and exploitation of the body's forces through the regulation of actions, postures and attention, constitution of constant supervision and an immediate punitive power, and, finally, organization of a regulatory power which is anonymous and non-individual in its operations, but which always ends up with an identification of subjected individualities. Broadly speaking, the singular body is taken charge of by a power that trains it and constitutes it as an individual, that is to say, as a subjected body. Very schematically, this is what we can say regarding the history of disciplinary apparatuses. To what does this history correspond? What is there behind this kind of extension that is easily identified on the surface of events and institutions?

My impression is that the question behind this general deployment of disciplinary apparatuses involved what could be called the accumulation of men. That is to say, alongside and, what's more, necessary for the accumulation of capital, there was an accumulation of men, or, if you like, a distribution of the labor force with all its somatic singularities. In what do the accumulation of men and the rational distribution of somatic singularities with the forces they carry consist?

First, they consist in bringing about the maximum possible use of individuals. They make all of them usable, not so that they can all be used in fact, but, precisely, so that they do not all have to be used; extending the labor market to the maximum in order to make certain of an unemployed reserve enabling wages to be lowered. As a result, making everyone usable.

Second, making individuals usable in their very multiplicity; ensuring that the force produced by the multiplicity of these individual forces of labor is at least equal to and, as far as possible, greater than the addition of these individual forces. How to distribute individuals so that as a group they are more than the pure and simple addition of these individuals set alongside each other?

Finally, to make possible the accumulation not only of these forces, but equally of time: the time of work, of apprenticeship, of improvement, of the acquisition of knowledge and aptitudes. This is the third aspect of the problem posed by the accumulation of men.

This triple function, this triple aspect of the techniques of the accumulation of men and of the forces of work, is, I think, the reason why the different disciplinary apparatuses were deployed, tried out, developed, and refined. The extension, movement, and migration of the disciplines from their lateral function to the central and general function they exercise from the eighteenth century are linked to this accumulation of men and to the role of the accumulation of men in capitalist society.

Considering things from a different angle, looking at it from the side of the history of the sciences, we could say that seventeenth and eighteenth century classical science responded to the empirical multiplicities of plants, animals, objects, values, and languages, with an operation of classification, with a taxonomic activity, which was, I think, the general form of these empirical forms of knowledge throughout the classical age.[15] On the other hand, with the development of the capitalist economy, and so when the problem of the accumulation of men arose alongside and linked with the accumulation of capital, it became clear that a purely taxonomic and simple classificatory activity was no longer valid. To respond to these economic necessities men had to be distributed according to completely different techniques than those of classification. Rather than use taxonomic schemas to fit individuals into species and genus, something other than a taxonomy had to be used that I will call a tactic, although this also involved questions of distribution. Discipline is a tactic, that is to say, a certain way of distributing singularities according to a non-classificatory schema, a way of distributing them spatially, of making possible the most effective temporal accumulations at the level of productive activity.

Okay, again very schematically, I think we could say that what gave birth to the sciences of man was precisely the irruption, the presence, or the insistence of these tactical problems posed by the need to distribute the forces of work in terms of the needs of the economy that was then developing. Distributing men in terms of these needs no longer entailed taxonomy, but a tactic, and the name of this tactic is "discipline." The disciplines are techniques for the distribution of bodies, individuals, time, and forces of work. It was these disciplines, with precisely these tactics with the temporal vector they entail, which burst into Western knowledge in the course of the eighteenth century, and which relegated the old taxonomies, the old models for the empirical sciences, to the field of an outmoded and perhaps even entirely or partially abandoned knowledge. Tactics, and with it man, the problem of the body, the problem of time, etcetera, replaced taxonomy.

We come here to the point at which I would like to go back to our question, that is to say, to the problem of asylum discipline as constitutive of the general form of psychiatric power. I have tried to show [that—and to show] how—what appeared openly, as it were, in the naked state, in psychiatric practice at the start of the nineteenth century, was a power with the general form of what I have called discipline.

⚜

In actual fact, there was an extremely clear and quite remarkable formalization of this microphysics of disciplinary power. It is found quite simply in Bentham's *Panopticon*. What is the Panopticon?[16]

It is usually said that in 1787 Bentham invented the model of a prison, and that this was reproduced, with a number of modifications, in some European prisons: Pentonville in England,[17] and, in a modified form, Petite Roquette in France,[18] and elsewhere. In fact, Bentham's Panopticon is not a model of a prison, or it is not only a model of a prison; it is a model, and Bentham is quite clear about this, for a prison, but also for a hospital, for a school, workshop, orphanage, and so on. I was going to say it is a form for any institution; let's just say that it is a form for a series of institutions. And again, when I say it is a schema for a series of possible institutions, I think I am still not exactly right.

In fact, Bentham does not even say that it is a schema for institutions, he says that it is a mechanism, a schema which gives strength to any institution, a sort of mechanism by which the power which functions, or which should function in an institution will be able to gain maximum force. The Panopticon is a multiplier; it is an intensifier of power within a series of institutions. It involves giving the greatest intensity, the best distribution, and the most accurate focus to the force of power. Basically these are the three objectives of the Panopticon, and Bentham says so: "Its great excellence consists, in the great strength it is capable of giving to *any* institution it may be thought proper to apply it to."[19] In another passage he says that what is marvelous about the Panopticon is that it "gives a herculean strength to those who direct the institution."[20] It "gives a herculean strength" to the power circulating in the institution, and to the individual who holds or directs this power. Bentham also says that what is marvelous about the Panopticon is that it constitutes a "new mode of obtaining power, of mind over mind."[21] It seems to me that these two propositions—constituting a Herculean strength and giving the mind power over the mind—are exactly typical of the Panopticon mechanism and, if you like, of the general disciplinary form. "Herculean strength," that is to say, a physical force which, in a sense, bears on the body, but which is such that this force, which hems in and weighs down on the body, is basically never employed and takes on a sort of immateriality so that the process passes from mind to mind, although in actual fact it really is the body that is at stake in the Panopticon system. This interplay between "Herculean strength" and the pure ideality of mind is, I think, what Bentham was looking for in the *Panopticon*. How did he bring it about?

There is a circular building, the periphery of the Panopticon, within which cells are set, opening both onto the inner side of the ring through an iron grate door and onto the outside through a window. Around the inner circumference of this ring is a gallery, allowing one to walk around the building, passing each cell. Then there is an empty space and, at its center, a tower, a kind of cylindrical construction of several levels at the top of which is a sort of lantern, that is to say, a large open room, which is such that from this central site one can observe everything happening in each cell, just by turning around. This is the schema.

What is the meaning of this schema? Why did it strike minds and why was it seen for so long, wrongly in my view, as a typical example of eighteenth century utopias? First, one and only one individual will be placed in each cell. That is to say, in this system, which can be applied to a hospital, a prison, a workshop, a school, and so on, a single person will be placed in each of these boxes; each body will have its place. So there is pinning down in space, and the inspector's gaze will encounter a body in whatever direction taken by his line of sight. So, the individualizing function of the coordinates are very clear.

This means that in a system like this we are never dealing with a mass, with a group, or even, to tell the truth, with a multiplicity: we are only ever dealing with individuals. Even if a collective order is given through a megaphone, addressed to everyone at the same time and obeyed by everyone at the same time, the fact remains that this collective order is only ever addressed to individuals and is only ever received by individuals placed alongside each other. All collective phenomena, all the phenomena of multiplicities, are thus completely abolished. And, as Bentham says with satisfaction, in schools there will no longer be the "*cribbing*" that is the beginning of immorality;[22] in workshops there will be no more collective distraction, songs, or strikes;[23] in prisons, no more collusion;[24] and in asylums for the mentally ill, no more of those phenomena of collective irritation and imitation, etcetera.[25]

You can see how the whole network of group communication, all those collective phenomena, which are perceived in a sort of interdependent schema as being as much medical contagion as the moral diffusion of evil, will be brought to an end by the panoptic system. One will be dealing with a power which is a comprehensive power over everyone, but which will only ever be directed at series of separate individuals. Power is collective at its center, but it is always individual at the point where it arrives. You can see how we have here the phenomenon of individualization I was talking about last week. Discipline individualizes below; it individualizes those on whom it is brought to bear.

As for the central cell, this kind of lantern, I told you that it was entirely glazed; in fact Bentham stresses that it should not be glazed or, if it is, one should install a system of blinds, which can be raised and lowered, and the room be fitted with intersecting, mobile partitions. This is so that surveillance can be exercised in such a way that those who are being supervised cannot tell whether or not they are being supervised; that is to say, they must not be able to see if there is anyone in the central cell.[26] So, on the one hand, the windows of the central cell must be shuttered or darkened, and there must be no backlighting which would enable prisoners to see through this column and see whether or not there is anyone in the central lantern; hence the system of blinds and the internal partitions that can be moved as desired.

So, as you can see, it will be possible for power to be entirely anonymous, as I was saying last week. The director has no body, for the true effect of the Panopticon is to be such that, even when no one is there, the individual in his cell must not only think that he is being observed, but know that he is; he must constantly experience himself as visible for a gaze, the real presence or absence of which hardly matters. Power is thereby completely de-individualized. If necessary, the central lantern could be completely empty and power would be exercised just the same.

There is a de-individualization and disembodiment of power, which no longer has a body or individuality, and which can be anyone whomsoever. Furthermore, one of the essential points of the Panopticon is that within the central tower, not only may anyone be there—surveillance may be exercised by the director, but also by his wife, his children, or his servants, etcetera—but an underground passage from outside to the center allows anyone to enter the central tower if they wish and to carry out supervision. This means that any citizen whomsoever must be able to supervise what is going on in the hospital, school, workshop, or prison: supervising what is going on, supervising to check that everything is in order, and supervising to check that the director is carrying out his functions properly, supervising the supervisor who supervises.

There is a sort of ribbon of power, a continuous, mobile, and anonymous ribbon, which perpetually unwinds within the central tower. Whether it has or does not have a figure, whether or not it has a name, whether or not it is individualized, this anonymous ribbon of power perpetually unwinds anyway and is exercised through this game of invisibility. What's more, this is what Bentham calls "democracy," since anyone can occupy the place of power and power is not the property of anyone since everyone can enter the tower and supervise the way in which power is exercised, so that power is constantly subject to control. Finally, power is as visible in its invisible center as those who occupy the cells; and, due to this, power supervised by anyone really is the democratization of the exercise of power.

Another feature of the Panopticon is that, to make the interior of the cells visible, on the side facing inwards there is, of course, a door with a window, but there is also a window on the outer side, indispensable for producing an effect of transparency and so that the gaze of the person in the central tower can pass through all the cells from one side to the other, seeing against the light everything the person—student, patient, worker, prisoner, or whomsoever—is doing in the cell. So the condition of permanent visibility is absolutely constitutive of the individual's situation in the Panopticon. You can see that the relationship of power really does have that immateriality I was just talking about, for power is exercised simply by this play of light; it is exercised by the glance from center to periphery, which can, at every moment, observe, judge, record, and punish at the first gesture, the first attitude, the first distraction. This power needs no instrument; its sole support is sight and light.

Panopticon means two things. It means that everything is seen all the time, but it also means that the power exercised is only ever an optical effect. The power is without materiality; it has no need of all that symbolic and real armature of sovereign power; it does not need to hold the scepter in its hand or wield the sword to punish; it does not need to intervene like a bolt of lightning in the manner of the sovereign. This power belongs rather to the realm of the sun, of never ending light; it is the non-material illumination that falls equally on all those on whom it is exercised.

Finally, the last feature of this Panopticon is that this immaterial power exercised in constant light is linked to an endless extraction of knowledge. That is to say, the center of power is, at the same time, the center of uninterrupted assessment, of the transcription of individual behavior. The codification and assessment of everything individuals are doing in their cells; the accumulation of knowledge and the constitution of sequences and series that will characterize these individuals; and a written, centralized individuality constituted in terms of a general network, forms the documentary double, the written ectoplasm, of the body's placement in its cell.

The first effect of this relationship of power is therefore the constitution of this permanent knowledge of the individual—pinned in a given space and followed by a potentially continuous gaze—which defines the temporal curve of his development, his cure, his acquisition of knowledge, or the acknowledgement of his error, and so forth. As you can see, the Panopticon is therefore an apparatus of both individualization and knowledge; it is an apparatus of both knowledge and power that individualizes on one side, and which, by individualizing, knows. Hence Bentham's idea of using it as an instrument for what he called "discovery in *metaphysics*." He thought that the panoptic apparatus could be used to conduct metaphysical experiments on children. Imagine taking foundlings, he said, right from birth, and putting them in a panoptic system, even before they have begun to talk or be aware of anything. In this way, Bentham says, we could follow "the genealogy of each observable idea"[27] and, as a result, repeat experimentally what Condillac deduced without any equipment for metaphysical experimentation.[28] As well as verifying Condillac's genetic conception, we could also verify the technological ideal of Helvétius when he said, "anyone can be taught anything."[29] Is this fundamental proposition for the possible transformation of humanity true or false? An experiment with a panoptic system would suffice to find out; different things could be taught to different children in different cells; we could teach no matter what to no matter which child, and we would see the result. In this way we could raise children in completely different systems, or even systems incompatible with each other; some would be taught the Newtonian system, and then others would be got to believe that the moon is made of cheese. When they were eighteen or twenty, they would be put together to discuss the question. We could also teach two different sorts of mathematics to children, one in which two plus two make four and another in which they don't make four; and then we would wait again until their twentieth year when they would be put together for discussions. And,

Bentham says, clearly having a bit of fun, this would be more worthwhile than paying people to give sermons, lectures, or arguments; we could have a direct experiment. Finally, of course, he says it would be necessary to conduct an experiment on boys and girls in which they are put together until they reach adolescence to see what happens. You see that this is the same story as *La Dispute* by Marivaux: a kind of panoptic drama that we find again, basically, in the piece by Marivaux.[30]

At any rate, you can see that the Panopticon is the formal schema for the constitution of an individualizing power and for knowledge about individuals. I think that the principal mechanisms of the panoptic schema, which we find at work in Bentham's *Panopticon*, are found again in most of the institutions which, as schools, barracks, hospitals, prisons, reformatories, etcetera, are sites both for the exercise of power and for the formation of a certain knowledge about man. It seems to me that the panoptic mechanism provides the common thread to what could be called the power exercised on man as a force of work and knowledge of man as an individual. So that panopticism could, I think, appear and function within our society as a general form; we could speak equally of a disciplinary society or of a panoptic society. We live within generalized panopticism by virtue of the fact that we live within a disciplinary system.

You will say that this is all very well, but can we really say that disciplinary apparatuses have extended over the whole of society, and that the mechanisms, apparatuses and powers of sovereignty have been eliminated by disciplinary mechanisms?

Just as the disciplinary type of power existed in medieval societies, in which schemas of sovereignty were nevertheless prevalent, so too, I think, forms of the power of sovereignty can still be found in contemporary society. Where do we find them? Well, I would find them in the only institution in the traditional dynasty of schools, barracks, prisons and so forth, that I have not yet spoken about, and the absence of which may have surprised you; I mean the family. I was going to say that the family is a remnant, but this is not entirely the case. At any rate, it seems to me that the family is a sort of cell within which the power exercised is not, as one usually says, disciplinary, but rather of the same type as the power of sovereignty.

I do not think it is true that the family served as the model for the asylum, school, barracks, or workshop. Actually, it seems to me that nothing in the way the family functions enables us to see any continuity between the family and the institutions, the disciplinary apparatuses, I am talking about. Instead, what do we see in the family if not a function of maximum individualization on the side of the person who exercises power, that is to say, on the father's side? The anonymity of power, the ribbon of undifferentiated power which unwinds indefinitely in a panoptic system, is utterly foreign to the constitution of the family in which the father, as bearer of the name, and insofar as he exercises power in his name, is the most intense pole of individualization, much more intense than the wife or children. So, in the family you have individualization at the top, which recalls and is of the very same type as the power of sovereignty, the complete opposite of disciplinary power.

Second, in the family there is constant reference to a type of bond, of commitment, and of dependence established once and for all in the form of marriage or birth. And it is this reference to the earlier act, to the status conferred once and for all, which gives the family its solidity; mechanisms of supervision are only grafted on to it, and membership of the family continues to hold even when these mechanisms do not function. Supervision is not constitutive of but supplementary to the family, whereas permanent supervision is absolutely constitutive of disciplinary systems.

Finally, in the family there is all that entanglement of what could be called heterotopic relationships: an entanglement of local, contractual bonds, bonds of property, and of personal and collective commitments, which recalls the power of sovereignty rather than the monotony and isotopy of disciplinary systems. So that, for my part, I would put the functioning and microphysics of the family completely on the side of the power of sovereignty, and not at all on that of disciplinary power. To my mind this does not mean that the family is the residue, the anachronistic or, at any rate, historical residue of a system in which society was completely penetrated by the apparatuses of sovereignty. It seems to me that the family is not a residue, a vestige of sovereignty, but rather an essential component, and an increasingly essential component, of the disciplinary system.

Inasmuch as the family conforms to the non-disciplinary schema of an apparatus (*dispositif*) of sovereignty, I think we could say that it is the hinge, the interlocking point, which is absolutely indispensable to the very functioning of all the disciplinary systems. I mean that the family is the instance of constraint that will permanently fix individuals to their disciplinary apparatuses (*appareils*), which will inject them, so to speak, into the disciplinary apparatuses (*appareils*). It is because there is the family, it is because you have this system of sovereignty operating in society in the form of the family, that the obligation to attend school works and children, individuals, these somatic singularities, are fixed and finally individualized within the school system. Does obligatory school attendance require the continued functioning of this sovereignty, the sovereignty of the family? Look at how, historically, the obligation of military service was imposed on people who clearly had no reason to want to do their military service: it is solely because the State put pressure on the family as a small community of father, mother, brothers and sisters, etcetera, that the obligation of military service had real constraining force and individuals could be plugged into this disciplinary system and taken into its possession. What meaning would the obligation to work have if individuals were not first of all held within the family's system of sovereignty, within this system of commitments and obligations, which means that things like help to other members of the family and the obligation to provide them with food are taken for granted? Fixation on the disciplinary system of work is only achieved insofar as the sovereignty of the family plays a full role. The first role of the family with regard to disciplinary apparatuses (*appareils*), therefore, is this kind of pinning of individuals to the disciplinary apparatus (*appareil*).

I think it also has another function, which is that it is the zero point, as it were, where the different disciplinary systems hitch up with each other. It is the switch point, the junction ensuring passage from one disciplinary system to another, from one apparatus (*dispositif*) to another. The best proof of this is that when an individual is rejected as abnormal from a disciplinary system, where is he sent? To his family. When a number of disciplinary systems successively reject him as inassimilable, incapable of being disciplined, or uneducable, he is sent back to the family, and the family's role at this point is to reject him in turn as incapable of being fixed to any disciplinary system, and to get rid of him either by consigning him to pathology, or by abandoning him to delinquency, etcetera. It is the sensitive element that makes it possible to determine those individuals inassimilable to any system of discipline, those who cannot pass from one system to the other and must finally be rejected from society to enter new disciplinary systems intended for this purpose.

The family, therefore, has this double role of pinning individuals to disciplinary systems, and of linking up disciplinary systems and circulating individuals from one to the other. To that extent I think we can say that the family is indispensable to the functioning of disciplinary systems because it is a cell of sovereignty, just as the king's body, the multiplicity of the king's bodies, was necessary for the mutual adjustment of heterotopic sovereignties in the game of societies of sovereignty.[31] What the king's body was in societies of mechanisms of sovereignty, the family is in societies of disciplinary systems.

To what does this correspond, historically? I think we can say that in systems in which the type of power was essentially that of sovereignty, in which power was exercised through apparatuses of sovereignty, the family was one of these apparatuses and was therefore very strong. The medieval family, as well as the family of the seventeenth or eighteenth centuries, were actually strong families owing their strength to their homogeneity with the other systems of sovereignty. However, to the extent that the family was thus homogeneous with all the other apparatuses of sovereignty, you can see that basically it had no specificity, no precise limits. That is why the family's roots spread far and wide, but it was quickly silted up and its borders were never well determined. It merged into a whole series of other relationships with which it was very close because they were of the same type: relationships of suzerain to vassal, of membership of corporations, etcetera, so that the family was strong because it resembled other types of power, but for the same reason it was at the same time imprecise and fuzzy.

On the other hand, in our kind of society, that is to say, in a society in which there is a disciplinary type of microphysics of power, the family has not been dissolved by discipline; it is concentrated, limited, and intensified. Consider the role played by the civil code with regard to the family. There are historians who will tell you that the civil code has given the maximum to the family; others say that it has reduced the power of the family. In fact, the role of the civil code has been to limit the family while, at the same time, defining, concentrating, and intensifying it. Thanks to the civil code the family preserved the schemas of sovereignty: domination, membership, bonds of suzerainty, etcetera, but it limited them to the relationships between men and women and parents and children. The civil code redefined the family around this micro-cell of married couple and parents and children, thus giving it maximum intensity. It constituted an alveolus of sovereignty through the game by which individual singularities are fixed to disciplinary apparatuses.

This intense alveolus, this strong cell, was necessary for bringing into play the major disciplinary systems that had invalidated the systems of sovereignty and made them disappear. I think this explains two phenomena.

The first is the very strong re-familialization we see in the nineteenth century, and particularly in the classes in society in which the family was in the process of breaking up and discipline was indispensable—basically, in the working class. At the time when, in the nineteenth century, the European proletariat was being formed, conditions of work and housing, movements of the labor force, and the use of child labor, all made family relationships increasingly fragile and disabled the family structure. In fact, at the beginning of the nineteenth century, entire bands of children, young people, and transhumant workers were living in dormitories and forming communities, which then immediately disintegrated. There was an increasing number of natural children, foundlings, and infanticides, etcetera. Faced with this immediate consequence of the constitution of the proletariat, very early on, around 1820-1825, there was a major effort to reconstitute the family; employers, philanthropists, and public authorities used every possible means to reconstitute the family, to force workers to live in couples, to marry, have children and to recognize their children. The employers even made financial sacrifices in order to achieve this refamilialization of working class life. Around 1830-1835, the first workers' cities were constructed at Mulhouse.[32] People were given houses in which to reconstitute a family, and crusades were organized against those who lived as man and wife without really being married. In short, there were a series of arrangements that were disciplinary.

Equally, in some towns, those living together without being properly married were rejected by workshops. There was a series of disciplinary apparatuses, which functioned as disciplinary apparatuses, within the workshop, in the factory, or in their margins anyway. But the function of these disciplinary apparatuses was to reconstitute the family cell. Or rather, their function was to constitute a family cell conforming to a mechanism that is not itself disciplinary but belongs, precisely, to the order of sovereignty, as if—and this is no doubt the reason—the only way disciplinary mechanisms could effectively function and get a grip with maximum intensity and effectiveness was if, alongside them, and to fix individuals, there was this cell of sovereignty constituted by the family. So, between familial sovereignty and disciplinary panopticism, the form of which is, I think, completely different from that of the family cell, there is a permanent game of cross-reference and transfer. In the course of the nineteenth century, in this project of refamilialization, the family, this cell of sovereignty is constantly being secreted by the disciplinary tissue, because however external it may be to the disciplinary system, however heterogeneous it may be because it is heterogeneous to the disciplinary system, it is in fact an element of that system's solidity.

The other consequence is that when the family breaks down and no longer performs its function—and this also appears very clearly in the nineteenth century—a whole series of disciplinary apparatuses are established to make up for the family's failure: homes for foundlings, orphanages, the opening, around 1840-1845, of a series of homes for young delinquents, for what will be called children at risk, and so on.[33] In short, the function of everything we call social assistance, all the social work which appears at the start of the nineteenth century,[34] and which will acquire the importance we know it to have, is to constitute a kind of disciplinary tissue which will be able to stand in for the family, to both reconstitute the family and enable one to do without it.

This was how young delinquents, most without a family, were placed at Mettray for example. They were regimented in an absolutely military, that is to say, disciplinary, non-familial way. Then, at the same time, within this substitute for the family, within this disciplinary system which rushes in where there is no longer a family, there is a constant reference to the family, since the supervisors, the chiefs, etcetera, are called father, or grandfather, and the completely militarized groups of children, who operate in the manner of decuries, are supposed to constitute a family.[35]

You have here then a [sort]* of disciplinary network which rushes in where the family is failing and which, as a result, constitutes the advance of a State controlled power where there is no longer a family. However, this advance of disciplinary systems never takes place without reference to the family, without a quasi or pseudo familial mode of functioning. I think this is a typical phenomenon of the necessary function of familial sovereignty with regard to disciplinary mechanisms.

What I will call the Psy-function, that is to say, the psychiatric, psychopathological, psycho-sociological, psycho-criminological, and psychoanalytic function, makes its appearance in this organization of disciplinary substitutes for the family with a familial reference. And when I say "function," I mean not only the discourse, but the institution, and the psychological individual himself. And I think this really is the function of these psychologists, psychotherapists, criminologists, psychoanalysts, and the rest. What is their function if not to be agents of the organization of a disciplinary apparatus that will plug in, rush in, where an opening gapes in familial sovereignty?

Consider what has taken place historically. The Psy-function was clearly born by way of psychiatry. That is to say, it was born at the beginning of the nineteenth century, on the other side of the family, in a kind of vis-à-vis with the family. When an individual escaped from the sovereignty of the family, he was put in a psychiatric hospital where it was a matter of training him in the apprenticeship of pure and simple discipline, some examples of which I gave you in the previous lectures, and where, gradually, throughout the nineteenth century, you see the birth of reference to the family. Psychiatry gradually puts itself forward as the institutional enterprise of discipline that will make possible the individual's refamilialization.

---

* (Recording:) kind, a constitution

The Psy-function is therefore born in this kind of vis-à-vis with the family. The family requested confinement and the individual was placed under psychiatric discipline and supposed to be refamilialized. Then, gradually, the Psy-function was extended to all the disciplinary systems: school, army, workshop, and so forth. That is to say, the Psy-function performed the role of discipline for all those who could not be disciplined. Whenever an individual could not follow school discipline or the discipline of the workshop, the army, and, if it comes to it, of prison, then the Psy-function stepped in. And it came in with a discourse attributing the individual's inability to be disciplined to the deficiency and failure of the family. This is how, in the second half of the nineteenth century, you see full responsibility for the individual's lack of discipline being laid at the door of familial deficiency. Then, finally, at the start of the twentieth century, the Psy-function became both the discourse and the control of all the disciplinary systems. The Psy-function was the discourse and the establishment of all the schemas for the individualization, normalization, and subjection of individuals within disciplinary systems.

This is how psycho-pedagogy appears within school discipline, the psychology of work within workshop discipline, criminology within prison discipline, and psychopathology within psychiatric and asylum discipline. The Psy-function is, then, the agency of control of all the disciplinary institutions and apparatuses, and, at the same time and without any contradiction, it holds forth with the discourse of the family. At every moment, as psycho-pedagogy, as psychology of work, as criminology, as psychopathology, and so forth, what it refers to, the truth it constitutes and forms, and which marks out its system of reference, is always the family. Its constant system of reference is the family, familial sovereignty, and it is so to the same extent as it is the theoretical authority for every disciplinary apparatus.

The Psy-function is precisely what reveals that familial sovereignty belongs profoundly to the disciplinary apparatuses. The kind of heterogeneity that seems to me to exist between familial sovereignty and disciplinary apparatuses is functional. And psychological discourse, the psychological institution, and psychological man are connected up to this function. Psychology as institution, as body of the individual, and as discourse, will endlessly control the disciplinary apparatuses on the one hand, and, on the other, refer back to familial sovereignty as the authority of truth on the basis of which it will be possible to describe and define all the positive or negative processes which take place in the disciplinary apparatuses.

It is not surprising that, from the middle of the twentieth century, the discourse of the family, the most "family discourse" of all psychological discourses, that is to say, psychoanalysis, can function as the discourse of truth on the basis of which all disciplinary institutions can be analyzed. And if what I am telling you is true, this is why you can see that a truth formed on the basis of the discourse of the family cannot be deployed as a critique of the institution, or of school, psychiatric, or other forms of discipline. To refamilialize the psychiatric institution, to refamilialize psychiatric intervention, to criticize the practice, institution, and discipline of psychiatry or the school in the name of a discourse of truth which has the family as its reference, is not to undertake the critique of discipline at all, but to return endlessly to discipline.*

By appealing to the sovereignty of the family relationship, rather than escape the mechanism of discipline, we reinforce this interplay between familial sovereignty and disciplinary functioning, which seems to me typical of contemporary society and of that residual appearance of sovereignty in the family, which may seem surprising when we compare it to the disciplinary system, but which seems to me in fact to function quite directly in harmony with it.

---

* The manuscript refers to the work of Gilles Deleuze and Félix Guattari, *L'Anti-Œdipe*, volume 1 of, *Capitalisme et Schizophrénie* (Paris: Éd. de Minuit, 1972), English translation by Robert Hurley, Mark Seem, and Helen Lane (New York: Viking, 1977), and R. Castel, *Le Psychanalysme* (Paris: Maspero, 1973).

---

1. Foucault is alluding here to the various reforms which, judging the Benedictine communities too open to society and reproaching them for having lost the spirit of penitential monasticism, sought to satisfy the requirements of Saint Benedict's rule. See, U. Berlière, *L'Ordre monastique des origines au XIIe siècle* (Paris: Desclée de Brouwer, 1921); *L'Ascèse bénédictine des origines à la fin du XIIe siècle* (Paris: Desclée de Brouwer, 1927); and, "L'étude des réformes monastiques des Xe et XIe siècles" *Bulletin de la classe des Lettres et des Sciences morales et politiques* (Brussels: Académie royale de Belgique, 1932) vol. 18; E. Werner, *Die Gesellschaftlichen grundlagender Klosterreform im XI. Jahrhundert* (Berlin: Akademie-Verlag, 1953); J. Lecler, S.J., "La crise du monachisme aux XIe-XIIe siècles" in *Aux sources de la spiritualité chrétienne* (Paris: Éd du Cerf, 1964). On the monastic orders in general, see P. Helyot and others, *Dictionnaire des ordres religieux, ou Histoire des ordres monastiques, religieux et militaires*, in 4 volumes (Paris: Éd. du Petit-Montrouge, 1847); P. Cousin, *Précis d'histoire monastique* (Paris: Bloud et Gay, 1956); D. Knowles, "Les siècles monastiques" in D. Knowles and D. Obolensky, *Nouvelle Histoire de l'Église, volume 2: Le Moyen Âge (600-1500)*, trans. L. Jézéquel (Paris: Le Seuil, 1968) pp. 223-240; and M. Pacaut, *Les Ordres monastiques et religieux au Moyen Âge* (Paris: Nathan, 1970).
2. Founded in 910 in the Mâconnais, the Cluny order, living under Saint Benedict's rule, developed in the eleventh and twelfth centuries in symbiosis with the seigniorial class, from which most of the abbots and prioresses came. See R.P. Helyot and others, *Dictionnaire des ordres religieux*, vol. 1, col. 1002-1036; U. Berlière, *L'Ordre monastique*, ch. 4, "Cluny et la réforme monastique" pp. 168-197; G. de Valous, *Le Monachisme clunisien des origines au XVe. Vie intérieure des monastères et organisation de l'ordre, Vol. II, L'Ordre de Cluny* (Paris: A. Picard, 1970); and "Cluny" in Cardinal A. Baudrillart, ed. *Dictionnaire d'histoire et de géographie ecclésiastiques* (Paris: Letouzey et Ané, 1956) vol. 2, col. 35-174; P. Cousin, *Précis d'histoire monastique*, p. 5; and A.H. Bredero, "Cluny et Cîteaux au XIIe siècle. Les origines de la controverse" *Studi Medievali*, 1971, pp. 135-176.
3. Citeaux, founded on 21 March 1098 by Robert de Molesmes (1028-1111), separated from the Cluny order in order to return to strict observance of Saint Benedict's rule, emphasizing poverty, silence, work, and renunciation of the world. See, R.P. Helyot and others, *Dictionnaire des ordres religieux*, vol. 1, col. 920-959; U. Berlière, "Les origines de l'ordre de Cîteaux de l'ordre bénédictin au XIIe siècle" *Revue d'histoire ecclésiastique*, 1900, pp. 448-471 and 1901, pp. 253-290; J. Besse, "Cisterciens" in A. Vacant, ed. *Dictionnaire de théologie catholique* (Paris: Letouzey et Ané, 1905) vol. 2, col. 2532-2550; R. Trilhe, "Cîteaux" in F. Cabrol, ed. *Dictionnaire d'archéologie chrétienne et de liturgie* (Paris: Letouzey et Ané, 1913) vol. 3, col. 1779-1811; U. Berlière, *L'Ordre monastique*, pp. 168-197; J.-B. Mahn, *L'Ordre cistercien et son gouvernement des origines au milieu du XIIIe siècle (1098-1266)* (Paris: E. de Boccard, 1945); J.-M. Canivez, "Cîteaux (Ordre dė)" in Cardinal A. Baudrillart, *Dictionnaire d'histoire et de géographie ecclésiastiques* (Paris: Letouzey et Ané, 1953) vol. 12, col. 874-997; and L.J. Lekai, *Les Moines blancs. Histoire de l'ordre cistercien* (Paris: Le Seuil, 1957).
4. In 1215, around the Castillian canon Dominique de Guzman, a community of evangelical preachers, living under the rule of Saint Augustine, was established, which in January 1217 received the name of "Preaching Friars" from Pope Honorius III. See, R.P. Helyot and others, *Dictionnaire des ordres religieux*, vol. 1, col. 86-113; G.R. Galbraith, *The Constitution of the Domenican Order, 1216-1360* (Manchester: Manchester University Press, 1925); M.-H. Vicaire, *Histoire de saint Dominique* (Paris: Éd. du Cerf, 1957) in 2 volumes; and *Saint Dominique et ses frères* (Paris: Éd. du Cerf, 1967). See also, P. Mandonnet, "Frères Prêcheurs" in A. Vacant and E. Mangenot, *Dictionnaire de théologie catholique* (Paris: Letouzey et Ané, 1905) vol. 6, col. 863-924; R.L. Œchslin, "Frères Prêcheurs" in A. Rayez, ed. *Dictionnaire de spiritualité ascétique et mystique. Doctrine et histoire* (Paris: Beauchesne, 1964) vol. 5, col. 1422-1524; and, A. Duval and M.-H. Vicaire, "Frères Prêcheurs (Ordre des)" in *Dictionnaire d'histoire et géographie ecclésiastiques*, vol. 18, col. 1369-1426.
5. The order founded at Monte Cassino in 529 by Benedict of Nursie (480-547), who drafted its rule in 534. See, R.P. Helyot, "Bénédictins (Ordre des)" in *Dictionnaire des ordres religieux* vol.1, col. 416-430; C. Butler, *Benedictine Monachism: Studies in Benedictine Life* (London: Longmans Green and Co., 1924), French translation by C. Grolleau, *Le Monachisme bénédictin* (Paris: J. de Gigord, 1924); C. Jean-Nesmy, *Saint Benoît et la vie monastique* (Paris: Le Seuil, 1959); and R. Tschudy, *Les Bénédictins* (Paris: Éd. Saint-Paul, 1963).

6. Founded in 1534 by Ignatius Loyola (1491-1556) to pursue the struggle against heresy, the order of Jesuits received the name "Company of Jesus" from Pope Paul III in his bull *Regimini Militantes Ecclesie*. See, R.P. Helyot and others, *Dictionnaire des ordres religieux*, vol. 1, col. 628-671; A. Demersay, *Histoire physique, économique et politique du Paraguay et des éstablissements des jésuites* (Paris: L. Hachette, 1860); J. Brucker, *La Compagnie de Jésus. Esquisse de son institut et de son histoire 1521-1773* (Paris: G. Beauchesne, 1919); H. Becher, *Die Jesuiten. Gestalt und Geschichte des Ordens* (Munich: Kösel-Verlag, 1951); A. Guillermou, *Les Jésuites* (Paris: Presses universitaires de France, 1963).
7. The "mendicant orders" were organized in the thirteenth century with a view to regenerating religious life; professing to live only by public charity and practicing poverty, they devoted themselves to preaching and teaching. The four first mendicant orders are the Dominicans, the Franciscans, the Carmelites, and the Augustinians.

   For the Dominicans, see above note 4.

   Constituted in 1209 by Francis of Assisi, the "Brotherhood of Penitents," devoted to the preaching of penitence, was transformed into a religious order in 1210 with the name "Friars Minor" (*minores*: humble) and intending to lead an itinerant life of poverty. See, R.P. Helyot and others, *Dictionnaire des ordres religieux*, vol. 2, col. 326-354; H.C. Lea, *A History of the Inquisition of the Middle Ages* (New York: Harper and Brothers, 1887) vol. 1, ch. 6, "The Mendicant orders," pp. 243-304 (French translation by S. Reinach, *Histoire de l'Inquisition au Moyen Âge* [Paris: Société nouvelle de librairie et d'éditions, 1900] vol. 1, ch. 6, "Les ordres mendiants"); E. d'Alençon, "Frères Mineurs" in *Dictionnaire de théologie catholique*, vol. 6, col. 809-863; P. Gratien, *Histoire de la fondation et de l'évolution de l'ordre des Frères Mineurs au XVIIIe siècle*, (Gembloux: J. Duculot, 1928); F. de Sessevalle, *Histoire générale de l'ordre de Saint-François* (Le-Puy-en-Velay, Éd. de la Revue d'histoire franciscaine, 1935-1937) 2 volumes; and J. Moorman, *A History of the Franciscan Order from its origins to the Year 1517* (Oxford: The Clarendon Press, 1968).

   In 1247 Pope Innocent IV entered the order of the Blessed Virgin Mary of Mount Carmel into the family of "mendicants." On the Carmelites, founded in 1185 by Berthold de Calabre, see, R.P. Helyot and others, *Dictionnaire des ordres religieux*, vol. 1, col. 667-705; and, B. Zimmerman, "Carmes (Ordre des)" in *Dictionnaire de théologie catholique, op. cit*, vol. 2, col. 1776-1792.

   Pope Innocent IV decided to unite the hermits of Tuscany into a single community within the framework of the Augustinian order. See J. Besse, "Augustin" in *Dictionnaire de théologie catholique*, vol. 1, col. 2472-2483. On the mendicant orders in general, see—in addition to the chapter devoted to them in H. C. Lea, *A History of the Inquisition*, vol. 1, pp. 275-346; *Histoire de l'Inquisition*, vol. 1, pp. 458-479; F. Vernet, *Les Ordres mendiants* (Paris: Bloud et Gay, 1933); J. Le Goff, "Ordres mendiants et urbanisation dans la France médiévale" in *Annales ESC*, no. 5, 1979, *Histoire et Urbanisation*, pp. 924-965. Foucault returns to the mendicant orders of the Middle Ages, in the context of an analysis of "cynicism," in the Collège de France course of 1983-1984, "Le Gouvernement de soi et des autres. Le courage de la vérité," lecture of 29 February 1984.
8. See above, lecture of 21 November 1973, note 4.
9. In 1343 Jan Van Ruysbroek (1294-1381) founded a community at Groenendaal, near Brussels, which he transformed in March 1350 into a religious order living under the Augustinian rule devoted to the struggle against heresy and lax morality within the Church. See, F. Hermans, *Ruysbroek l'Admirable et son école* (Paris: Fayard, 1958); J. Orcibal, *Jean de la Croix et les mystiques rhéno-flamands*, and A. Koyré, *Mystiques, spirituels, alchimistes du XVIe siècle allemand* (Paris: Gallimard, 1971).
10. One of the distinctive features of the schools of the "Brethren of the Common Life" was the distribution of students into decuries at the head of which a decurion was responsible for the supervision of conduct. See, M.J. Gaufrès, "Histoire du plan d'études protestant."
11. "Nowhere does the impression of order and religious emphasis appear better than in the use of time. Early in the morning the inhabitants go to mass, then the children go to school and the adults to the workshop or fields . . . When work has ended, religious exercises begin: the catechism, the rosary, prayers; the end of the day is free and left for strolling around and sport. A curfew marks the beginning of the night . . . This regime partakes of both the barracks and the monastery." L. Baudin, *Une théocratie socialiste: l'État jésuite du Paraguay* (Paris: M.-T. Génin, 1962) p. 23. See, L.A. Muratori, *I Cristianesimo felice nelle*

missioni de'padri della compagnia di Gesú nel Paraguai (Venice: G. Pasquali, 1743), French translation, *Relation des missions du Paraguay*, trans. P. Lambert (Paris: Bordellet, 1826) pp. 156-157; A. Demersay, *Histoire . . . du Paraguay et des établissements des jésuites*; J. Brucker, *Le Gouvernement des jésuites au Paraguay* (Paris: 1880); M. Fassbinder, *Der "Jesuitenstaat" in Paraguay* (Halle: M. Niemayer, 1926); C. Lugon, *La République communiste chrétienne des Guaranis* (Paris: Éditions Ouvrières, 1949). Foucault refers to the Jesuits in Paraguay in his lecture to the Cercle d'études architecturales, "Des espaces autres" *Dits et Écrits*, vol. 4, p. 761.

12. A congregation of priests and scholars founded in the sixteenth century by César de Bus (1544-1607), which in 1593 was established at Avignon. Inserted in the current of a renewal of the teaching of the catechism, it developed in the seventeenth and eighteenth centuries by turning to teaching in the colleges. See, R.P. Helyot and others, *Dictionnaire des ordres religieux*, vol. 2, col. 46-74.
13. See *Surveiller et Punir*, Part 3, ch. 1, pp. 137-138, 143, and 151-157; *Discipline and Punish*, Part 3, ch. 1, pp. 135-136, 141-142, and 149-156.
14. From 1781, the worker had to be provided with a "livret" or "cahier" which had to be stamped by the administrative authorities when he moved and which he had to present when he started work. Reinstated by the Consulate, the *livret* was only finally abolished in 1890. See, M. Sauzet, *Le Livret obligatoire des ouvriers*, (Paris: F. Pichon, 1890); G. Bourgin, "Contribution à l'histoire du placement et du livret en France" *Revue politique et parlementaire* vol. LXXI, January-March 1912, pp. 117-118; S. Kaplan, "Réflexions sur la police du monde du travail (1700-1815)" *Revue historique*, 103rd year, no. 529, January-March 1979, pp. 17-77; E. Dolleans and G. Dehove, *Histoire du travail en France. Mouvement ouvrier et législation social*, 2 volumes (Paris: Domat-Montchrestien, 1953-1955); In his course at the Collège de France for 1972-1973, "La Société punitive", in the lecture of 14 March 1973, Foucault presented the worker's *livret* as "an infra-judicial mechanism of penalization."
15. M. Foucault, *Les Mots et les Choses. Une archéologie des sciences humaines* (Paris: Gallimard, 1966) ch. 5, "Classer" pp. 137-176; English translation, *The Order of Things. An Archeology of the Human Sciences*, trans. A. Sheridan (London: Tavistock and New York: Pantheon, 1970) ch. 5, "Classifying," pp. 125-165.
16. J. Bentham, *The Panopticon; La Panoptique*. See above, lecture 21 November 1973, note 5.
17. A State penitentiary was built by Harvey, Busby, and Williams between 1816 and 1821 on a site at Pentonville acquired by Jeremy Bentham in 1795. It had a radiating structure of six pentagons around a central hexagon containing the chaplain, inspectors, and employees. The prison was demolished in 1903.
18. Petite Roquette was built following a competition for the construction of a model prison, the arrangement of which, according to the terms of the circular of 24 February 1825, must be "such that, with the aid of a central point or internal gallery, the whole of the prison can be supervised by one person, or at the most two people." C. Lucas, *Du système pénitentiaire en Europe et aux États-Unis* (Paris: Bossange, 1828) vol. 1, p. cxiii. "La Petite Roquette" or "central House for corrective education" was constructed in 1827 according to a plan proposed by Lebas. It was opened in 1836 and allocated to young prisoners until 1865. See, N. Barbaroux, J. Broussard, and M. Hamoniaux, "L'évolution historique de la Petite Roquette" *Revue "Rééducation"* no. 191, May 1967; H. Gaillac, *Les Maisons de correction (1830-1945)* (Paris: Éd. Cujas, 1971) pp. 61-66; and, J. Gillet, *Recherche sur la Petite Roquette* (Paris: 1975).
19. J. Bentham, *The Panopticon*, Letter 21, Schools, p. 93, emphasis in original; *La Panoptique*, p. 166.
20. Bentham writes that it gives "such herculean and ineludible strength to the grip of power" ibid. p. 88; ibid. p. 160.
21. Ibid. Preface, p. 31; ibid. p. 95.
22. Ibid. Letter, 21, Schools: "That species of fraud at *Westminster* called *cribbing*, a vice thought hitherto congenial to schools, will never creep in here" p. 86 (emphasis in original); ibid. p. 158.
23. Ibid. Letter 18, Manufactories, pp. 80-81; ibid. p. 150.
24. Ibid. Letter 7, Penitentiary-houses—safe-custody, p. 48; ibid. p. 115.
25. Ibid. Letter 19, Mad-houses, pp. 81-82; ibid. p. 152.

26. Ibid. Letter 2, Plan for a Penitentiary Inspection-house, pp. 35-36; ibid. pp. 7-8.
27. Ibid. Letter 21, Schools, p. 92; ibid. p. 164.
28. Foucault is alluding to Condillac's project of deducing the order of knowledge starting from sensation as the raw material of every development of the human mind. See, Étienne Bonnot de Condillac (1715-1780), *Essai sur l'origine des connaissances humaine, ouvrage où l'on réduit à un seul principe tout ce qui concerne l'entendement humain* (Paris: P. Mortier, 1746); English translation, *Essay on the origin of human knowledge*, trans. H. Aarsleff (Cambridge: Cambridge University Press, 2001); *Traité des sensations* (Paris: De Bure, 1754 [reprinted, Paris: Fayard, 1984]); English translation "A Treatise on the Sensations" in *Philosophical Writings of Etienne Bonnot, Abbé de Condillac*, trans. Franklin Philip in collaboration with Harlan Lane (Hillsdale and London: Lawrence Erlbaum, 1982). Foucault refers to this in an interview with C. Bonnefoy in June 1966: "L'homme est-il mort?" *Dits et Écrits*, vol. 1, p. 542, and in *Les Mots et le Choses*, pp. 74-77; *The Order of Things*, pp. 60-63.
29. This remark, which Bentham attributes to Helvétius, actually corresponds to the title of a chapter—"Education can do everything"—of the posthumous work of Claude-Adrien Helvétius, *De l'homme, de ses facultés intellectuelles et de son éducation*, published by Prince Gelitzin (Amsterdam: 1774) vol. 3; English translation, *A Treatise on Man; his intellectual faculties and his education*, trans. W. Hooper (London: 1777).
30. Pierre Carlet de Chamblain de Marivaux (1688-1763), *La Dispute, comédie en un acte et en prose, où pour savoir qui de l'homme ou de la femme donne naissance à l'inconstance, le Prince et Hermiane vont épier la rencontre de deux garçons et deux fillies élevés depuis leur enfance dans l'isolement d'une forêt* (Paris: J. Clousier, 1747).
31. Allusion to Ernst Kantorowicz, *The King's Two Bodies*.
32. See A. Penot, *Les Cités ouvrières de Mulhouse et des départements du Haut-Rhin* (Mulhouse: L. Bader, 1867). Foucault returns to this topic in his interview with J.-P. Barou and M. Perot, "L'œil du pouvoir"; "The Eye of Power."
33. See, J.-B. Monfalcon and J.-F. Terme, *Histoire des enfants trouvés* (Paris: J.-B. Baillière, 1837); E. Parent de Curzon, *Études sur les enfants trouvés au point de vue de législation, de la morale et de l'économie politique* (Poitiers: H. Oudin, 1847); H.J.B. Davenne, *De l'organisation et du régime des secours publics en France* (Paris: P. Dupont, 1865) vol. 1; L. Lallemand, *Histoire des enfants abandonnés et délaissés. Études sur la protection de l'enfance* (Paris: Picard et Guillaumin, 1885); J. Bouzon, *Cent Ans de lutte sociale. La législation de l'enfance de 1789 à 1894* (Paris: Guillaumin, 1894); C. Rollet, *Enfance abandonnée: vicieux, insoumis, vagabonds. Colonies agricoles, écoles de réforme et de préservation* (Clermont-Ferrand: G. Mont-Louis, 1899); and H. Gaillac, *Les Maisons de correctiont.* Michel Foucault returns to the topic in *Surveiller et Punir*, pp. 304-305; *Discipline and Punish* pp. 297-298.
34. The law of 10 January 1849 organized public Assistance in Paris under the Prefecture of the Seine and the Minister of the Interior. It appointed the director of this administration as guardian of foundlings, orphans, and abandoned children. See, A. de Watterwille, *Législation charitable, ou Recueil des lois arrêtés, décrets qui régissent les établissements de bienfaisance* (1790-1874) in 3 volumes (Paris: A. Hévis, 1863-1874); C.J. Viala, *Assistance de l'enfance pauvre et abandonnée* (Nîmes: Chastanier, 1892); F. Dreyfus, *L'Assistance sous la Seconde République* (1848-1851) (Paris: E. Cornély, 1907); and, J. Dehaussy, *L'Assistance publique à l'enfance. Les enfants abandonnés* (Paris: Librairie du Recueil, 1951).
35. Founded on 22 January 1840 by the magistrate Frédéric Auguste Demetz (1796-1873), the Mettray colony, near Tours, was devoted to children acquitted on the grounds of absence of responsibility and to children detained for paternal correction. See F.A. Demetz, *Fondation d'une colonie agricole de jeunes détenus à Mettray* (Paris: Duprat, 1839); A. Cochin, *Notice sur Mettray* (Paris: Claye et Taillefer, 1847); E. Ducpetiaux, (i) *Colonies agricoles, écoles rurales et écoles de réforme pour les indigents, les mendiants et les vagabonds, et spécialement pour les enfants des deux sexes, en Suisse, en Allemagne, en France, en Angleterre, dans les Pays Bas et en Belgique*, Report for the Minister of Justice (Brussels: printed by T. Lesigne, 1851), pp. 50-65; (ii) *La Colonie de Mettray* (Batignolles: De Hennuyer, 1856); (iii) *Notice sur la colonie agricole de Mettray* (Tours: Ladevèze, 1861); H. Gaillac, *Les Maisons de correction*, pp. 80-85. Foucault refers to Mettray in *Surveiller et Punir*, pp. 300-303; *Discipline and Punish*, pp. 293-296.

five

5 December 1973

[*The asylum and the family. From interdiction to confinement. The break between the asylum and the family.* ~ *The asylum; a curing machine.* ~ *Typology of "corporal apparatuses* (appareils corporels)". ~ *The madman and the child.* ~ *Clinics* (maisons de santé). ~ *Disciplinary apparatuses and family power.*]

I HAVE TRIED TO bring out at least some of the underlying disciplinary basis of the asylum, to show you how, from the eighteenth century, a sort of disciplinary network begins to cover society in which a number of specific disciplinary schemas appear, like the army, the school, the workshop, etcetera, and of which Bentham's *Panopticon* appears to me to be the formalization, or anyway the systematic and purified outline.

I would like now to examine more specifically how the asylum works, because it seems to me that the asylum has its particular features. On the one hand, it has a privileged and, what's more, difficult, problematic relationship with the family. On the other hand, as a disciplinary system, the asylum is also a site for the formation of a certain type of discourse of truth. I do not mean that the other disciplinary systems do not give rise to discourses of truth and have no relationship to the family, but in the case of the institution and discipline of the asylum I think the relationship to the family is very specific and surcharged. Moreover, it developed over a very long time and was constantly transformed throughout the nineteenth century. In addition to this, its discourse of truth is also a specific discourse.

Finally, the third characteristic feature is that, in all likelihood—this is my hypothesis and the line I would like to pursue—the discourse of truth developed in the asylum and the relationship to the family mutually support each other, lean on each other and will finally give rise to a psychiatric discourse which will present itself as a discourse of truth in which the family—family figures and family processes—is its fundamental object, target, and field of reference. The problem is how psychiatric discourse, the discourse arising from the exercise of psychiatric power, will be able to become the discourse of the family, the true discourse of the family, the true discourse about the family.

So, today: the problem of the asylum and the family.

I think we should start with the asylum without the family, with the asylum both violently and explicitly breaking with the family. This is the situation at the start that we find in the proto-psychiatry of which Pinel, but even more Fodéré and especially Esquirol, were the representatives and founders.

For the asylum breaking with the family I will take three accounts. The first is the actual juridical form of psychiatric confinement, with particular reference to the 1838 law, from which we have not yet escaped, since this law, with some modifications, more or less still governs confinement in an asylum. Given the period in which it is situated, it seems to me that this law should be interpreted as a break with the family and as the dispossession of the family's rights with regard to its mad members. In fact, before the 1838 law, the basic procedure, the fundamental juridical element that permitted taking charge of the madman, characterizing him and designating his status as insane, was essentially interdiction.

What was interdiction? First, it was a juridical procedure that was and had to be requested by the family. Second, interdiction was a judicial measure, that is to say, it was a judge who actually made the decision, but on the request of the family and after obligatory consultation of family members. Finally, third, the legal effect of this procedure of interdiction was the transfer of the interdicted individual's civil rights to a family council and his placement under a regime of guardianship. So, interdiction was, if you like, an episode of family law validated by judicial procedures.[1] This was the procedure of interdiction, and it was the basic procedure: the madman was essentially someone interdicted, and dissipate, spendthrift, mad, and similar individuals were recognized by their designated status as interdicted.

As for confinement, I was going to say that throughout the classical age it took place according to this legal procedure, but actually it did not take place in this way, but rather in an irregular manner. That is to say, confinement could occur either after the procedure of interdiction or independently of it, in which case it was always a de facto confinement obtained by the family who requested the intervention of the lieutenant of police, or of the intendant, etcetera, or even a confinement decided on by royal power, or by parliament, when someone had committed an irregularity, an infraction, or a crime, and it was thought better to confine him rather than go through the system of justice. The procedure of confinement, therefore, did not have a formal legal origin; it surrounded interdiction and could be substituted for it, but did not have a homogeneous or fundamental judicial status in this kind of taking charge of those who were mad.

Taking charge of those who were mad took place, then, by interdiction, and interdiction was an episode of family law validated by judicial procedure. I will skip a number of episodes that already foreshadow the 1838 law: the law of August 1790, for example, which gave certain rights to the municipal authority.[2]

I think the 1838 law consists in two fundamental things. The first is that confinement overrides interdiction. That is to say, in taking charge of the mad, the essential component is now confinement, interdiction only being added afterwards, if necessary, as a possible judicial supplement, when there is danger of the individual's legal situation, his civil rights, being jeopardized, or, alternatively, when the individual may jeopardize his family's situation by exercising his rights. But interdiction is no more than a component accompanying what is now the basic procedure of confinement.

One takes hold of the madman through confinement, that is to say, by seizing the body itself. The fundamental juridical component is no longer that of depriving the individual of his civil and family rights, but a real arrest. Who ensures this arrest, and how? Of course, most of the time, it takes place at the family's request, but not necessarily. In the 1838 law confinement may well be decided on prefectural authority, without having been requested by the family. In any case, whether or not it has been requested by the family, it is always prefectural authority, doubled by medical authority, which in the end must decide on someone's confinement. Someone arrives in a public hospital, or in a private clinic, with the diagnosis or presumption of madness: he will only be really, officially, designated and characterized as mad when someone qualified by the civil authorities has made an assessment, and when the civil authorities, that is to say, the prefectural authority, have thus made a decision on this assessment. That is to say, the madman is no longer distinguished and assigned a status in relation to the family field, but now appears within what we can call a technical-administrative field, or, if you like, a State-medical field, constituted by the coupling of psychiatric knowledge and power with administrative investigation and power. It is this coupling that will designate the mad individual as mad, and the family's power with regard to the mad individual will henceforth be relatively limited.

The mad individual now emerges as a social adversary, as a danger for society, and no longer as someone who may jeopardize the rights, wealth, and privileges of a family. The mechanism of the 1838 law designates a social enemy, and we can say that one consequence of this is that the family is dispossessed. I would say that when we read the justifications put forward for the 1838 law when it was being voted on, or the commentaries on it afterwards, it is always said that it really was necessary to give this preeminence to confinement over interdiction, to scientific-State power over family power, in order to protect both the life and rights of the family circle. Actually, as long as the lengthy, cumbersome, and difficult procedure of interdiction was the basic component, it was relatively difficult to gain control over someone who was mad, and meanwhile he could continue to wreak havoc in his family circle. He was a danger to those around him and his immediate family was exposed to his outbursts. It was necessary therefore to protect the family circle: hence the need for the procedure of speedy confinement before the lengthy procedure of interdiction.

On the other hand, it was stressed that giving too much importance to interdiction, making it the major component, opened the way to family plots and conflicts of interest. Here again it was necessary to protect the restricted, close family—ascendants and descendants—against the covetousness of the extended family.

This is true and, in a sense, the 1838 law really did function in this way, dispossessing the extended family to the advantage of, and in the interest of, the close family. But precisely this is quite typical of a whole series of processes that are found again throughout the nineteenth century, and which are not only valid for the insane, but also for pedagogy, delinquency, and so forth.*

The power of the State, or, let's say, a certain technical-State power, enters like a wedge, as it were, in the broad system of the family; it takes over a number of the extended family's powers in its own name, and, in order to exercise the power it has appropriated, rests on an entity, the small family cell, which I do not say is absolutely new, but which is carved out in a new way, strengthened, and intensified.

The small family cell of ascendants and descendants is a sort of zone of intensification within the larger family that is dispossessed and short-circuited. It is the power of the State, or, in this case, technical-State power, which will isolate and lean on this narrow, cellular, intense family that is the effect of the incidence of a technical-State power on the large, dispossessed family. This is what I think we can say about the mechanism of the 1838 law. You can see that, inasmuch as all the big asylums have functioned for 150 years now on the basis of this juridical form, it is important to note that it does not favor the family's powers. On the contrary, it divests the family of its traditional powers. In juridical terms, therefore, there is a break between the asylum and the family.

What do we see when we look at the medical tactic, that is to say, the way in which things unfold in the asylum?

The first principle, which is now consolidated, and which you will find practically throughout the life, I was going to say, the serene life of psychiatric discipline, that is to say, until the twentieth century, the principle, or precept rather, a rule of know-how, is that one can never cure a lunatic in his family. The family milieu is absolutely incompatible with the management of any therapeutic action.

---

* The manuscript adds: "In fact, we grasp here a process that will be found again throughout the history of psychiatric power."

We find hundreds of formulations of this principle throughout the nineteenth century. I will give you just one as a reference and example, because it is an old and, as it were, founding formulation. It is a text by Fodéré, from 1817, in which he says that someone admitted into an asylum "enters a new world in which he must be completely separated from his relatives, friends and acquaintances."[3] And I will quote a later text, from 1857, because it will serve us as a reference point and marks an important cleavage: "At the first glimmer of madness, separate the patient from his family, his friends, and his home. Immediately place him under the protection of the art."[4] So, a lunatic can never be cured in his family.

What's more, throughout the therapy, that is to say, the medical process that should lead to the cure, contact with the family is disruptive, dangerous, and as far as possible should be avoided. This is the principle, if you like, of isolation, or rather the principle of the foreign world, since the word 'isolation' is dangerous, appearing to suggest that the patient must be alone, whereas this is not how he is treated in the asylum. The family space and the space marked out by the disciplinary power of the asylum must be absolutely foreign to each other.[5] Why? I will just indicate the reasons here as points of reference. Some are extraordinarily banal, and others are quite interesting and, through successive transformations, will have a future in the history of psychiatric power.

The first reason is the principle of distraction, which is important despite its apparent banality. To be cured, a lunatic must never think of his madness.[6] One must act so that his madness is never present in his mind, is removed from his speech as far as possible, and cannot be seen by witnesses. Hiding his madness, not expressing it, putting it from his mind, thinking of something else: this is, if you like, a principle of non-association, of dissociation.

This is one of the great schemas of psychiatric practice in this period, up until the time when the principle of association triumphs in its place. And when I say, principle of association, I am not thinking of Freud, but of Charcot, that is to say, of the sudden emergence of hysteria, since hysteria will be the great dividing point in this history. So, if the family must be absent, if one must place the mad individual in an absolutely foreign world, it is because of the principle of distraction.

The second principle—again very banal, but interesting for its history—is that the family is immediately identified and indicated as, if not exactly the cause of insanity, at least its occasion. That is to say, what precipitates episodes of madness are vexations, financial worries, jealousy in love, grief, separations, ruin, and poverty, etcetera. All of this can set off madness and constantly feed it.[7] It is therefore with reference to the family as the permanent support of madness, and in order to short-circuit it, that patient and family must be separated.

The third, very interesting reason given, is the very strange notion introduced by Esquirol of "symptomatic suspicion," which will later break up and disappear, although it is still found for quite a while without Esquirol's term itself being used.[8] Esquirol says that the mental patient, and particularly the maniac, is struck by a "symptomatic suspicion." This means that insanity is a process during which the individual's mood changes: his sensations are altered, he experiences new impressions, he no longer sees things correctly, he does not see faces or understand words in the same way, and he may even hear voices with no real foundation, or see images, which are not exactly perceptual images but hallucinations. There are two reasons why the lunatic does not understand the causes of all these changes at the level of his body: on the one hand, he does not know that he is mad, and, on the other, he does not know the mechanisms of the madness.

Not understanding the cause of all these transformations, he looks for their origin elsewhere than in himself, than in his body, and elsewhere than in his madness. That is to say, he looks for their origin in his family circle. In this way he connects the cause of these impressions, rather than their strangeness, to everything around him. As a result, he thinks that the cause of this feeling of discomfort is nothing other than the malevolence of those around him, and he feels persecuted. Persecution, what Esquirol called "symptomatic suspicion," is a kind of ground on which the patient's relationships with his family circle develops. Obviously, if we want to break this symptomatic suspicion, if we want to make the patient aware that he is ill and that the strangeness of his sensations only comes from his illness, we must disconnect his existence from all those who have been around him, and who, since the onset of his illness, are now marked by this symptomatic suspicion.

Finally, the fourth reason advanced by psychiatrists to explain the need to break with the family is that in every family there are power relationships—which I would call the power of sovereignty, but it's not important—which are incompatible with the cure of madness for two reasons. The first is that, in themselves, these power relationships fuel the madness: a father's tyrannical exercise of his will over his children and family circle is part of the family's specific system of power, and will obviously reinforce the father's delusion of grandeur; a wife's legitimate pursuit of her whims, and her imposition of these whims on her husband, is based on the specific type of power relationships in the family space, but it can only fuel the wife's madness. Consequently, individuals must be deprived of the situation of power, of the points of support for their power in the family. A further reason, of course, is that medical power is, in itself, a different type of power from that of the family, and if we want the doctor's power to be exercised effectively, to get a real hold on the patient, we must of course suspend all the configurations, points of support, and relays specific to family power.

These, roughly, are the four reasons found in the psychiatry of the period for explaining the necessary therapeutic break between asylum and family. And there are endless highly edifying case histories in which you are told that just as a therapeutic procedure was about to be successful, everything was immediately upset by the slightest contact with the family.

Thus, in his treatise *Médecine mentale*, Berthier—who had been the student of Girard de Cailleux and had worked at the Auxerre hospital[9]—recounts a series of dreadful case histories of people who were on the way to being cured until contact with the family produced catastrophic effects. "M.B., a most respectable ecclesiastic who had always practiced an austere way of life, was affected, without noticeable cause, by monomania. As a suitable and precautionary measure, everyone he knew was banned from entering the asylum. Despite this enlightened advice, his father managed to get to him. The patient, who was getting better, immediately gets worse: his delirium takes on different forms. He has hallucinations, puts aside his breviary, swears, blasphemes, and becomes prey to an erotico-arrogant delirium."[10]

Another, even more beautiful case history: "Miss S. arrives in a deplorable state from a clinic of the Rhône department, suffering from melancholy, with maniacal excitement caused by sorrow and reversals of fortune. After two years of assiduous care we bring about a real improvement: convalescence approaches. Her son, delighted with the change, expresses the desire to see her. The head doctor agrees, but recommends a brief visit. The young man, having no idea of the importance of this recommendation, exceeds the limits. At the end of two hours the agitation is reborn."[11]

Ah! that's not the case history I wanted to tell you. It was the case history of a father at the Auxerre hospital who was on the way to recovery when he sees his son through a window. Seized by a frenetic desire to see his son, he smashes the window pane. The catastrophe occurred after he breaks the glass separating the asylum from the outside world, and so separating him from his son: he relapsed into his delirium. The process was immediately precipitated by contact with the family.[12]

So, entering the asylum, asylum life, necessarily involves breaking with the family.

If we now consider what takes place once entry has occurred, once the rite of purification and the break has been carried out, if we consider how the asylum is supposed to cure, how the asylum cure is supposed to take place, we see that we are still very far from the possibility of the family being the effective agent of cure. It must never be a question of the family. What's more, to bring about the cure one must never lean on elements, arrangements, or structures that might in any way evoke the family.

We will take Esquirol, and most of those who followed him up until the 1860s, as our basis. In this first episode of the history of psychiatric power, what is it in the hospital that cures? There are two things . . . no, actually there is basically one thing: in the hospital it is the hospital itself that cures. That is to say, the architectural arrangement itself, the organization of space, the way individuals are distributed in this space, the way they move around it, the way one looks or is looked at within it, all has therapeutic value in itself. In the psychiatry of this period the hospital is the curing machine. When I said there were two things, I was going to say that there is truth, but I will try to show you how the discourse of truth, or the emergence of truth as a psychiatric operation, are ultimately only effects of this spatial arrangement.

The hospital then is the curing machine. How does the hospital cure? It is absolutely not by reproducing the family that the hospital cures; the hospital is not in any way an ideal family. If the hospital cures it is because it puts to work those elements that I tried to show you were formalized in Bentham; it cures because the hospital is a panoptic machine, and it is as a panoptic apparatus that the hospital cures. The hospital is in fact a machine for exercising power, for inducing, distributing, and applying power according to Bentham's schema, even if, obviously, the specific architectural arrangements of Bentham's design are modified. Let's say, broadly speaking, that we can find four or five operational elements of the same order as Bentham's *Panopticon*, and which are supposed to play an effective role in the cure.

First, permanent visibility.[13] The madman must not only be someone who is watched; the fact of knowing that one is always being watched, better still, the fact of knowing that one *can* always be watched, that one is always under the potential power of a permanent gaze, has therapeutic value in itself, since it is precisely when one knows one is being looked at, and looked at as mad, that one will not display one's madness and the principle of distraction, of dissociation, will function to the full.

The madman then must be in the position of someone who can always be seen, from which you get the principle for the asylum's architectural organization. A different system than the circular *Panopticon* was preferred, but one that ensured just as much visibility. This was the principle of pavilion architecture, that is to say of small pavilions, which Esquirol explained should be laid out on three sides, the fourth opening onto the countryside. As far as possible, the pavilions thus arranged should only have a ground floor, because the doctor needed to be able to arrive stealthily and take in everything at a glance, without anyone, patients, warders, or supervisors, hearing him.[14] Moreover, in this transformed pavilion architecture, the model employed until the end of the nineteenth century, the cell—since, for Esquirol, the cell was at that time, if not preferable to the dormitory, at least the alternative to it—had to open on two sides in such a way that when the madman was looking out of one side, he could be watched through the other window to see how he was looking out the other side. What Esquirol says about asylum architecture is a strict transposition of the principle of panopticism.

Second, the principle of central supervision by means of a tower from where an anonymous power was constantly exercised is also modified. But it is found again, up to a point, first in the form of the director's building, which must be at the center and watch over all the pavilions set out around it. But, more particularly, central supervision is ensured in a different way than in Bentham's *Panopticon*, but in such a way as to produce the same effect. It is ensured by what we could call the pyramidal organization of supervisory observation.

That is to say, the relationships within the hierarchy of warders, nurses, supervisors, and doctors are formed in terms of a hierarchical channel culminating in the head doctor, the single person in charge of the asylum, because, and every psychiatrist of the period emphasizes this, administrative power and medical power must not be separated, and all these relays of supervision must finally converge on this kind of unitary and absolute knowledge-power constituted by the head doctor.

Third, the principle of isolation, which must also have a therapeutic value. Isolation and individualization are ensured by Esquirol's cell, which almost exactly reproduces the cell of Bentham's *Panopticon*, with its double opening and backlighting. In the standard practice of the period, which is the system of what could be called the triangular perception of madness, we also find this very curious principle of isolation, that is to say, of dissociation from all effects of the group, and of the assignation of the individual to himself as such.

That is to say, the asylum frequently met with the following objection: Is it really a good idea, medically, to put all the mad people together in the same space? First of all, won't the madness be contagious? And secondly, won't seeing others who are mad induce melancholy, sadness, etcetera, in those placed amongst them?

To which the doctors reply: Not at all. Quite the reverse, it is very good to see the madness of others, provided that each patient perceives the other madmen around him in the same way that the doctor sees them. In other words, we cannot ask a madman straightaway to adopt the same point of view on himself as the doctor, because he is too attached to his own madness. However, he is not attached to the madness of others. Consequently, if the doctor shows each patient how all the others around him are really ill and mad, as a result of this, perceiving the madness of others in a triangular fashion, the patient in question will end up understanding what it is to be mad, suffer delirium, be maniacal or melancholic, and suffer monomania. When someone who believes he is Louis XVI is confronted with someone who also thinks he is Louis XVI, and when he sees how the doctor judges this other person, he will then be able to arrive, indirectly, at a consciousness of himself that is analogous to medical consciousness.[15]

You have here an isolation of the madman in his own madness through this game of triangulation, which in itself has a curative effect,[16] or at any rate, which is the guarantee that there will be none of those corrosive phenomena of contagion in the asylum, those group phenomena, which it is precisely the function of the Panopticon to avoid in the hospital, school, or other institutions. The non-contagion, the non-existence of the group, is to be ensured by this kind of medical consciousness of others that each patient must have of those around him.

Finally, and here again you find the themes of the *Panopticon*, the asylum acts through the play of ceaseless punishment, which is ensured either by the personnel, of course, who must be present the whole time and close to each individual, or by a set of instruments.[17] Towards the 1840s in England, which was somewhat backward relative to Western psychiatric practice, a number of English and especially Irish doctors set out the principle of *no restraint*,* that is to say, of the abolition of instruments of physical restraint.[18] The demand created a considerable stir at the time and there was a sort of campaign for *no restraint* in all the hospitals of Europe and a quite important modification, in fact, in the way the mad were treated. However I do not think that the alternative, physical restraint or *no restraint*, was ultimately very serious.

As evidence for this I will take a letter sent by the reverend Mother Superior, in charge of the nuns at Lille, to her colleague, the Superior at Rouen, in which she said: You know, it's not that serious. You too can do what we do at Lille. You can easily remove these instruments on condition that you place "an imposing nun" beside all the lunatics you have set free.[19]

Ultimately, the choice between the intervention of personnel and the use of an instrument is superficial with regard to the deep mechanism of

* In English in original; G.B.

ceaseless punishment. Even so, I think that the system of *restraint*, of physical restraint, is in a sense more eloquent and more evident than the other. In the hospitals of this period—and so after Pinel's famous unchaining of the insane at Bicêtre—throughout the years from 1820 to 1845—the date of *no restraint*—there was a whole set of marvelous instruments: the fixed chair, that is to say, fixed to the wall and to which the patient was attached; the moving chair, which moved about according to the patient's restlessness;[20] handcuffs;[21] muffs;[22] straitjacket;[23] the finger-glove garment, which fit the individual tightly from his neck down so that his hands were pressed against his thighs; wicker caskets[24] in which individuals were enclosed; and dog collars with spikes under the chin. They make up an entire, highly interesting technology of the body, the history of which should perhaps be written, setting it in the general history of these physical apparatuses.

It seems to me that we can say that before the nineteenth century there were a fairly considerable number of these corporal apparatuses. I think we can identify three types. First, security and testing apparatuses, that is to say, apparatuses which prohibit a certain type of action, block a certain type of desire, the problem being the extent to which it is bearable and whether or not the prohibition materialized in the apparatus will be infringed. The classic example of these instruments is the chastity belt.

There is another type of corporal apparatuses used for extracting the truth and which conform to a law of gradual intensification, of quantitative increase—the water torture, the strappado,[25] for example—which were usually employed in the test of truth in judicial practice.

Finally, third, there are the corporal apparatuses with the basic function of both displaying and marking the force of power: branding the shoulder or forehead with a letter. Torturing regicides with pincers and burning them was both an apparatus of public torture and of branding; it was the demonstration of the power unleashed on the tortured and subjected body itself.[26]

We have here three major types of corporal apparatuses, and there is a fourth type of instrument that I think—but this is an hypothesis, for, again, the history of all this should be studied—appears precisely in the nineteenth century and in asylums. These are what we can call orthopedic instruments. By this I mean instruments whose function is not proof, branding by power, or extraction of truth, but correction, training, and taming of the body.

I think these apparatuses can be described in the following way. First, they are apparatuses of continuous action. Second, the progressive effect of these apparatuses must be to make themselves redundant, that is to say, ultimately one should be able to remove the apparatus and its effect will be definitively inscribed in the body. So, they are apparatuses with a self-nullifying effect. And finally, as much as possible they should be homeostatic apparatuses. That is to say, they are apparatuses such that the less one resists them the less one feels them, and the more one tries to escape them, the more one suffers. This is the system of the collar with iron spikes: if you do not lower your head you do not feel it, but the more you lower your head, the more you suffer; it is the system of the straitjacket: the more you struggle, the tighter it gets; it is the system of the chair which gives you vertigo: as long as you do not move you are comfortably seated, but if you are restless the chair's vibration makes you seasick.

This is the principle of the orthopedic instrument, which in the mechanics of the asylum is, I think, the equivalent of what Bentham dreamed of in the form of absolute visibility.

All of this directs us towards a psychiatric system in which the family has absolutely no role. Not only has the family been sterilized, excluded right from the start, but also, in what is supposed to be the therapeutic process of the asylum apparatus, there is nothing that recalls anything like the family. The model one thinks of, the model which operates, is clearly more that of the workshop, of big colonial kinds of agricultural exploitation, or of life in the barracks, with its parades and inspections.

And hospitals in this period really functioned in terms of this schematism. The Panopticon as a general system, as a system of permanent inspection, of uninterrupted observation, was obviously realized in the spatial organization of individuals set alongside each other, permanently under the eyes of the person responsible for supervising them. This is how a director of the Lille asylum puts it:[27] when he took over responsibility for the asylum, a bit before the *no restraint* campaign, he was surprised to hear dreadful cries everywhere, but was both reassured and, we should say, disturbed, when he saw that the patients were really very calm, because he had them all in view, pinned to the wall, each of them attached to a chair fixed to the wall—a system, as you can see, which reproduced the Panopticon mechanism.

We have then an entirely extra-familial type of restraint. I do not think that anything in the asylum brings to mind the organization of the family system; we think rather of the workshop, school, and barracks. Moreover, it is explicitly the military deployment of individuals that we see appearing [in] the work in the workshop, in agricultural work, and in work at school. For example, in his book of 1840 on *Traitement moral*, Leuret said that "whenever the weather permits, patients who are in a condition to march, and who cannot or do not wish to work, are brought together in the hospital courtyard and drilled like soldiers. Imitation is such a powerful lever, even on the laziest and most obstinate men, that I have seen several of the latter, who, resisting everything to start with, nonetheless agree to march. This is a start of methodical, regular, reasonable action, and this action leads to others."[28] With regard to one patient he says: "If I succeed in getting him to accept promotion, putting him in the place of commander, and if he acquits himself well, from that moment I would consider his cure almost certain. I never employ a supervisor to command the marching and maneuvers, only patients."

"With the help of this somewhat military organization [and so we pass from orthopedic exercise to the very constitution of medical knowledge; M.F.], inspection of the patients is facilitated, whether in the wards or courtyards, and every day I can give at least a glance to the incurably insane, keeping most of my time for the insane subject to active treatment."[29] So, with these methods of review, inspection, lining up in the courtyard, and the doctor's observation, we are effectively in the military world. This is how the asylum functioned until around the 1850s, at which point, it seems to me, we see something that indicates a shift.*

---

* The manuscript continues this analysis, noting: "All in all, a disciplinary apparatus which is in principle supposed to have therapeutic effectiveness. We see that under these conditions the correlate of this therapy, the object in its sights, is the will. Madness, no longer defined as blindness, but as affection of the will, and the insertion of the madman in a disciplinary therapeutic field, are two correlative phenomena which mutually support and reinforce each other."

Around 1850-1860 we begin to see the idea expressed that, first of all, the madman is like a child; second, that the madman must be placed in a milieu analogous to the family, although it is not a family; and finally, third, that these quasi familial elements have a therapeutic value in themselves.

You find the idea that the madman is like a child in, for example, a text by Fournet, to which I will return because it is important, "The moral treatment of insanity," which appeared in the *Annales médico-psychologique* in 1854. The madman must be treated like a child, and it is the family, "the true family in which the spirit of peace, intelligence and love reigns," that, "from the earliest time and the first human aberrations," must ensure "the moral treatment, the model treatment of the aberrations of heart and mind."[30]

This text from 1854 is all the more curious in that we see it taking a direction that is, I think, quite new at this time. Fournet says that the family has a therapeutic value, that the family is effectively the model on the basis of which one can construct a moral and psychological orthopedics, of which, he says, we have examples outside the psychiatric hospital: "The missionaries of civilization [and by this I think he means the soldiers then colonizing Algeria as well as missionaries in the strict sense; M.F.] who take from the family its spirit of peace, benevolence, devotion, and even the name of father, and who seek to cure the prejudices, false traditions, and errors of savage nations, are Pinels and Daquins in comparison with the conquering armies who claim to bring civilization through the brutal force of arms and who act on nations in the way that chains and prisons act on the unfortunate insane."[31]

In plain words this means that there were two ages of psychiatry; one in which chains were employed and the other where, let's say, humane feelings were employed. Well, in the same way, there are two methods and maybe two ages in colonization: one is the age of the pure and simple conquest by arms, and the other is the period of establishment and colonization in depth. And this in-depth colonization is carried out by the organization of the family model; it is by introducing the family into the traditions and errors of savage peoples that one begins the work of colonization. Fournet continues, saying that exactly the same thing is found with delinquents. He cites Mettray, founded in 1840, where, in what is basically a purely military schema, the names father, elder brother, and so on, were used in a pseudo-family organization. Fournet refers to this in order to say: You see that here as well the family model is used to try to "reconstitute . . . the elements and regime of the family around these unfortunates, orphaned through the deeds or vices of their parents." And he concludes: "It is not, gentlemen, that I wish from today to include insanity (*aliénation mentale*) in the same category as the moral alienation of peoples or individuals subject to the judgment of history or the law . . ."[32] This is another work, which he promises for the future, but never produced.

But you see that if he did not do it, many others did subsequently. You see delinquents as the residues of society, colonized peoples as the residues of history, and the mad as the residues of humanity in general, all included together in the same category, all the individuals—delinquents, peoples to be colonized, or the mad—who can only be reconverted, civilized and subjected to orthopedic treatment if they are offered a family model.

I think we have here an important point of inflexion. It is important because it takes place quite early, 1854, that is to say, before Darwinism, before *On the Origins of the Species*.[33] Certainly, the principle of ontogenesis-phylogenesis was already known, at least in its general form, but you see the strange use of it here and, especially—even more than the interesting bracketing together of the mad, the primitive, and the delinquent—the appearance of the family as the common remedy for being savage, delinquent, or mad. I am not in any way claiming that this text is the first, but it seems to me to be one of the most revealing and I have hardly found any earlier text that is so clear. So, we can say that the phenomenon I would like to talk about takes place roughly around the 1850s.

So, why did it take place then? What happened in this period? What is the basis of all this? For a long time I have looked for an answer to these questions, and it seemed that we could be put on the track by simply asking the Nietzschean question: "Who is speaking?" Who actually formulates this idea? Where do we find it?

You find it in people like Fournet,[34] in Casimir Pinel, a descendant of Pinel,[35] in Brierre de Boismont,[36] and you also begin to find it in

Blanche,[37] that is to say, in a series of individuals whose common characteristic is simply that of having at some time managed a public service, but especially private clinics, alongside and very different from hospitals and public institutions. Furthermore, all the examples they give of familialization as therapeutic milieu are based on the example of clinics. A fine discovery, you will say. Everyone knows that, from the nineteenth century, there were hospitals-barracks for the exploited and comfortable clinics for the rich. Actually, in relation to this I would like to bring out a phenomenon which goes a bit beyond this opposition, or, if you like, which is lodged in it but is much more precise.

I wonder if there was not a quite important phenomenon in the nineteenth century, of which this would be one of the innumerable effects. This important phenomenon, the effect of which arises here, would be the integration, organization, and exploitation of what I would call the profits of abnormalities, of illegalities or irregularities. I would say that the disciplinary systems had a primary, massive, overall function which appears clearly in the eighteenth century: to adjust the multiplicity of individuals to the apparatuses of production, or to the State apparatuses (*appareils*) which control them, or again, to adjust the combination of men to the accumulation of capital. Insofar as these disciplinary systems were normalizing, they necessarily produced, on their borders and through exclusion, residual abnormalities, illegalities, and irregularities. The tighter the disciplinary system, the more numerous the abnormalities and irregularities. Now, from these irregularities, illegalities, and abnormalities that the disciplinary system was designed to reduce, but that at the same time it created precisely to the extent that it functioned, the economic and political system of the bourgeoisie of the nineteenth century [drew]* a source of profit on the one hand, and of the reinforcement of power on the other.

I will take the example of prostitution, which is quite close to that of the psychiatric hospitals I will talk about after. Clearly, we don't have to wait until the nineteenth century for the existence of that famous triangle of prostitutes, clients and procurers, for the existence of brothels and established networks, etcetera. We don't have to wait until the

---

* (Recording:) found

nineteenth century for the employment of prostitutes and procurers as informers and for the circulation of large sums of money for sexual pleasure in general. However, in the nineteenth century I think we see the organization in European countries of a tight network resting first of all on a system of property, of hotels and brothels, etcetera, and which uses procurers as intermediaries and agents, who are at the same time informers recruited from a group about whose constitution I tried to say some things last year, that is, delinquents.[38]

If there was this kind of need for delinquents, and if, in the end, so much care was taken to form them into an "underworld," it is precisely because they were the reserve army of these important agents of which procurers-informers are only examples. Procurers, enframed by and coupled with the police, are the basic intermediaries of the system of prostitution. So what was the purpose of this system with its rigorous organization and its supports and relays? Its function is to bring back to capital itself, to the normal circuits of capitalist profit, all the profits that can be extracted from sexual pleasure, on the triple condition, of course, that, first, this sexual pleasure is marginalized, deprecated, and prohibited, and so then becomes costly solely by virtue of being prohibited. Second, if one wants to make a profit from sexual pleasure, then it must not only be prohibited, but it must actually be tolerated. And, finally, it must be supervised by a particular power, which is ensured by the coupling of criminals and police, through the procurer-informer. Brought back into the normal circuits of capitalism in this way, the profit from sexual pleasure will bring about the secondary effect of the reinforcement of all the procedures of surveillance and, consequently, the constitution of what could be called an infra-power, which is finally brought to bear on men's everyday, individual, and corporal behavior: the disciplinary system of prostitution. Because this is what is involved; alongside the army, school, and psychiatric hospital, prostitution, as it was organized in the nineteenth century, is again a disciplinary system, the economic and political impact of which can be seen straightaway.

First, sexual pleasure is made profitable, that is to say, it is made into a source of profit due to both its prohibition and its tolerance. Second, the profits from sexual pleasure flow back into the general circuits of capitalism. Third, leaning on this so as to fix even more firmly the extreme effects, the synaptic relays of State power, which end up reaching into men's everyday pleasure.

But prostitution is, of course, only one example of this kind of general mechanism which can be found in the disciplinary systems set up in the eighteenth century for a particular overall function, and which are then refined in the nineteenth century on the basis of this discipline which was essentially demanded by the formation of a new apparatus of production. Finer disciplines are adapted to these disciplines, or, if you like, the old disciplines are refined and thus find new possibilities for the constitution of profit and the reinforcement of power.

Let us now turn to the clinics of Brierre de Boismont, Blanche, and others. What basically is involved is the extraction of profit, and maximum profit, from the marginalization carried out by psychiatric discipline. For if it is clear that the basic aim of psychiatric discipline in its overall form is to take out of circulation individuals who cannot be employed in the apparatus of production, at another level, on a more restricted scale and with a very different social localization, they can be turned into a new source of profit.*

In fact, when a number of individuals from the wealthy classes are themselves marginalized, in the name of the same knowledge that determines confinement, then it will be possible to profit from them. That is to say, it will be possible to ask families who have the means to "pay to be cured." So you can see that the first step in the process will consist in demanding a profit from the family of the individual who is declared ill—on certain conditions.

Obviously it must not be possible to cure the patient at home. So the principle of isolation will continue to be emphasized for the patient who is a source of profit: "We will not cure you in your family. But if we ask your family to pay for you to be confined elsewhere, we must of course guarantee to restore to it something in its image." That is to say,

* In the manuscript Foucault adds: "It is the profit from irregularity which serves as a vector for importing the family model into psychiatric practice."

it is necessary to give back a certain benefit to the family proportionate to the profit demanded from it; a certain profit for the medical body is requested for confining an individual in this way, to pay a pension, etcetera, but the family must benefit from this. This benefit will be the renewal of the system of power within the family. The psychiatrists say to the family: "We will give back to you someone who will really conform and be adjusted and adapted to your system of power." Therefore, re-familialized individuals will be produced, inasmuch as it is the family that, by designating the mad person, provided the possibility of a profit to those who constitute the profit from marginalization. From this derives the need for clinics to be very closely adapted to the family model.

Thus in Brierre de Boismont's clinic, in the Saint-Antoine suburb, there was an organization completely modeled on the family, that is to say, with a father and mother. What's more, the model was not new: Blanche provided a first example of it during the Restoration.[39] The father is Brierre de Boismont himself, and the mother is his wife. Everyone lives in the family home, all are brothers, everyone takes their meals together, and all must have family feelings for each other. The reactivation of family feelings, the investment of every family function in the clinic, will be the effective agency of the cure.

There are some very clear accounts of this in Brierre de Boismont, in his quotation of the correspondence between his patients, after their cure, and himself or his wife. He quotes the letter of an old patient who wrote to Madame Brierre de Boismont: "Far from you, madame, I will often seek the memory so deeply engraved on my heart, in order to enjoy once more that calm filled with affection that you communicate to those who have the good fortune to be received into your home. I will often cast my mind back to your family milieu, so united in all its parts, so affectionate in each of its members, the eldest of whom is as gracious as she is intelligent. If, as is my wish, I return from my own family, you shall be my first visit, for it is a heartfelt debt" (20 May 1847).[40]

I think this letter is interesting. You see that the criterion, the form of the cure itself, is the activation of canonical types of family feelings: gratitude towards the mother and father. You also see at work here, or rising to the surface at least, the theme of a love which is both validated and quasi-incestuous, since the patient is supposed to be Brierre de Boismont's son, and so the brother of the eldest daughter for whom he experiences some feelings. What will be the effect of this reactivation of family feelings, what will he do when he returns to Paris? First of all he will see his family, the true family—that is to say, the family that will get the benefit of the medical process—and, only secondly, he will see Brierre de Boismont's family, this quasi-family, which therefore plays a role of both super- and sub-family. It is a super-family inasmuch as it is the ideal family, which functions in the pure state, the family as it should be always; and it is inasmuch as it is the true family that it is attributed an orthopedic function. Second, it is a sub-family inasmuch as its role is to efface itself before the real family, to activate family feelings by means of its internal mechanism only so that the real family benefits from this, and, at that point, it is no more than the kind of schematic support which, discreetly, constantly sustains the functioning of the real family. This super-family and sub-family is constructed in these clinics, the social and economic location of which is, as you can see, very different from that of the asylum.

However, if the bourgeois, paying clinic is thus familialized—functioning on the family model—then the family, in turn, outside the clinic, must play its role. It is not just a question of saying to the family, if you pay me, I will make your madman able to function in the family; the family still has to play its role, that is to say, actually designate those who are mad. It must play a disciplinary role for itself, as it were, that is to say, it must say: Here is our mad, abnormal member, who is a matter for medicine. That is to say, you have familialization of the therapeutic milieu for the clinics on one side, and, on the other, disciplinarization of the family, which at that point becomes the agency of the abnormalization of individuals.

Whereas the question of the abnormal individual did not arise for the sovereign family—which was concerned rather with the hierarchical order of births, the order of inheritance, relationships of allegiance, obedience, and preeminence between them, with the name and all the sub-functions of the name—the disciplinarized family will begin to substitute for this sovereign function of the name the psychological function of the designation of abnormal individuals, of the abnormalization of individuals.

What I am saying about the clinics is also valid for the school, and to a certain extent for health in general, and for military service, and so on. What I have wanted to show you is that, however much the family continued to conform to a model of sovereignty in the nineteenth century, it may be that, from the middle of the nineteenth century perhaps, there was a sort of internal disciplinarization of the family, that is to say, a kind of transfer of disciplinary forms and schemas, of those techniques of power given by the disciplines, into the very heart of the game of family sovereignty.

Just as the family model is transferred into disciplinary systems, disciplinary techniques are transplanted into the family. And at that point the family, while retaining the specific heterogeneity of sovereign power, begins to function like a little school: the strange category of student parents appears, home duties begin to appear, the control of school discipline by the family; the family becomes a micro-clinic which controls the normality or abnormality of the body, of the soul; it becomes a small scale barracks, and maybe it becomes, we will come back to this, the place where sexuality circulates.

I think we can say that, on the basis of disciplinary systems, family sovereignty will be placed under the following obligation: "You must find for us the mad, feeble minded, difficult, and perverse, and you must find them yourself, through the exercise of disciplinary kinds of control within family sovereignty. And when, through the operation of this disciplinarized sovereignty, you have found your mad, abnormal, feeble minded, and difficult members in your home, we, say the disciplines, will put them through the filter of normalizing apparatuses and restore them to you, the family, for your greater functional benefit. We will make them conform to your needs, even if, obviously, we have made our profit on this."

This is how disciplinary power lives off family sovereignty, requiring the family to play the role of the agency that decides between normal and abnormal, regular and irregular, asking the family to hand over its abnormal, irregular individuals, etcetera, and making a profit from this, which enters into the general system of profit and can be called, if you like, the economic benefit of irregularity. After which, what's more, the family is supposed to find again, at the end of the process, an individual who has been disciplined in such a way that he can be effectively subjected to the family's specific schema of sovereignty. Being a good son, a good husband, and so on, is really the outcome offered by all these disciplinary establishments, by schools, hospitals, reformatories, and the rest. This means that they are machines thanks to which it is thought that disciplinary apparatuses will constitute characters who can take their place within the specific morphology of the family's power of sovereignty.

---

1. "*Les furieux* must be placed in a place of safety, but they can only be detained by virtue of a judgment which must be prompted by the family (...). It is to the Tribunals alone that it [the Civil Code; J.L.] entrusts the care of establishing their condition." Circular of Portalis, 30 Fructidor Year 12 (17 September 1804) cited in G. Bollotte, "Les malades mentaux de 1789 à 1838 dans l'œuvre de P. Sérieux" *Information psychiatrique*, vol. 44, no. 10, 1968, p. 916. The Civil Code of 1804 reformulated the old jurisdiction in article 489 (Title XI, ch. 2): "The person who has reached the age of majority and is in a habitual state of imbecility, dementia, or frenzy, must be interdicted, even when this state has intervals of lucidity." See, "Interdit" in C.J. de Ferriere, ed., *Dictionnaire de droit et de pratique* (Paris: Brunet, 1769) vol. 2, pp. 48-50; H. Legrand du Saulle, *Étude médico-legale sur l'interdiction des aliénés et sur le conseil judiciaire* (Paris: Delahaye et Lecrosnier, 1881); P. Sérieux and L. Libert, *La Régime des aliénés en France au XVIII*[e] *siècle* (Paris: Masson, 1914); P. Sérieux and M. Trénel, "L'interdiction des aliénés par voie judiciaire (sentence d'interdiction) sous l'Ancien Régime" *Revue historique de droit français et étranger*, 4th series, 10th year, July-September 1931, pp. 450-486; A. Laingui, *La Responsabilité pénale dans l'ancien droit (XVI*[e]*-XVIII*[e] *siècles)* (Paris: Librairie générale de droit et de jurisprudence, 1970) vol. 2, pp. 173-204. Foucault refers to interdiction in *Histoire de la folie*, pp. 141-143 (omitted from *Madness and Civilization*). He returns to the topic in the lecture of 12 January 1975 of his course at the Collège de France, 1974-1975, *Les Anormaux*, eds. V. Marchetti and A. Salomoni (Paris: Gallimard/Seuil, 1999) pp. 131-136; English translation, Michel Foucault, *Abnormal. Lectures at the Collège de France 1974-1975*, English ed. Arnold I. Davidson, trans. Graham Burchell (New York: Picador, 2003) pp. 141-145.
2. The law of 16-24 August 1790 made confinement a police measure by entrusting "to the vigilance and authority of municipal bodies ... the responsibility for avoiding or remedying unfortunate events which could be occasioned by the insane or the *furieux* left in liberty" (Title XI, article 3) in *Législation sur les aliénés et les enfants assistés. Recueil des lois, décrets et circulaires (1790-1879)* (Paris: Ministère de l'Intérieur et des Cultes, 1880) vol. 1, p. 3. See, M. Foucault, *Histoire de la folie*, p. 443; *Madness and Civilization*, pp. 238-239.
3. F.E. Fodéré, *Traité du délire*, vol. 2, p. 252.
4. P. Berthier, *Médecine mentale, vol. 1; De l'isolement* (Paris: J.-B. Baillière, 1857) p. 10.
5. The principle is stated by Esquirol in his "Mémoire sur l'isolement des aliénés" (read at the Institut on 1 October 1852): "The isolation of the insane (sequestration, confinement) consists in withdrawing him from all his habits, in separating him from his family, his friends, and his servants; in surrounding him with strangers; in changing his whole way of life" *Des maladies mentales considérées sous les rapports médical, hygiénique et médico-légal*, vol. 2, p. 745. J.-P. Falret, "Du traitement général des aliénés" (lecture at Salpêtrière, 1854) in *Des maladies mentales et des asiles d'aliénés* (Paris: J.-B. Baillière, 1864) pp. 677-699, see p. 685 sq.; J. Guislain, *Traité sur les phrénopathies*, p. 409; J.-M. Dupuy, *Qulques considérations sur la folie. Visite au Castel d'Andorte, établissement destiné aux aliénés de la classe riche* (Périgueux: Dupont, 1848) pp. 7-8.
6. François Leuret states that "whenever one can, one should impose silence on the patient on the subject of his delirium and occupy him with something else" *Du traitement moral de la folie, op. cit.*, p. 120. See also his "Mémoire sur la révulsion morale dans le traitement de la folie" in *Mémoires de l'Académie royale de médecine*, 1841, p. 658. However, it is J.-P. Falret who, in a faithful summary of Esquirol's conceptions, states the principle most explicitly in an unpublished manuscript: "Isolation is obviously of prime importance ... But, once the patient has been withdrawn from external influences, should he be left to himself without seeking to destroy the fixity of his unhealthy preoccupations? Obviously not. Not content with having removed the causes which may foment it, one must combat the delirium itself, and to this end experience recognizes no more effective means than, for some, fixing their attention on objects most likely to fascinate them, and, for others, diverting them from their fixed ideas, distracting them from their preoccupations by constantly presenting them with objects foreign to their delirium, and by completely directing their attention on every kind of occupation, so that it is impossible for them to think of the subject of their illness." Quoted by G. Daumezon and P. Koechlin, "La psychothérapie institutionelle

française contemporaine" *Annais portugueses de psiquiatria*, vol. 4, no. 4, 1952, p. 274. See also, J.-P. Falret, *Des maladies mentales et des asiles d'aliénés*, p. 687.

7. "The moral cause of insanity often exists in the bosom of the family, and gets its source from sorrows, domestic disputes, setbacks, etcetera (...) the first shock to the intellectual and moral faculties often takes place in the insane person's own home, amongst his acquaintances, his relatives, and his friends." J.E.D. Esquirol, *Des passions, considérées comme causes, symptômes et moyens curatifs de l'aliénation mentale*, Paris Medical Thesis no. 574 (Paris: Didot Jeune. 1805), p. 43. See J. Fournet, "Le traitement moral de l'aliénation mentale, soit morale, a son principe et son modèle dans la famille" (Report read to the *Société médicale d'émulation*, 4 March 1854): "A good number of the insane find in what we call the family not only the conditions which irritate, aggravate and precipitate these kinds of affections, but in virtue of this, the conditions which give birth to them" *Annales médico-psychologiques*, 2nd series, vol. 6, October 1854, pp. 523-524; and A. Brierre de Boismont, "De l'utilité de la vie de famille dans le traitement de l'aliénation mentale, et plus spécialement de ses formes tristes" (Report read to the *Académie des sciences*, 21 August 1865) *Annales médico-psychologiques*, 4th series, vol. 7, 1866 (Paris: Martinet, 1866), pp. 40-68.
8. J.E.D. Esquirol, "De la folie" in *Des maladies mentales*, vol. 1, p. 120; English translation, J.E.D. Esquirol, *Mental Maladies. A Treatise on Insanity*, trans. E.K. Hunt (New York and London: Hafner, 1965) p. 74: "The insane man becomes timid and suspicious. He fears every one that he approaches; and his suspicions extend to those who were most dear to him. The conviction that every one is endeavouring to torment and slander him, to render him miserable, and to ruin him, in body and estate, puts the finishing stroke to this moral perversion. Hence that *symptomatic suspicion*, which often grows up without motive."
9. In 1849, Pierre Berthier (1830-1877) became intern under his uncle, Henri Girard de Cailleux, head doctor and director of the Auxerre mental asylum. After the defense of his thesis, "De la nature de l'aliénation mentale d'après ses causes et son traitement," at Montpellier in 1857, Berthier returned to Auxerre for two years before his appointment as head doctor at Bourg (Ain), before becoming resident doctor at Bicêtre in 1865.
10. P. Berthier, *Médecine mentale*, vol. 1, Observation C, p. 25.
11. Ibid. Observation D, p. 25.
12. Ibid. Observation B: "M.G., suffering from acute melancholy (...) arrives in the most unfortunate state (...). After some months of treatment, and not without many efforts, improvement arrives (...). In spite of the express prohibition of the doctor director, the patient sees his son; he breaks a glass window pane and throws himself through the opening he has made, with the intention of joining him. From that moment (...) the hallucinations reappear with greater intensity, sleep vanishes, the delirium increases; and the patient's situation constantly gets worse" pp. 24-25.
13. In *Histoire de la folie*, pp. 517-519, this principle was considered under the heading "Mirror Recognition"; *Madness and Civilization*, pp. 262-265.
14. "In a ground floor building, at any moment and without a sound he can arrive close to the patients and servants." J.E.D. Esquirol, *Des établissements consacrés aux aliénés en France*, p. 36; reprinted in *Des maladies mentales*, vol. 2, p. 426.
15. P. Pinel, *Traité médico-philosophique sur l'aliénation mentale, ou la Manie*, section II, § xxii: "Habilité dans l'art de diriger les aliénés, en paraissant se prêter à leurs idées imaginaires," pp. 93-94; *A Treatise on Insanity*, Section II, "The propriety of appearing to assent to the absurd propositions and fanciful ideas of maniacs" pp. 96-97. In fact, Pinel says: "Three insane persons, each of whom believed himself to be a king, and each of whom took the title Louis XVI, quarreled one day over the prerogatives of royalty, and defended them somewhat too energetically. The keeper approached one of them, and drawing him aside, asked: 'Why do you argue with these men who are evidently mad? Doesn't everyone know that you should be recognized as Louis XVI?' Flattered by this homage, the madman immediately withdrew, glancing at the others with a disdainful hauteur. The same trick succeeded with a second, and thus it was that in an instant there remained no trace of the dispute." This passage is quoted, with a somewhat different commentary, in *Histoire de la folie*, pp. 517-518; *Madness and Civilization*, pp. 262-263.
16. J.E.D. Esquirol, "De la folie" in *Des maladies mentales*, vol. 1, p. 124; *Mental Maladies. A Treatise on Insanity*, pp. 75-76. Evoking the "strongest objection that can be urged against

establishments devoted to this kind of treatment," Esquirol counters that "the frightful effects that may result from mingling with companions in misfortune" are compensated for by a cohabitation that "does not injure them,—that it is not an obstacle to a cure—that it is a valuable means of treatment, because it obliges the insane to reflect upon their condition (...) to occupy their thoughts with what is going on around them,—to forget themselves, as it were, which is, in itself, a means of cure." Falret also claims that the asylum makes it possible "to prompt reflection on oneself through the contrast between everything around the patient and his only family circle." J.-P. Falret, "Du traitement général des aliénés" (1854) in *Des maladies mentales et des asiles d'aliénés*, p. 687.

17. *Histoire de la folie* evokes the "almost arithmetical obviousness of punishment" p. 521; *Madness and Civilization*, p. 267.
18. The roots of the principle of *no restraint* are found in the reforms undertaken by the Englishmen W. Tuke, J. Haslam, and E. Charlesworth, and the Irishman J. Conolly. Following the death at York asylum of a woman belonging to the Quakers, William Tuke founded on 11 May 1796 an establishment for the insane for members of the Society of Friends: the *Retreat.* Samuel Tuke (1784-1857), William's grandson, published *Description of the Retreat, an Institution near York for Insane Persons of the Society of Friends* (York: W. Alexander, 1813). See, R. Semalaigne, *Aliénistes et Philanthropes: les Pinel et les Tuke* (Paris: Steinheil, 1912); M. Foucault, *Histoire de la folie*, pp. 484-487, 492-496, 501-511, *Madness and Civilization*, pp. 243-255 (pages 484-501 of the French edition are omitted from the English translation); John Haslam, apothecary at the Bethlehem hospital in London, devoted a work to him: *Considerations on the Moral Management of Insane Persons* (see also above notes 6 and 13 to the lecture of 7 November 1973); in 1820, Edward Charlesworth (1783-1853), consultant doctor at the Lincoln Asylum, attacked the coercive methods then much in evidence: *Remarks on the Treatment of the Insane and the Management of Lunatics Asylums* (London: Rivington, 1825); John Conolly (1794-1866), promoter of *no restraint*, applied it from 1 June 1839 after his arrival at the Middlesex asylum at Hanwell, near London. He set out his conceptions in, *The Construction and Government of Lunatics Asylums and Hospitals for the Insane* (London: J. Churchill, 1847), and in *The Treatment of the Insane without Mechanical Restraint* (London: Smith and Elder, 1856). See also, H. Labatt, *An Essay on Use and Abuse of Restraint in the Management of the Insane* (London: Hodges and Smith, 1847).
19. Letter of the Mother Superior of the asylum for women at Lille to the Mother Superior of the nuns of Saint Joseph of Cluny who ministered to the asylum of Saint Yon (Lower Seine)—of which Bénédict Augustin Morel (1807-1873) was the head doctor from 23 May 1856—in which she set out the way in she controlled agitated patients: "We set to work... taking an agitated woman so as to put her under the supervision of a nun who knew how to impress." Quoted in B.A. Morel's report, *Le Non-Restraint, ou De l'abolition des moyens coercitifs dans le traitement de la folie* (Paris: Masson, 1860) p. 77.
20. An armchair resting on bellows so that "at the slightest movement the insane person is bounced about in every direction, and the unpleasant sensation caused by this movement forces him to be keep calm." J. Guislain, *Traité sur les phrénopathies*, p. 414.
21. Iron handcuffs covered with leather are recommended by Esquirol as one of the "many means more gentle than chains," J.E.D. Esquirol, "Des Maisons d'aliénés" in *Des maladies mentales*, vol. 2, p. 533. See also, J. Guislain, *Traité sur l'aliénation mentale et sur les hospices des aliénés*, vol. 2, book 12, "Institutions for the insane. Means of repression," pp. 271-272.
22. The "strong muffs" are a piece of cloth holding the hands together in front of the body.
23. The straitjacket was invented in 1790 by Guilleret, an upholsterer of Bicêtre, and consists of a shirt made of strong cloth or canvas, open at the back, with long sleeves crossing over in front and fastened at the back, immobilizing the arms. See, J. Guislain, *Traité sur l'aliénation mentale*, vol. 2, pp. 269-271; E. Rouhier, *De la camisole ou gilet de force* (Paris: Pillet, 1871); A. Voisin, "D l'utilité de la camisole de force et des moyens de contention dans le traitement de la folie" (Communication to the Société médico-psychologiques, 26 July 1860) *Annales médico-psychologiques*, 3rd series, vol. 6, November 1860, pp. 427-431; V. Magnan, "Camisole," in *Dictionnaire encyclopédique des sciences médicales* (Paris: Masson/Asselin, 1880) 1st series, vol. 11, pp. 780-784. Foucault analyses the meaning of its use in *Histoire de la folie*, p. 460 (omitted from the English translation).

24. An instrument of restraint, the wicker casket is a cage, a man's length, in which the patient is laid out on a mattress. It has a lid and is cut off at the neckline. See, J. Guislain, *Traité sur l'aliénation mentale*, vol. 2, p. 263.
25. The strappado (*l'estrapade*) hoisted the guilty person, attached by a rope and tied hands and feet, to the top of a bracket, and then let him fall towards the ground several times. On the test of truth in judicial procedure, see Foucault's course at the Collège de France for 1971-1972, "Penal Theories and Institutions," sixth lecture, and *Surveiller et Punire*, pp. 43-46, *Discipline and Punish*, pp. 39-42.
26. On the public torture and execution of Damien, see *Surveiller et Punir*, pp. 9-11 and 36-72; *Discipline and Punish*, pp. 3-6 and 32-69.
27. This is Doctor Gosseret, recounting his having discovered "patients of both sexes fixed to wall by iron chains," quoted by B.A. Morel, *Le Non-Restraint*, p. 14. Guillaume Ferrus also says that "in some places the unfortunates are fixed to the wall, to which they are attached in an upright position by means of a strap," quoted in R. Semelaigne, *Les Pioniers de la psychiatrie française avant et après Pinel* (Paris: Baillière, 1930) vol. 1, pp. 153-154.
28. F. Leuret, *Du traitement moral de la folie*, p. 178.
29. Ibid. p. 179.
30. J. Fournet, "Le traitement moral de l'aliénation" *Annales médico-psychologiques*, p. 524. See also, J. Parigot, *Thérapeutique naturelle de la folie. L'air libre et la vie de famille dans la commune de Ghéel* (Brussels: J.B. Tircher, 1852) p. 13: "We think that the sick man needs the sympathy that family life gives birth to right from the start."
31. J. Fournet, "Le traitement moral de l'aliénation" pp. 526-527. Joseph Daquin (1732-1815) was born in Chambéry where he was appointed in 1788 to the Incurables where he encountered the conditions imposed on the insane. See J. Daquin, *La Philosophie de la folie, ou Essai philosophique sur le traitement des personnes attaquées de folie* (Chambéry: Gorin, 1791). A revised and expanded edition appeared in 1804 dedicated to Philippe Pinel: *La Philosophie de la folie, où l'on prouve que cette maladie doit plutôt être traitée par les secours moraux que les secours physique* (Chambéry: Cléaz, 1804). See also, J.R. Nyffeler, *Joseph Daquin und seine "Philosophie de la folie"* (Zurich: Juris, 1961).
32. J. Fournet, "Le traitement moral de l'aliénation" p. 527. On Mettray, see above note 35 to the lecture of 28 November.
33. Charles Robert Darwin (1809-1882), *On the Origins of the Species by means of Natural Selection, or the Preservation of Favoured Races in the Struggle for Life* (London: J. Murray, 1859); French translation of the 6th edition, *De l'origine des espèces au moyen de la sélection naturell, ou la Lutte pour l'existence dans la nature*, trans. E Barbier (Paris: Reinwald, 1876).
34. Jules Fournet (1811-1885), head of the clinic at the Hôtel-Dieu, author of, *Doctrine organo-psychique de la folie* (Paris: Masson, 1867), and the discourse given at the Congrés médico-psychologique in 1878, *De l'hérédité physique ou morale* (Paris: Imprimerie nationale, 1880).
35. Jean Pierre Casimir Pinel (1800-1866), nephew of Philippe Pinel, worked in 1829 at 76 rue de Chaillot, a clinic devoted to the treatment of mental illnesses, before transferring it in 1844 to Neuilly in 1844, in the old Saint-James folly. See his, *Du traitement de l'aliénation mentale en général, et principalement par les bains tièdes prolongés et les arrosements continus d'eau froide su la tête* (Paris: J.-B. Baillière, 1853).
36. Alexandre Brierre de Boismont (1798-1881), after being employed in 1825 as doctor to the Sainte-Colombe clinic, rue de Picpus, took over management of a clinic at 21 rue Neuve Saint-Geneviève in 1838, which was transferred in 1859 to Saint-Mandé, where he died on 25 December 1881. See: "Maison de Santé du Docteur Brierre de Boismont, rue Neuve Sainte-Geneviève, no. 21, près du Panthéon, Prospectus" *Observations médico-légales sur la monomanie homicide* (Paris: Mme. Auger Méquignon, 1826—taken from the *Revue médicale*, October and November 1826); and, *Des hallucinations, ou Histoire raisonée des apparitions, des visions, des songes* (Paris: J.-B. Baillière, 1845).
37. In 1821, Esprit Sylvestre Blanche (1796-1852) took over management of a clinic founded in 1806 in Montmartre by P.A. Prost, then rented, in 1846, the old town mansion of Princess de Lamballe at Passy. He made himself known through his criticisms of François Leuret's application of moral treatment (see below, note 8 to the lecture of 19 December). See, J. Le Breton, *La Maison de santé du docteur Blanche, ses médecins, ses malades* (Paris: Vigné, 1937);

R. Vallery-Radot, "La maison de santé du docteur Blanche" *La Presse médicale*, no. 10, 13 March 1943, pp. 131-132.

38. The lecture of 21 February 1973 of Foucault's Collège de France course "The punitive society" was devoted to the organization of the world of delinquency. See also *Surveillir et Punir*, pp. 254-260 and pp. 261-299; *Discipline and Punish*, pp. 252-256 and pp. 257-290.
39. In his clinic in the Saint-Antoine suburb, which Doctor Pressat handed over to him in 1847.
40. A. Brierre de Boismont, "De l'utilité de la vie de famille dans le traitement de l'aliénation mentale" *Annales médico-psychologiques*, pp. 8-9.

six

12 December 1973

[*Constitution of the child as target of psychiatric intervention. ~ A family-asylum utopia: the Clermont-en-Oise asylum. ~ From psychiatry as "ambiguous master" of reality and truth in proto-psychiatric practices to psychiatry as "agent of intensification" of reality. ~ Psychiatric power and discourse of truth. ~ The problem of simulation and the insurrection of the hysterics. ~ The question of the birth of psychoanalysis.*]

I WILL CONTINUE WITH last week's lecture for a while because last week I found a marvelous institution that I was vaguely aware of but did not realize how well it suited me. So I would like to say something about it because it seems to me to show very well this connection between asylum discipline and, let's say, the family model.

Contrary to a rather loose hypothesis, which I have myself maintained, that the asylum was constituted through the extension of the family model, I have tried to show you that the nineteenth century asylum functioned in fact on a model of micro-power close to what we can call disciplinary power that functions in a way that is completely heterogeneous to the family. And then I tried to show that the insertion, the joining of the family model to the disciplinary system takes place relatively late in the nineteenth century—I think we can put it around the years 1860 to 1880—and it was only then that the family could not only become a model in the functioning of psychiatric discipline, but also, and especially, the horizon and object of psychiatric practice.

A time came, albeit late, when psychiatry really was concerned with the family. I have tried to show you that this occurred at the point of intersection of two processes which mutually supported each other: one was the constitution of what could be called the profits of abnormalities or irregularities, and the other was the internal disciplinarization of the family. There is evidence for both of these processes.

On the one hand, of course, there is the growing extension throughout the nineteenth century of those profitable institutions whose aim is basically to make both abnormality and, at the same time, its correction, costly; let's say, roughly, clinics for children, adults, etcetera. On the other hand, there is the deployment of psychiatric techniques at the heart of the family, their use in family pedagogy. It seems to me that if we look at how this took place, at least in families which could yield a profit from abnormality, that is to say bourgeois families, [by following] the evolution of the internal pedagogy of these families, we would see how the vigilant family eye, or, if you like, family sovereignty, gradually came to resemble the disciplinary form. The watchful family eye became a psychiatric gaze, or, at any rate, a psycho-pathological, a psychological gaze. Supervision of the child became supervision in the form of deciding on the normal and the abnormal; one began to keep an eye on the child's behavior, character, and sexuality, and it is here that we see the emergence of precisely all that psychologization of the child within the family itself.

It seems to me that both the notions and apparatuses of psychiatric control were gradually imported into the family. With regard to the famous instruments of restraint found in asylums from around 1820 to 1830—binding hands, holding the head up, keeping in an upright position, etcetera—my impression is that, initially established as instruments of and within asylum discipline, they gradually advance and take root in the family. The control of posture, of gestures, of the way to behave, the control of sexuality, with instruments for preventing masturbation, etcetera, all penetrate the family through a disciplinarization which develops during the nineteenth century and the effect of which is that, through this disciplinarization, the child's sexuality finally becomes an object of knowledge within the family itself. And as a result of this the child will become the central target of psychiatric intervention. The child becomes the central target in two senses.

On the one hand, directly, since the institution of profit plugged into psychiatry will effectively ask the family to provide it with the material it needs in order to make its profit. Psychiatry says, more or less: "let your mad little children come to me," or, "you're never too young to be mad," or, "don't wait for the age of majority or adulthood to be mad." And all of this is translated into the institutions of supervision, detection, training, and child therapy that you see developing at the end of the nineteenth century.

And then, in a second sense, childhood becomes the center, the target of psychiatric intervention indirectly, insofar as what one asks the mad adult about is, precisely, his childhood: let your childhood memories come, and through this you will be psychiatrized. This is more or less what I tried to set out last week.

All this brings me to this institution, which, around the 1860s, displays the asylum-family link up so well. I cannot say it is the first link up, but certainly its most perfect, best adjusted, almost utopian form. I have found hardly any other examples, in France at least, which are so perfect as this establishment, which constitutes at this time, and early on therefore, a kind of family-asylum utopia, the meeting point of family sovereignty and asylum discipline. This institution is the coupling of the Clermont-en-Oise asylum with the Fitz-James clinic.

At the end of the eighteenth century, in the neighborhood of Beuvais, there is a small house of confinement, in the classic sense of the term. It is run by Cordelier monks who, in return for an allowance, accept twenty residents either at the request of families or on the basis of *lettres de cachet*. The house is opened in 1790 and all its fine society is freed. However, obviously, some families are burdened with these dissolute, disorderly, mad people, and so they are then sent to someone at Clermont-en-Oise who has opened a kind of boarding house. At this time, just as Parisian restaurants were opening up on what was left of the great aristocratic houses broken up as a result of the Emigration, so, in the same way, many of these boarding houses arose on the ruins of houses of confinement that had been thrown open. So there is a boarding house at Clermont-en-Oise in which, under the Revolution, during the Empire, and even at the beginning of the Restoration, there were twenty residents. Then, when the great institutionalization of psychiatric practice takes place, this boarding house becomes increasingly important and the prefectural administration of the Oise department and the founder of the boarding house come to an arrangement whereby the department's destitute insane will be sent to the Clermont boarding house in return for a payment by the department. What's more, the agreement is extended to the departments of Seine-et-Oise, Seine-et-Marne, Somme, and l'Aisne, and in 1850 a total of five departments send more than a thousand people to this boarding house, which then simply resembles a multi-departmental asylum.[1]

At this point the asylum splits, or rather, puts out a sort of pseudopodium, in the form of what is called the "colony."[2] This "colony" is made up of a number of the asylum's residents with the ability to [work].* On the pretext that they can be useful and, at the same time, that work is useful for their cure anyway, they are subjected to a very strict regime of agricultural work.

A second pseudopodium, linked to the farm, is established for wealthy residents who do not come from the Clermont asylum, but who were sent directly by their families and who pay a very high price for a completely different kind of boarding based on a different, family model.[3]

In this way we have an institution with three levels: the Clermont asylum with its thousand patients; the farm with 100-150 men and women who are required to work;[4] and then a boarding house for paying residents, who are further separated, the men living in the management quarters with the director of the institution himself, and the wealthy women living in a different building with the typical name of "*petit château*," where the general form of their existence follows the family model.[5] This was established in the decade 1850 to 1860. In 1861, the director publishes a balance sheet, which is at the same time a sort of prospectus, which is therefore highly eulogistic and slightly utopian, but which gives an exact picture of the meticulous and subtle way the system operates.

In this kind of establishment—the Clermont asylum, the farm, and the Fitz-James petit château—there are a number of levels. On the one

---

* (Recording:) are able to work

hand, you have an easily identifiable economic circuit: first, a departmental grant for poor patients allocated by the general council according to their numbers; second, withdrawal from the poor patients of the number of people necessary and sufficient for running a farm; and finally, the creation and maintenance of a petit château with the profit from the farm, taking in a number of paying residents, their payment constituting the profit for those in charge of the general system. So, you have the system: community subsidy-work-exploitation-profit.

Second, you can see that there is a sort of perfect social microcosm, a sort of little utopia of general social functioning. The asylum is the reserve army of the farm proletariat; it is all those who, potentially, could work, and who, if they cannot work, wait for the moment when they can, and, if they do not have the ability to work, remain in the asylum vegetating. Then there is the place of productive work, which is represented by the farm. Then you have the institution in which those who benefit from the work and the profit are found. And to each of these levels corresponds a specific architecture: that of the asylum; that of the farm, which in reality is a model practically bordering on slavery and colonization; and then the petit château with the management quarters.

You also have two types of power, the first of which is split. You have the traditional disciplinary power of the asylum, which is negative in a way, since its function is to keep people calm without getting anything positive from them. Then you have a second disciplinary type of power, but slightly modified, which is, roughly, the power of colonization: putting people to work, with the insane divided into squads and brigades, etcetera, under the authority and supervision of those who regularly put them to work. And then there is power on the family model for residents of the petit château.

In short, you have three types of psychiatric intervention or manipulation, corresponding to these three levels. One is, if you like, the degree zero of psychiatric intervention, that is to say, pure and simple penning within the asylum. Second, there is the psychiatric practice of putting patients to work on the pretext of curing them: ergotherapy. And then, third, for paying residents, you have individual, individualizing psychiatric practice on the family model.

In the middle of all this, the most important and typical element is undoubtedly the way in which psychiatric knowledge and treatment are connected to the practice of putting those residents to work who are capable of working. Actually, very strangely, it is clear that the psychiatric categories developed by the psychiatry of the time, since Esquirol—and which I will try to show got absolutely no hold on therapy itself—are not in fact employed here at all as a classification of the curability of different people and the form of treatment that should be applied to them. Nosological classification is not linked to any therapeutic prescription but serves instead solely to define the possible utilization of individuals for the work they are offered.

Thus the directors of the Clermont asylum and the Fitz-James farm realized that if a patient was maniacal, monomaniacal, or demented, they were good for work in the fields and workshops looking after and managing animals and plowing tools.[6] On the other hand, "imbeciles and idiots are responsible for cleaning the courtyards and stables and all the transport necessary for the service."[7] The use of women according to their symptomatology is much more discriminating. Thus "those in the washhouse and laundry are almost always affected by a noisy delirium and would not be able to abide by the peace and quiet of workshop life."[8] In the washhouse and laundry, therefore, one can rave at the top of one's voice, talk loudly, and shout. Second, "those occupied with hanging out the washing are melancholics in whom this kind of work can restore the vital activity they so often lack. The imbeciles and idiots are responsible for taking laundry from the washhouse to the drying room. The workshops for sorting and folding the laundry are the remit of calm patients, monomaniacs, whose fixed ideas or hallucinations make possible a fairly sustained attention."[9]

I have cited this establishment because it seemed to me to represent, around the 1860s, both the first form and most perfect realization of this family-discipline adjustment, and, at the same time, of the deployment of psychiatric knowledge as discipline.

✣

This example leads us, moreover, to the problem that I would now like to consider, which is this: How and to what extent can one attribute a therapeutic effect to this disciplinary, not yet familialized space, to this disciplinary system that we see being constituted between 1820 and 1830 and which will constitute the broad basis for the asylum institution? For, after all, it should not be forgotten that even if this disciplinary system is in many respects isomorphic with other disciplinary systems, like the school, the barracks, the workshop, and suchlike, it puts itself forward and justifies itself by its therapeutic function. What is it in this disciplinary space that is supposed to cure? What medical practice inhabits this space? This is the problem I would like to begin to address today.

To do this I would like to start with a type of example about which I have already spoken, which is what we can call the classical cure, meaning by classical the cure still current in the seventeenth and eighteenth centuries, and even at the beginning of the nineteenth century. I have given you a number of examples of this. There is the case of Pinel's patient who thought he was being pursued by revolutionaries, was waiting to be brought before the courts, and was consequently threatened with the death penalty. Pinel cured him by organizing a pseudo-trial around him, with pseudo-judges, in the course of which he was acquitted—thanks to which he was cured.[10]

In the same way, someone like Mason Cox, at the beginning of the nineteenth century gives the following example of a cure. It involves a man of forty years, who "had injured his health by too close attention to extensive mercantile concerns."[11] This passion for commerce had put into his head the idea that "his body was universally diseased."[12] And the main one of these, the one by which he felt most threatened, was what was called at the time "repelled itch," that is to say, an irruption of scabies which had not reached its term, which had spread throughout the organism, and manifested itself in a number of symptoms. The classical technique for curing it was to bring out this famous scabies and treat it as such.

For some time attempts were made to get the patient to understand that he did not have any of the illnesses in question: "no arguments could divert him . . . a formal consultation of medical men was therefore determined on, who, having previously agreed on the propriety of humouring the patient, professed to be unanimously of the opinion that his apprehension was just, a medical plan was laid down, some rebefacient application to different parts of the body occasioned crops of eruptions from time to time which were washed with some simple preparation. This farce continued a few weeks, and the patient at length was perfectly restored to health and reason."[13] His delirium had been satisfied, as it were.

What do these procedures of Pinel and Mason Cox presuppose and what do they bring into play? They presuppose—this is well known, I will not return to it—that the kernel of madness is a false belief, an illusion or an error. They also presuppose—which is already a bit different—that for the illness to disappear it is enough to dispel the error. The procedure of cure is therefore the reduction of the error; except the mad person's error is not just anyone's error.

The difference between the error of someone who is mad and someone who is not mad is not so much in the extravagance of the idea itself, because, after all, it is not very extravagant to believe one has "repelled itch." And moreover, as Leuret will say later in his *Fragments psychologiques sur la folie*, between Descartes who believed in vortices and a patient at Salpêtrière who imagined that a council was being held in his lower abdomen,[14] the extravagance is not especially on the patient's side. What makes a mad person's error the error of someone who is, precisely, mad? It is not then so much the extravagance, the final effect of the error, as the way in which the error can be overcome, dispelled. The mad person is someone whose error cannot be dispelled by a demonstration; he is someone for whom demonstration does not produce the truth. Consequently, one will have to find a different method of dispelling the error—since madness really is, in fact, the error—without using demonstration.

This means that, instead of attacking the erroneous judgment and showing that it has no correlation with reality, which is roughly the process of demonstration, one will let the false judgment be taken as true while transforming reality so that it is adapted to the mad, erroneous judgment. Now, when an erroneous judgment thus finds that it has a correlate in reality, which verifies it, from then on, the mental content coinciding with something in reality, there is no longer error and so no more madness.

So it is not by treating the false judgment, by trying to correct it or dismiss it by demonstration, but rather by dressing up and manipulating reality that reality is placed on the same level, as it were, as the delirium. When the false judgment of the delirium is found to have a real content in reality, it will as a result become a true judgment and the madness will cease being madness, since the error will have ceased being error. So one makes reality delirious so that the delirium is no longer delirium; one puts the delirium in the right so that it is no longer deceived. It is a matter, in short, of introducing reality into the delirium behind the mask of delirious figures, so that the delirium is satisfied by reality; through a game of transformations, of masks, one surreptitiously introduces a reality beneath all the false propositions of the delirium, or beneath the main false propositions of delirium, and in this way the delirium is verified.*

You see that this practice of the cure is, in a sense, absolutely homogeneous with the classical conception of judgment and error; we are in line with, say, the Port-Royal conception of the proposition and judgment.[15] However, you see that there is a difference between the teacher or demonstrator, the person who possesses the truth, and the psychiatrist. Whereas the master of truth, the teacher or scientist, manipulates judgment, the proposition, and thought, the doctor will manipulate reality in such a way that the error becomes true. In this kind of process the doctor is the intermediary, the ambivalent person who [on the one hand] looks from the side of reality and manipulates it, and, on the other, looks from the side of truth and error and arranges it that the form of reality comes up to the level of the error in order to transform it thereby into truth.

He manipulates reality by making it wear a mask; he makes this reality a little less real, or at any rate he deposits a film of unreality on it; he puts it between the brackets of the theater, of the "as if," of the pseudo-, and by making reality unreal in this way he carries out the transformation of error into truth. Consequently he is the agent of reality—and in this he is not like the scientist or the teacher; he is however someone

* The manuscript clarifies: "Since it is as a comic, theatrical reality, as a pseudo-reality that it is introduced into the delirium, and by according a second effectiveness to reality, since for the delirium to fail it is enough that the false judgment become true through the masking of reality."

who makes reality unreal in order to act on the erroneous judgment maintained by the patient.[16]

I think we can say that the psychiatrist, as he will function in the space of asylum discipline, will no longer be the individual who considers what the mad person says from the standpoint of truth, but will switch resolutely, definitively, to the standpoint of reality.* He will no longer be the ambiguous master of reality and truth that he was still with Pinel and Mason Cox; he will be the master of reality. He will no longer have anything to do with somehow smuggling reality into the delirium; it is no longer a question of the psychiatrist being a smuggler of reality as Pinel and Mason Cox were. The psychiatrist is someone who must give reality that constraining force by which it will be able to take over the madness, completely penetrate it, and make it disappear as madness. The psychiatrist is someone who—and this is what defines his task—must ensure that reality has the supplement of power necessary for it to impose itself on madness and, conversely, he is someone who must remove from madness its power to avoid reality.

From the nineteenth century, the psychiatrist is then a factor of the intensification of reality, and he is the agent of a surplus-power of reality, whereas, in the classical period he was, in a way, the agent of a power of the 'derealization' of reality. You will say that if it is true that the nineteenth century psychiatrist crosses over completely to the side of reality, and if he becomes for madness the agent of the intensification of the power of reality, thanks precisely to the disciplinary power he gives himself, it is not true however that he does not pose the question of truth. I will say that, of course, the problem of truth is posed in nineteenth century psychiatry, despite the nevertheless quite considerable negligence it manifests with regard to the theoretical elaboration of its practice. Psychiatry does not avoid the question of truth, but, instead of placing the question of the truth of madness at the very heart of the cure, at the heart of its relationship with the mad person, which was still the case for Pinel and Mason Cox, instead of bringing the problem of truth out into the open in the confrontation between doctor and

---

* The manuscript adds: "In asylum psychiatry, the psychiatrist plays the role of master of reality in a completely different way."

patient, psychiatric power only poses the question of truth within itself. It gives itself the truth right from the start and once and for all by constituting itself as a medical and clinical science. This means that rather than the problem of the truth being at stake in the cure, it is resolved once and for all by psychiatric practice as soon as this practice assumes the status of a medical practice founded as the application of a psychiatric science.

So that if one had to define this power that I would like to talk to you about this year, I would suggest, provisionally, the following: Psychiatric power is that supplement of power by which the real is imposed on madness in the name of a truth possessed once and for all by this power in the name of medical science, of psychiatry. On the basis of this definition, which I put forward in this provisional form, I think we can understand some general features of the history of psychiatry in the nineteenth century.

First there is the very strange relationship—I was going to say the absence of relationship—between psychiatric practice and, say, discourses of truth. On the one hand, it is true that with the psychiatrists of the beginning of the nineteenth century psychiatry very quickly shows great concern to constitute itself as a scientific discourse. But to what scientific discourses does psychiatric practice give rise? It gives rise to two types of discourse.

One of these we can call the clinical or classificatory, nosological discourse. Broadly speaking, this involves describing madness as an illness or, rather, as a series of mental illnesses, each with its own symptomatology, development, diagnostic and prognostic elements, etcetera. In this, the psychiatric discourse that takes shape takes normal clinical medical discourse as its model; it aims to constitute a sort of *analogon* of medical truth.

Then, and very soon too, even before Bayle's discovery of general paralysis, anyway from 1822 (the date of Bayle's discovery),[17] you see the development of an anatomical-pathological knowledge which poses the question of the substratum or organic correlatives of madness, the problem of the etiology of madness, of the relationship between madness and neurological lesions, etcetera. This is no longer a discourse analogous to medical discourse, but a real anatomical-pathological or physiological-pathological discourse that is to serve as the materialist guarantee of psychiatric practice.[18]

Now, if you look at how psychiatric practice developed in the nineteenth century, how madness and mad people were actually handled in the asylum, you notice that, on the one hand, this practice was placed under the sign of and, so to speak, under the guarantee of these two discourses, one nosological, of kinds of illnesses, and the other anatomical-pathological, of organic correlatives. Psychiatric practice developed in the shelter of these two discourses, but it never used them, or it only ever used them by reference, by a system of cross-references and, as it were, of pinning. Psychiatric practice, such as it was in the nineteenth century, never really put to work the knowledge, or quasi-knowledge, which was being built up in psychiatric nosology or in anatomical-pathological research. Basically, distributions in the asylum, the ways in which patients were classified and divided up, the ways in which they were subjected to different regimes and given different tasks, and the ways in which they were declared cured or ill, curable or incurable, did not take these two discourses into account.

The two discourses were just sorts of guarantees of truth for a psychiatric practice that wanted to be given truth once and for all and for it never to be called into question. The two big shadows of nosology and etiology, of medical nosography and pathological anatomy, were behind it to constitute, before any psychiatric practice, the definitive guarantee of a truth which this practice will never bring into operation in the practice of the cure. In crude terms, psychiatric power says: The question of truth will never be posed between madness and me for the very simple reason that I, psychiatry, am already a science. And if, as science, I have the right to question what I say, if it is true that I may make mistakes, it is in any case up to me, and to me alone, as science, to decide if what I say is true or to correct the mistake. I am the possessor, if not of truth in its content, at least of all the criteria of truth. Furthermore, because, as scientific knowledge, I thereby possess the criteria of verification and truth, I can attach myself to reality and its power and impose on these demented and disturbed bodies the surplus-power that I give to reality. I am the surplus-power of reality inasmuch as I possess, by myself and definitively, something that is the truth in relation madness.

This is what a psychiatrist of the time called "the imprescriptible rights of reason over madness," which were for him the foundations of psychiatric intervention.[19]

I think the reason for this absence of a connection between discourses of truth and psychiatric practice, for this gap, pertains to this function of the enhanced power of the real, which is the basic function of psychiatric power and which must, as it were, slip behind its back a truth considered to be already acquired. This makes it possible to understand that the great problem of the history of psychiatry in the nineteenth century is not a problem of concepts, and not at all the problem of this or that illness: neither monomania nor even hysteria was the real problem, the cross psychiatry had to bear in the nineteenth century. If we accept that the question of truth is never posed in psychiatric power, then it is easy to understand that the cross nineteenth century psychiatry has to bear is quite simply the problem of simulation.[20]

By simulation I do not mean the way in which someone who is not mad could pretend to be mad, because this does not really call psychiatric power into question. Pretending to be mad when one is sane is not something like an essential limit, boundary, or defect of psychiatric practice and psychiatric power, because, after all, this happens in other realms of knowledge, and in medicine in particular. We can always deceive a doctor by getting him to believe that we have this or that illness or symptom—anyone who has done military service knows this—and medical practice is not thereby called into question. On the other hand, and this is the simulation I want to talk to you about, the simulation that was the historical problem of psychiatry in the nineteenth century is simulation internal to madness, that is to say, that simulation that madness exercises with regard to itself, the way in which hysteria simulates hysteria, the way in which a true symptom is a certain way of lying and the way in which a false symptom is a way of being truly ill. All this constituted the insoluble problem, the limit and, ultimately, the failure of nineteenth century psychiatry that brought about a number of sudden developments.

If you like, psychiatry said more or less: I will not pose the problem of truth with you who are mad, because I possess the truth myself in terms of my knowledge, on the basis of my categories, and if I have a power in relation to you, the mad person, it is because I possess this truth. At this point madness replied: If you claim to possess the truth once and for all in terms of an already fully constituted knowledge, well, for my part, I will install falsehood in myself. And so, when you handle my symptoms, when you are dealing with what you call illness, you will find yourself caught in a trap, for at the heart of my symptoms there will be this small kernel of night, of falsehood, through which I will confront you with the question of truth. Consequently, I won't deceive you when your knowledge is limited—that would be pure and simple simulation—but rather, if one day you want really to have a hold on me, you will have to accept the game of truth and falsehood that I offer you.

Simulation: the whole history of psychiatry can be said to be permeated by this problem of simulation, from the two simulators at Salpêtrière in 1821, when it looms up before Georget, one of the leading psychiatrists of the period, until the 1880s and the important episode with Charcot. And when I say this problem, I am not talking about the theoretical problem of simulation, but the processes by which those who were mad actually responded with the question of falsehood to this psychiatric power that refused to pose the question of truth. The untruthfulness of simulation, madness simulating madness, was the anti-power of the mad confronted with psychiatric power.

I think the historical importance of this problem of both simulation and hysteria derives from this. It also enables us to understand the collective character of this phenomenon of simulation. We see it emerge around 1821 in the behavior of the two hysterics called "Pétronille" and "Braguette."[21] I think these two patients founded an immense historical process in psychiatry; they were imitated in all the asylums in France because ultimately it was their weapon in the struggle with psychiatric power. And with the serious crisis of asylum psychiatry, which broke out at the end of the nineteenth century, around 1880, the problem of truth really was imposed by the mad on psychiatry when, in front of Charcot the great miracle worker, it became evident that all the symptoms he was studying were aroused by him on the basis of his patients' simulation.

I emphasize this history for a number of reasons. The first is that it is not a matter of symptoms. It is often said that hysteria has disappeared, or that it was the great illness of the nineteenth century. But it was not the great illness of the nineteenth century; it was, to use medical terminology, a typical asylum syndrome, or a syndrome correlative to asylum power or medical power. But I don't even like the word syndrome. It was actually the process by which patients tried to evade psychiatric power; it was a phenomenon of struggle, and not a pathological phenomenon. At any rate, that is how I think it should be viewed.

Second, we should not forget that if there was so much simulation within asylums after Braguette and Pétronille, this was not only because it was made possible by the coexistence of patients within the asylums, but also because of sometimes spontaneous and sometimes involuntary, sometimes explicit and sometimes implicit complicity with the patients on the part of the personnel, of warders, asylum doctors, and medical subordinates. We should not forget that Charcot practically never examined a single one of these hysterics, and that all his observations, falsified by simulation, were actually given to him by the personnel surrounding the patients, and who, together with the patients, with greater or lesser degrees of complicity, constructed this world of simulation as resistance to psychiatric power that, in 1880 at Salpêtrière, was incarnated in someone who, precisely, was not even a psychiatrist, but a neurologist, and so someone most able to base himself on the best constituted discourse of truth.

The trap of falsehood, then, was set for the person who came armed with the highest medical knowledge. So the general phenomenon of simulation in the nineteenth century should be understood not only as a process of the patients' struggle against psychiatric power, but as a process of struggle at the heart of the psychiatric system, of the asylum system. And I think we arrive here at the episode that must be the aim of my course, which is the moment when, precisely, the question of truth, put aside after Pinel and Mason Cox by the disciplinary system of the asylum and by the type of functioning of psychiatric power, was forcibly reintroduced through all these processes.*

---

* The manuscript adds: "We can, then, call antipsychiatry any movement by which the question of truth is put back in play within the relationship between the mad person and the psychiatrist."

We may say that psychoanalysis can be interpreted as psychiatry's first great retreat, as the moment when the question of the truth of what is expressed in the symptoms, or, in any case, the game of truth and lie in the symptom, was forcibly imposed on psychiatric power; the problem being whether psychoanalysis has not responded to this first defeat by setting up a first line of defense. At any rate, credit should not be given to Freud for the first depsychiatrization. We owe the first depsychiatrization, the first moment that made psychiatric power totter on the question of truth, to this band of simulators. They are the ones who, with their falsehoods, trapped a psychiatric power which, in order to be the agent of reality, claimed to be the possessor of truth and, within psychiatric practice and cure, refused to pose the question of the truth that madness might contain.

There was what could be called a great simulator's insurrection that spread through the whole of the asylum world in the nineteenth century, and the constant and endlessly rekindled source of which was Salpêtrière, an asylum for women. This is why I don't think we can make hysteria, the question of hysteria, the way in which psychiatrists got bogged down in hysteria in the nineteenth century, a kind of minor scientific error, a sort of epistemological blockage. It is clearly very reassuring to do this, because it makes it possible to write the history of psychiatry and the birth of psychoanalysis in the same style as the explanation of Copernicus, Kepler, or Einstein. That is to say, there is a scientific blockage, an inability to get free from the excessive number of spheres of the "Ptolemaic" world, or from Maxwell's equations, etcetera. We find secure footing in this scientific knowledge and, starting from this kind of dead-end, see an epistemological break and then the sudden appearance of Copernicus or Einstein. By posing the question in these terms, and by making the history of hysteria the *analogon* of these kinds of episodes, the history of psychoanalysis can be placed in the calm tradition of the history of the sciences. However, if, as I would like to do, we make simulation—and so not hysteria—the militant underside of psychiatric power rather than an epistemological problem of a dead-end, if we accept that simulation was the insidious way for the mad to pose the question of truth forcibly on a psychiatric power that only wanted to impose reality on them, then I think that we could write a history of psychiatry that would no longer revolve around psychiatry and its knowledge, but which finally would revolve around the mad.

And you can see that if we take up the history of psychiatry in this way, then it can be seen that what we can call the institutional perspective, which poses the problem of whether or not the institution is the site of violence, is in danger of suppressing something. It seems to me that it delineates the historical problem of psychiatry—that is to say, the problem of this power of reality that it was the psychiatrist's task to re-impose and which was trapped by the questioning falsehood of the simulators—in an extraordinarily narrow way.

This is the kind of general background I would like to give to the following lectures. So, next week, I will try to resume this history, which I have suggested to you in a sketchy way, by taking up the problem of how psychiatric power functioned as a surplus-power of reality.

---

1. In 1861 the asylum received 1227 insane persons, 561 men and 666 women, divided into 215 paying and 1212 destitute residents. See the work by the asylum's director, Gustave Labitte, *De la colonie de Fitz-James, succursale de l'asile privé de Clermont (Oise), considérée au point de vue de son organisation administrative et médicale* (Paris: J.-B. Baillière, 1861) p. 15. On the history of the Clermont asylum, see E.-J. Woillez, *Essai historique, descriptif et statistique sur la maison d'aliénés de Clermont (Oise)* (Clermont: V. Danicourt, 1839).
2. The Fitz-James colony was created in 1847.
3. "In creating the Fitz-James colony, first of all we wanted the patients to be in a completely different environment than that of Clermont" G. Labitte, *De la colonie de Fitz-James*, p. 13.
4. In 1861, the farm comprised "170 patients," ibid. p. 15.
5. According to G. Labitte's description: "1. The management section allocated to living quarters for the director and male residents. 2. The Farm section, where the colonists stay. 3. The Petit Château section, inhabited by resident women. 4. The Bévrel section, occupied by women employed in laundering the linen" ibid. p. 6.
6. "On the farm ... work in the fields and workshops, looking after and managing animals and plowing tools, are the remit of maniacs, monomaniacs and the demented" ibid. p. 15.
7. Ibid.
8. Ibid. p. 14.
9. Ibid.
10. P. Pinel, *Traité médico-philosophique*, section VI, § iv: "Essai tenté pour guérir une mélancolie profonde produite par une cause morale" pp. 233-237; A *Treatise on Insanity*, "An attempt to cure a case of melancholia produced by a moral cause" pp. 224-227.
11. Joseph Mason Cox, *Practical Observations on Insanity*, Case II, p. 51; *Observations sur la démence*, (1806), p. 77.
12. Ibid. p. 51; ibid. p. 78.
13. Ibid. p. 52; ibid. pp. 78-79.
14. F. Leuret, *Fragments psychologiques sur la folie* (Paris: Crochard, 1834) ch. 2: "Delirium of intelligence": "The chair hirer of a Parisian parish, treated by Monsieur Esquirol, ... said he had bishops in his belly who were holding a council ... Descartes thought it an established fact that the pineal gland is a mirror which reflected the image of external bodies ... Is one of these assertions better proved than the other?" p. 43. Leuret is referring to Descartes' analysis of the role of the pineal gland in the formation of ideas of objects which strike the senses: R. Descartes, *Traité de l'Homme* (Paris: Clerselier, 1664) in Descartes, *Œuvres et Lettres*, ed. A. Bridoux, pp. 850-853; English translation, "Treatise on Man," trans. Robert Stoothoff, in *The Philosophical Writings of Descartes*, trans. John Cottingham, Robert Stoothoff, Dugald Murdoch (Cambridge: Cambridge University Press, 1985) vol. 1, p. 106.
15. In this conception, "*Judging* is the action in which the mind, bringing together different ideas, affirms of one that it is the other, or denies of one that it is the other. This occurs when, for example, having the idea of the earth and the idea of round, I affirm or deny of the earth that it is round" A. Arnauld and P. Nicole, *La Logique, ou l'Art de penser, contenant, outre les règles communes, plusieurs observations nouvelles propres à former le jugement* (1662) (Paris: Desprez, 1683, 5th edition) p. 36; English translation, *Logic, or, The art of thinking*, trans. J.V. Buroker (Cambridge: Cambridge University Press, 1996) p. 23. See, L. Marin, *La Critique du discours. Sur la "Logique de Port-Royal" et les "Pensées de Pascal"* (Paris: Éd. de Minuit, 1975) pp. 275-299; and Foucault's comments in *Les Mots et les Choses*, Part One, "Représenter," pp. 72-81; *The Order of Things*, pp. 58-67; and, "Introduction" to A. Arnauld and C. Lancelot, *Grammaire génerale et raisonnée contenant les fondements de l'art de parler expliqués d'une manière claire et naturelle* (Paris: Républications Paulet, 1969), reprinted in *Dits et Écrits*, vol. 1, pp. 732-752.
16. On this theatrical production, see Michel Foucault, *Histoire de la folie*, pp. 350-354; *Madness and Civilization*, pp. 187-191. The second lecture of the Collège de France course of 1970-1971, "The Will to Knowledge," speaks of this "theatricalization" of madness as an "ordeal test" which involves "seeing which of the two, patient or doctor, would keep up the game of truth the longest, all this theater of madness by which the doctor objectively realized as it were the patient's delirium and, on the basis of this feigned truth, reached the patient's truth" (personal notes; J.L.).

17. Whereas paralytic disorders were considered to be intercurrent affections of the development of dementia or, as Esquirol said, a "complication" of the illness (see the article "Démence" in *Dictionnaire des sciences médicales, par une société de médecins et de chirurgiens* [Paris: C.L.F. Panckoucke, 1814] vol. VIII, p. 283, and the article "Folie" vol. XVI, 1816), in 1822, Antoine Laurent Jessé Bayle (1799-1858), on the basis of six observations followed by anatomical checks, gathered in the department of Royer-Collard at Salpêtrière, identified a morbid entity which, following the anatomical cause to which he attributed it, he called "chronic arachnitis," using the fact that "in all the periods of the illness, there is a constant relationship between the paralysis and the delirium . . . we therefore could not refuse to accept that these two orders of phenomena are the symptoms of a single illness, that is to say of a chronic arachnitis," to which he devotes a first part of his thesis defended on 21 November 1822 (*Recherches sur les maladies mentales*, Medical Thesis, Paris, no. 147 [Paris: Didot Jean, 1822]): *Recherches sur l'arachnitis chronique, la gastrite, la gastro-entérite, et la goutte, considérées comme causes de l'aliénation mentale* (Paris: Gabon, 1822; centenary republication Paris: Masson, 1922) vol. 1, p. 32. Bayle later extended his conception to most mental illnesses: "Most mental illnesses are the symptoms of an original chronic phlegmasia of the 'membranes of the brain' " *Traité des maladies et de ses membranes* (Paris: Gabon, 1826) p. xxiv. See also his text, "De la cause organique de l'aliénation mentale accompagnée de paralysie générale" (read at the Imperial Academy of Medicine) *Annales médico-psychologiques*, 3rd series, vol. 1, July 1855, pp. 409-425.
18. In the 1820s, a group of young doctors turned to pathological anatomy on which it tried to graft clinical psychiatry. Félix Voisin set out the programme: "Given the symptoms, how can the seat of the disease be determined. This is the problem that medicine illuminated by physiology can address today" *Des causes morales et physiques des maladies mentales, et de quelques autres affections telles que l'hysterie, la nymphomanie et le satyriasis* (Paris: J.-B. Baillière, 1826) p. 329. In 1821, two students of Léon Rostan (1791-1866), Achille [de] Foville (1799-1878) and Jean-Baptiste Delaye (1789-1879), presented a paper for the Prix Esquirol: "Considérations sur les causes de la folie et de leur mode d'action, suivies de recherches sur la nature et le siège spécial de cette maladie" (Paris: 1821). On 31 December 1819, Jean-Pierre Falret (1794-1870) defended his thesis: *Observations et propositions médico-chirurgicales*, Medical Thesis, Paris, no. 296 (Paris: Didot, 1919) before publishing his, *De l'hypocondrie et du suicide. Considérations sur les causes, sur le siège et le traitement du ces maladies, sur les moyens d'en arrêter les progrès et d'en prévoir les développements* (Paris: Croullebois, 1822). On 6 December 1823, Falret gave a lecture to the Athénée de Médecine: "Inductions tirées de l'ouverture des corps des aliénés pour servir au diagnostic et au traitement des maladies mentales" (Paris: Bibliothèque Médicale, 1824).

    In 1830 a debate on the organic causes of madness was started on the occasion of the thesis of one of Esquirol's students, Étienne Georget (who entered Salpêtrière in 1816 and in 1819 won the Prix Esquirol with his paper: "Des ouvertures du corps des aliénés") which was defended on 8 February 1820, *Dissertation sur les causes de la folie*, Medical Thesis, Paris, no. 31 (Paris: Didot Jeune, 1820), and in which he criticizes Pinel and Esquirol for being satisfied with observation of the phenomena of madness without seeking to connect them to a productive cause. In his work, *De la folie*, p. 72, Georget declares: "I must not fear finding myself in opposition to my teachers . . . by demonstrating that madness is a cerebral idiopathic affection."
19. It was Jean-Pierre Falret who asserted that, thanks to isolation, "the family, in the silence of a positive law, overcoming the fear of committing an arbitrary act, and making use of the imprescriptible right of reason over delirium, subscribes to the teachings of science in order to obtain the benefit of the cure of the insane." J.-P. Falret, *Observations sur le projet de loi relatif aux aliénés, présentés le 6 janvier 1837 à la Chambre des députés par le ministre de l'Intérieur* (Paris: Éverat, 1837) p. 6.
20. The problem of simulation was raised in 1800 by P. Pinel who devoted a chapter to it in his *Traité médico-philosophique* section VI, § xxii: "Mania simulée; moyens de la reconnoître" pp. 297-302; A *Treatise on Insanity*, "Feigned mania: the method of ascertaining it," pp. 282-287. See also, A. Laurent, *Étude médico-légale sur la simulation de la folie. Considérations cliniques et pratiques à l'usage des médecins experts, des magistrats et des jurisconsultes* (Paris: Masson, 1866); H. Bayard, "Mémoire sur les maladies simulées," *Annales d'hygiène publique et de médecine*

légale, 1st series, vol. XXXVIII, 1867, p. 277; E. Boisseau, "Maladies simulées" in A. Dechambre and others, eds. *Dictionnaire encyclopédique des sciences médicales*, 2nd series, vol. 2 (Paris: Masson/Asselin, 1876) pp. 266-281; G. Tourdès, "Simulation" ibid. pp. 681-715. Charcot dealt with the question on several occasions: (1) "Ataxie locomotrice, forme anormale" (20 March 1888) in *Leçons du mardi à la Salpêtrière. Policlinique 1887-1888*, notes of the course of M. Blin, J. Charcot, and H. Colin (Paris: Lecrosnier & Babé, 1889) vol. 1, pp. 281-284; (2) Lecture IX: "De l'ischurie hystérique," (1873) in *Leçons sur les maladies du système nerveux*, vol. 1, collected and published by D.M. Bourneville (Paris: Delahaye et Lecroisner, 1884, 5th edition) pp. 281-283; English translation, J.M. Charcot, *Clinical Lectures on Diseases of the Nervous System*, vol. 1, trans. George Sigerson (London: New Sydenham Society, 1877) Lecture 10, "Hysterical ischuria" pp. 230-232; (3) Lecture 1: "Leçon d'ouverture de la chaire de clinique des maladies du système nerveux" (23 April 1882), and Lecture XXVI: "Cas du mutisme hystérique chez l'homme," both in *Leçons sur les maladies du système nerveux*, vol. 3, collected and published by Babinski, Bernard, Féré, Guinon, Marie and Gilles de La Tourette (1887) (Paris: Lecroisner & Babé, 1890), pp. 17-22 and 432-433; English translation, J.M. Charcot, *Clinical Lectures on Diseases of the Nervous System*, trans. Thomas Savill (London and New York: Tavistock/Routledge, 1991) vol. 3, Lecture I, "Introductory," pp. 14-19, and Lecture 26, "A Case of Hysterical Mutism in a man," pp. 368-370.

21. In 1821, at Salpêtrière, Étienne Georget, attracted by the experiments conducted by the Baron Jules Dupotet de Sennevoy in October 1820 at the Hôtel Dieu in the department of Hussun, with the help of Léon Rostan, converted two patients into somnambulistic experimental subjects: Pétronille and Manoury, the widow Brouillard, called "Braguette." See A. Dechambre, "Nouvelles expériences sur le magnétisme animal" *Gazette médicale de Paris*, 12 September 1835, p. 585. Georget reports these experiments, without revealing the identity of the patients, in *De la physiologie du système nerveux, et spécialement du cerveau*, vol. 1, ch. 3: "Somnambulisme magnétique" (Paris: J.-B. Baillière, 1821) p. 404. See also, A. Gauthier, *Histoire du somnambulisme: chez tous les peuples, sous les noms divers d'extases, songes, oracles, visions, etc.* (Paris: F. Maltese, 1842) vol. 2, p. 324; A. Dechambre, "Deuxième lettre sur le magnétisme animal," *Gazette médicale de Paris*, 1840, pp. 13-14, and "Mesmérisme," in *Dictionnaire encyclopédique des sciences médicales*, 2nd series (Paris: Masson/Asselin, 1877) vol. VII, pp. 164-165.

seven

19 DECEMBER 1973*

Psychiatric power. ~ A treatment by François Leuret and its strategic elements: 1–creating an imbalance of power; 2–the reuse of language; 3–the management of needs; 4–the statement of truth. ~ The pleasure of the illness. ~ The asylum apparatus (dispositif).

THE ESSENTIAL FUNCTION OF psychiatric power is to be an effective agent of reality, a sort of intensifier of reality to madness. In what respect can this power be defined as a surplus-power of reality?

To begin to sort out this question a little, I would like to take the example of a psychiatric treatment of around the years 1838-1840. How did psychiatric treatment take place at this time?

At first sight, at the time of the establishment, the organization, of the asylum world, there was no treatment, because recovery was expected as a sort of, if not spontaneous, at least automatic process of reaction to the combination of four elements. These were: first, isolation in the asylum; second, physical or physiological medication with opiates,[1] laudanum,[2] etcetera; third, a series of restraints peculiar to asylum life, such as discipline, obedience to a regulation,[3] a precise diet,[4] times of sleep and of work,[5] and physical instruments of constraint; and then, finally, a sort of psychophysical, both punitive and therapeutic medication,

* In the manuscript this lecture is given the title: "The psychiatric cure."

like the shower,[6] the rotary swing,[7] etcetera. These combined elements defined the framework of treatment from which recovery was expected without any theory or explanation ever being given for this recovery.*

Despite this initial appearance, I think psychiatric treatment developed in terms of a number of plans, tactical procedures, and strategic elements that can be defined and are, I believe, very important for the constitution of psychiatric knowledge, maybe up until our own time.

I will take one cure as an example that, to my knowledge, is the most developed example in the French psychiatric literature. Sadly the psychiatrist who provided this example has an unfortunate reputation: Leuret, the man of moral treatment, who for a long time was reproached for his abuse of punishment and the shower, and other such methods.[8] He is certainly the person who not only defined the classical psychiatric cure in the most precise, meticulous way, and who left the most documents concerning his treatments, but I think he is also the person who developed his practices, his strategies of treatment, and pushed them to a point of perfection which makes it possible both to understand the general mechanisms which were put to work by other psychiatrists, his contemporaries, and to see them in slow motion, as it were, in detail and in terms of their subtle mechanisms.

The treatment is that of a M. Dupré and is reported in the final chapter of the *Traitement moral de la folie* in 1840.[9] "M. Dupré is a short, fat man, given to stoutness; he walks alone and never addresses a word to anyone. His gaze is uncertain, his countenance vacant. He is constantly belching and farting, and he frequently makes a very disagreeable little grunt with the aim of ridding himself of the emanations that have entered his body by means of necromancy. He is insensitive to the kindnesses he may be shown and even seeks to avoid them. If one insists it puts him in a bad mood, but without him ever becoming violent, and he says to the supervisor, if one is there: 'Make these madmen who come to torment me go away.' He never looks anyone in the face, and if one succeeds in drawing him out from uncertainty and daydreaming for an instant, he immediately falls back into it (. . .). There are three families

* The manuscript adds: "A code, in short, not a linguistic code of signifying conventions, but a tactical code enabling the establishment and definitive inscription of a certain relationship of force."

on Earth whose nobility makes them pre-eminent over all others; these are the families of the Tartar princes, of Nigritie, and of the Congo. One particular race, the most illustrious of the family of Tartar princes, is that of the Halcyons, of which he is the head, Dupré so-called, but in reality born in Corsica, descendant of Cosroës: he is Napoleon, Delavigne, Picard, Audrient, Destouches, Bernardin de Saint-Pierre, all at the same time. The distinctive sign of his Halcyon status is his constant ability to enjoy the pleasures of love. Beneath him are degenerate, less favored beings of his race, called three quarters, one quarter, or one fifth Halcyons, according to their amorous abilities. As a result of his excesses, he fell into a state of chronic illness, for the treatment of which his adviser sent him to his Saint-Maur château (this is what he calls Charenton), then to Saint-Yon, then to Bicêtre. The Bicêtre in which he finds himself is not the one near Paris, and the town one points out to him, some distance from the home, is none other than the town of Langres, in which, in order to deceive him, there are representations of monuments which bear some resemblance to those of the true Paris. He is the only man in the home; all the others are women, or rather combinations of several women, wearing well arranged masks provided with beards and side-whiskers. He positively recognizes the doctor who looks after him as a cook who was once in his service. The house in which he slept, when coming from Saint-Yon to Bicêtre, vanished when he left it. He never reads a newspaper and would not touch one for anything in the world; the newspapers he is given are false, they do not speak of him, Napoleon, and those who read them are accomplices in league with those who produce them. Money has no value; there is nothing but counterfeit money. He often hears the bears and apes talking in the jardin des Plantes. He remembers his stay in his Saint-Maur château, and even some of the people he met there (. . .). The multiplicity of his false ideas is no less remarkable than the confidence with which he spouts them."[10]

In the subsequent analysis of the lengthy treatment I think we can distinguish a number of game plans or maneuvers, which Leuret never theorizes and for which he provides no explanation founded on an etiology of mental illness, or on a physiology of the nervous system, or even, more generally, on a physiology of madness. He merely dissects the different operations he tried out and these maneuvers can, I think, be divided into four or five major types.

First, there is the maneuver of creating an imbalance of power, that is to say, right from the start or, anyway, as quickly as possible, making power flow in one and only one direction, that is to say, from the doctor. And this is what Leuret hastens to do; his first contact with Dupré consists in creating an imbalance of power: "The first time I approach M. Dupré in order to treat him, I find him in a huge room filled with the supposedly incurably insane. He is sitting, waiting for his meal with his stupid look, indifferent to everything going on around him, completely unaffected by the dirtiness of his neighbors and himself, and seeming to have only the instinct to eat. How to bring him out of his torpor, to give him some real sensations, to make him a bit attentive? Kind words do nothing; would severity be better? I pretend to be unhappy with his words and conduct; I accuse him of laziness, vanity and untruthfulness, and I demand that he stand upright and bareheaded before me."[11]

I think this first meeting fully reveals what we could call the general ritual of the asylum. Basically, and Leuret is in no way different from his contemporaries in this respect, in all the asylums of this period, the first episode of contact between the doctor and his patient is indeed this ceremony, this initial show of force; that is to say, the demonstration that the field of forces in which the patient finds himself in the asylum is unbalanced, that there is no sharing out, reciprocity, or exchange, that language will not pass freely and neutrally from one to the other, that all possible reciprocity or transparency between the different characters inhabiting the asylum must be banished. Right from the start one must be in a different world in which there is a break, an imbalance, between doctor and patient, a world in which there is a slope one can never reascend: at the top of the slope is the doctor; and at the bottom, the patient.

It is on the basis of this absolutely statutory difference of level, of potential, which will never disappear in asylum life, that the process of treatment can unfold. It is a commonplace of the advice given by alienists concerning different treatments that one should always begin by marking power in this way. Power is all on one side, Pinel said when he recommended approaching the patient with "a sort of ceremony of fear, an imposing air, which can act strongly on the imagination [of the maniac; J.L.] and convince him that all resistance is pointless."[12] Esquirol said the same: "In a home for the insane there must be one and only one chief to whom everything is subordinate."[13]

Clearly, it is the "principle of the foreign will" again, which we can call Falret's principle, which is the substitution of a "foreign will" for the patient's will.[14] The patient must feel himself immediately confronted by something in which all the reality he will face in the asylum is summed up and concentrated in the doctor's foreign and omnipotent will. By this I do not mean that every other reality is suppressed to the advantage of the single will of the doctor, but that the element which carries all the reality that will be imposed on the patient, the support for this reality the task of which is to get a hold on the illness, must be the doctor's will as a foreign will that is officially superior to the patient's will and so inaccessible to any relationship of exchange, reciprocity, or equality.

This principle has basically two objectives. Its first objective is to establish a sort of state of docility that is necessary for the treatment: the patient, in fact, must accept the doctor's prescriptions. But it is not just a question of subjecting the patient's wish to recover to the doctor's knowledge and power; establishing an absolute difference of power involves above all breaking down the fundamental assertion of omnipotence in madness. In every madness, whatever its content, there is always an assertion of omnipotence, and this is the target of the first ritual of the assertion of a foreign and absolutely superior will.

In the psychiatry of this time, the omnipotence of madness may manifest itself in two ways. In some cases it will be expressed within the delirium in the form of ideas of grandeur for example: thinking one is a king. In M. Dupré's case, believing he is Napoleon,[15] that he is sexually superior to all humanity,[16] that he is the only man and all the others are women,[17] are all so many assertions, within the delirium itself, of a sort of sovereignty or omnipotence. But clearly this only applies to cases of delusions of grandeur. Outside of this, when there is no delusion of grandeur, there is still an assertion of omnipotence, not in the way the delirium is expressed, but in the way it is exercised.

Whatever the content of the delirium, even when one thinks one is persecuted, the fact of asserting one's delirium, that is to say refusing all discussion, reasoning, and proof, is in itself an assertion of omnipotence, and this is absolutely coextensive with all madness, whereas expressing omnipotence within the delirium is only the fact of having delusions of grandeur.

Asserting one's omnipotence in the delirium simply by the fact of being delirious is typical of all madness.

Consequently, you can see how and why this first move, this first maneuver of the psychiatric operation is justified: it is a matter of breaking down the omnipotence of madness, of reducing it by demonstrating a different, more vigorous will endowed with greater power. Georget advises doctors: "Instead of . . . refusing to accord a lunatic the status of king that he claims, prove to him that he is powerless and that you, who are anything but powerless, can do anything to him; perhaps he will reflect that actually, it may well be that he was in error."[18]

So, this first contact, which I illustrated with the case of M. Dupré, is inserted in the general context of asylum practice of this time, obviously with many variants, in the form of the delirium's omnipotence countered by the doctor's reality and omnipotence, which is accorded him by, precisely, the statutory imbalance of the asylum. And all the internal discussions of psychiatric discourse take place around this: some doctors think the doctor's power should be marked from time to time with violence, but also, on occasion, with the demand for esteem and trust, in a compromise mode, with a sort of pact imposed on the patient. Then, on the other hand, there are psychiatrists who recommend fear, violence, and threats in every case. Some see the fundamental imbalance of power as sufficiently assured by the asylum system itself, its system of surveillance, internal hierarchy, and the arrangement of the buildings, the asylum walls themselves, carrying and defining the network and gradient of power. And then other psychiatrists consider rather that the doctor's own person, his prestige, presence, aggressiveness, and polemical vigor all give him this mark. All these variants do not seem to me to be important with regard to the basic ritual, which I will show you that Leuret then develops throughout the treatment by clearly opting for the solution of the medical individualization of this surplus power conferred by the asylum, and by giving it the very direct form of aggression and violence.

One of the themes of Dupré's delirium was belief in his sexual omnipotence, and that those around him in the asylum were women. Leuret asks Dupré if all the people around him really are women: "Yes" says Dupré. "Me too" asks Leuret. "Of course, you too." At this point Leuret takes hold of Dupré and, "shaking him vigorously, asks him if this is a woman's arm."[19] Dupré is not very convinced, so to convince him more Leuret puts some "grains of calomel" in his evening food and the unfortunate Dupré suffers violent diarrhea during the night. This enables Leuret to say to Dupré the next morning: "The only man in the asylum is so afraid of the night that it's given him the runs."[20] This is how he marked his virile and physical supremacy, by producing this artificial sign of fear in Dupré.

We could cite a series of elements like this throughout the treatment. Leuret puts Dupré in the shower. Dupré struggles, comes out with his delirious themes again, and says: "A woman is insulting me!" "*A woman*?" says Leuret, and directs the shower on him violently, deep in his throat, until the struggling Dupré recognizes that this really is a man's behavior, and "ends by agreeing that it is a man."[21] So, there is a ritual imbalance of power.

A second maneuver is what could be called the reuse of language. In fact, Dupré did not recognize people for what they were, believed his doctor was his cook, and gave himself a series of successive and simultaneous identities, since he was "Destouches, Napoleon, Delavigne, Picard, Audrieux, Bernardin de Saint-Pierre, all at the same time."[22] Therefore—and this is what characterizes the second maneuver, which, with some overlap, more or less follows the first chronologically—Dupré must first of all relearn the names and be able to give each person his correct name: "As a result of being pestered, he becomes attentive and obeys."[23] He is made to repeat them until he knows them: "He must learn my name, those of the students, supervisors, and nurses. He must name all of us."

Leuret makes him read books, recite verse, and forces him to speak the Latin he learned at school; he forces him to speak in Italian, which he had learned when he was in the army; he makes him "tell a story."[24]

Finally, on another occasion, he puts him in the bath, puts him under the shower as usual and, having done this, contrary to the usual practice, orders him to empty the bath. Now Dupré is not accustomed to obeying orders. He is forced to obey this order and, when Dupré is emptying the bath with his pails, as soon as his back is turned, Leuret refills the bath again so that he can repeat the order a number of times until the mechanism of order and obedience are completely locked together.[25]

In this series of operations, which basically focus on language, it seems to me to be, first of all, a matter of correcting the delirium of polymorphous naming and of constraining the patient to restore to each person the name by which he gets his individuality within the disciplinary pyramid of the asylum. In a way which is quite typical, Dupré is not required to learn the names of the patients but rather those of the doctor, of the doctor's students, and of the supervisors and nurses: the apprenticeship of naming will be an apprenticeship in hierarchy at the same time. Naming and showing respect, the distribution of names and the way in which individuals are placed in a hierarchy, amount to one and the same thing.

You see too that he is required to read and recite verse, etcetera. This is, of course, a matter of occupying the mind, of diverting the delirious use of language, but it is equally a matter of re-teaching the subject to use the forms of language of learning and discipline, the forms he learned at school, that kind of artificial language which is not really the one he uses, but the one by which the school's discipline and system of order are imposed. Finally, in the episode of the bath that is filled and he is made to empty on an indefinitely repeated order, it really is this language of orders, but this time of precise orders that the patient must be taught.

In general, I think what is at stake for Leuret here is making the patient accessible to all the imperative uses of language: the use of proper names with which one greets, shows one's respect and pays attention to others; school recital and of languages learned; language of command. You can see that it is not at all a sort of re-apprenticeship—that one might call dialectical—of the truth. It is not a question of showing Dupré, on the basis of language, that his judgments were false; there is no discussion about whether or not it is right to consider everyone

"Halcyons," as Dupré believes in his delirium.[26] It is not a matter of turning the false into truth in a dialectic peculiar to language or discussion. In this game of orders and commands, it is simply a matter of putting the subject back in contact with language inasmuch as it is the carrier of imperatives; it is the imperative use of language that refers back to and is organized by a whole system of power. This is the language peculiar to the asylum; it fixes the names that define the asylum hierarchy; it is the master's language. It is this whole web of power that must be visible as reality behind the language one teaches. The language one re-teaches to the patient is not the language through which he will be able to rediscover the truth; the language he is forced to re-learn is a language in which the reality of an order, of a discipline, of a power imposed on him, must appear. This is what Leuret says, moreover, at the end of these language exercises: "Here is M. Dupré who has become attentive [attention being the faculty of reality of course; M.F.], he has entered into a relationship with me; I bring an action to bear on him, he obeys me."[27] "Attention," that is to say, a relationship with the doctor—that is to say, with the person who gives orders and holds the power—a relationship that consists precisely in the doctor, who holds the power, performing an action in the form of an order. It is a language, therefore, which is transparent to this reality of power.

Here again we see that, in a sense, Leuret is much more subtle, and more of a perfectionist, than the psychiatrists of his time. Even so, what was called "moral treatment" at this time really was something like this, although less directly focused on the uses of language, of course, on that kind of rigged dialogue that was really a game of order and obedience, because, unlike Leuret, most psychiatrists put their faith in the internal mechanisms of the asylum institution rather than in this direct action of the psychiatrist as holder of power.[28] However, in the end, if you look at what the functioning of the asylum institution itself was for the psychiatrists of this period, and where they sought the therapeutic character of the asylum's action, you see that the asylum was thought to be therapeutic because it obliged people to submit to regulation, to a use of time, it forced them to obey orders, to line up, to submit to the regularity of certain actions and habits, to submit to work. And for the psychiatrists of the time, this whole system of order, both as orders given and, equally, as institutional regularities and constraints, is ultimately one of the major factors of asylum therapy. As Falret said in 1854, in a rather late text, "a strictly observed positive regulation, which fixes the use of every hour of the day, forces every patient to react against the irregularity of his tendencies by submitting to the general law. Instead of being left to himself to follow the impulse of his whim or his disordered will, the insane person is constrained to bend before a rule which is all the more powerful for being established for everyone. He is obliged to place himself in the hands of a foreign will and to make a constant effort on himself so as not to incur the punishments attached to infringements of the rule."[29]

Esquirol too thought that this system of the order, of the order given and the order followed, of the order as command and the order as regularity, was the major effective agent of asylum treatment: "In such a home there is a movement, an activity, a whirl into which every person gradually enters; the most stubborn, defiant lypemaniac is forced to live outside of himself and, without being aware of it, is carried away by the general movement and example of others (...); the maniac himself, restrained by the harmony, order and rule of the home, defends himself better against his impulses and abandons himself less to his eccentric activities."[30] In other words, order is reality in the form of discipline.

The third maneuver in the apparatus of asylum therapy is what could be called the management or organization of needs. Psychiatric power ensures the advance of reality, the hold of reality on madness, through the management of needs, and even through the emergence of new needs, through the creation, maintenance and renewal of needs.

Here again, as a starting point, I think we can take the very subtle, very curious version that Leuret gives of this principle.

His patient, M. Dupré, did not want to work on the grounds that he did not believe in the value of money: "Money has no value; there is nothing but counterfeit money" said Dupré,[31] since I, Napoleon, am the only person who has the right to mint coins. Consequently, the money given to him is counterfeit money: It's pointless to work! Now, the problem is precisely that of getting Dupré to understand the need for this money. One day he is forced to work, but he hardly does any work. At the end of the day it is suggested that he take a salary corresponding to his day's work; he refuses, giving as his reason that "money has no value."[32] He is seized and money forced into his pocket, but he is confined "without food or drink" for the night and following day as punishment for having resisted. A nurse however, who has been duly prepared in advance, is sent to him, and says: "Ah! Monsieur Dupré, how I pity you not eating! If I was not afraid of Monsieur Leuret's authority and punishment I would bring you something to eat; I am prepared to take this risk if you give me a little reward." So in order to eat M. Dupré is obliged to take from his pocket three of the eight sous he had been given.

No doubt the meaning or, at least, the usefulness of money is already beginning to emerge for him on the basis of this artificially created need. He is well fed and, here again, a "dozen grains of calomel" are mixed in with "the vegetables eaten by M. Dupré who, quickly feeling the need to go to the lavatory, calls the servant and begs her to give him a free hand. A new pecuniary arrangement."[33] The following day Dupré goes to work and "seeks the price for his day's work." This is, says Leuret, "the first reasonable act, made voluntarily and with reflection, that I have got from him."[34]

Of course, we might wonder about this astonishing relationship Leuret establishes between money and defecation, but, as you can see, in the form of an imperative intervention. You can see that it is not a symbolic relationship of two terms—money-excrement—but a tactical relationship between four terms: food, defecation, work, and money, and in which the fifth term, which runs through the four points of the tactical rectangle, is medical power. I think we see the relationship between money and defecation, which, as you know, was to have a well-known future, emerging here for the first time and it is established through this game of medical power passing between these four terms.[35]

It seems to me that generally, and here again in a particularly subtle, clever form, Leuret provided the formula of something very important in the system of psychiatric treatment at this time. Basically it involves establishing the patient in a carefully maintained state of deprivation: the patient's existence must be kept just below a certain average level. Hence a number of tactics, less subtle than Leuret's, but which also had a long future in the asylum institution and in the history of madness.

The clothing tactic: Ferrus, in his treatise *Des aliénés*, from 1834, provides a whole theory of asylum clothing, in which he says: "The clothing of the insane calls for special attention: almost all the mad are vain and proud. Before the onset of their illness, most of them led a life full of adventures; they often had wealth which their mental disorder led them to squander."[36] They therefore had fine clothes and jewelry, and in the asylum they recreate these costumes which are, at the same time, the sign of their old splendor, of their current poverty, and of the way in which their delirium operates: the mad must be deprived of all this. However, says Ferrus, we must not go too far, because in asylums the mad are often allowed only torn and shameful clothes, which humiliate them too much and may excite their delirium or their disgust, and then they walk about naked. Something must be found between the ornaments of delirium and obscene nudity, and this will be "clothing of unrefined and sturdy materials, but cut in a single style and kept clean, so as to moderate the puerile vanities of madness."[37]

There is also the tactic of food, which must be plain, uniform, and not given on demand but in rations that, as far as possible, are slightly less than the average. Furthermore, in addition to this general rationing of food within the asylum is added a policy of punishment by withholding food, especially after the policy of *no restraint*, that is to say, after the suppression of some of the contraptions of constraint:[38] the great asylum punishment was deprivation of courses, fasting, etcetera.

Then there is the tactic of setting to work. Work is highly overdetermined in the asylum system since, on the one hand, it ensures the necessary order, discipline, regularity, and constant occupation. Thus, very quickly, around the 1830s, work becomes obligatory within asylums. The Sainte-Anne farm was initially an extension of the Bicêtre hospital before taking over from it.[39] As Girard de Cailleux said when he was the director of the Auxerre hospital: "peeling and preparing vegetables is frequently a highly beneficial occupation in treatment."[40] The interesting thing about this is that this work is not just imposed because it is a factor in order, discipline, and regularity, but because it enables one to slip in a system of reward. Asylum work is not free; it is paid, and this payment is not a supplementary favor but at the very heart of the function of work, for the remuneration must be sufficient to satisfy certain needs created by the underlying asylum deprivation: insufficient food, the absence of any extras (tobacco, a dessert, etcetera, must be paid for).

For the system of remuneration imposed with work to function, one has to have wanted, to have needed, and to have been deprived. So, these remunerations must be sufficient to satisfy the needs created by the basic deprivation and, at the same time, sufficiently low to remain below, of course, normal and general remunerations.

Finally, and above all, the great deprivation developed by asylum discipline is, perhaps, quite simply deprivation of freedom. And you see how, in the psychiatrists of the first half of the nineteenth century, the theory of isolation gradually changes or, if you like, is deepened and completed. The theory of isolation I was talking about last week was basically demanded by the obligation to create a break between the therapeutic framework and the patient's family, the milieu in which the illness developed. Subsequently you see the birth of the idea that isolation has a supplementary advantage: it not only protects the family but gives rise to a new need in the patient, the need for freedom, of which he was previously unaware. Treatment can be developed on the basis of this artificially created need.

In the asylum form of this period, psychiatric power is therefore the creator of needs and the management of the deprivations it establishes. There are a number of easily identifiable reasons for this administration of needs, this institutionalization of deprivation.

First, because the reality of the things one needs will be imposed through the game of needs; money, which previously had no value, will now acquire value when one is deprived and needs it to make up for this deprivation. So, the reality of what one needs will be perceived through this game of deprivation. This is the first effect of the system.

The second effect is that the reality of an external world, which previously the omnipotence of madness was inclined to deny, takes shape through the asylum lack, and this reality beyond the asylum's walls is increasingly imposed as being inaccessible, but as inaccessible only during the time of madness. This external world will be real in basically two ways. On the one hand it will be the world of non-lack in contrast to the asylum world, and so it will appear as a desirable reality. On the other hand, the external world will appear at the same time as a world into which one is initiated by learning to react to one's own lack, to one's own needs: When you have learned that you must work to feed yourself, to earn money even to defecate, then you will be able to reach the outside world. The outside world is thus real as the world of non-lack in contrast to the asylum world of deprivations, and as the world to which the lack of the asylum will serve as a propaedeutic.

The third effect of this policy of deprivation is that in this materially reduced status in comparison with the real world, with life outside the asylum, the patient will recognize his unsatisfied state, his reduced status, his lack of rights to anything, and the reason for his lack being that he is, quite simply, ill. It won't be the reality of the external world that he sees, but the reality of his own madness through the system of deprivations that have been established around him. In other words, he must learn that he must pay for his madness, because madness really exists as something by which he is affected; and madness will be paid for by a general lack of existence, by this systematic deprivation.

Finally, the fourth effect of the organization of asylum deprivation is that by learning deprivation, by learning that to make up for this deprivation he must work, concede certain things, submit to discipline, etcetera, the patient will learn that basically the care given him, the cure that one attempts to obtain for him, are not owed to him; he is obliged to get them through the efforts of obedience to work, discipline, and remunerated production; he will pay with his work for the good that society does him. As Belloc said: "... if society gives the insane the care they need, the latter must relieve it of the burden according the degree of their strength."[41] In other words, the mad person learns the fourth aspect of reality: as a patient he must provide for his own needs by his work so that society does not have to pay for them. So we arrive at the conclusion that, on the one hand, one pays for one's madness, but that, on the other hand, recovery is purchased. The asylum is precisely what makes one pay for one's madness with artificially created needs, and, at the same time, pay for one's treatment through a certain discipline, a certain output. The asylum, by establishing a deprivation, makes possible the creation of a currency with which one will pay for this cure. At bottom, what constitutes the asylum is the creation of the means of payment for the therapy on the basis of systematically created needs, the moral reward of madness. And you can see that the problem of money linked to the needs of madness, which has its price, and of the recovery, which must be purchased, is deeply inscribed in the psychiatric maneuver and the asylum apparatus.

Finally, the [fifth] apparatus is that of the statement of truth. This is the final phase, although in the therapy proposed by Leuret it is the penultimate episode: the patient must be got to tell the truth. You will say that if this is true, and if this episode is so important in the unfolding of the therapy, how could I say that the problem of truth was not posed in the practice of the classical treatment?[42] But you will see how this problem of truth is posed.

This is what Leuret did with Dupré. Dupré asserted that Paris was not Paris, that the king was not the king, that he himself was Napoleon, and that Paris was only the town of Langres that some people had disguised as Paris.[43] According to Leuret, there is only one thing to do, which is to take his patient to Paris, and, in fact, he organizes a walk through Paris under the direction of an intern. He shows him the different monuments of Paris, and says to him: "Do you not recognize Paris?—No, no, Dupré replies, we are here in the town of Langres. Several of the things in Paris have been copied."[44] The intern pretends not to know his way and asks Dupré to guide him to Place Vendôme. Dupré finds it easily and the intern then says to him: "So we are in Paris since you can find Place Vendôme so well!—No, I recognize Langres disguised as Paris."[45] Dupré is taken back to the hospital at Bicêtre where he refuses to recognize that he has visited Paris, and, "since he persists in his refusal, he is put in the bath and cold water is poured over his head. Then he agrees to anything one likes," and that Paris really is Paris. However, out of the bath "he returns to his mad ideas. He is made to undress again and the affusion is repeated: he gives way again," recognizes that Paris is Paris, but, as soon as he is dressed again "he maintains he is Napoleon. A third affusion corrects him; he gives way and goes to bed."[46]

However, Leuret is not fooled and is fully aware that these kinds of exercises are not sufficient. He moves on to an exercise at a higher level, as it were: "The following day I have him brought to me, and after some words about his trip the day before, I ask him. Your name?—I have been using another; my real name is Louis-Napoleon Bonaparte.—Your profession?—Lieutenant discharged from the 19th line; but I must explain. Lieutenant means army chief.—Where were you born?—Ajaccio, or, if you like,

Paris.—I see from this certificate that you were insane at Charenton.—I was not insane at Charenton. I was at my château of Saint-Maur for nine years. Displeased with his answers, I have him taken to the bath; under the shower I give him a newspaper and want him to read out aloud. He obeys. I question him and satisfy myself that he has understood what he has read. Then, after asking out loud if the shower tank is quite full, I have a notebook given to Dupré on which I order him to give written answers to the questions I put to him. Your name?—Dupré.—Your profession?—Lieutenant.—Your place of birth?—Paris.—How long were you at Charenton?—Nine years.—And at Saint-Yon?—Two years and two months.—How long have you been in the section for the treatment of the insane at Bicêtre?—Three months; for three years I have been incurably insane.—Where did you go yesterday?—In the town of Paris.—Do the bears talk?—No."[47] Progress, you see, compared with the earlier episode. And now we reach the third stage in the exercise of the statement of the truth, which is a crucial moment as you will see. "From his answers we can see that Monsieur Dupré is in a sort of *uncertainty between madness and reason*."[48] He has been insane for fifteen years! And, Leuret thinks, "now is the time to require him to make a decisive resolution, that of writing the story of his life."[49] He only carries it out after several showers and "devotes the rest of the day and the following day to writing his story, with many details. He knows and writes everything that a man can recall of his childhood. He gives the names of his lodgings and of the schools where he studied, of his teachers and fellow students in great numbers. In his whole account there is not a false thought or a word out of place."[50]

The problem arises here, which I am quite unable to resolve at present, of the way in which the autobiographical account was actually introduced into psychiatric practice, and criminological practice, around 1825 to 1840, and how, in fact, the account of one's own life came to be an essential component, with several uses, in all those processes of taking charge of individuals and disciplining them. Why did telling one's life story become an episode within the disciplinary enterprise? How was recounting one's past, how was the memory of childhood, able to find a place within this? I don't really know. Anyway, concerning this maneuver of the statement of the truth, I would like to say that it seems to me we can accept certain things.

First of all, you can see that the truth is not what is perceived. Basically, when M. Dupré was taken to see Paris, it was not so much in order that his perception revealed to him that Paris really was there, and that it was Paris. This is not what was asked of him; we know full well that so far as he will perceive anything, he will perceive Paris as the imitation of Paris. What is asked of him—and this is how the statement of the truth becomes effective—is that he avow it. It does not have to be perceived, it has to be said, even if it is said under the constraint of the shower. The fact alone of saying something that is the truth has a function in itself; a confession, even when constrained, is more effective in the therapy than a correct idea, or an idea with exact perception, which remains silent. So, the statement of the truth has a performative character in the game of the cure.

Second, I think we should note that the essential point of the truth, what Leuret is especially attached to, is in part, of course, that Paris is Paris, but what he wants above all is that his patient pin himself to his own history. What is required is that the patient recognizes himself in a kind of identity constituted by certain episodes in his life. In other words, it is in this recognition of certain biographical episodes that the patient must firstly state the truth; the most effective statement of the truth will not bear on things, but rather on the patient himself.

Finally, third, I think we should notice that this biographical truth which is asked of the patient, and the confession of which is so effective in the therapy, is not so much the truth that he could say about himself, at the level of his actual experience, but a truth imposed on him in a canonical form: cross-examination of identity, the recall of certain episodes already known to the doctor, acknowledgement that he really was at Charenton at a given moment, that he really was ill between certain dates, etcetera.[51] A biographical corpus is established from the outside through the system of family, employment, civil status, and medical observation. Ultimately the patient must own to this entire corpus of identity, and it has to be one of the most fruitful moments of the therapy when he does so; it is when this does not take place that we must despair of the illness.

I will quote, just for the beauty of the dialogue, from another of Leuret's cases. It is the story of a woman whom he said he would never be able to cure. And the fact that he could never cure this woman is attributed precisely to her inability to own to this biographical schema that carries her identity. Here is the dialogue that, according to Leuret, reveals her incurability: "How are you madam?—The person of myself is not a Mrs. (*une dame*), please call me Miss.—I do not know your name; would you like to tell me?—The person of myself does not have a name: she wishes that you do not write.—I would however really like to know what to call you, or rather what your name was formerly.—I understand what you mean. It was Catherine X, one must speak no more of what took place. The person of myself has lost her name, she gave it on entering Salpêtrière.—How old are you?—The person of myself has no age.—But this Catherine X you were talking about, how old is she?—I do not know (...)—If you are not the person about whom you speak, perhaps you are two people in one?—No, the person of myself does not know the one who was born in 1799. Maybe it is that lady whom you see there (...)—What have you done, and what has happened to you since you have been the person of yourself?—The person of myself has lived in the clinic for (...). Physical and metaphysical experiments have been made on her and are still being made on her (...). There is an invisible who comes down, she wants to mix her voice with mine. The person of myself does not want this, she sends her away gently.—What are they like, these invisibles of which you speak?—They are small, impalpable, barely formed.—How are they dressed?—In a coat.—What language do they speak?—They speak French; if they spoke another language the person of myself would not understand them.—Are you certain that you see them?—Certainly, the person of myself sees them, but metaphysically, in invisibility, never materially, because then they would no longer be invisible (...)—Do you sometimes feel the invisibles on your body?—The person of myself feels, and is very angry at it; they have done all sorts of indecent things to her (...)—How are you finding it at Salpêtrière?—The person of myself finds it very well; she is treated very kindly by M. Pariset. She never asks anything from the maids (...)—What do you think of the ladies with you here in this ward?—The person of myself thinks they have lost their reason."[52]

In a sense this is the most marvelous description of asylum existence to be found. Once the name has been given on entering Salpêtrière, once this administrative, medical individuality has been constituted, all that remains is "the person of myself," who only speaks in the third person. In such a case, in which confession is not possible and with the endless statement in the third person of this someone who only expresses herself in the form of the person who is not anyone, Leuret clearly sees that the therapeutic processes organized around the statement of the truth were no longer possible. As soon as one has left one's name on entering Salpêtrière and one is no more than "the person of myself" in the asylum, when, consequently, one can no longer recount one's childhood memories and recognize oneself in this statutory identity, then one is definitely good for the asylum.

We could say that at bottom the asylum machine owes its effectiveness to a number of things: uninterrupted disciplinary training; the dissymmetry of power inherent in this; the game of need, money, and work; statutory pinning to an administrative identity in which one must recognize oneself through a language of truth. However, you can see that this truth is not the truth of madness speaking in its own name but the truth of a madness agreeing to first person recognition of itself in a particular administrative and medical reality constituted by asylum power. The operation of truth is accomplished when the patient has recognized himself in this identity. Consequently, the operation of truth takes place in the form of charging discourse with the task of this institution of individual reality. The truth is never at issue between doctor and patient. What is given at the start, established once and for all, is the biographical reality with which the patient must identify if he wants to be cured.

There remains a final, supplementary episode in this Dupré affair. When Leuret has got this true account, but true precisely in terms of a biographical canon constituted in advance, he does something astonishing: he releases Dupré while telling him that he is still ill but no longer in need of the asylum at this time. What was Leuret doing in releasing his patient? In a way, certainly, it was a matter of continuing that kind of intensification of reality for which the asylum had been responsible. That is to say, we will see Leuret again plotting exactly the same kind of maneuvers around his patient, now living in freedom, as those I have been talking about. He is trapped with problems of truth; when he claims to know Arabic he is placed in a situation in which he is forced to confess that he does not know it.[53] He is caught in the same constraints of language as those in which he was held in the asylum. The job Leuret found for his patient to lead him to the cure, that is to say, so that reality has a total grip on him, was as a printer's corrector,[54] so that he is effectively inserted into that constraining order of language which, again, is not that of language as the bearer of truth, in its dialectical use, but of language in its imperative use. What he reads must actually conform to statutory and school orthography.

In the same way, Leuret explains that he created needs by taking him to the Opéra so that he acquire the desire to go to performances. Hence the need for him to earn some money. It is still the same [enterprise] of the renewal of or identification with reality through a disciplinary game, now extended rather than concentrated and intense as in the asylum: "I increased his enjoyments so as to extend his needs and thus gain many means for directing him."[55]

However, there is a much stronger, more subtle and interesting reason. This is that, in fact, Leuret identified something in his patient that had three forms: the pleasure of the asylum,[56] the pleasure of being ill, and the pleasure of having symptoms. This triple pleasure is the underlying basis of the omnipotence of madness.

When we go back over the whole development of the treatment, we see that from the start Leuret tried to attack this pleasure of the illness that he had detected in his patient. He uses the famous shower, the straitjacket, and deprivation of food right from the start, and these repressions have a double, physiological and moral, justification. The moral justification corresponds to two objectives. On the one hand, it involves, of course, making the reality of the doctor's power felt against the omnipotence of madness. But it is also a matter of taking the pleasure out of madness, that is to say, wiping out the pleasure of the symptom through the displeasure of the cure. Here again I think Leuret reproduces techniques that were employed by the psychiatrists of his time without being reflected or theorized.

However, what is particular about Leuret—and here he takes things further—is that in Dupré he found a special case. He had a patient who, when under the shower, and even when cauterized on the skin of his head,[57] hardly protested and found that it was completely bearable so long as it was part of his treatment.[58] Now it is here that Leuret no doubt goes further than most of the psychiatrists of the time who—as sign, moreover, of their omnipotence facing the patient—basically required the patient to accept treatment without a word. In this case he has a patient who accepts the treatment, and whose acceptance is, in a way, part of the illness.

Leuret identifies this acceptance as a bad sign for his therapy; treatment is being incorporated within the delirium. When given a shower, Dupré says: "A woman is insulting me!"[59] Things must therefore be arranged so that treatment and delirium are disconnected, so that treatment is confiscated from the delirium constantly invading it. It is thus necessary to give an especially painful edge to the treatment, so that reality will establish its hold on the illness through the treatment.

We find some fundamental ideas in this technique: madness is linked to a pleasure; through pleasure, treatment may be integrated into the madness itself; the impact of reality may be neutralized by a mechanism of pleasure intrinsic to the treatment; and, consequently, the cure must not only work at the level of reality, but also at the level of pleasure, and not only at the level of the pleasure the patient takes in his madness, but at the level of the pleasure the patient takes in his own treatment.*

Hence, when Leuret realized that Dupré found a whole series of pleasures in the asylum—in the asylum he could be delirious at ease, he could integrate his treatment in his delirium, and all the punishments inflicted on him were reinvested in his illness—then, at that point, Leuret concluded that he had to get his patient out of the asylum and to deprive him of the pleasure of the illness, the hospital, and of the cure. As a result, he put him back into circulation, consequently taking the pleasure out of the treatment and making it function in an absolutely non-medical mode.

In this way Leuret is entirely resorbed as a medical personage. He has ceased playing his aggressive and imperious role, and in its place he brings a number of accomplices into play in order to construct the

* The manuscript adds: "There is both power and pleasure in every symptom."

following kind of scenarios. Despite his job as a corrector at a printing house, M. Dupré continued to make systematic spelling mistakes, since in his delirium he wanted to simplify the spelling system. A pseudo-letter of appointment was sent to him for a job that would have brought him a lot of money. M. Dupré drafts a letter of acceptance of this new, well remunerated situation, but he lets by one or two spelling mistakes, so that Leuret's accomplice can send him a letter in which he says: "I would have employed you, if you had not made dreadful spelling mistakes."[60]

So you see that all the mechanisms here, which are of the same type as those in the asylum, are now demedicalized. The medical personage, as Leuret says himself, must become instead a benign personage who tries to arrange things, who acts as an intermediary between harsh reality and the patient.[61] However, as a result of this, the patient will no longer be able to take pleasure either in his illness, which causes so many unfortunate consequences, or in the asylum, since he is no longer there, or even in his doctor, since the doctor will have disappeared as such. M. Dupré's cure was wholly successful; it ended in the Spring of 1839 with a complete recovery. However, Leuret noted that at Pâques in 1840 some unfortunate signs proved that a new illness was overcoming "the patient."[62]

✣

In summary, we can say that in the way that it functions through this kind of treatment, the asylum is a curing apparatus in which the doctor's action is part and parcel of the institution, the regulations, and the buildings. Basically, it is a question of a sort of great single body in which the walls, the wards, the instruments, the nurses, the supervisors, and the doctor are elements which have, of course, different functions to perform, but the essential function of which is to bring about a collective effect. And, according to different psychiatrists, the main accent, the most power, will sometimes be fixed on the general system of supervision, sometimes on the doctor, and sometimes on spatial isolation itself.

The second thing I would like to emphasize is that the asylum has been a site for the formation of several series of discourse. It was possible to construct a nosography, a classification of illnesses, on the basis of these observations. Also, on the basis of the free disposal of the corpses of the mad, it was possible to outline a pathological anatomy of mental illness. However, you can see that none of these discourses, neither nosography nor pathological anatomy, served as a guide in the formation of psychiatric practice. In actual fact, although we have had some protocols of this practice, we can say that it remained silent in that for years and years psychiatric practice did not produce an autonomous discourse other than the protocol of what was said and done. There have been no real theories of the cure, nor even attempts to explain it; the cure has been a corpus of maneuvers, tactics, and gestures to be made, actions and reactions to be activated, the tradition of which has been carried on through asylum life, in medical teaching, and with just some of those cases, the longest of which I have quoted, as surfaces of emergence. All we can say about the way in which the mad were treated amounts to a body of tactics, a strategic ensemble.

Third, I think we should talk of an asylum tautology, in the sense that, through the asylum apparatus itself, the doctor is given a number of instruments whose basic function is to impose reality, to intensify it, and add to it the supplement of power that will enable the doctor to get a grip on madness and reduce it, and therefore, to direct and govern it. These supplements of power added to reality by the asylum are disciplinary asymmetry, the imperative use of language, the management of lack and needs, the imposition of a statutory identity in which the patient must recognize himself, and the removal of pleasure from madness. These are the supplements of power by which, thanks to the asylum and its processes, reality will be able to fix its grip on madness. But, you see—and it is in this sense that there is a tautology—that all of this—the dissymmetry of power, the imperative use of language, etcetera—is not merely a supplement of power added to reality, but the real form of reality itself. To be adapted to the real, [. . .*] to want to leave the condition of madness, is just precisely to accept a power that one recognizes is insurmountable and to relinquish the omnipotence of madness. To stop being mad is to agree to be obedient, to be able to earn one's living, to

* (Recording:) to relinquish the omnipotence of madness,

recognize oneself in the biographical identity that has been formed of you, and to stop taking pleasure in madness. So as you can see, the instrument by which madness is reduced, the supplement of power added to reality so that it masters madness, is at the same time the criterion of the cure, or again, the criterion of the cure is the instrument by which one cures. So, we can say that there is a great asylum tautology in that the asylum is that which must give a supplementary intensity to reality and, at the same time, the asylum is reality in its naked power, it is reality medically intensified, it is medical action, medical power-knowledge, which has no other function than to be the agent of reality itself.

The asylum tautology is this action of the supplement of power accorded to reality, which consists in nothing other than the reproduction of this reality itself within the asylum. And you can see why the doctors of the time could say both that the asylum had to be something absolutely cut off from the outside world, that the asylum world of madness had to be an absolutely specialized world entirely in the hands of a medical power defined by the pure competence of knowledge—confiscation, therefore, of the asylum space for the benefit of medical knowledge—and, on the other hand, that the same doctors said that the general forms of the asylum had to recall everyday life as much as possible, that the asylums had to be similar to the colonies, workshops, colleges, and prisons, that is to say, that the specificity of the asylum is to be exactly homogeneous to that from which it is differentiated, by virtue of the line separating madness and non-madness.

Finally, the last point on which I will stop, and about which I will talk later, is that when we follow a cure like Leuret's in some detail—with, of course, the qualification that this is the most sophisticated of all the cures for which we have an account—simply quoting the different episodes, without adding, I think, to what Leuret said, and by taking into account the fact that Leuret did not in any way theorize what he meant, you see a number of notions appearing: the doctor's power, language, money, need, identity, pleasure, reality, childhood memory. All of this is completely inscribed within the asylum strategy, but not yet constituting anything more than points of support for this asylum strategy. Later, you know what their future will be; you will find them again in a completely extra-asylum discourse, or at any rate in a discourse that will present itself as extra-psychiatric.* However, before taking on this status of object or concept, in the kind of slow-motion which M. Dupré's cure offers us, we see them at work as tactical points of support, strategic elements, maneuvers, plans, and nodes in the relationships between the patient and the asylum structure itself.

Later, we will see how they are detached from it in order to enter another type of discourse.

* The manuscript adds: "it is there that Freud will look for them."

---

1. Opiates, preparations with an opium base, renowned for suspending attacks of fury and restoring order between ideas, were recommended, in preference to purgatives and bleedings, by Jean-Baptiste Van Helmont (1577-1644) and Thomas Sydenham (1624-1689). Their use in treating "maniacal" or "furious" forms of madness developed in the eighteenth century. See, Philippe Hecquet (1661-1737) *Réflexions sur l'usage de l'opium, des calmants et des narcotiques pour la guérison des maladies* (Paris: G. Cavalier, 1726) p. 11; J. Guislain, *Traité sur l'aliénation mentale et sur les hospices des aliénés*, vol. I, book IV: "Moyens dirigés sur le système nerveux central. Opium," pp. 345-353. See also the pages devoted to this substance by M. Foucault, in *Histoire de la folie*, pp. 316-319 (omitted from the English translation).

   In the nineteenth century, Joseph Jacques Moreau de Tours (1804-1884) recommended the use of opiates in the treatment of mania: "In the opiates (opium, datura, belladonna, henbane, aconite, etcetera) we can still find an excellent means of calming the usual agitation of maniacs and the passing fits of rage of monomaniacs." "Lettres médicales sur la colonie d'aliénés de Ghéel" *Annales médico-psychologiques*, vol. V, March 1845, p. 271. See, C. Michéa, *De l'emploi des opiacés dans le traitement d'aliénation mentale* (Paris: Malteste, 1849), and *Recherches expérimentales sur l'emploi des principaux agents de médication stupéfiante dans le traitement de l'aliénation mentale* (Paris: Labé, 1857); H. Legrand du Saulle, "Recherches cliniques sur le mode d'administration de l'opium dans la manie" *Annales médico-psychologiques*, 3rd series, vol. V, January 1857, pp. 1-27; H. Brochin, "Maladies nerveuses. § Narcotiques" in *Dictionnaire encyclopédique des sciences médicales*, 2nd series, vol. XII (Paris: Masson/Asselin, 1877), pp. 375-376; and, J.-B. Fonssagrives, "Opium" ibid. 2nd series, vol. XVI, 1881, pp. 146-240.
2. Laudanum, a preparation in which opium was combined with other ingredients, of which the most widely used was the liquid laudanum of Sydenham, or "*vin d'opium composé*," was recommended for digestive disorders, the treatment of nervous illnesses and hysteria; see, T. Sydenham, "Observationes Medicae" (1680) in *Opera Omnia* (London: W. Greenhill, 1844) p. 113; English translation, "Medical Observations" in *The Works of Thomas Sydenham*, trans. R. G. Latham (London: The Sydenham Society, mdcccxlviii) vol. 1, p. 173. See *Dictionnaire encyclopédique des sciences médicales*, 2nd series, vol. II (Paris: Masson/Asselin, 1876) pp. 17-25.
3. Since Pinel, who asserted "the absolute necessity for an invariable order of work" (*Traité médico-philosophique*, section V: "Police générale et ordre journalier du service dans les hospices d'aliénés" p. 212; *A Treatise on Insanity*, "General police and daily distribution of services in lunatic asylums," p. 206) the alienists constantly stressed the importance of regulations. Thus, J.-P. Falret, "Du traitement générale des aliénés" *Des maladies mentales et des asiles d'aliénés*, p. 690: "What do we see in modern asylums? We see a strictly observed positive regulation, which fixes the use of every hour of the day and forces every patient to react against the irregularity of his tendencies by submitting to the general law. He is obliged to place himself in the hands of a foreign will and to make a constant effort on himself so as not to incur the punishments attached to infringements of the rule."
4. The problem of the dietary regime occupied a privileged place, both as a component of the daily organization of asylum time, and as a contribution to treatment. Thus, François Fodéré states that "food is the first medicine" *Traité du délire*, vol. II, p. 292. See, J. Daquin, *La Philosophie de la folie*, republished with a presentation by C. Quétel (Paris: Éditions Frénésie, 1987) pp. 95-97; and, J. Guislain, *Traité sur l'aliénation mentale*, vol. II, book 16: "Régime alimentaire à observer dans l'aliénation mentale" pp. 139-152.
5. Work, an essential component of moral treatment, was conceived of in the double perspective of therapy (isolation) and discipline (order). See, P. Pinel, *Traité médico-philosophique*, section V, § xxi: "Loi fondamentale de tout hospice d'aliénés, celle d'un travail mécanique": "Constant work changes the vicious circle of ideas, clarifies the faculties of understanding by exercising them, alone keeps order wherever the insane are assembled, and dispenses with a host of detailed and often pointless rules in order to maintain internal police" p. 225; *A Treatise on Insanity*, "Mechanical employment essential to the successful management of lunatic hospitals" p. 217. Cf., C. Bouchet, "Du travail appliqué aux aliénés" *Annales médico-psychologiques*, vol. XII, November 1848, pp. 301-302. In *Histoire de*

la folie, pp. 505-506; *Madness and Civilization*, pp. 247-249, Foucault refers to a study by Jean Calvet, from 1952, on the historical origins of the work of patients in insane asylums.

6. P. Pinel lends his authority to the shower by making it an instrument of both treatment and conditioning. See the second, revised and expanded edition of his *Traité médico-philosophique sur l'aliénation mentale* (Paris: Caille et Ravier, 1809) pp. 205-206. See also, H. Girard de Cailleux, "Considérations sur le traitement des maladies mentales" *Annales médico-psychologiques*, vol. IV, November, 1844, pp. 330-331; H. Rech (de Montpellier), "De la douche et des affusions d'eau froide sur la tête dans le traitement des aliénations mentales" ibid. vol. IX, January 1847, pp. 124-125. It is François Leuret especially who makes use of it in *Traitement moral de la folie*, ch. 3, § "Douches et affusions froides" pp. 158-162. See Foucault's discussion of M. Dupré's cure in this and the following lecture (above, French p.143 *sq. and below*, French p.173 sq). Foucault devotes several pages to this cure in: *Maladie mentale et Psychologie* (Paris: P.U.F., 1962) pp. 85-86; English translation, *Mental Illness and Psychology*, trans. Alan Sheridan (New York: Harper and Row, 1976) p. 72; *Histoire de la folie*, p. 338 and pp. 520-521; *Madness and Civilization*, p. 172 and pp. 266-267; and "L'eau et la folie" *Dits et Écrits*, vol. 1, pp. 268-272. He returns to it in "Sexuality and Solitude" *London Review of Books*, 21 May-5 June 1981, p. 3 and pp. 5-6, reprinted in *The Essential Works of Foucault, 1954-1984*, vol. 1: *Ethics: subjectivity and truth*, ed. Paul Rabinow, trans. Robert Hurley and others (New York: The New Press, 1997) pp. 175-176; French translation, "Sexualité et solitude," trans. F. Durand-Bogaert, *Dits et Écrits*, vol. 4., pp. 168-169.
7. The rotary swing was perfected by the English doctor Erasmus Darwin (1731-1802) and used to treat madness by Mason Cox, who praised its effectiveness: "I think it can be put to both a moral and a physical use, and be employed with success both as a means of relief and as a means of discipline, in order to make the patient more adaptable and docile" *Observations sur la démence*, p. 58. [It has not been possible to consult the first, 1804, edition of *Practical Observations on Insanity*, on which the French translation is based, and the passage quoted here does not appear in the second, 1806, edition. However, reference is made to the rotary swing elsewhere in the 1806 edition, e.g., p. 137; G.B.] See, L. Amard, *Traité analytique de la folie et des moyens de la guerir* (Lyon: printed by Ballanche, 1807) pp. 80-93; J. Guislain, *Traité sur l'aliénation mentale*, vol. I, book IV, and, *Moyens dirigés sur le système nerveux cérébral. De la rotation* (Amsterdam: Van der Hey, 1826) p. 374 and p. 404; C. Buvat-Pochon, *Les Traitements de choc d'autrefois en psychiatrie. Leurs liens avec les thérapeutiques modernes*, Medical thesis, Paris, no. 1262 (Paris: Le François, 1939). See *Histoire de la folie*, pp. 341-342; *Madness and Civilization*, pp. 176-177.
8. While he was alive, Leuret had to defend himself from critics who condemned his practice as, in his own words, "retrograde and dangerous" (*Du traitement moral de la folie*, p. 68). His main opponent was E.S. Blanche, in his paper to the royal Academy of medicine, *Du danger des rigueurs corporelles dans le traitement de la folie* (Paris: Gardembas, 1839), as well as in his short work, *De l'état actuel du traitement de la folie en France* (Paris: Gardembas, 1840). These polemics were echoed in Leuret's obituary notices: U. Trélat, "Notice sur Leuret" *Annales d'hygiène publique et de médecine légale*, vol. 45, 1851, pp. 241-262; and A. Brierre de Boismont, "Notice biographique sur M.F. Leuret" *Annales médico-psychologiques*, 2nd series, vol. III, July 1851, pp. 512-527.
9. It is Observation XXII: "Bearers of imaginary titles and ranks" *Du traitement moral de la folie*, pp. 418-462.
10. Ibid. pp. 421-424.
11. Ibid. p. 429.
12. P. Pinel, *Traité médico-philosophique, op. cit.*, section II, § ix: "Intimider l'aliéné, mais ne point se permettre aucun acte de violence" p. 61; *A Treatise on Insanity*, "Intimidation too often associated with violence" pp. 64-65.
13. J.E.D. Esquirol, "De la folie" (1816) in *Des maladies mentales* vol. 1, p. 126; *Mental Maladies*, "Insanity," p. 76.
14. See above note 3. Already, for J. Guislain, this was one of the advantages of "isolation in the treatment of insanity": "Based on a feeling of dependence that he makes the insane person feel (...) forced to conform to a foreign will" *Traité sur l'alienation mentale*, vol. I, p. 409.

15. F. Leuret, *Du traitement moral de la folie*, p. 422: "Dupré is a name of convenience, a name of disguise; his true name, as we well know, is Napoleon."
16. Ibid. p. 423: "The distinctive sign of his Halcyon status is his constant ability to enjoy the pleasures of love."
17. Ibid. p. 423: "Only he in the home is a man; all the others are women."
18. E.J. Georget, *De la folie. Considérations sur cette maladie*, p. 284.
19. F. Leuret, *Du traitement moral de la folie*, p. 429.
20. Ibid. p. 430.
21. Ibid. p. 430.
22. Ibid. p. 422.
23. Ibid. p. 431.
24. Ibid. p .431.
25. Ibid. p. 432.
26. Ibid. p. 422.
27. Ibid., p. 432.
28. Leuret defined his treatment thus: "I understand by moral treatment of madness the reasoned use of all means that act directly on the intelligence and passions of the insane" ibid. p. 156.
29. J.P. Falret, *Des maladies mentales et des asiles d'aliénés*, p. 690.
30. J.E.D. Esquirol, "De la folie" (1816) in *Des maladies mentales*, vol. I, p. 126; *Mental Maladies*, "Insanity," p. 76.
31. F. Leuret, *Du traitement moral de la folie*, p. 424.
32. Ibid. p. 434.
33. Ibid. p. 435.
34. Ibid.
35. Michel Foucault is alluding here to the "money-excrement" relationship, which had a great future in psychoanalytic literature. Mentioned by Freud in a letter to Fliess of 22 December 1897 (French translation in *La Naissance de la psychanalyse. Lettres à Wilhelm Fliess, 1887-1902*, trans. A Berman [Paris: P.U.F., 1956] p. 212; English translation, *The Complete Letters of Sigmund Freud to Wilhelm Fliess, 1887-1904*, trans. J.M. Masson [Cambridge, Mass.: The Belknap Press of Harvard University Press, 1985] p. 288), this symbolic relationship is developed in the theory of anal eroticism. See, S. Freud, "Charakter und Analerotik" (1908) in *Gesammelte Werke* [hereafter, *GW*] (Frankfurt: S. Fischer Verlag, 1941) vol. VII, pp. 201-209; English translation "Character and Anal Eroticism" in *The Standard Edition of the Complete Psychological Works of Sigmund Freud* [hereafter *Standard Edition*], trans. under General Editorship of James Strachey (London: The Hogarth Press, 1953-1974) vol. 9; "Über Triebumsetzung insbesondere der Analerotik" (1917) in *GW* (1946) vol. X, pp. 401-410; "On Transformations of Instinct as Exemplified in Anal Eroticism," *Standard Edition*, vol.17. See also, E. Borneman, *Psychoanalyse des Geldes. Eine kritische Untersuchung psychoanalytisher Geldtheorien* (Frankfurt: Suhrkamp Verlag, 1973); French translation, *Psychanalyse de l'argent. Une recherche critique sur les théories psychanalytiques de l'argent*, trans. D. Guérineau (Paris: P.U.F., 1978); English translation, *The Psychoanalysis of Money* (New York: Urizen Books, 1976).
36. G. Ferrus, *Des aliénés. Considérations sur l'état des maisons qui leur sont destinées, tant en France qu'en Angleterre; sur le régime hygiénique et moral auquel ces malades doivent être soumis; sur quelques questions de médecine légale et de législation relatives à leur état civil* (Paris: printed by Mme. Huzard, 1834) p. 234.
37. Ibid.
38. See above, lecture of 5 December 1973, note 18.
39. The "Sainte-Anne farm" derived from the donation made by Anne of Austria in 1651 for the construction of an establishment for taking in the sick during epidemics. Partially constructed, the land remained under cultivation. In 1833, Guillaume Ferrus (1784-1861), head doctor at Bicêtre, decided to use it to put to work convalescents and able-bodied incurables from the three sections of the asylum. A decision of the commission set up on 27 December 1860 by the prefect Haussmann to "study the improvements and reforms to be carried out in the service for the insane of the Seine department" marked the end of the farm. The construction of an asylum, begun in 1863 according to the plans established

under the directive of Girard de Cailleux, was inaugurated on 1 May 1867. See, C. Guesstel, *Asile d'aliénés de Sainte-Anne à Paris* (Versailles: Aubert, 1880).

40. Henri Girard de Cailleux (1814-1884) filled the posts of head doctor and director of the Auxerre insane asylum from 20 June 1840 until his appointment in 1860 as Inspector General for the Seine service for the insane. The quotation comes from his article: "De la construction et de la direction des asiles d'aliénés" *Annales d'hygiène publique et de médecine légale*, vol. 40, 1st Part, July 1848, p. 30.
41. H. Belloc, *Les Asiles d'aliénés transformés en centres d'exploitation rurale, moyen d'exonérer en tout ou en partie les départements des dépenses qu'ils font pour leurs aliénés en augmentant le bien-être de ces malades, et en les rapprochant des conditions d'existence de l'homme en société* (Paris: Béchet, 1862) p. 15.
42. Foucault is alluding here to several earlier propositions: (a) In the lecture of 7 November 1973 he argues that the doctor's therapeutic process does not require "any discourse of truth" (above, p. 10); (b) in that of 14 November Foucault claims that the "game of truth, within delirium and of delirium, will be completely suppressed in the psychiatric practice that commences at the start of the nineteenth century" (above, p. 35); and (c) in the lecture of 12 December 1973 he concludes that in psychiatric power the question of truth is never posed (above, p. 134).
43. F. Leuret, *Du traitement moral de la folie*, p. 423 and pp. 435-436.
44. Ibid. p. 438.
45. Ibid. p. 439.
46. Ibid. p. 440.
47. Ibid. pp. 440-442.
48. Ibid. p. 444.
49. Ibid.
50. Ibid. pp. 444-445.
51. Ibid. pp. 441-442.
52. F. Leuret, *Fragments psychologiques sur la folie*, pp. 121-124.
53. F. Leuret, *Du traitement moral de la folie*, pp. 449-450.
54. Ibid. p. 449.
55. Ibid. p. 451.
56. Ibid. p. 425: "He does not dream of leaving the hospital and no longer fears the treatments with which he is threatened or that he has been made to undergo."
57. Ibid. p. 426: "A red hot iron was applied once to the top of his head, and twice to the nape of his neck."
58. Ibid. p. 429: "He then asks me if it is a question of his treatment; in which case he will resign himself to whatever I would like to do."
59. Ibid. p. 430.
60. Ibid. p. 453: "In a very short letter he let pass a dozen spelling mistakes, and it would have been better if he had not aspired for a job of this kind."
61. Ibid. p. 454: "I let the struggle get under way; M. Dupré defended himself the best he could, then, when he was too greatly pressed, I came to his aid, taking the role of conciliator."
62. Ibid. p. 461.

eight

9 JANUARY 1974

[*Psychiatric power and the practice of "direction". ~ The game of "reality" in the asylum. ~ The asylum, a medically demarcated space and the question of its medical or administrative direction. ~ The tokens of psychiatric knowledge: (a) the technique of questioning; (b) the interplay of medication and punishment; (c) the clinical presentation. ~ Asylum "microphysics of power." ~ Emergence of the Psy-function and of neuropathology. ~ The triple destiny of psychiatric power.*]

I HAVE SHOWN THAT psychiatric power in its both archaic and elementary form, as it functioned in the proto-psychiatry of the first thirty or forty years of the nineteenth century, essentially operated as a supplement of power given to reality.

This means, first of all, that psychiatric power is above all a certain way of managing, of administering, before being a cure or therapeutic intervention: it is a regime. Or rather, it is because and to the extent that it is a regime of isolation, regularity, the use of time, a system of measured deprivations, and the obligation to work, etcetera, that certain therapeutic effects are expected from it.

Psychiatric power is a regime, but at the same time—and I have stressed this aspect—it seems to me that in the nineteenth century it is a struggle against madness conceived as a will in revolt, as an unbounded will, whatever nosographic analysis or description may ultimately be given of its phenomena. Even in a case of delirium, it is the will to believe in that delirium, the will to assert that delirium, the will at the heart of that assertion of the delirium, which is the target of the struggle that runs through and drives the psychiatric regime throughout its development.

Psychiatric power is therefore mastery, an endeavor to subjugate, and my impression is that the word that best corresponds to this functioning of psychiatric power, and which is found in all the texts from Pinel to Leuret,[1] the term that recurs most frequently and appears to me to be entirely typical of this enterprise of both regime and mastery, of regularity and struggle, is the notion of "direction" (*direction*).* The history of this notion should be studied, because it did not originate in psychiatry—far from it. In the nineteenth century this notion still carries a whole set of connotations arising from religious practice. For three or four centuries before the nineteenth century, "spiritual direction" (*direction de conscience*) defined a general field of techniques and objects.[2] At a certain point, some of these techniques and objects, along with this practice of direction, were imported into the psychiatric field. It would be a history worth doing. Anyway, there's a track here: the psychiatrist is someone who directs the operations of the hospital and who directs individuals.

Just to indicate not only its existence, but also the clear awareness of this practice on the part of psychiatrists themselves, I will quote a text from 1861 which comes from the director of the Saint-Yon asylum: "In the asylum I direct, I praise, reward, reprimand, command, constrain, threaten, and punish every day; and for why? Am I not then a madman myself? And everything I do, my colleagues all do likewise; all, without exception, because it derives from the nature of things."[3]

What is the aim of this "direction"? This is the point I got to last week. I think it is basically to give reality a constraining power. This means two things.

First of all it means making this reality inevitable and, as it were, commanding, making it function like power, giving it that supplement

* Nineteenth century English psychiatrists, and English translations of French psychiatrists, such as Pinel, generally use "management," or "moral treatment" etcetera, where the French use "direction," although the latter is occasionally used as well. Since Foucault explicitly draws attention to the term and its history I have left it as direction in English.

of vigor which will enable it to match up to madness, or to give it that extra reach which will enable it to get through to those individuals who are mad who flee it or turn away from it. So it is a supplement given to reality.

But at the same time, and this is the other aspect of psychiatric power, its aim is to validate the power exercised within the asylum as being quite simply the power of reality itself. What does this intra-asylum power claim to bring about by the way it functions within this planned space, and in the name of what does it justify itself as power? It justifies itself as power in the name of reality itself. Thus you find both the principle that the asylum must function as a closed milieu, absolutely independent of pressures like those exerted by the family, etcetera—an absolute power therefore—and, at the same time, the principle that this asylum, in itself, entirely cut off, must be the reproduction of reality itself. Its buildings must be as similar as possible to ordinary dwellings; relationships between those within the asylum must be like those between citizens; the general obligation to work must be represented within the asylum, and the system of needs and the economy must be reactivated. So, there is the reduplication of the system of reality within the asylum.

So, giving power to reality and founding power on reality is the asylum tautology.

But in fact, and more exactly, what is actually introduced within the asylum in the name of reality? What is given power? What is it exactly that is made to function as reality? What is given the supplement of power, and on what type of reality is asylum power founded? This is the problem, and it was in an attempt to disentangle it a little that last week I quoted the long account of a cure that appeared to me to be absolutely exemplary of how psychiatric treatment functions.

I think we can identify precisely how the game of reality within the asylum is introduced and how it functions. I would like to summarize schematically what emerges from it quite naturally. What basically can we identify as reality in "moral treatment" in general, and in the case we have been considering in particular?

I think it is, first of all, the other's will. The reality the patient must confront, the reality to which his attention—distracted by his insubordinate will—must submit and by which he must be subjugated, is first of all the other as a center of will, as a source of power, the other inasmuch as he has, and will always have, greater power than the mad person. The greater part of power is on the other's side: the other is always the holder of a greater part of power in relation to the mad person's power. This is the first yoke of reality to which the mad person must be subjected.

Second, we found another type, or another yoke of reality to which the mad person is subjected. This was shown by the apprenticeship of the name, of the past, the obligation of anamnesis—you remember [the way in which] Leuret required and got his patient to recount his life, under the threat of eight pails of water.[4] So: name, identity, the biography recited in the first person, and recognized consequently in the ritual of something close to confession. This is the reality imposed on the mad person.

The third reality is the reality of the illness itself or, rather, the ambiguous, contradictory, vertiginous reality of the madness, since, on the one hand, in a moral cure it is always a question of showing the mad person that his madness is madness and that he really is ill, thus forcing him to abandon any possible denial of his own madness and subjecting him to the inflexibility of his real illness. And then, at the same time, he is shown that at the heart of his madness is not illness but fault, wickedness, lack of attention, presumption. At every moment—you remember M. Dupré's cure—Leuret requires his patient to acknowledge that, in the past, he was at Charenton and not in his château of Saint-Maur,[5] that he really is ill, and that his status is that of a patient. This is the truth to which the subject must be subjected.

However, at the same time, when he is subjecting him to a shower, Leuret actually says to M. Dupré: But I am not doing this in order to care for you, because you are ill; I am doing this because you are bad, because you harbor an unacceptable desire.[6] And you know how far Leuret pushed the tactic, since he goes so far as to force his patient to leave so that he does not enjoy his illness within the asylum, and so that he does not shelter the symptoms of his illness in the surrounds of the asylum. Consequently, in order to deny illness its status as illness, the bad desire within it and sustaining it, must be driven out. So it is necessary both to impose the reality of the illness and also to impose on the consciousness of the illness the reality of a desire that is not ill, which sustains and is the very root of the illness. Leuret's tactic broadly revolves around this reality and unreality of the illness, this reality and unreality of madness, and this constitutes the third yoke of reality to which, generally speaking, patients are subjected in moral treatment.

Finally, the fourth form of reality is everything corresponding to the techniques concerning money, need, the necessity to work, the whole system of exchanges and services, and the obligation to provide for his needs.

These four elements—the other's will and the surplus power situated definitively on the side of the other; the yoke of identity, of the name and biography; the non-real reality of madness and the reality of the desire which constitutes the reality of madness and nullifies it as madness; and the reality of need, exchange, and work—are, I think, the kind of nervures of reality which penetrate the asylum and constitute the points within the asylum on which its system is articulated and on the basis of which tactics are formed in the asylum struggle. Asylum power is really the power exerted to assert these realities as reality itself.

It seems to me that the existence of these four elements of reality, or the filtering that asylum power carries out in reality in order to let these four elements penetrate the asylum, is important for several reasons.

The first is that these four elements introduce a number of questions into psychiatric practice that stubbornly recur throughout the history of psychiatry. First, they introduce the question of dependence on and submission to the doctor as someone who, for the patient, holds an inescapable power. Second, they also introduce the question, or practice rather, of confession, anamnesis, of the account and recognition of oneself. This also introduces into asylum practice the procedure by which all madness is posed the question of the secret and unacceptable desire that really makes it exist as madness. And finally, fourth, they introduce, of course, the problem of money, of financial compensation; the problem of how to provide for oneself when one is mad and how to establish the system of exchange within madness which will enable the mad person's existence to be financed. You see all of this taking shape, already fairly clearly, in these techniques of proto-psychiatry.

I think these elements are equally important, not only through these techniques, through these problems deposited in the history of psychiatry, in the corpus of its practices, [but also]* because through these elements we see the definition of the cured individual. What is a cured individual if not precisely someone who will accept these four yokes of dependence, of confession, of the unacceptability of desire, and of money? The cure is the process of daily, immediate physical subjection carried out in the asylum that constitutes the cured individual as the bearer of a fourfold reality. And this fourfold reality of which the individual must be the bearer, that is to say, the receiver, is the law of the other, self-identity, the unacceptability of desire, and the insertion of need in an economic system. These are the four elements which, when they have been effectively taken on by the individual treated, will qualify him as a cured individual. The fourfold system of adjustment,† which cures by itself, through its effectuation, restores the individual.

I would now like to deal with another set of consequences that I would like to develop further and which will be the object of my remarks. This fourfold subjection is brought about therefore in a disciplinary space, and thanks to this disciplinary space. To that extent, and until now, what I have been able to tell you about the asylum does not differ that much from what we could have said about barracks, schools, orphanages, and prisons for example. Nevertheless, there is a fundamental difference between these establishments or institutions and the asylum. The difference is, of course, that the asylum has a medical stamp.

How did the things I have been talking about—the general regime of the asylum, the technique of struggle, and the extra power given to reality in this intra-asylum struggle—concern medicine, and why was a doctor needed? What is the meaning of the hospital's medical status? What is the meaning of the fact that, at a certain moment, and precisely at the start of the nineteenth century, the mad had to be put not only in a disciplinary place, but, what's more, in one that was medical? In other words, why was a doctor needed to convey this supplementary power of reality?

* (Recording:) it is equally important
† The manuscript has "subjection" rather than "adjustment."

Concretely, again, you know that until the end of the eighteenth century the places in which the mad were put, the places which served to disciplinarize their mad existence, were not medical places: neither Bicêtre,[7] nor Salpêtrière,[8] nor Saint-Lazare[9] were medical institutions, nor even, when it comes to it, was Charenton,[10] even though, unlike the other establishments, it was specifically intended for the cure of the mad. None of these were really medical places. Certainly, there were doctors, but what doctors there were had the responsibilities and role of an ordinary doctor, that is to say, providing the care entailed by the condition of the individuals confined and by the treatment itself. The cure of the mad was not demanded from the doctor as doctor; the framework ensured by religious personnel, the discipline imposed on individuals, did not need a medical guarantee for one to expect them to provide what was considered to be a cure.

All this, which is very clear until the end of the eighteenth century, suddenly changes in the last years [of the] century, and in the nineteenth century we find, then, on the one hand, an absolutely general assertion that the mad need to be directed, that they need a regime, and, on the other hand, the paradoxical assertion, which up to a point is not entailed by the first assertion, that this direction must be in the hands of medical personnel. Why is there this requirement of medicalization at the moment that the discipline I have been talking about is redefined? What is the meaning of the fact that henceforth the hospital must be the place where a medical knowledge is put to work? Does it mean that the direction of the mad must be organized on the basis of a knowledge, of an analysis, nosography, and etiology of mental illness?

I don't think so. I think we must absolutely insist on the fact that in the nineteenth century there was, on the one hand, a development of nosographies, of etiologies of mental illness, of the research of pathological anatomy on the possible organic correlations of mental illness, and then, on the other hand, the set of these tactical phenomena of direction. This gap, this discrepancy, between what could be called a medical theory and what was the actual practice of direction, is revealed in many ways.

First, in a hospital the relationship that was possible between confined individuals and a doctor as someone with a particular knowledge that he can apply to the patient was infinitely slight or, if you like, completely random. Leuret, who conducted lengthy and difficulty therapies, of which I have given you one example, said that we should never forget that in an ordinary hospital a head doctor could devote roughly thirty-seven minutes a year to each of his patients, and he cited one hospital, probably Bicêtre, in which the head doctor could devote a maximum of eighteen minutes a year to each patient.[11] You can see that the relationship between the asylum population and medical technique strictly speaking was completely random.

We find another, no doubt more serious proof of this discrepancy in the fact that if we look at how patients were actually distributed within asylums at this time, we see that it had strictly nothing to do with the nosographic division of mental illnesses found in theoretical texts. In the actual organization of asylums you see no trace or effect of the distinction between mania and lypemania,[12] between mania and monomania,[13] and the series of manias and dementias.[14] However, the divisions you do see being established concretely in the hospitals are completely different: these are the differences between the curable and the incurable, between calm and agitated patients, obedient and insubordinate patients, patients able to work and those unable to work, those punished and those unpunished, and patients to be placed under constant surveillance and those under surveillance from time to time or not at all. This is the distribution that effectively measured out the intra-asylum space, and not the nosographic frameworks being constructed in theoretical treatises.

Yet another proof of this discrepancy between medical theory and asylum practice was, if you like, the fact that everything medical theory defined through symptomatological analysis or pathological-anatomy as possible medication for mental illness was constantly and very quickly reused, not with a therapeutic aim, but within a technique of direction. What I mean is that medication like the shower or even cauterization,[15] moxas,[16] etcetera, were indeed initially prescribed in terms of a conception of the etiology of mental illness or of its organic correlations—like the need to facilitate the circulation of blood, for example, or to relieve congestion in a part of the body—but insofar as such methods were unpleasant for the patient they were very quickly taken up for use within the specific regime of direction, that is to say, as punishment. You know that this is still going on, and that the way in which electroshock therapy is used is exactly this kind of thing.[17]

Even more precisely, the use of medication itself was generally the extension of asylum discipline to the surface of the body, or into the body. What was bathing a patient really about? At one level, in theory, it really was a matter of improving the circulation of the blood. What was the reason for using laudanum or ether,[18] as was frequently the case in asylums around 1840-1860? Apparently it was to calm the patient's nervous system, but it was, in fact, quite simply the extension of the asylum regime, the regime of discipline, inside the patient's body. The current use of tranquilizers is still the same kind of practice. So, in asylum practice, you very quickly had this kind of reversion to the use of what medical theory defined as possible medication as a component of the disciplinary regime. So I don't think we can say that the doctor functioned within the asylum on the basis of his psychiatric knowledge. At every moment, what was given as psychiatric knowledge, and formulated in the theoretical texts of psychiatry, was converted into something else in real practice, and we can say that this theoretical knowledge never had a real hold on asylum life strictly speaking. Once again, this is true of the first years of this proto-psychiatry, and it is no doubt true, to a considerable extent, for the whole history of psychiatry up to the present. So how did the doctor function, and why was he necessary, if the frameworks he established, the descriptions he gave, and the medication he defined on the basis of this knowledge, are not put to work, and are not even put to work by him?

What does it mean to stamp this asylum power as medical? Why must asylum power be exercised by a doctor? It seems to me that the interior of the asylum is given a medical stamp by the physical presence of the doctor: it is through his omnipresence, the assimilation, if you like, of asylum space to the psychiatrist's body. The asylum is the psychiatrist's body, stretched and distended to the dimensions of an establishment, extended to the point that his power is exerted as if every part of the asylum is a part of his own body, controlled by his own nerves. More precisely, I would say that this assimilation, psychiatrist's body-asylum space, is revealed in different ways.

First of all, the first reality the patient must encounter, and which is, in a way, the reality through which all the other elements of reality will have to pass, is the psychiatrist's body itself. You recall those scenes I talked about to start with: every therapy begins with the sudden appearance of the psychiatrist in person, in flesh and blood, looming up in front of his patient, either on the day of his arrival or when his treatment begins, and with the prestige of this body of which it was indeed said that it must be without defect, that it must impose itself through its own stature and weight. This body must impress itself on the patient as reality, or as that through which the reality of every other reality will have to pass; this is the body to which the patient must be subjected.

Second, the psychiatrist's body must be present everywhere. Asylum architecture—as defined in the 1830s and 1840s by Esquirol,[19] Parchappe,[20] Girard de Cailleux,[21] and others—was always calculated so that the psychiatrist could be present virtually everywhere. He must be able to take in everything in a glance, and by taking a stroll, inspect the situation of each of his patients; at any moment he must be able to see and make a complete survey of the establishment, patients and personnel; he must see everything and everything must be reported to him: what he does not see himself, he must be informed about by supervisors completely subservient to him, so that he is always present, at every moment, in the asylum. The entire asylum space is covered with his eyes, ears, and actions.

What's more, the psychiatrist's body must communicate directly with every part of the asylum administration: supervisors are basically the cogs of the machine, the hands, at any rate the instruments, directly under the psychiatrist's control. Girard de Cailleux—the great organizer of all the asylums built on the outskirts of Paris from 1860[22]—said: "It is, of course, through a hierarchy that the impulse given by the head doctor is communicated to every part of the service; he is its regulator, but his subordinates are the essential cogs."[23]

All in all, I think we can say that the psychiatrist's body is the asylum itself; ultimately, the asylum machinery and the psychiatrist's organism must form one and the same thing. And this is what Esquirol says in his treatise *Des maladies mentales*: "The doctor must be, as it were, the principle of a hospital's life for the insane. It is through him that everything must be put in motion; he directs every action, called upon as he is to be the regulator of every thought. Everything concerning the inhabitants of the establishment must be submitted to him as the center of action."[24]

So I think the need to give the asylum a medical stamp, the assertion that the asylum must be a medical place, signifies first of all—this is the first stratum of meaning we can draw out—that the patient must find himself faced with the doctor's omnipresent body, as it were, that ultimately he must be enveloped within the doctor's body. But, you will say, exactly why must it be a doctor? Why could not any director play this role? Why must this individual body, which becomes the power, the body through which all reality passes, be precisely a doctor's body?

Oddly enough, the problem was both always being taken up and never debated head on. In the texts of the nineteenth century you find it repeatedly asserted, as a principle, as an axiom, that the asylum really must be directed by a doctor and that the asylum will have no therapeutic function if the doctor does not direct it entirely. And then, at the same time, you see the difficulty of explaining this constantly recurring principle, with the revival of the worry that since it is, after all, a disciplinary establishment, a good administrator would suffice. In fact, for a long time there was a constant conflict between the medical director of the hospital, who had therapeutic responsibility, and the person with responsibility for supplies, administration of the personnel, and management, etcetera. Pinel himself had a kind of anxiety from the start, since he said: Basically, my job is to care for the patients, but, when we come down to it, Pussin, who has been the porter, concierge, and supervisor at Bicêtre for many years, knows just as much as me; and, after all, it was actually by leaning on his experience that I was able to learn what I did.[25]

This will be found throughout the nineteenth century, transposed to another scale, with the problem of who, manager or doctor, ultimately must prevail in the running of the hospital. The doctors' answer—and in the end this is the solution adopted in France—is that the doctor must prevail.[26] The doctor will have the main responsibility and will ultimately be the director, with, alongside him, someone in charge of, the tasks of management and supply, but under the doctor's control and, to an extent, responsibility. So, why the doctor? Answer: because he knows. But since it is precisely not his psychiatric knowledge that is actually put to work in the asylum regime, since it is not psychiatric knowledge that is actually used by the doctor when he directs the regime of the insane, what is it that he knows? So, how can we say that a doctor must direct an asylum because the doctor knows? And in what respect is this knowledge necessary? I think that what is thought to be necessary in the good running of the asylum, what makes it necessary that the asylum is given a medical stamp, is the effect of the supplementary power given, not by the content of a knowledge, but statutorily, by the formal stamp of knowledge. In other words, it is through the tokens of his possession of a knowledge, and only through the action of these tokens, whatever the actual content of this knowledge, that medical power, as necessarily medical power, functions within the asylum.

What are these tokens of knowledge? How are they put to work in the proto-asylum of the first years of the nineteenth century, and how will they work, moreover, for years afterwards? It is fairly easy to follow the series of formulae by which these tokens of knowledge worked in the organization and functioning of the hospital.

First, Pinel said: "When you question a patient, you should first of all inform yourself about him, you should know why he is there, what the complaint is against him, his biography; you should have questioned his family or circle, so that when you question him you know more about him than he does or, at least, you know more than he imagines you do, so that when he says something you think is untrue you will then be able to intervene and stress that you know more about it than he does, and that you attribute what he says to lying, to delirium . . ."[27]

Second, the technique of psychiatric questioning (*l'interrogatoire*) as defined in fact, if not theoretically, and no doubt less by Pinel than by Esquirol and his successors,[28] is not a way of getting information from the patient that one does not possess. Or rather, if it is true that, in a way, it really is necessary, by questioning the patient, to get information from him that one does not possess, the patient does not have to be aware that one is dependent upon him for this information. The questioning must be conducted in such a way that the patient does not say what he wants, but answers questions.[29]* Hence the strict advice: never

* The manuscript also refers to a form of questioning by "the doctor's silence" and illustrates it with this observation by F. Leuret: "Partial dementia with a depressive character. Auditory hallucinations" in *Fragments pyschologiques sur la folie* (Paris: Crochard, 1834) p. 153.

let the patient spin out an account, but interrupt him with questions which are both canonical, always the same, and also follow a certain order, for these questions must function in such a way that the patient is aware that his answers do not really inform the doctor, but merely provide a hold for his knowledge, give him the chance to explain; the patient must realize that each of his answers has meaning within a field of an already fully constituted knowledge in the doctor's mind. Questioning is a way of quietly substituting for the information wormed out of the patient the appearance of an interplay of meanings which give the doctor a hold on the patient.

Third—still with these tokens of knowledge that enable the doctor to function as a doctor—the patient must be constantly supervised, a permanent file must be kept on him, and when dealing with him one must always be able to show that one knows what he has done, what he said the day before, what faults he committed, and what punishment he received. So, a complete system of statements and notes on the asylum patient must be organized and made available to the doctor.[30]

Fourth, the double register of medication and direction must always be brought into play. When a patient has done something that one wants to curb, he must be punished, but in punishing him one must make him think that one punishes him because it is therapeutically useful. One must therefore be able to make the punishment function as a remedy and, conversely, when one fixes a remedy for him, one must be able to impose it knowing that it will do him good, but making him think that it is only to inconvenience and punish him. This double game of remedy and punishment is essential to how the asylum functions and can only be established provided that there is someone who presents himself as possessing the truth concerning what is remedy and what is punishment.

Finally, the last element in the asylum by which the doctor gives himself the insignia of knowledge, is the great game of the clinic that is so important in the history of psychiatry. The clinic is basically a staged presentation of the patient in which questioning the patient serves the purpose of instructing students, and in which the doctor operates on the double register of someone who examines the patient and someone who teaches the students, so that he will be both the person who cares and the person who possesses the master's word; doctor and teacher at the same time. And [...] this practice of the clinic is established very early on within asylum practice.

In 1817, Esquirol started the first clinics at Salpêtrière,[31] and from 1830 regular clinical lessons were given at Bicêtre[32] and Salpêtrière.[33] Finally, from around 1830 to 1835, every important head of a service, even if he is not a professor, uses this system of the clinical presentation of patients, that is to say, this interplay between medical examination and professorial performance. Why is the clinic important?

We have a really fine theory of the clinic from Jean-Pierre Falret, someone who actually practiced it. Why was it necessary to use this method of the clinic?

First, the doctor must show the patient that he has around him a number of people, as many as possible, who are ready to listen to him, and that, consequently, the patient, who may possibly object to the doctor's words, who may not pay any attention to them, nevertheless cannot fail to notice that they really are listened to, and listened to with respect by a number of people. The effect of power of his words is thus multiplied by the presence of auditors: "The presence of a large and deferential public imparts the greatest authority to his words."[34]

Second, the clinic is important because it allows the doctor not only to question the patient, but also, by questioning him or by commenting on his answers, to show the patient himself that he is familiar with his illness, that he knows things about his illness, that he can talk about it and give a theoretical account of it before his students.[35] In the patient's eyes, the status of the dialogue he has with the doctor will change its nature; he will understand that something like a truth that everyone accepts is being formulated in the doctor's words.

Third, the clinic is important because it consists not only in questioning the patient, but also in making the general anamnesis of the case before the students. The whole of the patient's life will be summarized before [them,]* he will be got to recount it, or, if he does not want to recount it, the doctor will do so in his place; the questioning will carry on and, in the end—with his assistance if he wants to speak, or even

* (Recording:) the students

without it if he shuts himself up in silence—the patient will see his own life unfolding before him, which will have the reality of illness, since it is actually presented as illness before students who are medical students.[36]

And, finally, by playing this role, by accepting to come to the front of the stage, on display with the doctor, exposing his own illness, answering his questions, the patient, says Falret, will take note that he is giving pleasure to the doctor and that, to some extent, he is paying him for the trouble he is taking.[37]

You can see that in the clinic we find again the four elements of reality I spoke about earlier: power of the other, the law of identity, confession of the nature of the madness in its secret desire, and remuneration, the game of exchanges, the economic system controlled by money. In the clinic, the doctor's words appear with a greater power than those of anyone else. In the clinic, the law of identity weighs on the patient, who is obliged to recognize himself in everything said about him, and in the entire anamnesis of his life. By answering the doctor's questions in public, in having the final confession of his madness dragged from him, the patient recognizes and accepts the reality of the mad desire at the root of his madness. Finally, he enters in a particular way into the systems of satisfactions and compensations, and so on.

As a result, you see that the great support of psychiatric power, or rather the great amplifier of the psychiatric power woven into the daily life of the asylum, will be this famous ritual of the clinical presentation of the patient. The enormous institutional importance of the clinic in the daily life of psychiatric hospitals from the 1830s until today is due to the fact that the doctor constituted himself as a master of truth through the clinic. The technique of confession and of the account becomes an institutional obligation, the patient's realization that his madness is illness becomes a necessary episode, and the patient enters in turn into the system of profits and satisfactions given to the person who looks after him.

You can see how the tokens of knowledge are magnified in the clinic, and how, in the end, they function. The tokens of knowledge, and not the content of a science, allow the alienist to function as a doctor within the asylum. These insignia of knowledge enable him to exercise an absolute surplus-power in the asylum, and ultimately to identify himself with the asylum body. These tokens of knowledge allow him to constitute the asylum as a sort of medical body that cures through its eyes, ears, words, gestures, and machinery. And, finally, these tokens of knowledge will enable psychiatric power to play its real role of the intensification of reality. You see how it is not so much contents of knowledge as tokens of knowledge that are put to work in this clinical scene. Through these tokens of knowledge, you see the emergence and work of the four tentacles of reality I have been talking about: the surplus-power of the doctor, the law of identity, the unacceptable desire of madness, and the law of money.

I think we could say that through this identification of the psychiatrist's body and the asylum, through this game of the tokens of knowledge and the four forms of reality which pass through them, we can identify the formation of a medical figure who is at the opposite pole to another medical figure taking on a completely new form at this time—the surgeon. The surgical pole began to take shape in the medical world of the nineteenth century with the development of pathological anatomy, broadly speaking, let's say with Bichat.[38] On the basis of a real content of knowledge, it involved the doctor identifying a reality of the illness in the patient's body, and the use of his own hands, of his own body, to nullify the disease.

At the other end of this field is the psychiatric pole, which operates in a completely different way. On the basis, then, not of the content of knowledge, but of tokens of knowledge qualifying the medical figure, the psychiatric pole involves making the asylum space function as a body which cures by its own presence, its own gestures, its own will, and, through this body, it involves giving a supplement of power to the fourfold form of reality.

In conclusion, I would like to say that, as you can see, we arrive at this paradox of the completely specific constitution of a space of discipline, of an apparatus of discipline, which differs from all the others because it has a medical stamp. But this medical stamp, which distinguishes the asylum space from all the other disciplinary spaces, does not function by putting a theoretically formulated psychiatric knowledge to work within the asylum. This medical distinction is in reality the establishment of a game between the mad person's subjected body and the psychiatrist's institutionalized body, the psychiatrist's body extended to the dimensions of an institution. We should think of the asylum as the psychiatrist's body; the asylum institution is nothing other than the set of regulations that this body effectuates in relation to the body of the subjected mad person in the asylum.

✤

In this, I think we can identify one of the fundamental features of what I will call the microphysics of asylum power: this game between the mad person's body and the psychiatrist's body above it, dominating it, standing over it and, at the same time, absorbing it. This, with all the specific effects of such a game, seems to me to be the typical feature of the microphysics of psychiatric power.

We can pick out three phenomena from this that I will try to analyze a bit more precisely in the following lectures. The first is that from around 1850 to 1860 this proto-psychiatric power that I have tried to define in this way will, of course, be considerably transformed as the result of certain phenomena that I will try to point out to you. Nonetheless, it lives on, surcharged and modified, not only in asylums, but also outside. That is to say, around 1840 to 1860, there was a sort of diffusion, a migration of this psychiatric power, which spread into other institutions, into other disciplinary regimes that it doubled, as it were. In other words, I think psychiatric power spread as a tactic for the subjection of the body in a physics of power, as power of the intensification of reality, as constitution of individuals as both receivers and bearers of reality.

I think we find it under what I will call the Psy-functions: pathological, criminological, and so on. Psychiatric power, that is to say, the function of the intensification of reality, is found wherever it is necessary to make reality function as power. If psychologists turn up in the school, the factory, in prisons, in the army, and elsewhere, it is because they entered precisely at the point when each of these institutions was obliged to make reality function as power, or again, when they had to assert the power exercised within them as reality. The school, for example, calls on a psychologist when it has to assert that the knowledge it provides and distributes is reality, when it ceases to appear to be real to those to whom it is offered. The school has to call in the psychologist when the power exercised at school ceases to be a real power, and becomes a both mythical and fragile power, the reality of which must consequently be intensified. It is under this double condition that one needs the educational psychologist who reveals the differential abilities of individuals on the basis of which they will be placed at a certain level in a field of knowledge, as if this was a real field, as if it was a field which had in itself its power of constraint, since one has to remain where one is in this field of knowledge defined by the institution. In this way knowledge functions as power, and this power of knowledge presents itself as reality within which the individual is placed. And, at the end of the educational psychologist's treatment, the individual actually is the bearer of a double reality: the reality of his abilities on the one hand, and the reality of the contents of knowledge he is capable of acquiring on the other. It is at the point of articulation of these two "realities" defined by the educational psychologist that the individual appears as an individual. We could undertake the same kind of analysis of prisons, the factory, and so forth.

The fundamental role of the psychological function, which historically is entirely derived from the dissemination of psychiatric power in other directions beyond the asylum, is to intensify reality as power and to intensify power by asserting it as reality. I think this is, if you like, the first point to be stressed.

Now, how did this kind of dissemination come about? How was it that this psychiatric power, which seemed to be so firmly tied up with the specific space of the asylum, began to drift? At any rate, what were the intermediaries? I think the intermediary is easily found and is basically the psychiatrization of abnormal children, and more precisely the psychiatrization of idiots. It is when the mad were separated from idiots within the asylum that a kind of institution began to take shape in which psychiatric power was put to work in the archaic form I have just been describing.[39] For years, we can say for almost a century, this archaic form remained what it was at the beginning. I think it is on the basis of this mixed form, between psychiatry and pedagogy, on the basis of this psychiatrization of the abnormal, of the feeble minded, mentally defective, etcetera, that the system of dissemination took place that allowed psychology to become that kind of permanent doubling of the functioning of every institution. So, next week I would like to say something about this organization and establishment of the psychiatrization of idiots.

Then I would also like to pick out other phenomena based on this proto-psychiatry. The other series of phenomena is this: whereas in the psychiatrization of idiots the psychiatric power I have described continues to advance within the asylum almost without change, on the other hand, a number of utterly fundamental and essential things take place, a double process in which (as in every battle) it is very difficult to know who started it, who takes the initiative and even who gains the upper hand in the end. What were these two twin processes?

First, the appearance of neurology, or more precisely, of neuropathology, was a fundamental event in the history of medicine, that is to say, when certain disorders began to be dissociated from madness and it became possible to assign them a neurological seat and neuropathological etiology that made it possible to distinguish those who were really ill at the level of their body from those for whom one could assign no etiology at the level of organic lesions.[40] This raised the question of the seriousness, of the authenticity, of mental illness, which generated the suspicion that, after all, should a mental illness without any anatomical correlation really be taken seriously?

And, opposite this—correlative to this kind of suspicion that neurology began to cast over the whole world of mental illness—there was the game of patients who never ceased to respond to psychiatric power in terms of truth and falsehood. To psychiatric power, which said "I am only a power, and you must accept my knowledge solely at the level of its tokens, without ever seeing the effects of its content," patients responded with the game of simulation. When, with neuropathology, doctors finally introduced a new content of knowledge, patients responded with another type of simulation, which was, broadly speaking, the hysterics' great simulation of nervous illnesses like epilepsy, paralysis, and so on. And the game, the kind of endless pursuit between patients, who constantly trapped medical knowledge in the name of a certain truth and in a game of lies, and doctors, who endlessly tried to recapture patients in the trap of a neurological knowledge of pathological signs, of a serious medical knowledge, finally permeated the whole history of nineteenth century psychiatry as a real struggle between doctors and patients.

Finally, the last point is how the principal elements we saw taking shape within psychiatric power, and which were its main supports, were taken up outside the asylum institution. That is to say, how were those elements of reality—the law of the power of the other, the prestige given to the doctor's words, the law of identity, the obligation of anamnesis, the attempt to drive out the mad desire that constitutes the reality of madness, and the problem of money, etcetera—brought into play within a practice like psychoanalysis that claims it is not psychiatric, and yet in which one sees how its different elements were inscribed within the game of psychiatric power that isolated them and brought them out?[41]

So, if you like, psychiatric power will have a triple destiny. We will find it persisting for a long time in its archaic form, after the period 1840 to 1860, in the pedagogy of mental deficiency. You will find it being re-elaborated and transformed in the asylum through the interplay of neurology and simulation. And then, a third destiny will be its take up within a practice that puts itself forward however as a practice that is not exactly psychiatric.

---

1. Apart from the many occurrences of the term "direction" (*diriger*) in his *Traité médico-philosophique* (pp. xlv, 46, 50, 52, 194, 195, and 200), Pinel devotes two passages to the direction of the insane: section II, § vi: "Advantages of the art of directing (*diriger*) the insane in order to promote the effect of medicines" pp. 57-58; and § xxii: "Skill in directing (*diriger*) the insane by seeming to go along with their imaginary ideas" pp. 92-95; *A Treatise on Insanity*, pp. 59-60 and pp. 95-98 (the English translation generally renders *diriger* as "management"; G.B.). For his part, Esquirol defines moral treatment as "the art of directing (*diriger*) the intelligence and passions of the insane" *Des maladies mentales*, vol. I, p. 134; *Mental Maladies*, p. 79. Leuret states that "it is necessary to direct (*diriger*) the intelligence of the insane and to excite passions in them which can divert their delirium" *Du traitement moral de la folie*, p. 185.
2. The practice of "direction" or "conduct" was instituted on the basis of the pastoral of Carlo Borromeo (1538-1584), *Pastorum instructiones ad concionandum, confessionisque et eucharistiae sacramenta ministrandum utilissimae* (Antwerp: C. Plantini, 1586), and in connection with Catholic reform and the development of "retreats." Among those who laid down its rules, we can refer to (a) Ignace de Loyola, *Exercitia spiritualia* (Rome: A. Bladum, 1548); English translation, Ignatius Loyola, *The Spiritual Exercises of St. Ignatius Loyola*, trans. Elisabeth Meier Tetlow (Lanham and London: University Press of America, 1987). See, P. Dudon, *Saint Ignace de Loyola* (Paris: Beauchesne, 1934); P. Doncœur, "Saint Ignace et la direction des âmes" in *La Vie Spirituelle*, vol. 48, Paris, 1936, pp. 48-54; M. Olphe-Galliard, "Direction spirituelle," III: "Période moderne" in *Dictionnaire de spiritualité ascétique et mystique. Doctrine et histoire*, vol.III (Paris: Beauchesne, 1957) col. 1115-1117. (b) François de Sales (1567-1622) *Introduction à la vie dévote* (1608), of which chapter 4 became the directors' bible: "De la nécessité d'un directeur pour entrer et fair progrès en la dévotion" in *Œuvres*, vol. III (Annecy: Niérat, 1893) pp. 22-25; English translation, St. Francis de Sales, *Introduction to the Devout Life*, trans. Michael Day (Wheathampstead: Anthony Clarke, 1990), "The necessity of a guide," pp. 12-15. See F. Vincent, *François de Sales, directeur d'âmes. L'éducation de la volonté* (Paris: Beauchesne, 1923). And (c) Jean-Jacques Olier (1608-1657), founder of the Saint-Sulpice seminary, "L'esprit d'un directeur des âmes" in *Œuvres complètes* (Paris: J.-P. Migne, 1856) col. 1183-1240.

   On "direction" we can refer to the following works: E.M. Caro, "Les direction des âmes au XVIIe siècle" in *Nouvelles Études morales sur le temps présent* (Paris: Hachette, 1869) pp. 145-203; H. Huvelin, *Quelques directeurs d'âmes au XVIIe siècle: saint François de Sales, M. Olier, saint Vincent de Paul, l'abbé de Rancé* (Paris: Gabalda, 1911). Foucault returns to the notion of "direction" in his lectures at the Collège de France of 1974-1975, *Les Anormaux*, lectures of 19 February and 26 February 1975, pp. 170-171 and pp. 187-189; *Abnormal*, pp. 182-184 and pp. 201-204; of 1977-1978, *Sécurité, Territoire, Population*, ed. Michel Senellart (Paris: Gallimard/Seuil, 2004) lecture of 28 February 1978; and 1981-1982, *L'Herméneutique du sujet*, ed. F. Gros (Paris: Gallimard/Seuil, 2001) lectures of 3 and 10 March, pp. 315-393; English translation, *The Hermeneutics of the Subject. Lectures at the Collège de France 1981-82*, ed. Frédéric Gros, English series ed. Arnold I. Davidson, trans. Graham Burchell (New York: Palgrave Macmillan, 2005) pp. 331-412; and in his lecture at the University of Stanford, 10 October 1979, " 'Omnes et singulatim': Towards a Critique of Political Reason" in *The Essential Works of Michel Foucault 1954-1984, vol. 3: Power*, ed. James D. Faubion, trans. Robert Hurley and others (New York: New Press, 2000) pp. 310-311; French translation, "'Omnes et singulatim': vers une critique de la raison politique" trans. P. E. Dauzat, *Dits et Écrits*, vol. 4, pp. 146-147.
3. H. Belloc, "De la responsabilité morale chez les aliénés," *Annales médico-psychologiques*, 3rd series, vol. III, July 1861, p. 422.
4. F. Leuret, *Du traitement moral de la folie*, pp. 444-446.
5. Ibid. p. 441, p. 443, and p. 445.
6. Ibid. p. 431: "I direct a jet of water on his face and body, and when he seems disposed to bear everything *for his treatment*, I am very careful to tell him that it is not a question of treating him, but of offending and punishing him" (Leuret's emphasis).
7. Constructed in 1634 with the view to being an asylum for poor nobility and wounded soldiers, the Bicêtre château was incorporated in the Hôpital général created by the edict

of 27 April 1656, ordering that "the able-bodied and disabled mendicant poor, of both sexes, be confined in a hospital to be employed in works, manufacture, and other work according to their ability." It was in the "Saint-Prix employment" [special quarters for the ill; J.L.], created in 1660 to take in the insane, that Pinel took up the post of "infirmary doctor" on 11 September 1793; he occupied this post until 19 April 1795. See, P. Bru, *Histoire de Bicêtre (hospice, prison, asile), d'après des documents historiques* (Paris: Éd. du Progrès médical, 1890); F. Funck-Brentano and G. Marindaz, *L'Hôpital général de Bicêtre* (Lyon: Laboratoires Ciba, 1938); and J.M. Surzur, "L'Hôpital-hospice de Bicêtre. Historique, fonctions sociales jusqu'à la Révolution française," Medical Thesis, Paris, 1969, no. 943 (Paris: 1969).

8. La Salpêtrière owed its name to the saltpeter factory erected on the spot under Louis XIII. The edict of 27 April 1656 incorporated it in the Hôpital générale for the "confinement of the mendicant poor" of the town and inner suburbs of Paris, for "incorrigible women," and for some "mad persons." On the suppression of its carceral function in 1793, the home became the "Maison nationale des femmes," until 1823. The General Council for hospitals and homes of the Seine, founded in 1801 by Jean-Antoine Chaptal (1756-1832) by a decree of 27 March 1802, ordered the transfer to Salpêtrière of mad women hospitalized at the Hôtel-Dieu. See, L. Boucher, *La Salpêtrière. Son histoire de 1656 à 1790. Ses origines et son fonctionnement au XVIIIe siècle* (Paris, Éd. du Progrès médical, 1883); G. Guillain and P. Mathieu, *La Salpêtrière* (Lyon: Laboratoires Ciba, 1939); J. Couteaux, "L'histoire de la Salpêtrière" *Revue hospitalière de France*, vol. 9, 1944, pp. 106-127 and 215-242. Since then a well-documented study has become available: N. Simon and J. Franchi, *La Pitié-Salpêtrière* (Saint-Benoît-la-Forêt: Éd. de l'Arbre à images, 1986).

9. Saint-Lazare, founded in the ninth century by the hospitaller friars of Saint Lazare for the care of lepers, was transformed by Saint Vincent de Paul on 7 January 1632 to take in "persons detained by order of His Majesty" and the "insane poor." In 1794 it became a prison for streetwalkers. See, E. Pottet, *Histoire de Saint-Lazare, 1122-1912* (Paris: Société française d'imprimerie et de librairie, 1912); J. Vié, *Les Aliénés et les correctionnaires à Saint-Lazare au XVIIe et au XVIIIe siècle* (Paris: F. Alcan, 1930). Foucault refers to it in *Histoire de la folie*, p. 62 and p. 136; *Madness and Civilization*, p. 42 (page 136 of the French edition is omitted from the English translation).

10. The Charenton home was the result of a foundation of the King's counsellor, Sébastien Leblanc, in September 1641. In February 1644 it was handed over to the St-Jean-de-Dieu order of hospitallers, created in 1537 by the Portuguese Jean Cindad for the service of the poor and sick. See, J. Monval, *Les Frères hospitaliers de Saint-Jean-de-Dieu en France* (Paris: Bernard Grasset, 1936); A. Chagny, *L'Ordre hospitalier de Saint-Jean-de-Dieu*, two volumes (Lyon: Lescuyer et fils, 1953). See also, P. Sevestre, "La maison de Charenton, de la fondation à la reconstruction: 1641-1838" *Histoire des sciences médicales*, vol. 25, 1991, pp. 61-71.

Closed in July 1795, the home was reopened and nationalized under the Directory, on 15 June 1797, to replace the quarters for the insane at the Hôtel-Dieu. Its direction was then entrusted to an old member of the regular order of Premonstratensians, François de Coulmiers, and Joseph Gastaldy was appointed head doctor. See, C.F.S. Giraudy, *Mémoire sur la Maison nationale de Charenton, exclusivement detinée au traitement des aliénés* (Paris: Imprimerie de la Société de Médecine, 1804); J.E.D. Esquirol, "Mémoire historique et statistique sur la Maison Royale de Charenton" (1835) in *Des maladies mentales considérées sous les rapports médical, hygiénique et médico-légale*, vol. II, 1838, pp. 539-736; and, C. Strauss, *La maison nationale de Charenton* (Paris: Imprimerie nationale, 1900).

11. F. Leuret, *Du traitement moral de la folie*, p. 185: "In an establishment for the insane that I could name, the number of patients is such that in the course of a whole year the head doctor can give only thirty seven minutes to each patient, and in another, where the number of patients is even greater (...) each patient has the right to see the head doctor for only eighteen minutes a year."

12. Foucault refers here to the distinction established by Esquirol in the field of madness defined as a "usually chronic cerebral affection, without fever, characterized by disorders of sensibility, intelligence, and the will" J.E.D. Esquirol, "De la folie" (1816) in *Des maladies mentales*, vol. I, p. 5; *Mental Maladies*, p. 21. Within the field marked out by this tripartite division of psychological faculties will be inserted the clinical varieties differing

from each other in terms of (a) the nature of the disorder affecting the faculties; (b) the extension of the disorder; (c) the quality of the humor which affects it. Thus, whereas mania is characterized by "disturbance and over-excitement of the sensibility, intelligence, and will" ("De la manie" [1818], ibid. vol. II, p. 132; English, ibid. p. 378), in lypemania—a neologism created by Leuret in 1815 on the basis of Greek root, λύπη, sadness, affliction—"sensibility is painfully excited or injured; the sad, oppressive passions modify the intelligence and will" ("De la lypémanie ou mélancoli" [1820], ibid. pp. 398-481; English, ibid. pp. 199-233).

13. The criterion for the distinction between mania and monomania was the extension of the disorder, general or partial, that is to say, localized in a faculty (intellectual or instinctive monomania, etcetera), an object (erotomania), or a theme (religious or homicidal monomania). Thus mania is characterized by the fact that "the delirium is general, all the faculties of the understanding are over-excited and disrupted," whereas in monomania "the sad or gay, concentrated or expansive delirium is partial and circumscribed to a small number of ideas and affections" ibid. vol. II, "De la manie" p. 133; English, ibid. "Mania" p. 378.
14. In contrast with mania characterized by "over-excitement of the faculties," the group of dementias—with "acute," "chronic" and "senile" varieties—are distinguished by their negative aspects: "Dementia is a usually chronic cerebral affection without fever, characterized by deterioration of the sensibility, intelligence and will" ibid. "De la démence" (1814); p. 219; English, ibid. "Dementia" p. 417.
15. Cauterization or "actual cautery" consisted in the application of an iron heated in the fire or in boiling water to the top of the head or the nape of the neck. See, L. Valentin, "Mémoire et observations concernant les bons effets du cautère actuel, appliqué sur la tête dans plusieurs maladies," Nancy, 1815. Esquirol recommended the use of the moxa and "red-hot iron applied to the nape of the neck in mania complicated by fury" *Des maladies mentales*, vol. I, "De la folie" (1816) p. 154; *Mental Maladies*, p. 87: "I have many times applied the iron at a red heat to the neck, in mania complicated with fury," and ibid., vol. II, "De la manie" p. 191 and 217; English, ibid. "Mania" pp. 400-401 and p. 411. See, J. Guislain, *Traité sur l'aliénation mentale et sur les hospices des aliénés*, vol. II, ch. vi, "Moxa et cautère actuel" pp. 52-55.
16. "Moxas" are cylinders made from a material the progressive combustion of which was supposed to excite the nervous system and have a function of sensory arousal through the pain it caused. See, A.E.M. Bernardin, *Dissertation sur les avantages qu'on peut retenir de l'application du moxa* (Paris: Lefebvre, 1803); E.J. Georget, *De la folie*, p. 247: Georget recommended its use in forms of insanity involving stupor and insensibility; J. Guislain, *Traité sur les phrénopathies*, section IV, p. 458: "This powerful irritant acts on the physical sensibility through pain and the destruction of living parts, but it also has a moral action through the fear it inspires."
17. Ugo Cerletti (1877-1963), dissatisfied with the cardiazol shock used by the Milanese psychiatrist Laszlo von Meduna since 1935, perfected electroshock therapy with Lucio Bini. On 15 April 1938, a schizophrenic was subjected to this therapy for the first time. See, U. Cerletti, "L'elettroshock" *Rivista sperimentale di freniatria*, Reggio Emilia, vol. XVIII, 1940, pp. 209-310; "Electroshock therapy," in A.M. Sackler and others, *The Great Physiodynamic Therapies in Psychiatry: An Historical Appraisal* (New York: Harper, 1956) pp. 92-94.
18. From the second half of the nineteenth century, the use of ether developed in psychiatry for both therapeutic purposes—notably for calming "states of nervous excitement" (see, W. Griesinger, *Die Pathologie und Therapie der psychischen Krankheiten* [Stuttgart: A. Krabbe, 1845] p. 544; English translation, *Mental Pathology and Therapeutics*, trans. C. Lockhart Robertson and James Rutherford [New York and London: Hafner, 1965] p. 478)—and for diagnosis. See, H. Bayard, "L'utilisation de l'éther et le diagnostic des maladies mentales" *Annales d'hygiène publique et médicale*, vol. 42, no. 83, July 1849, pp. 201-214; B.A. Morel, "De l'étherisation dans la folie du point de vue du diagnostic et de la médecine légale" *Archives générales de médecine*, 5th series, vol. 3, 1, February 1854, p. 135: "In certain definite circumstances, etherisation is a precious means for modifying the unhealthy condition and for enlightening the doctor as to the real neuropathic character of the affection"; and, H. Brochim, "Maladies nerveuses," § "Anesthésiques: éther et chloroforme" in *Dictionnaire encyclopédique des sciences médicales*, 2nd series, vol. XII, 1877, pp. 376-377.

19. On his return from his travels in France, Italy, and Belgium, Esquirol opened up the discussion of the construction of asylums for the insane, first in his report, *Des établissements consacrés aux aliénés en France*, republished in *Des maladies mentales*, vol. II, pp. 339-431, and then in his article "Maisons d'aliénés" in *Dictionnaire des sciences médicales*, vol. XXX (Paris: C.L.F. Panckoucke, 1818) pp. 47-95, republished in *Des maladies mentales*, vol. II, pp. 432-538.
20. Jean-Baptiste Parchappe de Vinay (1800-1866), appointed General Inspector of the Service for the insane in 1848, drew up plans for an asylum that would be able to separate categories of patients and put to work a therapeutic project: *Des principes à suivre dans la fondation et la construction des asiles d'aliénés* (Paris: Masson, 1853). See J.G.H. Martel, *Parchappe. Signification de son œuvre, sa place dans l'évolution de l'assistance psychiatrique*, Medical Thesis, Paris, 1965, no. 108 (Paris: R. Foulon and Co., 1965).
21. Henri Girard de Cailleux (1813-1884), appointed head doctor and director of the Auxerre insane asylum on 20 June 1840, proposed the construction of asylums in which, in line with the principles of moral treatment, the insane would be isolated, classified, and put to work. His ideas are developed in, "De l'organisation et de l'administration des établissements d'aliénés" *Annales médico-psychologiques*, vol. II, September 1843, pp. 230-260; "De la construction, de l'organisation, et de la direction des asiles d'aliénés," *Annales d'hygiène publique et de médecine légale*, vol. 40, Part 2, July 1848, p. 5 and p. 241.
22. Appointed by Haussman in 1860 to the post of Inspecteur général of the Service for insane for the Seine, Girard de Cailleux, within the framework of the reorganization of the Service of assistance to the insane, in 1861 proposed a program for the construction of a dozen asylums in the Paris suburbs, modeled on the Auxerre asylum which he had transformed after his appointment as director (see the previous note). In May 1867, Saint-Anne opened, followed in 1868 by Ville-Évrard, then Perray-Vaucluse in 1869, and later by Villejuif in 1884. See, G. Daumezon, "Essai d'historique critique de l'appareil d'assistance aux malades mentaux dans le département de la Seine depuis le début du xixe siècle" *Information psychiatrique*, vol. I, 1960, no. 5, pp. 6-9; and, G. Bleandonu and G. Le Gaufey, "Naissance des asiles d'aliénés (Auxerre-Paris)" *Annales ESC*, 1975, no. 1, pp. 93-126.
23. H. Girard de Cailleux, "De la construction de l'organisation et de la direction des asiles d'aliénés," p. 272.
24. J.E.D. Esquirol, "Des maisons d'aliénés" (1818) in *Des maladies mentales*, vol. II, pp. 227-528. This metaphor is promised a fine future. Thus, in 1846, Paul Balvet, old director of the Saint-Alban hospital and initiator of the movement of institutional psychiatry, stated: "The asylum is homogeneous to the psychiatrist, who is its head. Being the head is not an administrative grade: it is an organic relationship with the body that one commands (...). He commands in the way that we say the brain commands the nerves. The asylum must therefore be conceived as the psychiatrist's body." P. Balvet, "De l'autonomie de la profession psychiatrique" in *Documents de l'Information psychiatrique*, vol. I: *Au-delà de l'asile d'aliénés et de l'hôpital psychiatrique* (Paris: Desclée de Brouwer, 1946) pp. 14-15.
25. Born 28 September 1745 at Lons-le-Saulner, Jean-Baptiste Pussin, after having been the head of the division of "confined boys" at Bicêtre in 1780, was promoted to governor of the seventh *emploi*, or the Saint-Prix *emploi*, corresponding to the "quarters for the agitated insane." Pinel met him there when taking up his post as hospital doctor at Bicêtre on 11 September 1793 following his appointment on 6 August 1793. Appointed head doctor at the hospital of Salpêtrière on 13 May 1795, Pinel obtained Pussin's transfer there on 19 May 1802, and worked with him in the section for the mad until his death on 7 April 1811. In his "Recherches et observations sur le traitement moral des aliénés" p. 220, Pinel praises Pussin and acknowledges his role in the "first developments of moral treatment." In the 1809 edition of his *Traité médico-philosophique*, he declares that "fully confident of the rectitude and skill of the head of internal police, I allowed him free exercise of the power at his command" p. 226. On Pussin, see, R. Semelaigne, "Pussin," in *Alénistes et philanthropes: les Pinel et les Tuke*, Appendice, pp. 501-504; E. Bixler, "A forerunner of pyschiatric nursing: Jean-Baptiste Pussin" *Annals of Medical History*, 1936, no. 8, pp. 518-519. See also, M. Caire, "Pussin avant Pinel" *Information psychiatrique*, 1993, no. 6, pp. 529-538; J. Juchet, "Jean-Baptiste Pussin et Philippe Pinel à Bicêtre en 1793: une rencontre, une complicité, une dette" in J. Garrabé, ed., *Philippe Pinel* (Paris: Les Empêcheurs de penser en rond,

1994) pp. 55-70; and, J. Juchet and J. Postel, "Le surveillan Jean-Baptiste Pussin" *Histoire des sciences médicales*, vol. 30, no. 2, 1996, pp. 189-198.

26. On the basis of the law of 30 June 1838 a debate began on the nature of the powers in charge in the asylums. Thus, the Prefect of the Seine, the Baron Haussmann, on the 27 December 1860, set up a commission for "the improvement and reforms to be carried out in the services for the insane" which, from February to June 1861, discussed whether an administrative director should be appointed alongside the asylum doctor or whether medical and administrative powers should both be in the hands of a doctor director, as foreseen in article 13 of the order of application of the law of 18 December 1839. On 25 November 1861, the report concluded that "a single authority would be desirable, that every administrative or medical element work under a single impulse towards the good that is offered" *Rapport de la Commission instituée pour la réforme et l'aménagement du service d'aliénés du departement de la Seine* (Paris: 1861).
27. P. Pinel, *La Médecine clinique rendue plus précise et plus exacte par l'application de l'analyse, ou Recueil et résultats d'observations sur les maladies aiguës, faites à la Salpêtrière* (Paris: Brosson et Gabon, 1804, 2nd edition) pp. 5-6.
28. Falret, for example, puts questioning in the forefront of clinical examination by laying down as principle that "if you wish to know the tendencies, the direction of the mind, and the dispositions of feelings which are the source of every symptom, do not reduce your duty as observer to the passive role of secretary to the patients, of stenographer of their words or narrator of their actions . . . The first principle to be followed . . . is therefore to change one's passive role of the observer of the patient's words and actions into an active role, and frequently seek to provoke and call forth symptoms which would never arise spontaneously" J.-P. Falret, "Discours d'ouverture: De la direction à imprimer à l'observation des aliénés," in *Leçons cliniques de médecine mentale faites à l'hospice de la Salpêtrière* (Paris: J.-B. Baillière, 1854) pp. 19-20.
29. Ibid. 8th Lesson, pp. 221-222: "Sometimes one must artfully lead the conversation to certain subjects one supposes are related to unhealthy ideas or sentiments; these calculated interviews act as touchstones for bringing to light morbid preoccupations. Considerable experience and much art is often necessary to observe certain insane people appropriately." See also, J.-P. Falret, *De l'enseignement clinique des maladies mentales* (Paris: Martinet, 1850) pp. 68-71.
30. Hence the numerous declarations that insist on the need to collect observations on the patients in "registers" which recapitulate the history of their illness. P. Pinel recommends "keeping exact journals of the progress and diverse forms taking by the insanity throughout its course, from its onset to its end" *Traité médico-philosophique*, section VI, § xii, p. 256; *A Treatise on Insanity*, Section VI, p. 246. C.F.S. Giraudy stresses this in his *Mémoire sur la Maison nationale de Charenton*, pp. 17-22. Moreau de Tours notes: "Information obtained about the patient are kept in the register, which must also contain the necessary details on the progress of the illness (. . .) This register is a veritable notebook of observations, a statistical study of which is made at the end of each year, which is a source of precious documents" J.J. Moreau de Tours, "Lettres médicales sur la colonie d'aliénés de Ghéel" p. 267. On this form of disciplinary writing, see M. Foucault, *Surveiller et Punish*, pp. 191-193; *Discipline and Punish*, pp. 191-192.
31. In 1817 Esquirol began a clinical class of mental illnesses at Salpêtrière, which he continued until his appointment as head doctor at Charenton in 1826. See, R. Semelaigne, *Les Grands Aliénistes français* (Paris: G. Steinheil, 1894) p. 128; and, C. Bouchet, *Quelques mots sur Esquirol* (Nantes: C. Mellinet, 1841) p. 1.
32. At Bicêtre from 1833 to 1839, Guillaume Ferrus, appointed head doctor at the beginning of 1826, gave "Clinical lessons on mental illnesses," which are reproduced in the *Gazette médicale de Paris*, vol. I, no. 65, 1833; vol. II, no. 39, 1834, p. 48; vol. IV, no. 25, 1836, pp. 28, 44 and 45; and in the *Gazette des hôpitaux*, 1838, pp. 307, 314, 326, 345, 352, 369, 384, 399, 471, 536, 552, 576, 599 and 612; 1839, pp. 5, 17, 33, 58, 69, 82, 434 and 441. In 1840, after the departure of Ferrus, Leuret organized clinical lessons which he continued until 1847, published in part in the *Gazette des hôpitaux*, vol. II, 1840, pp. 233, 254, 269 and 295.
33. At Salpêtrière, Jules Baillarger (1809-1890) took up clinical teaching in 1841. Jean-Pierre Falret, appointed doctor of a section for the insane, in turn began clinical teaching in 1843,

part of which is published in the *Annales médico-psychologiques*, vol. IX, September 1847, pp. 232-264, and vol. XII, October 1849, pp. 524-579. These lessons are reprinted (with the same title) in: *De l'enseignement clinique des maladies mentale.* See, M. Wiriot, *L'Enseignement clinique dans les hôpitaux de Paris entre 1794 and 1848*, Medical Thesis, Paris, 1970, no. 334 (Vincennes: Chaumé, 1970).

34. J.-P. Falret, *De l'enseignement clinique*, p. 126.
35. Ibid. p. 127: "The public narration of their illness made by the insane is an even more precious help to the doctor . . . , the doctor must be powerful in a very different way in the wholly new conditions of the clinic, that is to say, when the professor makes all the phenomena of his illness perceptible to the patient in the presence of more or less numerous auditors."
36. Ibid. p. 119: "If the patients accept . . . he will give the history of their illness with the fixed principle of recounting only that which is completely known to them, and he will frequently stop to ask them if he is truthfully expressing the facts that they themselves have told him earlier."
37. Ibid. p. 125: "The account of their illness, given in all its developments, often makes a strong impression on the insane, who themselves testify to its truth with visible satisfaction, and enjoy entering into the greatest detail in order to complete the account, as if they were astonished and proud that someone should take such an interest in them so as to know their entire history."
38. Marie François Xavier Bichat (1771-1802), after having been introduced to surgery in Lyon in the department of Marc-Antoine Petit (1762-1840) and, in June 1794, becoming the student of Pierre Joseph Delsaut (1744-1795), surgeon at the Hôtel-Dieu, devoted himself, after his appointment in 1800, to pathological anatomy, undertaking to establish the definite relationships between alterations of tissues and clinical symptoms. See, *Traité des membranes en général et des diverses membranes en particulier* (Paris: Gabon, 1800). He set out his conceptions in *Anatomie générale appliquée à la physiologie et à la médecine*, in four volumes (Paris: Brosson et Gabon, 1801); English translation, *General Anatomy, applied to Physiology and the Practice of Medicine*, trans. C. Coffyn (London: 1824).

But it was above all Gaspard Llaurent Bayle (1774-1816) and René Théophile Laënnec (1781-1826) who strove to found clinical medicine and pathological anatomy in a single discipline. Bayle was one of the first to formulate the methodology of the young school of clinical anatomy in his thesis defended 4 Ventôse Year X/24 February 1802: *Considérations sur la nosologie, la médecine d'observation et la médecine pratique, suiviies d'observations pour servir à l'histoire des pustules gangreneuses*, Medical Thesis, Paris, no. 70 (Paris: Boiste [Gabon], 1802). He sets out the ideas that he will develop and clarify in, *Recherches sur la phtisie pulmonaire* (Paris: Gabon, 1810); English translation, *Researches on Pulmonary Phthisis*, trans. W. Barrow (London: Longman, 1815), and in "Considérations générales sur les secours que l'anatomie pathologique peut fournir à la médecine," in *Dictionnaire des sciences médicales*, vol. II (Paris: C.L.F. Panckoucke, 1812) pp. 61-78. R.T. Laënnec renewed pulmonary pathology by endeavouring to "put the diagnosis of internal organic lesions on the same level as the diagnosis of surgical illnesses," *De l'auscultation médiate, ou Traité du diagnostic des malades des poumons et du cœur, fondé principalament sur ce nouveau moyen d'exploration*, two volumes (Paris: Brosson and Chaudé, 2nd revised and expanded edition, 1826) vol. 1, p. xxv; English translation, *A Treatise on Mediate Auscultation, and on Diseases of the Lungs and Heart*, translated by a Member of the College of Physicians (London: J.B. Bailliere, 1846), and in his posthumous work, *Traité inédit sur l'anatomie pathologique, ou Exposition des altérations visible qu'éprouve le corps humain dans l'état de maladie* (Paris: Alcan, 1884).

On Bichat, see the pages in chapter 8, "Ouvrez quelques cadavres" of M. Foucault, *Naissance de la clinique. Une archéologie du regard médical* (Paris: P.U.F., 1963) pp. 125-148; English translation, *The Birth of the Clinic. An Archeology of Medical Perception*, trans. A.M. Sheridan Smith (London: Tavistock and New York: Pantheon, 1973), ch. 8, "Open Up a Few Corposes" pp. 124-148. More generally, see, J.E. Rochard, *Histoire de la chirurgie française au XIXe siècle* (Paris: J.-B. Baillière, 1875); O. Temkin, "The role of surgery in the rise of modern medical thought" *Bulletin of the History of Medicine*, Baltimore, Md: vol. 25, no. 3, 1951, pp. 248-259; E.H. Ackerknecht, (i) "Pariser chirgurgie von 1794-1850" *Gesnerus*, vol. 17, 1960, pp. 137-144, and (ii) *Medicine at the Paris Hospitals, 1794-1848*

(Baltimore Md: The Johns Hopkins Press, 1967); French translation, *La Médecine hospitalière à Paris, 1794-1848*, trans. F. Blateau (Paris, Payot, 1986); P. Huard and M. Grmeck, eds., *Sciences, médecine, pharmacie, de la Révolution à l'Empire, 1789-1815* (Paris: Éd. Dacosta, 1970) pp. 140-145; M.-J. Imbault-Huart, *L'École pratique de dissection de Paris de 1750 à 1822, ou l'influence du concept de médecine pratique et de médecine d'observation dans l'enseignement médico-chirurgical au XVIII*[e] *siècle*, Thèse de doctorat ès lettres, University-Paris-I, 1973, reprinted University of Lille-III, 1975; P. Huard, "Concepts et réalités de l'éducation et de la profession médico-chirurgicales pendant la Révolution" *Journal des savants*, April-June 1973, pp. 126-150.

On G.L. Bayle, see, M.-J. Imbault-Huart, "Bayle, Laënnec et la méthode anatomo-clinique" *Revue du Palais de la Découverte*, special number, 22 August 1981, pp. 179-89. Later, J. Duffin, "Gaspard Laurent Bayle et son legs scientifique: au-delà de l'anatomie pathologique" *Canadian Bulletin of Medical History*, Winnipeg, vol. 31, 1986, pp. 167-184.

On Laënnec, see, P. Huard, "Les chirurgiens et l'esprit chirurgical en France au XVIIIe siècle," *Clio Medica*, vol. 15, nos. 3-4, 1981. Later, J. Duffin (i) "The medical philosophy of R.T. Laënnec (1781-1826)" *History and Philosophy of the Life Sciences*, vol. 8, 1986, pp. 195-219, and (ii) "La médecine anatomo-clinique: naissance et constitution d'une médecine moderne" *Revue médicale de la Suisse Romande*, no. 109, 1989, pp. 1005-1012.

39. In the 1830s we begin to see the separation of the insane from idiot children, in the form of both statements of principle and the beginning of institutional realizations. Appointed to Bicêtre in 1826, in 1834 Guillaume Ferrus called for the creation of "special establishments in which every curative technique was brought together" *Des aliénés*, p. 190. In 1839, in a report of the Medical Commission of Paris Hospitals, Ferrus emphasized again "the usefulness of the creation of a children's section at Bicêtre" (quoted by D.M. Bourneville, *Assistance, Traitement et Éducation des enfants idiots et dégénérés. Rapport fait au congrès national d'Assistance publique, Lyon, juin 1894* [Paris: Publications du Progrès médical, 1895] p. 142). One of the first institutional realizations was that of Jean-Pierre Falret who, after his appointment to Salpêtrière on 30 March 1831, decided to bring together 80 idiots and imbeciles in a common section. However, their slowness is such that, in 1835, J.-B. Parchappe can still write that the presence of young idiots in "insane asylums, in the absence of special quarters, offers every kind of drawback (. . .) I consider the creation of a quarter for children in insane asylums to be an indispensable necessity" *Des principes à suivre dans la fondation et la construction des asiles d'aliénés* (Paris: Masson, 1853) p. 89. On this point, see the historical account of D.M. Bourneville, *Assistance, Traitement et Éducation des enfants idiots*, ch. 1: "Aperçu historique de l'assistance et du traitement des enfants idiots et dégénérés," pp. 1-7. See below, lecture of 16 January 1974.
40. In the 1880s, when the nosology of neurological disorders reaches its completion, the field of the neuroses jettisons the mass of organic symptoms (paralysis, anesthesia, sensorial disorders, algia, etcetera) which are supplanted by the new clinical neuropathology attached to the study of localized lesions of the nerves and marrow and specialized structures of the encephalon. What remains of this field tends, around 1885 to 1890, to be organized around four major clinical groups: (a) choreic neuroses (hysterical chorea, St. Vitus's dance); (b) neurasthenia; (c) hysteria; and (d) obsessions and phobias.
41. Foucault's analysis is inspired here by R. Castel, *Le Psychanalysme* (Paris: Maspero, 1973) about which he wrote in the manuscript for the lecture of 7 November 1973: "This is a radical book because, for the first time, psychoanalysis is situated solely within psychiatric practice and power."

nine

16 January 1974

The modes of generalization of psychiatric power and the psychiatrization of childhood. ~ 1. The theoretical specification of idiocy. The criterion of development. ~ Emergence of a psychopathology of idiocy and mental retardation. Édouard Seguin: instinct and abnormality. ~ 2. The institutional annexation of idiocy by psychiatric power. ~ The "moral treatment" of idiots: Seguin. ~ The process of confinement and the stigmatization of the dangerousness of idiots. ~ Recourse to the notion of degeneration.

I WOULD LIKE TO try to pick out the points and forms of the generalization of psychiatric power, which I have the impression took place fairly early on. I do not think, if you like, that the generalization of psychiatric power is contemporary with or an effect of psychoanalytic practice. It seems to me that there was a diffusion of psychiatric power very early on, a transmission that dates from a much earlier period and the effect of which is, of course, transmission of an archaic form of psychiatric power.

It seems to me that this diffusion of psychiatric power was carried out on the basis of childhood, that is to say, starting from the psychiatrization of childhood. Of course, you find sketches and forms of this generalization based on personages other than the child—we find them quite early on, for example, in connection with the criminal, with the development of psychiatric legal expertise and of the notion of monomania—but in the end it seems to me that it was especially the child much more than the adult who provided the support for the diffusion of psychiatric power in the nineteenth century.

In other words—anyway, this is the hypothesis I would like to try out before you—I think that we should look for the principle of diffusion of psychiatric power in the direction of the coupling of the hospital and the school, of health institution and the system of learning (pedagogical institution, model of health). And as an epigraph for what follows I would like to quote one of those short and dazzling sentences loved by Canguilhem. He wrote: " 'Normal' is the term used by the nineteenth century to designate the scholastic prototype and the state of organic health."[1] It seems to me that, in the end, the diffusion of psychiatric power takes place by way of this development of the concept of the "normal."

It would be quite natural to expect the psychiatrization of childhood to take place by two routes apparently laid down in advance: by way of the discovery of the mad child on the one hand, and, on the other, by way of bringing childhood to light as the locus of the foundation and origin of mental illness.*

Now, my impression is that things did not happen in this way exactly. In actual fact, it seems to me that the discovery of the mad child took place rather late and was much more the secondary effect of the psychiatrization of the child than its place of origin. I think the mad child appeared rather late in the nineteenth century;[2] we see it emerging around Charcot, that is to say, around hysteria, around the 1880s, and it does not enter psychiatry by the royal road of the asylum, but by way of private consultation. The first children you see appearing in the file of the history of psychiatry are the children of private clients; they are generally, with regard to Charcot, idiot grandsons of Russian grand dukes, or somewhat hysterical Latin American granddaughters.[3] It is these children, framed moreover by the parents, this trinity, who appeared in Charcot's offices around the 1880s. And it was not at all the tightening of family discipline, or the imposition of school discipline, which allowed the mad child to be picked out in the course of the nineteenth century.

* The manuscript clarifies: "through the action of anamnesis, the questioning of patients and their family, and the accounts of their life."

On the other hand, neither was a fundamental, privileged, founding relationship between childhood and madness brought to light by the anamneses, the autobiographical accounts, to which psychiatric power constrained patients throughout the nineteenth century. When the mad were asked to recount their life, this was not at all an attempt to account for their madness on the basis of what happened in their childhood, but in order to grasp a madness already constituted, as it were, in this childhood, or at any rate, some forewarning signs of a predisposition to madness, which would already mark their childhood, or in order to find the signs of hereditary predisposition. And nor was the mad content of childhood experience questioned through anamnesis. So, the mad child, the child as object of psychiatry, appeared late, and a fundamental relationship between childhood and madness was not a question early on.

I would say then—this is the hypothesis I want to consider—that psychiatrization of the child, however paradoxical this may be, did not come about by way of the mad child or the madness of childhood, by way of the constitutive relationship between madness and childhood. It seems to me that psychiatrization of the child came about through a completely different figure: the imbecilic child, the idiot child, the child who will soon be called retarded, that is to say, a child about whom one was careful to say, right from the start, in the first thirty years of the nineteenth century, that he was not mad.[4] Psychiatrization of the child took place through the intermediary of the child who was not mad and this was the point from which psychiatric power was generalized.

I think we can pick out two apparently completely divergent processes. One is of a purely theoretical order. It can be analyzed on the basis of medical texts, observations, and nosographic treatises. This is the process of the theoretical elaboration of the notion of imbecility or idiocy as a phenomenon absolutely distinct from madness.

Summarizing things very schematically, we can say that until the end of the eighteenth century, what was called imbecility, stupidity and, already, idiocy, had no distinctive features in comparison with madness in general. It was nothing other than a species of madness, distinguished, of course, from a series of other species, but which in any case belonged to the general category of madness. Sometimes, for example, you had a sort of major opposition between madness in the form of "frenzy" ("*fureur*"),[5] that is to say, of violence, of temporary agitation, if you like, a madness in the form of "more," and then a madness in the form of "less," which was instead a kind of dejection, inertia, on non-agitation,[6] and which was in fact what was called "dementia,"[7] "stupidity,"[8] "imbecility," etcetera. Or again, imbecility or stupidity was defined as a particular form in a series in which one could find mania, melancholy, and dementia.[9] At the most we can [pick out]* some indications identifying idiocy as an illness that it was easier to find in children; dementia, on the other hand, being an illness exactly similar in its content, but only occurring after a certain age.[10]

The place occupied by imbecility or idiocy in the nosographic tables may seem surprising—it is either a broad notion, generally opposed to agitation and frenzy (*fureur*), or a precise notion—in any case, one is a little surprised to see imbecility appear within madness at a time when, precisely, madness was essentially characterized by delirium, that is to say, by error, false belief, licentious imagination, and assertion without any connection with reality.[11] Except, if it is true that madness is essentially defined by this core delirium, can idiocy or imbecility be seen as part of this large family of deliria? Actually, the nature of imbecility is assimilated—along with dementia, moreover—to a sort of delirium that either arrives late, as in the case of dementia, when it has reached its most acute point, that is to say, the stage when it is disappearing and where, pushed to its extreme point of exasperation, of violence, it falls in on itself, collapses and is nullified as delirium, or else it arrives much earlier, as in the case of idiocy. In this kind of eighteenth century nosography, imbecility is the error of delirium, but so generalized, so total, that it can no longer conceive the least truth or form the least idea; it is, as it were, error that has become obnubilation, that is to say, delirium that has fallen into its own night. This is what Jacquelin Dubuisson, a psychiatrist who was a contemporary of Pinel, said about idiotism in 1816, and so fairly late: "Idiotism is a condition of stupor or of the abolition of the intellectual and affective functions, the result of which is a more or less complete obtuseness; in addition there are often alterations of the vital functions. These sort of insane individuals, deprived of the

* (Recording:) find

sublime faculties that distinguish thinking and social man, are reduced to a purely mechanical existence that makes their condition abject and wretched. *Causes*. The causes are more or less the same as those of dementia, from which idiotism only differs by a more intense and profound alteration in the injured functions."[12]

Idiotism, therefore, is not at all the kind of first, elementary ground on the basis of which other, more violent or intense pathological conditions could develop; it is instead the absolute, total form of madness. It is the vertigo of madness, turning on itself so quickly that none of the elements, the beliefs of the delirium can be detected; it is the non-color produced by colors whirling on themselves. It is this effect of the "obnubilation" of all thought, and even of all perception, which is defined in idiotism, so that in this period it is nonetheless thought of as a category of delirium, despite the absence of symptoms.[13] This, more or less, is the, hastily reconstructed, theoretical situation at the end of the eighteenth century.

How will the new notion of idiocy, of mental retardation, of imbecility be developed in the first forty years of the nineteenth century, that is to say, from Esquirol to Seguin in 1843? Here again, I refer just to texts, to theoretical developments, and say nothing about institutions or real practices.

I think we can fix two important moments in the development of this notion of idiocy in the theoretical texts of psychiatry at the beginning of the nineteenth century.* The moment typified by Esquirol and his texts of 1817, 1818, and 1820,[14] and then Belhomme's book of 1824.[15] At this point you see a completely new notion of idiocy emerging, which you would not be able to find in the eighteenth century. Esquirol defines it in this way: "Idiocy is not a disease, but a condition in which the intellectual faculties are never manifested, or have never been sufficiently developed . . ."[16] And, in 1824, Belhomme more or less textually summarizes the same definition; he says that "idiocy is . . . a constitutional condition in which the intellectual functions have never developed . . ."[17]

This definition is important because it introduces the notion of development; it makes development, or rather the absence of development the [distinctive] criterion for distinguishing between madness and idiocy.

---

* The manuscript says at this point: "The specification of idiocy in comparison with dementia—that is to say the form or stage of mental illness to which it is closest—is carried out in two stages."

Idiocy is not defined therefore with reference to truth or error, or with reference to the ability or inability to control oneself, or with reference to the intensity of the delirium, but with reference to development. Now, in these definitions, and in the descriptions following them, Esquirol and Belhomme make a sort of binary use of development. Development, for both Esquirol and Belhomme, is something one may or may not have, from which one has or has not benefited; one is developed in the same way as one has will or intelligence; one is not developed in the same way as one lacks intelligence or will. There is still a sort of very simplistic use of this notion of development.

However, despite this simplistic use of the notion, the criterion of a development one does or does not have, from which one does or does not benefit, allows a certain number of developments for covering this theoretical domain.

First, it allows a clear chronological distinction. If idiocy is an absence of development, then it is necessary, it is normal, that madness* is something that appears from the outset—and this in contradistinction to other forms of the weakening of thought, intellect, or perception, such as dementia, which, like the other mental illnesses of mania, monomania, lypemania, etcetera, appears at the earliest with puberty.[18] So, a chronological distinction is established at this time.

Second, there is a difference in the type of evolution involved. If idiocy is non-development, then it is stable and acquired once and for all: the idiot does not develop. Dementia, however, which is also an enfeeblement of thought, in contrast with idiocy, is a mental illness that evolves, which gets worse from year to year, which may stabilized for a time, and [which] may possibly be cured.[19]

The third difference is that idiocy is always linked to organic defects of the constitution.[20] It is therefore a kind of disability,[21] or is even included in the general table of monstrosities,[22] whereas dementia may be accompanied by accidental lesions that occur at a particular moment.[23]

Finally, there is a difference in the symptoms. Since dementia is a late illness which arises on the basis of certain processes and, possibly, organic lesions, it will always have a past, that is to say, in dementia we

* The argument here suggests that this should be 'idiocy'; G.B.

will always find some remains, either of intelligence, or even of delirium, but in any case something either positive or negative from the past of this condition will remain. The idiot, however, is someone without a past, someone for whom nothing remains, whose existence has not left, and will never leave, the least trace in his memory. And so you end up with Esquirol's canonical formulations that were repeated for more than a century: "The man suffering dementia is deprived of goods he previously enjoyed: he is a rich man who has become poor. The idiot has always been in a state of misfortune and wretchedness."[24]

You can see that this notion of development, despite its crude, strictly binary use, nonetheless allows certain distinctions to be made and enables a dividing line to be drawn between two kinds of features: those of something that defines an illness, and those of something belonging to disability or monstrosity, but not illness.

The second stage, some years later, around the 1840s, is Seguin, whom we will find throughout the process of the institutionalization and psychiatrization of childhood, and who, in his *Traitement moral des idiots*, provides the major concepts on the basis of which the psychology, the psychopathology, of mental retardation will be developed throughout the nineteenth century.[25]

Seguin makes a distinction between idiots strictly speaking and retarded children: "I was the first to point out the extreme difference separating them . . . Even the superficial idiot displays an arrested physiological and psychological development."[26] So, we do not have an absence of development, but arrested development. As for the retarded child, according to Seguin, what distinguishes him from the idiot is that he is not someone whose development has been halted. He is not someone whose development is arrested, but someone who "develops more slowly than children his age; he is behind their progress from start to finish, and this daily increasing backwardness ends up establishing an enormous difference, an insurmountable distance, between him and them."[27] This is the outcome of a continuous development.

I think the two related definitions, of the idiot as someone affected by arrested development, and of the retarded individual as someone whose development, while continuous, is simply slower, are important theoretically. They bring in several notions that will be influential in the practice of the psychiatrization of the child.

First, the way in which Seguin conceives of development in his *Traitement moral des idiots* is no longer, as it was in Esquirol, something with which one is endowed or of which one is deprived, as with intelligence or will; development is a process which affects organic life and psychological life, a dimension along which neurological or psychological organizations, functions, behaviors, and acquisitions are spread out. It is a temporal dimension and no longer a kind of faculty or quality with which one is endowed.

Second, this temporal dimension is, in a sense, common to everyone. No one escapes it, but it is a dimension along which one may be halted. To that extent, development is common to everyone, but it is common more as a sort of optimum, as a rule of chronological succession with an ideal outcome. Development is therefore a kind of norm with reference to which one is situated, much more than a potentiality that is possessed in itself.

Third, you can see that this norm of development has two variables in the sense that, either one may be halted at this or that stage in this scale of development, along this dimension—and the idiot is precisely someone who is halted very early on at a certain stage—[or], it is no longer the stage at which one is halted, but the speed with which one crosses this dimension—and someone who is retarded is precisely someone who, without being blocked at a certain stage, is checked at the level of his speed. Hence there are two pathologies, which complement one another moreover, one being the final effect of the other: a pathology of being blocked [at a] stage [which, as it happens, will be] terminal, and a pathology of slowness.

Hence, the fourth important thing is that we see a double normativity taking shape. On the one hand, inasmuch as the idiot is someone halted at a certain stage, the scale of idiocy will be assessed by reference to the adult as the norm: the adult will appear as both the real and ideal end of development; so that the adult will function as the norm. On the other hand, the variable of slowness—Seguin's text says it very clearly—is defined by other children: a retarded child is someone who develops more slowly than the others. A consequence of this is that some kind of childhood average, or a particular majority of children, will constitute the other norm in relation to which the retarded child will be situated. So these two phenomena of mental deficiency—idiocy in the strict sense, and retardation—will be situated by reference to two normative levels: the adult, representing the final stage, and other children, defining the average speed of development.

The fifth point in this development is that idiocy and, with greater reason, mental retardation, can no longer be defined as illnesses. There was still ambiguity in Esquirol with regard to whether idiocy should be accorded the status of illness or non-illness. After all, in Esquirol, idiocy was the absence of something, and to that extent could be characterized as an illness. In Seguin, the idiot and the mentally retarded are not patients: they cannot be said to lack stages; they have either not reached a stage or they have reached it too slowly. Seguin's idiot or mentally retarded individual is someone who has not left the normal, or rather, he is situated at a lower degree within something that is the norm itself, that is to say, child development. The idiot is a particular sort of child, not someone who is ill; the idiot is someone more or less sunk within a childhood that is normal childhood itself. The idiot is a certain degree of childhood, or again, if you like, childhood is a certain way of passing more or less quickly through the degrees of idiocy, debility, or mental retardation. Consequently, you can see that idiocy or mental retardation cannot really be considered as pathological deviations, even if, in the end, it really is an illness, or something like a disability or organic lesion, which causes them. They are temporal varieties of stages within the normative development of the child. The idiot belongs to childhood, as previously he belonged to illness.

A number of consequences follow from this, the main one of which is obviously this: If it is true that the idiot or retarded child is someone stuck at a certain level, not within the field of illness, but within the temporality of childhood, then the treatment he is to be given will be no different in kind than that given to any child. That is to say, the only way to treat an idiot or retarded child is quite simply to impose education on them, obviously with possible variations and specifications concerning method, but there is nothing else to do but impose the educational schema itself. The therapy for idiocy will be pedagogy itself, a more radical pedagogy which will search further, which will go back deeper into the archaic roots of all this, but a pedagogy all the same.

Finally, the sixth and final point I want to emphasize here is that, for Seguin, these halts and this delay or slowness in the developmental process do not belong to the order of illness.[28] But they quite evidently bring with them the sanctions of phenomena that fail to appear, of organizations that do not emerge, and of acquisitions of which the child is not capable: this is the negative side of mental retardation. However, there are also positive phenomena which are nothing other than the bringing to light, the emergence, the failure to integrate certain elements that normal development would have had to cover up, resist or integrate. This is what Seguin calls "instinct," which becomes blatant due to arrested or extremely slow development. Instinct, which belongs to childhood, is given from the start and it appears within idiocy or mental retardation in the wild state without being integrated. "Idiocy" says Séguin, "is an infirmity of the nervous system the radical effect of which is to withdraw all or part of the child's organs and faculties from the regular action of his will, which hands him over to his instincts and removes him from the moral world."[29]

So you can see that, all in all, what appears through this analysis of mental deficiency is the specification of organizations, conditions, or behaviors within childhood which are not strictly pathological, but which are deviant with respect to two norms: that of other children and that of the adult. What we see appearing here is precisely abnormality: the idiot or retarded child is not a child who is ill; he is an abnormal child.

What then, secondly, are the positive phenomena of this abnormality, or what is it, beyond divergence, deviation from the norm, that this abnormality frees? It is instinct. That is to say, these phenomena are not symptoms, they are kinds of both natural and anarchical elements. In short, instincts are to abnormality what symptoms are to illness. Abnormality does not have symptoms so much as instincts, which are, as it were, its natural element.* I think instinct as the real content of abnormality is what we see taking shape in Seguin's analysis of retardation

* The manuscript says: "Whereas illness is characterized by symptoms and manifests itself in dysfunctions or deficiencies, instinct is more the nature of abnormality than its symptom."

and idiocy. This is what can be said at the simple level of discourse and theory about the establishment of this profoundly new category of abnormality as distinct from illness. And I think that the confiscation of this new category of abnormality by medicine, its psychiatrization, was precisely the principle on which the diffusion of psychiatric power was based.

Actually, in the same period as the theoretical domain I have rapidly surveyed was being constituted, at the same time as this was taking place, not in the background, not as a consequence, but at the same time and, in truth, as a real condition of possibility of this development, a completely different and apparently contradictory process was taking place. Since if you go from Pinel or Dubuisson to Seguin, by way of Esquirol, you see the series of steps by which idiocy was specified in relation to madness, by which idiocy and mental illness were disconnected: theoretically, idiocy is no longer an illness at the level of its medical status. Now, at the same time, there is a contrary process, which is not theoretical, but a process of institutionalization, and this is the establishment of idiocy within the psychiatric space, a colonization of idiocy by psychiatry. And this is an extremely strange phenomenon.

In fact, if you go back to the situation at the end of the eighteenth century, to the time of Pinel, you still find people classified as "imbeciles" in the deepest depths of houses of confinement. Most of these people are adult, and one imagines that some at least of these were later described as "lunatics," but you also find twelve-year-old children.[30] Now, when the question of imbecility really began to be posed, and posed in medical terms, the first treatment was precisely to get rid of them, to deport them from that kind of confused space of confinement, and to annex them, basically, to institutions for the deaf and dumb, that is to say, to strictly pedagogical institutions where one had to compensate for certain defects, inadequacies, and disabilities, so that at the end of the eighteenth century you see the first practical approach to the treatment of idiots in homes for the deaf and dumb, and precisely with Itard, with whom, moreover, Seguin was initially trained.[31]

And then you see them gradually brought back into the asylum space. In 1834, Voisin, one of the important psychiatrists of the time, opens an institute of "orthophrenia" at Issy, where what was involved was precisely having a place for the treatment of poor, mentally defective children; but this was still an institution half-way, as it were, between the specialized pedagogy for the deaf and dumb and a psychiatric center in the strict sense.[32] Then, in the years immediately following this, from 1835 to 1845, in the period when Seguin defines idiocy outside of mental illness, in the recently organized or reorganized big asylums, you see wings being opened, for the retarded, idiots, often hysterics and epileptics, and all of them children. In the years 1831 to 1841, J.-P. Falret organizes a wing at Salpêtrière;[33] in 1833, Ferrus opens a wing for idiot children at Bicêtre,[34] for which Seguin becomes responsible in 1842.[35]

Throughout the second half of the nineteenth century you find the colonization of idiot children within the psychiatric space. And even if an establishment is opened specifically for these children at Perray-Vaucluse in 1873,[36] it remains the case that at the end of the century, at Bicêtre,[37] Salpêtrière,[38] and Villejuif,[39] there are still psychiatric wings for these mentally defective children. Moreover, not only is this colonization effectuated, de facto, by the opening of these sections within the psychiatric space, but a decision of the Minister of the Interior in 1840 states explicitly that the 1838 law on the confinement of the insane applies equally to idiots: this is no more than a matter of a simple ministerial decision that is based on the principle that idiots are still a category of the insane.[40]

So, at a moment when there is this clear theoretical division between insanity and idiocy, there are a whole series of institutions and administrative measures which lump together what was in the process of being distinguished. To what does this institutional annexation, contemporary with the theoretical distinction, correspond?

It might be thought that this theoretical distinction is quite simply the effect of the organization of primary education at this time: Guizot's law dates from 1833.[41] It might be thought that with mental retardation or mental deficiency being filtered through the primary education then being developed, idiots identified as problems within these educational establishments will be gradually expelled into the asylums. This is in fact true, but not for the period I am considering. In actual fact it is at the end of the nineteenth century that generalized primary education will act as a filter, and the major inquiries which take place at the end of the century on mental deficiency take place in an educational milieu, that is to say, the schools are asked for the facts for the inquiry.[42] These inquiries are indeed conducted with primary school teachers, and the question will focus on the nature and possibilities of schooling. For example, in 1892-1893, when Rey conducts an inquiry into mental deficiency in the Bouches-du-Rhône, he addresses himself to primary school teachers and, in order to identify the idiots, imbeciles, and mentally deficient, he asks which children do not follow school activities in an appropriate way, which children make themselves noted by their unruliness, and which children cannot even attend school.[43] This is the basis on which the great patchwork will be established. Primary education acts in fact as the filter and reference for the phenomena of mental retardation.

However, this does not apply to the period I am considering, that is to say, around 1830 to 1840. In other words, it is not so as to provide children with schools, or because of a failure to provide them with schools, that the problem arises of where to put them. The problem of where to put them does not arise in terms of their schooling, of their ability or inability to be educated at school, but in terms of their parents' work. That is to say: what can be done so that the care needed by an idiot child does not make him an obstacle to working parents? What's more, this exactly corresponds to the government's concern at the time that the law on primary education was being made. You know that if "nursery schools" ("*salles d'asile*") were created in the 1830s, that is to say, crèches and kindergartens, and if schooling was provided for children in this period, it was not so much in order to equip them for future employment, as to free their parents for work by no longer having to concern themselves with their children.[44] The organization of these educational establishments at this time corresponded to the aim of releasing parents from taking care of their children so as to put them on the labor market.

The people who created the specialized establishments for idiots in this period had exactly the same concern. I remind you that Voisin opened his institute of "orthophrenia" on the rue de Sèvres, not for the rich, who could pay, but for the poor. I will quote you a text by Fernald, which is a bit later but reflects this concern exactly, and which says: "Whereas care of an idiot child at home takes up the time and energy of one person, the proportion of people employed in asylums is one person for five idiot children. The care at home of one idiot, especially if disabled, consumes the wages and abilities of the people of the household, so that an entire family falls into poverty. Humanity and good policy call for families to be relieved of responsibility for these unfortunates."[45]

In this way, and on the basis of this concern, it was decided to apply the law of confinement and assistance for inmates to poor idiot children as well. The institutional assimilation of idiots and the mad takes place precisely on the basis of this concern to release parents for possible work. In 1853 Parchappe comes to this conclusion in his *Principes à suivre dans la fondation et la construction des asiles d'aliénés*: "Mental alienation includes not only all the forms and degrees of madness in the strict sense (. . .) but also idiocy which depends on a congenital defect, and imbecility produced by an illness after birth. Lunatic asylums must therefore be founded to receive all the insane, that is to say, the mad, the idiots, and the imbeciles."[46]

And now, some years after the clear distinction between madness and idiocy, you see the notion of mental alienation move back a degree, as it were, and become the general category embracing all the forms of madness and idiocy and imbecility as well. "Mental alienation" will become the practical concept on the basis of which one will be able to cover the need to confine the mentally ill and the mentally defective using the same mechanisms and in the same places of assistance. The practical nullification of the distinction between idiocy and mental illness is sanctioned by the very strange and abstract notion of "mental alienation" as a general term covering the whole.

Now, once placed within the asylum space, the power exercised on idiot children is precisely psychiatric power in the pure state, and remains so with practically no elaboration. In the asylum for the mad a series of processes take place which by which psychiatric power is considerably elaborated, but when it is connected up with the confinement of idiots this power is simply put to work and kept going for years. At any rate, if you look at the way in which Seguin himself—who so clearly defined a difference between mental illness and idiocy in his *Traitement moral des idiots*—actually treated the idiots and mentally deficient at Bicêtre, you see that he applied exactly the same schemas of psychiatric power, but with, as it were, a magnifying and purifying effect. And within this practice, which was absolutely canonical for defining the methods for educating idiots, we find exactly the same mechanisms of psychiatric power. The education of idiots and the abnormal is psychiatric power in the pure state.

What in fact did Seguin do at Bicêtre in 1842-1843? First, he conceived of the education of idiots, which he called "moral treatment" moreover, using the same term as Leuret, to whom he refers, as first of all the confrontation of two wills: "The struggle of the two wills may be long or short, finish to the advantage of the teacher or of the pupil."[47] You recall the way in which, in psychiatric "moral treatment," the confrontation of patient and doctor was indeed the confrontation of two wills in a struggle for power. You find exactly the same formulation and the same practice in Seguin; except, one might wonder how Seguin can speak of the confrontation of two wills when it is a case of an adult and a retarded child or an idiot. We really must speak of two wills and of a confrontation between teacher and idiot, Seguin says, because the idiot seems not to have any will, but in actual fact he has the will not to will, and this is precisely what characterizes instinct. What is "instinct"?

It is a certain anarchic form of will which consists in never wanting to submit to the will of others; it is a will which refuses to organize itself in the mode of the individual's monarchical will, which consequently refuses any order and any kind of integration within a system. Instinct is a will which "*wills* not *to will*,"[48] and which stubbornly insists on not constituting itself as an adult will—the adult will being characterized, for Seguin, as a will that can obey. Instinct is an indefinite series of small refusals opposed to any will of the other person.

Again we find again a contrast with madness here. The idiot is someone who stubbornly says "no"; the mad person is someone who says a "yes," a presumptuous "yes" to all his crazy ideas, and the exasperation of the mad person's will consists precisely in saying "yes" even to things that are false. For Seguin, the idiot is someone who anarchically and stubbornly says "no" to everything, and so the teacher's role is absolutely similar to the psychiatrist's role facing the mad person: the psychiatrist must master this "yes" and transform it into a "no"; the teacher's role in his confrontation with the idiot consists in mastering this "no" and making it into a "yes" of acceptance.* The idiot's "energetic no, no, no, repeated without respite, arms crossed or hanging down, or while biting his fist,"[49] must be countered with a "power which tires him out and constantly says to him: On! On! It is up to the teacher to say it to him loudly enough, firmly enough, early enough and for long enough so that he can toe the line and show to what extent he is a man."[50]

There is confrontation, then, which is of the same type as that found in psychiatric power, and which takes place in the form of a certain surplus-power, as in psychiatric power, constituted definitively on the teacher's side. And it is in relation to the teacher's body, as to the psychiatrist's body, that special education must be conducted. Seguin emphasizes and practices this omnipotence of the teacher in his visible body.

First, the teacher must block all family power; the teacher becomes the absolute master of the child: "So long as the child is entrusted to the Master," Seguin says in an expression not lacking in style, "parents have the rights of grief, the Master has the rights of authority. Master of the application of his method, Master of the child, Master of the family's relationships with the child, *Magister*, he is thrice Master or not at all," says Seguin, who could not have had a very good grasp of Latin.[51] He is master at the level of his body and, like the psychiatrist, he must have an impeccable physique. "A clumsy, common bearing and gestures, poorly shaped, lackluster eyes set far apart, and a lifeless, expressionless gaze; or again, a fleshy mouth, thick, soft lips, incorrect pronunciation, drawling, guttural, nasal or poorly accented voice," are all absolutely proscribed for someone who wants to be Master of the idiot.[52] He must appear physically impeccable before the idiot, as a both powerful and unknown personage: "The Master must have a straightforward bearing, distinct speech and gestures, a clear-cut manner, to make him noted, listened to, seen, and recognized" straightaway by the idiot.[53]

The idiot's education must take place through its connection with this impeccable and omnipotent body. It is a physical connection, and it really is precisely through the master's body that the reality itself of the

* The manuscript adds: "Special education is the confrontation with this 'no'."

pedagogical content must pass. Seguin produces the theory and practice of this physical clinch of idiot child and omnipotent master. For example, he tells how he succeeded in subduing an unruly child: "A.H. was uncontrollably lively; climbing like a cat, slipping away like a mouse, one shouldn't have thought of getting him to stand upright and still for three seconds. I put him on a chair and sat down opposite him, holding his feet and knees between mine; one of my hands held his two on his knees, while the other constantly brought his mobile face back in front of me. Apart from eating and sleeping, we stayed like that for five weeks."[54] Consequently there is a total physical capture that serves to subject and master the body.

The same goes for looking. How do you teach an idiot to look? At any rate, you do not start by teaching him to look at things; you teach him to look at the master. His access to the reality of the world, the attention he will pay to differences between things, will begin with his perception of the master. When the idiot child's gaze wanders or gets lost, "you approach, the child struggles; your eyes seek his, he avoids your eyes; you pursue, he escapes again; you think you have got him, he closes his eyes; you are there, attentive, ready to surprise him, waiting for him to reopen his eyelids in order to penetrate his eyes with your gaze; and if, as reward for your efforts, the day he sees you for the first time, the child pushes you away, or if, in order to forget his primitive condition, his family present to the world a distorted picture of the constant care you have given him, then you will begin again to expend your life anxiously in this way, no longer for the love of this or that, but for the triumph of the doctrine of which you alone still have the secret and the courage. This was how, for four months, I pursued the elusive gaze of a child in the void. The first time his eyes met mine, he broke away, letting out a loud cry (. . .)."[55] Here again we find the feature of psychiatric power that is so prominent; the organization of all power around and with the psychiatrist's body.

Third, in this moral treatment of idiot children you find again the organization of a disciplinary space like that of the asylum. We see, for example, learning the linear distribution of bodies, individual places, gymnastic exercises—the full use of time. As Bourneville will say later, "the children must be busy from getting up until going to bed. Their activities must be constantly varied (...). From waking up, washing oneself, getting dressed, brushing one's clothes, cleaning one's shoes, making the bed, and, after that, keeping the attention constantly alert (school, workshop, gymnastics, singing, recreations, walks, games, etcetera) (...) until going to bed, when the children must be taught to lay out their clothes in an orderly way on their chair."[56] Full use of time, work.

In 1893, there were about two hundred children at Bicêtre, some of whom worked from 8.00 a.m. until 11.00 a.m., and the others from 1.00 p.m. until 5.00 p.m., as brush, shoe, and basket makers, etcetera.[57] This all went very well, since, even selling the product of their work at a very low, wholesale and not market, price, they succeeded in making "a profit of seven thousand francs";[58] after wages for the masters, running costs, and repayment of loans for the construction of the buildings, there are seven thousand francs that Bourneville thinks will give the idiots a sense of being useful to society.[59]

Finally, the last point, in which we also find again all the asylum mechanisms, is that like psychiatric power, the power over idiots is tautological in the sense I have tried to explain. That is to say, what is this psychiatric power entirely canalized through the master's body supposed to introduce, to convey within this asylum for idiots? It must introduce nothing other than the outside, that is to say, ultimately, the school itself, the school to which the children could not adapt and in relation to which, precisely, it was possible to designate them as idiots. That is to say, the psychiatric power at work here makes school power function as a sort of absolute reality in relation to which the idiot will be defined as an idiot, and, after making school power function as reality in this way, it will give it that supplement of power which will enable school power to get a hold as the general rule of treatment for idiots within the asylum. What does the psychiatric treatment of idiots do, if not precisely repeat the content of education itself in a multiplied and disciplinary form?

Consider, for example, the program of Perray-Vaucluse at the end of the nineteenth century. In 1895, there were four sections within the division for idiots. In the fourth section, the lowest, teaching was simply by sight with wooden objects: Bourneville says that this was exactly the level of infant classes. In the third section, a bit higher, there are "practical lessons, exercises in reading, reciting, sums and writing"; this is the level of preparatory classes. In the second section the children learn grammar, history, and slightly more difficult arithmetic; this is the level of the final year at primary school. In the first section the children are prepared for the school certificate.[60]

You see the tautology of psychiatric power with regard to schooling. On the one hand, school power functions as reality in relation to the psychiatric power that posits it as being that in relation to which it will be able to identify and specify those who are mentally retarded; and then, on the other hand, it will make it function within the asylum, given a supplement of power.

We have two processes therefore: the theoretical specification of idiocy and the practical annexation by psychiatric power. How could these two processes, pulling in opposite directions, give rise to medicalization?*

For the coupling of these two processes of opposing tendencies there was, I think, a simple economic reason, which, in its very humbleness, and certainly much more than the psychiatrization of mental deficiency, was at the origin of the generalization of psychiatric power. The famous 1838 law, then, which defined the modalities of confinement and the conditions of assistance to poor inmates, had to be applied to idiots. Now, in the terms of this law, the cost of board and lodgings for someone confined in the asylum was paid by the *département* or the local community from which he came; that is to say, the local community became financially responsible for those who were confined.[61] The reason why the local authorities hesitated for years to confine the mentally deficient, even after the 1840 decision, was precisely the increased burden of their financial obligations.[62] There are texts which are perfectly clear about this. For the council of a *département*, a prefecture, a town hall, to accept and support an idiot's confinement, the doctor had to guarantee to the authority in question that the idiot was not only an idiot, that he was not only unable to provide for his own needs—it was not even enough to say that his family could not provide for his needs—but, and this was the

* The manuscript specifies: "psychiatric."

only condition on which the local authorities agreed to support him, he had to say that he was dangerous, that is to say, that he could commit arson, murder, rape, etcetera. The doctors of the period from 1840 to 1860 say this clearly. They say: In order to get care for him we have to write false reports, to make the situation look worse than it is and depict the idiot or mental defective as someone who is dangerous.

In other words, the notion of danger becomes necessary in order to transform an act of assistance into a phenomenon of protection and thus enable those responsible for assistance to accept that responsibility. Danger is the third element enabling the procedure of confinement and assistance to be set going, and the doctors actually give certificates in these terms. Now what is strange is that, on the basis of this kind of minor circumstance, which raises quite simply the problem of the cost of abnormality that we always come across in the history of psychiatry, the problem of the cost of abnormality will have a major effect, because, with the complaints of these doctors who, from 1840 to 1850, complain about being forced to accuse idiots of being dangerous, you see the gradual development of a whole medical literature that increasingly takes itself seriously, which will, if you like, stigmatize the mentally deficient and actually make him into someone who is dangerous.[63] Which means that fifty years later, when Bourneville writes his report, *Assistance, Traitement et Éducation des enfants idiots et dégénérés*, idiot children have become dangerous.[64] Cases are regularly cited proving that idiots are dangerous: they are dangerous because they masturbate in public, commit sexual offences, and are arsonists. And in 1895,* someone as serious as Bourneville tells this story in order to prove that idiots are dangerous: in the Eure *département*, someone raped a young girl who was an idiot who had become a prostitute; so that the idiot proves the danger of idiots "at the very moment she was a victim."[65] We could find a number of similar statements; I am summarizing them. In 1895 Bourneville says: "Criminal anthropology has demonstrated that a high proportion of criminals, inveterate drunks, and prostitutes are, in reality, imbeciles at birth whom no one has ever sought to improve or discipline."[66]

In this way you see the reconstitution of the broad category of all those who may represent a danger for society, those moreover whom Voisin, in

---

* 1894; 1895 is the date of publication.

1830, was already wanting to confine when he said that one should also look after those who "are . . . noticeable for their difficult character, a profound dissimulation, a wild self-esteem, a boundless pride, burning passions and terrible tendencies."[67] All of these will begin to be confined through this stigmatization of the idiot that is necessary for assistance to come into play. The outline emerges of that great reality of the both abnormal and dangerous child, the pandemonium of whom Bourneville will recount in his 1895 text when he says that, ultimately, we are dealing with idiots and through them, alongside them and absolutely linked to idiocy, a whole series of perversions, which are perversions of the instincts. You see here how this notion of instinct serves as a peg for Seguin's theory and for psychiatric practice. The children who must be confined are "children more or less defective from the intellectual point of view, but affected by perversions of the instincts: thieves, liars, masturbators, pederasts, arsonists, destroyers, murderers, poisoners, etcetera."[68]

This whole family, thus reconstituted around the idiot, constitutes, precisely, abnormal childhood. In the psychiatric order—I completely leave aside for the moment the problems of physiology and pathological anatomy—the category of abnormality did not apply to the adult at all in the nineteenth century; it was only applied to the child. In other words, I think we could summarize things by saying that in the nineteenth century, those who were mad were adults and, prior to the final years of the century, a mad child was not thought to be a real possibility; furthermore, the idea that the mad child had been discovered only arose through a retrospective projection of the adult onto the child; Charcot's mad children first, and then those of Freud soon after. However, in the nineteenth century, it is basically the adult who is mad and, on the other hand, children who are abnormal. The child was the bearer of abnormalities, and around the idiot, around the problems raised by his exclusion, this entire family, this general field of abnormality, was constituted—from the liar to the poisoner, from the pederast to the murderer, from the onanist to the arsonist—at the center of which appears the retarded child, the mentally deficient child, the idiot. Through these practical problems raised by the idiot child you see psychiatry becoming something infinitely more general and dangerous than the power that controls and corrects madness; it is becoming power over the abnormal, the power to define, control, and correct what is abnormal.

This double function of psychiatry, as power over madness and power over abnormality, corresponds to the gap between practices concerning the mad child and practices concerning the abnormal child. The disjunction between the mad child and the abnormal child seems to me to be an absolutely fundamental feature of the exercise of psychiatric power in the nineteenth century. I think it is easy to draw the following main consequences from this.

The first consequence is that psychiatry will now be able to plug into a whole series of disciplinary regimes existing around it, on the grounds of the principle that it alone is both the science and power of the abnormal. Psychiatry will be able to claim for itself everything abnormal, all these deviations and abnormalities in relation to school, military, family and other forms of discipline. The generalization, diffusion, and dissemination of psychiatric power took place in our society by way of this carving out of the abnormal child.

The second consequence is a matter of the internal rather than external consequences of diffusion. Psychiatry, as power over madness and power over abnormality, will find itself under a kind of internal obligation to define possible relationships between the abnormal child and the mad adult. It is to this end that, basically in the second half of the nineteenth century, two concepts are developed that will enable the link to be made, that is to say, the notion of instinct on the one hand, and the notion of degeneration on the other.

Actually, instinct is precisely that element whose existence is natural, but which is abnormal in its anarchical functioning, which is abnormal whenever it is not mastered or repressed. So it is the fate of this both natural and abnormal instinct, of instinct as element, as unity of nature and abnormality, which psychiatry will gradually try to reconstruct from childhood to adulthood, from nature to abnormality, and from abnormality to illness.[69] Psychiatry will expect to find the link between the abnormal child and the mad adult in the fate of instinct from childhood to adulthood.

On the other hand, "degeneration," the other great concept alongside that of "instinct," is an unfortunate concept; instinct had a career in which it remained valid as a concept for much longer. However, the notion of degeneration is also very interesting, because it is not, as is usually said, the projection of biological evolutionism onto psychiatry.

Biological evolutionism will intervene in psychiatry, take up this notion and overload it with certain connotations, but it will do this later.[70]

Degeneration, as Morel defines it, arises before Darwin and before evolutionism.[71] What is degeneration in Morel's time, and what will it basically remain until its abandonment at the beginning of the twentieth century?[72] A child who carries the traces of his parents' or ancestors' madness, as stigmata or signs, will be called "degenerate." Degeneration is therefore, as it were, the effect of abnormality produced on the child by his parents. And, at the same time, the degenerate child is an abnormal child whose abnormality is such that, in certain determinate circumstances and following certain accidents, it may produce madness. Degeneration is therefore the predisposition of abnormality in the child that will make possible the adult's madness, and, in the form of abnormality, it is the sign on the child of his ancestors' madness.

Consequently, you see this notion of degeneration pick out the family and ancestors, as a package without strict definition for the moment, and the child, and it makes the family the collective support of this double phenomenon of abnormality and madness. If abnormality leads to madness and if madness produces abnormality, it is actually because we are already within this collective support that is the family.[73]

I come to the third and last consequence. Studying the point of departure and functioning of the generalization of psychiatry, we now find ourselves faced with these two notions: degeneration and instinct. That is to say, we are seeing the emergence of something that will become what we can call, very roughly as I quite realize, the field of psychoanalysis, that is to say, of the familial destiny of instinct. What does instinct become in the family? What is the system of exchanges that take place between ancestors and descendants, children and parents, and which calls instinct into question? Take these two notions, make them function together, and it is right there that psychoanalysis will at any rate get going, will start talking.

So, the principle of the generalization of psychiatry is found on the child's side, not the adult's; it is not found in the generalized use of the notion of mental illness, but rather in the practical carving out of the field of abnormalities. It is precisely in this generalization, starting from the child and abnormality, and not from the adult and illness, that we see the emergence of the future object of psychoanalysis.

1. G. Canguilhem, *Le Normal et le Pathologique* (Paris: P.U.F., 1972, 2nd revised edition) p. 175; English translation, *On the Normal and the Pathological,* trans. Carolyn R. Fawcet (Dordrecht, Boston and London: D. Reidel, 1978) p. 145.
2. In 1856 C.S. Le Paulmier presented a study devoted specifically to the mad child: *Des affections mentales chez les enfants, et en particulier de la manie,* Paris Medical Thesis, no. 162 (Paris: Rignoux, 1856). Paul Moreau de Tours (1844-1908) published what may be considered to be the first treatise of infant psychiatry: *La Folie chez les enfants* (Paris: J.-B. Baillière, 1888).
3. After his journey in Russia in 1881 to look after the daughter of an old mayor of Moscow and that of a grand duke of Saint Petersburg, in his private practice on the Boulevard Saint Germain Charcot had to accept several children, from wealthy Russian circles, suffering from nervous ailments. As a Parisian journalist noted: "His Russian clientele in Paris is quite sizeable" (*Le Temps,* 18 March, 1881, p. 3). These cases, like those of the Latin American children, were not made the subjects of publications, apart from the case of a young "Russian Israelite" of 13 years referred to in a lecture: "De l'hystérie chez les jeunes garçons," *Progrès médical,* vol. X, no. 50, 16-23 December 1882, pp. 985-987, and no. 51, 24-31 December 1882, pp. 1003-1004; and those of Miss A. aged 15 years, and S., 17 years, originally from Moscow, referred to in *Leçons sur les maladies du système nerveux,* vol. III, Lesson VI, pp. 92-96; *Clinical Lectures on Diseases of the Nervous System,* vol. 3, pp. 77-83. See, A. Lubimov, *Le Professeur Charcot,* trans. L.A. Rostopchine (Saint Petersburg: Souvorina, 1894).
4. Thus Esquirol, while treating idiocy in connection with mental illness, distanced himself from any assimilation of the idiot to the insane by suggesting that "idiocy cannot be confused with dementia and other mental alienations, to which it belongs moreover through the lesion of intellectual and moral faculties" ("Idiotisme" in *Dictionnaire des sciences médicales,* vol. XXIII, [Paris: C.L.F. Panckoucke, 1818] p. 509). Similarly, Jacques Étienne Belhomme (1800-1880), attached to the section for idiots in Esquirol's department at Salpêtrière, suggested that "this ailment belongs exclusively to childhood, and any mental illness presenting similar phenomena to the latter after puberty should be carefully distinguished from it" *Dissertation inaugurale présentée et soutenue à la faculté de Médecine de Paris, le 1er juillet 1824* (Paris: Germer-Baillière, 1843) p. 52.
5. "Frenzy (*fureur*) is an over-excitement of nervous and muscular forces, excited by a false perception, a memory, or a false idea, characterized by an exasperation, a violent anger against present or absent individuals or objects, causes or witnesses of the event. Bouts of *fureur* are veritable paroxysms of delirium, which vary in their duration and the frequency of their recurrence" E.J. Georget, *De la folie. Considérations sur cette maladie* pp. 106-107.
6. Hence the opposition made by Joseph Daquin between the "extravagant" and the "stupid madman": "The extravagant madman comes and goes, and is continually physically agitated; he fears neither danger nor threats (...) In the imbecilic madman, the intellectual organs appear to be completely lacking; he conducts himself on the impulse of the other person, without any kind of discernment" *La Philosophie de la folie,* 1791 edition, p. 22, 1987 edition, p. 50.
7. William Cullen (1710-1790) speaks of "innate dementia," which he defines as an "imbecility of the mind for judging, by which men do not perceive or recall the relationships between things" *Apparatus ad nosologiam methodicam, seu Synopsis nosologiae methodicae in usum studiosorum,* Part IV, "Vesania" (Edinburgh: W. Creech, 1769). According to Désiré Magloire Bourneville (1840-1909), *Recueil de mémoires, notes et observations sur l'idiotie,* vol. I: *De l'idiotie* (Paris: Lecroisner and Babé, 1891) p. 4, Jean-Michel Sagar (1702-1778) devotes one and a half pages to a form of imbecility he calls *amentia* in his work, *Systema morborum sympltomaticum secundum classes, ordines, genera et species* (Vienna: Kraus, 1776). François Fodéré stated that "innate dementia seems to be the same thing as idiocy," defining it as an "Entire or partial obliteration of the affective faculties, with no appearance of either innate or acquired intellectual faculties," *Traité du délire,* vol. I, pp. 419-420.
8. (a) Under the name of *stupiditas sive morosis* Thomas Willis isolates a class of mental illnesses in chapter XIII of his *De Anima Brutorum, quae hominis vitalis ac sensitiva est* (London: R. Davis, 1672); English version, *Two Discourses concerning the Soul of Brutes,*

Which Is That of the Vital and Sensitive of Man, ed. S. Pordage (London: Harper and Leigh, 1683). From this, chapter III, "Of Stupidity or Foolishness," is reproduced in P. Cranefield, "A seventeenth-century view of mental deficiency and schizophrenia: Thomas Willis on 'Stupidity or Foolishness'," *Bulletin of the History of Medicine*, vol. 35, no. 4, 1961, pp. 291-316. See p. 293: "Stupidity, or *Morosis*, or Foolishness, although it most chiefly belongs to the Rational Soul, and signifies a defect of the Intellect and Judgment, yet it is not improperly reckoned among the Diseases of the Head or Brain; forasmuch as this *Eclipse* of the superior soul, proceeds from the Imagination and the Memory being hurt, and the failing of these depends upon the faults of the Animal Spirits, and the Brain itself." Foucault refers to this in *Histoire de la folie*, pp. 270-271 and 278-280 (both passages omitted from the English translation). See, J. Vinchon and J. Vié, "Un maître de la neuropsychiatrie au xviie siècle: Thomas Willis (1662-1675)," *Annales médico-psychologiques*, 12th series, vol. II, July 1928, pp. 109-144.

(b) François Boissier de Sauvages (1706-1767) *Nosologia methodica sistens morborum classes, genera et species, juxta Sydenhami mentem et bontanicorum ordinem*, vol. II (Amsterdam: De Tournes, 1763); French translation, *Nosologie méthodique, ou Distribution des maladies en classes, en genres et en espèces suivant l'ésprit de Sydenham et l'ordre des botanistes*, trans. Gouvion (Lyon: Buyset, 1771) vol. II. The chapter devoted to *amentia* distinguishes an eighth species: *amentia morosis*, or Stupidity: "Imbecility, dullness, foolishness, stupidity: this is a weakness, a slowness or abolition of the faculty of imagination or judgment, without the accompaniment of delirium" p. 340. See, L.S. King, "Boissier de Sauvages and eighteenth-century nosology," *Bulletin of the History of Medicine*, vol. 40, no. 1, 1966, pp. 43-51.

(c) Jean-Baptiste Théophile Jacquelin Dubuisson (1770-1836) defines "idiotism" by "a condition of stupor or of the abolition of the intellectual and affective functions, the result of which is a more or less complete obtuseness" *Des vésanies ou maladies mentales* (Paris: Méquignon, 1816) p. 281.

(d) Georget adds to the genres of insanity defined by Pinel a "Fourth genre that we could designate as stupidity," characterized by "the accidental absence of the manifestation of thought, either because the patient has no ideas, or because he cannot express them" *De la folie*, p. 115. See, A. Ritti, "Stupeur-Stupidité" in *Dictionnaire encyclopédique des sciences medicales* (Paris: Masson/Asselin, 1883) 3rd series, vol. XII, pp. 454-469.

9. Thus Boissier de Sauvages inserts the *ingenii imbecillitas* in the 18th classification of his nosography devoted to *amentia*. See his *Nosologie méthodique*, vol. II, pp. 334-342. For Joseph Daquin, "the words dementia and imbecility are roughly synonymous, with this difference however between them: the former is an absolute deprivation of reason, while the latter is only an enfeeblement of it" *La Philosophie de la folie*, p. 51.

10. J.E. Belhomme: "Idiocy is easily distinguished from dementia ... One begins with life, or in an age which precedes the full development of intelligence; the other appears after puberty; the former belongs exclusively to childhood, the latter is mainly an illness of old age" *Essai sur l'idiotie. Propositions sur l'éducation des idiots mise en rapport avec leur degré d'intelligence* (Paris: Didot Jeune, 1824) pp. 32-33. On the history of idiocy, see, E. Seguin, *Traitement moral, hygiène et éducation des idiots et des autres enfants arriérés ou retardés dans leur développement* (Paris: J.-B. Baillière, 1846) pp. 23-32; D.M. Bourneville, *Assistance, Traitement et Éducation des enfants idiots et dégénérés*, ch. 1: "Aperçu historique de l'assistance et du traitement des enfants idiots et dégénérés," pp. 1-7; L. Kanner, *A History of the Care and Study of the Mentally Retarded* (Springfield, Ill: C.C. Thomas, 1964); G. Netchine, "Idiots, débiles et savants au xixe siècle" in R. Zazzo, *Les Débilités mentales*, pp. 70-107; and, R. Myrvold, *L'Arriération mentale, de Pinel à Binet-Simon*, Medical Thesis, Paris, 1973, no. 67.

11. See J.E.D. Esquirol, "Délire," in *Dictionnaire des sciences médicales* (Paris: C.L.F. Panckoucke, 1814) vol. VIII, p. 255: "Apyretic delirium [i.e., without fever; J.L.] is the pathognomic sign of vesania"; E.J. Georget, *De la folie*, p. 75: "The essential symptom of this illness (...) consists in intellectual disorders to which the name delirium has been given; there is no madness without delirium." Michel Foucault notes that for eighteenth century medicine an "implicit delirium exists in all the alterations of the mind." *Histoire de la folie*, p. 254; *Madness and Civilization*, p. 99.

12. J.-B. Jacquelin Dubuisson, *Des vésanies*, p. 281.
13. P. Pinel classifies "idiotism" among the "species" of mental alienation: *Traité médico-philosophique*, section IV, pp. 166-176; *A Treatise on Insanity*, "Mental Derangement Distributed into Different Species. Fifth species of mental derangement: Idiotism, or obliteration of the intellectual and affective faculties," pp. 165-173.
14. J.E.D. Esquirol, "Hallucinations" in *Dictionnaire des sciences médicales*, vol. XX (Paris: C.L.F. Panckoucke, 1817) pp. 64-71; "Idiotisme," ibid. vol. XXIII, 1818, pp. 507-524; and "De l'idiotie" (1820) in *Des maladies mentales*, vol. II, pp. 286-397; *Mental Maladies*, "Idiocy," pp. 445-496.
15. This is the medical thesis defended by Jacques Étienne Belhomme on 1 July 1824: *Essai sur l'idiotie. Propositions sur l'éducation des idiots mise en rapport avec leur degré d'intelligence*, Medical Thesis, Paris, no. 125 (Paris: Didot Jeune, 1824), reprinted with some corrections: Paris: Germer-Baillière, 1843.
16. J.E.D. Esquirol, "De l'idiotie" in *Des Maladies mentales*, p. 284; *Mental Maladies*, "Idiocy," p. 446.
17. J.E. Belhomme, *Essai sur l'idiotie*, 1843 ed., p. 51.
18. J.E.D. Esquirol, "De l'idiotie," p. 284: "Idiocy begins with life or in the age which precedes the full development of the intellectual and affective faculties . . . Dementia, like mania and monomania, only begins with puberty"; "Idiocy" p. 446. See also, J.E. Belhomme, (note 10 above).
19. J.E.D. Esquirol, "De l'idiotie,"pp. 284-285: "Idiots are what they must be throughout their life . . . We do not imagine the possibility of changing this condition," whereas "dementia (. . .) has a period of more or less rapid growth. Chronic, senile dementia gets worse from year to year (. . .). We can cure dementia, we conceive of the possibility of suspending its accidents"; "Idiocy,"pp. 446-447. It is precisely because alienists like Louis Florentin Calmeil, Achille [de] Foville, Étienne Georget, Louis François Lélut (1804-1877), and François Leuret consider idiots incurable that they recommend their isolation in asylums.
20. J.E.D. Esquirol, ibid. p. 284: "Everyone detects an imperfect organization or halted development in them. On opening the cranium we almost always find defects of conformation"; ibid.p. 446; J.E. Belhomme, 1824 edition, p. 33: "The idiot presents traces of an incomplete organization . . . The autopsy of idiots reveal defects of conformation, of organization"; E.J. Georget, *De la folie*, p. 105: "Idiots and imbeciles not only have a badly formed intellectual organ (see, the opening of bodies), but their whole system usually shares this unhealthy condition. In general, they are little developed (. . .) many are rachitic, scrofulous, paralytics, or epileptics, and sometimes combine several of these illnesses (. . .). The organization of the brain in these case is no better than those of all the other organs."
21. On 1 November 1852, Henri Jean Baptiste Davenne, general director of Public Assistance, sending the Seine Prefect a report, the fourth chapter of which concerned the education of idiot and imbecile children, stated: "The idiot is nothing other than a poor cripple to whom the doctor will never give what nature has denied him." *Rapport du Directeur de l'adminstration de l'Assistance Publique à M. le Préfet de la Seine sur le service des aliénés du département de la Seine* (Paris: Imprimerie de l'adminstration de l'Assistance Publique, 1852).
22. For Étienne Georget, since idiots are characterized by "an original defect of development, they must be ranked among the monsters; this is truly the case in the intellectual respect" *De la folie*, p. 102, n. 1. On the connotations of the term at this time, see C. Davaine, "Monstres," in *Dictionnaire encyclopédique des sciences médicales*, vol. LXI (Paris: Asselin, 1874) pp. 201-264.
23. J.E.D. Esquirol, "De l'idiotie," p. 285: "On opening the body we sometimes find organic lesions, but these are accidental, for the thickening of the bones of the cranium, and the separation of their tables, coinciding only with dementia, do not characterize any defects of conformation"; "Idiocy" p. 447.
24. Ibid.
25. In 1831, Édouard Seguin (1812-1880), assistant teacher to Jean Itard, doctor of the National Institution for deaf-mutes, was entrusted by the latter, and by Esquirol, with the education of an idiot child. He reports this experience in *Essai sur l'éducation d'un enfant*

(Paris: Porthman, 1839). In 1840, he put his method into practice in the Hospice des Incurables in the Saint-Martin district, and published, *Théorie pratique de l'éducation des enfants arriérés et idiots. Leçons aux jeunes idiots de l'Hospice des Incurables* (Paris: Germer-Baillière, 1842). In October 1842, the Conseil général des Hospices decided to transfer the children from Bicêtre into Doctor Félix Voisin's department, which Seguin leaves in 1843 after disagreements. Before emigrating to the United States in 1850, he drew up a balance sheet of his experiences in *Traitement moral, hygiène et éducation des idiots*, in which he defines his principles of "physiological education." No publication in France dealt with Seguin between the thesis of I. Saint-Yves, *Aperçus historiques sur les travaux concernant l'éducation médico-pédagogique: Itard, Bourneville*, Medical Thesis, Lyon, no. 103, 1913-1914 (Paris: P. Lethielleux, 1914) and the article by H. Beauchesne, "Seguin, instituteur d'idiots à Bicêtre, ou la première équip médico-pédagogique," *Perspectives psychiatriques*, vol. 30, 1970, pp. 11-14. See, since then, Y. Pelicier and G. Thuillier, (i) "Pour une histoire de l'éducation des enfants idiots en France, 1830-1914," *Revue historique*, vol. 261, no. 1, January 1979, pp. 99-130, and (ii) *Édouard Seguin (1812-1880). L'instituteur des idiots* (Paris: Éd. Economica, 1980); A. Brauner, ed. *Actes du colloque international: Cent ans après Édouard Seguin* (Saint-Mandé: Groupement du recherches pratiques pour l'enfance, 1981); J.G.G. Martin, "Une biographie française d'Onésime-Edouard Seguin (20 January 1812—28 October 1880), premier thérapeute des enfants arriérés, d'après ses écrits et les documents historiques," Medical Thesis, Paris-Saint Antoine, 1981, no. 134.

26. E. Seguin, *Traitement moral, hygiène et éducation des idiots*, p. 72: "It has been said that I confused idiot children with merely backward or retarded children; and it has been said precisely because I was the first to point out the extreme difference separating them."
27. Ibid.: "The retarded child is not halted in himself, except he develops more slowly than children his age . . ."
28. Ibid. p. 26: "No, idiocy is not an illness."
29. Ibid. p. 107.
30. At the beginning of the nineteenth century asylums took in, and sometimes mixed together, both adults and a child population of "idiots," "imbeciles," and "epileptics," who were poorly distinguished medically until 1840 and even after. Thus in 1852, at Bicêtre, the third section of the quarters housing the insane included epileptic adults and children, and some idiots. See D.M. Bourneville, *Assistance, Traitement et Éducation des enfants idiots et dégénérés*, p. 4. For an inventory of the places, see, H.J.B. Davenne, *Rapport . . . sur le service des aliénés du département de la Seine.*
31. Jean Marc Gaspard Itard (1774-1838), was trained as a surgeon and was appointed on 31 December 1800 as resident doctor of the National Institution for the deaf and dumb, directed by the abbot Sicard. There, with the help of the governess Madame Guérin, for more than four years he undertook the "moral treatment" of a twelve-year-old child, captured in 1799 in the forests of Lacaume (Aveyron). See, J.M.G. Itard, (i) *De l'éducation d'un homme sauvage, ou des premiers développements physiques et moraux du jeune sauvage de l'Aveyron* (Paris: Goujon, 1801); (ii) *Rapport fait à S.E. le Ministre de l'Intérieur sur les nombreux développements et l'état actuel du sauvage de l'Aveyron* (Paris: Imprimerie impériale, 1807); republished by D.M. Bourneville under the title: *Rapports et mémoires sur le sauvage de l'Aveyron, l'idiotie et la surdi-mutité*, vol. II (Paris: Alcan, 1814); reprinted in L. Malson, *Les Enfants sauvage, mythe et réalité*, followed by, J. Itard, *Mémoire et Rapport sur Victor d'Aveyron* (Paris: Union générale d'édition, 1964); English translation in Lucien Malson and Jean Itard, *Wolf Children*, trans. L. Malson, and *The Wild Boy of Aveyron* (London: NLB, 1972).
32. In 1822, with Jean-Pierre Falret, Félix Voisin (1794-1872), a student of Esquirol attracted by the problems of treating idiot children, founded a clinic at Vanves (see, *Établissement pour le traitement des aliénés des deux sexes, fondé en juillet 1822 à Vanves* [Paris: A. Belin, 1828]). In 1833, the Conseil générale des Hospices entrusted him with the organization of a service for idiots and epileptics at the Hospice des Incurables on the rue de Sèvres. In 1834 he created an "orthophrenic establishment" at 14 avenue de Vaugirard at Issy-les-Moulineaux, for idiot children. In 1836, the residents of this establishment, along with those of the Hospice, were transferred to Bicêtre, where Voisin arrived in 1840. The only document on this establishment comes from Charles Chrétien Marc (1771-1840), "Rapport à M. le Conseiller d'État, Préfet de police, sur l'établissement orthophrénique de M. Félix

Voisin," *Le Moniteur*, 24 October 1834, and reprinted as an appendix to F. Voisin, *De l'idiotie chez les enfants, et les autres particularitiés d'intelligence ou de caractère qui nécessitent pour eux une instruction et une éducation spéciales de leur responsabilité moral* (Paris: J.-B. Baillière, 1843) pp. 87-91. See also, F. Voisin, *Applications de la physiologie du cerveau à l'étude des enfants qui nécissitent une éducation spéciale* (Paris: Éverat, 1830), and *Aperçu sur les règles de l'éducation et de l'instruction des idiots et des arriérés* (Paris: Doin, 1882).

33. Jean-Pierre Falret was appointed doctor for the section for idiots at Salpêtrière on 30 March 1831 and brought together "eighty idiots and imbeciles in a common school" which he directed until his appointment in 1841 as director of a section for insane adults.

34. It was in fact in 1828, two years after his appointment in 1826 as head doctor at Bicêtre, that Guillaume Ferrus organized "a sort of school" for idiot children. See F. Voisin, "De l'idiotie," Report read to the Academy of medicine on 24 January 1843, republished by D.M. Bourneville in *Recueil de mémoires*, vol. I, p. 268. He begins his clinical teaching there in 1833: "De l'idiotie ou idiotisme (Cours sur les malades mentales)," *Gazette des hôpitaux civils ou militaires*, vol. XII, 1838, pp. 327-397.

35. At the instigation of Ferrus, then Inspecteur général des Hospices, Édouard Seguin was asked in November 1842 to direct the center for idiot and epileptic children in Félix Voisin's department, transferred from the Hospice des Incurables. See above note 25.

36. On 27 November 1873, the General Council of the Seine decided to appropriate the farm of the Vaucluse asylum to be used as a colony for young idiots. It opened on 5 August 1876. See, D.M. Bourneville, *Recueil de mémoires*, ch. 4: "L'assistance des enfants idiots et épileptiques à Paris et dans la Seine: 1. Colonie de Vaucluse" pp. 62-65.

37. Begun in 1882, the special section for idiot and epileptic children only opened in 1892. See, D.M. Bourneville, ibid. ch. 4: "Section des enfants idiots et épileptiques de Bicêtre" pp. 69-78, and *Histoire de la section des enfants de Bicêtre, 1879-1899* (Paris: Lecrosnier and Babé, 1889).

38. In 1894, the population of children hospitalized at Salpêtrière numbered 135, of which 35 were idiots and 71 epileptic idiots. See, D.M. Bournevill, *Recueil*, pp. 67-69.

39. In 1888, a wing of the division for women in the Villejuif asylum was allocated for the hospitalization and treatment of retarded, idiot or epileptic girls from Salpêtrière and Saint-Anne, under the direction of Doctor Briand. In 1894, 75 idiots and epileptics are hospitalized there.

40. The circular of 14 August 1840 states: "the Minister of the Interior, having decided that the law of 1838 was applicable to idiots and imbeciles, children could no longer reside in any establishment other than an insane asylum. As a consequence of this, the Conseil général des Hospices transferred to the Bicêtre asylum those who were in other establishments" H.J.B. Davenne, *Rapport ... sur le service des aliénés du département de la Seine*, p. 62.

41. This is the law of 28 June 1833 on elementary education. See, M. Gontard, *L'Enseignement primaire en France de la Révolution à la loi Guizot. Des petites écoles de la monarchie d'Ancien Régime aux écoles primaires de la monarchie bourgeoise*, doctoral thesis, Lyon, 1955 (Lyon: Audin, 1959).

42. In the context of the creation of special classes for retarded children, in 1891 Bourneville asked the delegation to the canton from the 5th arrondissement of Paris to establish statistics for retarded children. The first screening took place in 1894 in the public schools of the 5th and 6th arrondissements. See, D.M. Bourneville, "Note à la Commission de surveillance des asiles d'aliénés de la Seine," 2 May 1896, and *Création de classes spéciales pour les enfants arriérés* (Paris: Alcan, 1898).

43. In 1892, Philippe Rey, chief doctor of the Saint-Pierre asylum of Marseille and Conseiller général of the Vaucluse, with a view to the creation of an "interdepartmental asylum for taking in and treating retarded or abnormal children," undertook their census with the help of a questionnaire sent to primary school teachers of the Bouches-du-Rhône and Vaucluse départements. See, D.M. Bourneville, *Assistance, Traitement et Éducation, op. cit*, p. 45 and pp. 197-198.

44. As was said by Jean Denys Marie Cochin (1789-1841), founder in 1828, with the marchioness of Pastoret, of the "*salles d'asile*": "their effect is to procure, free or at little expense, considerable facilities for the well-being of the population, by reducing the burden of each household and increasing the resources of the heads of the family, both in

connection with the freedom to work, and by allowing a reduction in the number of persons involved in the supervision of the children" *Manuel des fondateurs et des directeurs des premières écoles de l'enfance connues sous le nom de "salles d'asile"* (1833), 4th edition, with a notice by Austin Cochin (Paris: Hachette, 1853) p. 32. They were recognized by an edict of 28 March 1831. Subsequent to the law of 28 June 1833 on primary instruction, an edict of 22 December 1837 defined their status in its first article: "The *salles d'asile*, or schools of the first age, are charitable establishments to which children of both sexes may be admitted, up to the age of six full years, in order to receive the care and attention of maternal supervision and primary education that their age calls for" ibid. p. 231. See, Laurent Cerise (1807-1869), *Le Médecin de salle d'asile, ou Manuel d'hygiène et d'éducation physique de l'enfanc* (Paris: Hachette, 1836); A. Cochin, *Notice sur la vie de J.D.M. Cochin, et sur l'origine et les progrès des salles d'asile* (Paris: Duverger, 1852); and H.J.B. Davenne, *De l'organisation et du régime des secours publics en France*, vol. I, pp. 76-82.

45. W. Fernald, *The History of the Treatment of Feeble Mind* (Boston, Mass.: 1893), quoted by D.M. Bourneville in *Assistance, Traitement et Éducation*, p. 143.
46. J.-B. Parchappe de Vinay, *Principes a suivre dans la fondation et la construction des asiles d'aliénés*, (Paris: Masson, 1853) p. 6.
47. E. Seguin, *Traitement moral, hygiène et éducation des idiots*, p. 665. See, I. Kraft, "Edward Seguin and 19th century moral treatment of idiots," *Bulletin of the History of Medicine*, vol. 35, no. 5, 1961, pp. 393-418.
48. E. Seguin, *Traitement moral*, p. 665.
49. Ibid. p. 664.
50. Ibid.p. 666.
51. Ibid.p. 662.
52. Ibid.p. 656.
53. Ibid.p. 659.
54. Ibid.p. 366.
55. Ibid.ch. xxxix: "Gymnastics and education of the nervous system and sensory apparatus" § v; "Sight" pp. 418-419.
56. D.M. Bourneville, "Summary considerations on the medico-pedagogical treatment of idiocy" in *Assistance, Traitement et Éducation*, p. 242.
57. Ibid. p. 237: "At the end of 1893, two hundred children were employed in the workshops and divided up as follows: 14 brush makers, 52 shoe makers, 13 printers, 19 carpenters, 14 locksmiths, 57 tailors, 23 basket makers, and 8 straw and cane workers."
58. Ibid. p. 238.
59. "The children themselves are happy to see that their work is productive, that it is translated into practical results, and that all that they do contributes to their well-being, education and the upkeep of their section" D.M. Bourneville, *Compte rendu du Service des enfants idots, épileptiques et arriérés de Bicêtre* (Paris: Publications du Progrès médical, 1900) vol. XX, p. xxxv.
60. On 27 November 1873, the Conseil général de la Seine decided to appropriate the farm buildings of the lunatic asylum of Vaucluse (Seine-et-Oise) for a colony of idiot children. When it opened on 5 August 1876, the Perray-Vaucluse colony comprised four divisions: "4th division. Teaching by sight, practical lessons (...); memory exercises; alphabet and printed figures and letters in wood (Bicêtre model). 3rd division. Children who have acquired the most elementary knowledge. Practical lessons, exercises in reading, reciting, arithmetic and writing... 2nd division. Children able to read, write and add up (...); notions of grammar, arithmetic, French history and geography (...). 1st division. Preparation for school certificate. For these, instruction is not noticeably different from that of primary school" D.M. Bourneville, *Assistance, Traitement et Éducation*, pp. 63-64.
61. The provisions were specified in section III of the law of 30 June 1838: Costs of the service for the insane. Article 28 established that in the absence of resources stated in article 27, "the expense shall be met out of the special percentage added, by the finance law, to the normal expenses of the department to which the insane person belongs, without prejudice to the support of the commune in which the insane person is domiciled, upon a basis proposed by the Conseil Général (Department Council), upon the advice of the prefect, and approved by the government" quoted by R. Castel, *L'Ordre psychiatrique*, p. 321; *The Regulation of Madness*, p. 249.

62. In his Report of June 1894, D.M. Bourneville emphasizes the financial reasons for resistance from the department and commune administrations who, carefully managing their budgets, delayed admission of idiot children to the asylum until they became a danger: see, *Assistance, Traitement et Éducation*, p. 84.
63. Thus, for G. Ferrus, if idiot and imbecile children come under the jurisdiction of the 1838 law, it is because, like every lunatic, they can be considered dangerous: "It only needs a circumstance to arouse their violent instincts and lead them to actions which endanger safety and public order" quoted in H.J.B. Davenne, *Rapport... sur le service des aliénés du département de la Seine*, Appendix, p. 130. Jules Falret also stresses "the dangers of every kind they could pose to themselves or to society, idiots and imbeciles as well as lunatics" J. Falret, "Des aliénés dangereux," § 10: "Idiots et imbéciles," Report to the Société médico-psychologique, 27 July 1868, in *Les Aliénés et les Asiles d'aliénés. Assistance, législation et médecine légale* (Paris: J.-B. Baillière, 1890) p. 241.
64. Bourneville: "No week passes without the newspapers reporting cases of crimes and offences committed by idiots, imbeciles or the mentally retarded" *Assistance, Traitment et Éducation*, p. 147.
65. "A man called Many..., says La Vallée de l'Eure (1891), made a violent sexual assault on a young idiot girl, who, what's more, was engaged in prostitution."
66. Ibid. p. 148.
67. F. Voisin, *De l'idiotie chez les enfants*, p. 83.
68. D.M. Bourneville, *Assistance, Traitement et Éducation*, p. 145.
69. In the second half of the nineteenth century the research of psychiatrists concerning instinct developed on two fronts: one, natural, of cerebral physiology, and the other, cultural, of the relationships between sociability and morality. See, G. Bouchardeau, "La notion d'instinct, dans la clinique psychiatrique au XIXe" *Évolution psychiatrique*, vol. XLIV, no. 3, July-September 1979, pp. 617-632.

    Valentin Magnan (1835-1916) established a link between the instinctive perversions of degenerates and anatomico-physiological disorders of the cerebral-spinal system, in a classification which connected the different perversions to processes of excitation or inhibition of corresponding cerebral-spinal structures. See his "Étude clinique sur les impulsions et les actes des aliénés" (1861) in *Recherches sur les centres nerveux*, vol. II (Paris: Masson, 1893) pp. 353-369. See also, Paul Serieux (1864-1947), *Recherches cliniques sur les anomalies de l'instinct sexuel*, Medical Thesis, Paris, no. 50, 1888 (Paris: Lecrosnier and Babé, 1888-1889), and Charles Féré (1852-1907) *L'instinct sexuel. Évolution et dissolution* (Paris: Alcan, 1889). Foucault returns to this point in *Les Anormaux*, lectures of 5 and 12 February and 21 March 1975, pp. 120-125, pp. 127-135, and pp. 260-271; *Abnormal*, pp. 129-134, 137-145, and 275-287.
70. Thus, in 1886, Joseph Jules Déjerine (1849-1917) reviews Darwin's work very positively in *L'Hérédité dans les maladies du système nerveux* (Paris: Asselin and Houzeau, 1886). But it was V. Magnan who developed Morel's theory by introducing a reference to the notion of evolution and of the neurological localization of the degenerative process. See his *Leçons cliniques sur les maladies mentales* (Paris: Battaille, 1893); V. Magnan and P. Legrain, *Les Dégénérés (état mental et syndromes épisodiques)* (Paris: Rueff, 1895); and A. Zaloszyc, *Éléments d'une histoire de la théorie des dégénérescences dans la psychiatrie française*, Medical Thesis, Strasbourg, July 1975.
71. Two years before the publication of Charles Darwin's *On the Origin of the Species by means of Natural Selection, or the Preservation of Favoured Races in the Struggle for Life* (London: J. Murray, 1859), B.A. Morel published his *Traité des dégénérescences physique, intellectuelles et morales de l'espèce humaine, et des causes qui produisent ces variétés maladives* (Paris: J.-B. Baillière, 1857) in which he defines degeneration: "The clearest idea we can give ourselves of the degeneration of the human species is to think of it as a primitive type of unhealthy deviation. This deviation, however simple we imagine it to be in its origin, nonetheless contains elements of transmissibility of such a kind that the person who carries its germ becomes increasingly incapable of fulfilling his functions in humanity, and intellectual progress, already checked in his person, is still threatened in his descendants" (p. 5). The psychiatry that comes from Morel will only convert to evolutionism by ceasing

to see "perfection" as the most exact conformity to a "original (*primitif*)" type, and by seeing it instead as the greatest possible divergence from that type.

72. See, I.R. Dowbiggin, *Inheriting Madness: Professionalization and Psychiatric Knowledge in Nineteenth-Century France* (Berkeley: University of California Press, 1991); French translation, *La Folie héréditaire, ou Comment la psychiatrie française s'est constituée en un corps de savoir et de pouvoir dans la seconde moitié du XIXe siècle*, trans. G. Le Gaufrey, preface by G. Lanteri-Laura (Paris: Éd. Epel, 1993).
73. After reaching its peak in the 1880s, the theory of degeneration began to decline. Freud criticized it in 1894 in his article on "Die Abwehr-Neuropsychosen" *Neurologisches Zentralblatt*, vol. 13, 1894, no. 10, pp. 362-364 and no. 11, pp. 402-409, reprinted in *GW*, vol. I, 1952, pp. 57-74; French translation, "Les psychonévroses de défese" trans. J. Laplanche, in S. Freud, *Névrose, Psychose et Perversion* (Paris: Presses universitaires de France, 1973); English translation, "The Neuro-Psychoses of Defence, *Standard Edition*, vol. 3. Also: *Drei Abhandlungen zur Sexualtheorie* (Vienna: Deuticke, 1905) in *GW*, vol. V, 1942, pp. 27-145; French translation, *Trois Essais sur la théorie de la sexualité*, trans. B. Reverchon-Jouve (Paris: Gallimard, 1923); English translation, "Three Essays on the Theory of Sexuality, *Standard Edition* (1953-1974) vol. 7. In 1903, Gilbert Ballet (1853-1916) wrote in a *Traité de pathologie mentale* published under his editorship (Paris: Doin, 1903), that he saw no advantages in including the term "degeneration" in the vocabulary of twentieth century psychiatry (pp. 273-275). See, G. Génil-Perrin, *Histoire des origines et de l'évolution de l'idée de dégénérescence en médecine mentale* (Paris: A. Leclerc, 1913).

ten

23 JANUARY 1974

Psychiatric power and the question of truth: questioning and confession; magnetism and hypnosis; drugs. ~ Elements for a history of truth: 1. The truth-event and its forms: judicial, alchemical and medical practices. ~ Transition to a technology of demonstrative truth. Its elements: (a) procedures of inquiry; (b) institution of a subject of knowledge; (c) ruling out the crisis in medicine and psychiatry and its supports: the disciplinary space of the asylum, recourse to pathological anatomy; relationships between madness and crime. ~ Psychiatric power and hysterical resistance.

I HAVE ANALYZED THE level at which psychiatric power appears as a power in which and by which truth is brought into play. It seems to me that, at a certain level at least, let's say the level of its disciplinary operation, the function of psychiatric knowledge is by no means to found a therapeutic practice in truth, but much rather to give the psychiatrist's power a particular stamp, to give it an additional, supplementary distinction; in other words, the psychiatrist's knowledge is one of the components by which the disciplinary apparatus organizes the surplus-power of reality around madness.

But this leaves out of account certain elements that are nevertheless present in this historical period of what I call proto-psychiatry, extending, roughly, from the 1820s to the 1860s and 1870s, until what we can call the crisis of hysteria. In one sense the elements I have left to one side are fairly unobtrusive, dispersed, not very prominent, and they have certainly not occupied a large space in the organization of psychiatric power in the operation of the disciplinary regime, and yet I think these elements were switch points in the process of the internal and external transformation of psychiatric power. These few, unobtrusive, dispersed points are those where madness was posed the question of truth despite the overall working of the disciplinary apparatus. In saying that there are three such points, I do not claim that this is an exhaustive list; it seems to me that we can say provisionally that there were three in which the question of truth addressed to madness creeps in.

These points are, first of all, the practice or ritual of questioning and the extortion of confession, which is the most important and most constant process, and which ultimately has not changed much within psychiatric practice. Second, a different process which had a cyclical fortune, which disappeared at one point, but which, through the havoc it wreaked in the disciplinary world of the asylum, was extremely important historically: the procedure of magnetism and hypnosis. And finally, third, a well-known element about which the history of psychiatry has been significantly quiet, which is the use, I do not say the absolutely constant use, but from around 1840 to 1850 the very general use of drugs—mainly ether,[1] chloroform,[2] opium,[3] laudanum,[4] and hashish,[5] a whole panoply—which for a dozen years were used on a daily basis in the asylum world of the nineteenth century, and on which the historians of psychiatry have been prudently silent, although, along with hypnosis and the technique of questioning, it is probably the point on which the history of psychiatric practice and power took a sudden turn or, at any rate, was transformed.

Of course, these three techniques are ambiguous, that is to say, they function at two levels. On the one hand, they function at the disciplinary level; in this sense, questioning is really a particular way of fixing the individual to the norm of his own identity—Who are you? What is your name? Who are your parents? What about the different episodes of your madness?—of pinning the individual to his social identity and to the madness ascribed to him by his own milieu. Questioning is a disciplinary method and its effects can in fact be identified at that level.

Magnetism was introduced into the nineteenth century asylum very early on, that is to say around 1820 to 1825, at a time when its use was still at an empirical level and other doctors generally rejected it. It was very clearly used as an adjunct of the doctor's physical, corporal power.[6] In this space of the extension of the doctor's body organized by the asylum, in this kind of process, this game, by which the working parts of the asylum must be like the psychiatrist's own nervous system, so that the psychiatrist's body and the asylum space itself form a single body, it is clear that magnetism, with all its physical effects, was a functional component in the mechanism of discipline. Finally, drugs—mainly opium, chloroform, and ether—were, like drugs still today, an obviously disciplinary instrument for maintaining order, calm, and keeping patients quiet.

At the same time, the use of these three perfectly decipherable elements whose disciplinary effects make their insertion into the asylum quite comprehensible, and despite what was expected of them, had an effect in which they brought with them or introduced a question of truth. It may be that it was the cross-examined, magnetized, hypnotized, and drugged madman himself who posed the question of truth. And, to that extent, it seems to me that these three elements really were the elements of the disciplinary system's fracture, the moment at which medical knowledge, which again was only a token of power, found itself required to speak, no longer just in terms of power, but in terms of truth.

⚜

I would like to open a parenthesis here and insert a little history of truth in general. It seems to me that we could say that knowledge of the kind we call scientific basically presupposes that there is truth everywhere, in every place and all the time. More precisely, this means that while there are of course moments for scientific knowledge when the truth is grasped more easily, points of view that allow it to be perceived more easily or certainly, and instruments for discovering it where it is hidden, remote or buried, nonetheless, for scientific practice in general, there is always the truth; the truth is always present, in or under every thing, and the question of truth can be posed about anything and everything. The truth may well be buried and difficult to reach, but this only directs us to our own limits and circumstances. The truth in itself permeates the entire world, without break. There is no black hole in the truth. This means that for a scientific type of knowledge nothing is too small, trivial, ephemeral, or occasional for the question of truth, nothing too distant or close to hand for us to put the question: what are you in truth? The truth dwells in everything and anything, even Plato's famous nail clippings.[7] This means not only that the truth lives everywhere and that the question of truth can be posed at every [moment], but it also means that no one is exclusively qualified to state the truth, if, of course, they have the instruments required to discover it, the categories necessary to think it, and an adequate language for formulating it in propositions. Speaking even more schematically, let's say that we have here a philosophico-scientific standpoint of truth linked to a technology for the construction of truth, or for finding it in principle, a technology of demonstration. Let's say that we have a technology of demonstrative truth joined, in short, to scientific practice.

Now I think there has been a completely different standpoint of truth in our civilization. This completely different standpoint of truth, no doubt more archaic than the one I am talking about, was gradually pushed aside or covered over by the demonstrative technology of truth. This other standpoint of truth, which is, I think absolutely crucial in the history of our civilization by virtue of it being covered over and colonized by the other, is that of a truth which, precisely, will not be everywhere and at all times waiting for us whose task is to watch out for it and grasp it wherever it happens to be. It will be the standpoint of a dispersed, discontinuous, interrupted truth which will only speak or appear from time to time, where it wishes to, in certain places; a truth which does not appear everywhere, at all times, or for everyone; a truth which is not waiting for us, because it is a truth which has its favorable moments, its propitious places, its privileged agents and bearers. It is a truth which has its geography. The oracle who speaks the truth at Delphi[8] does not express it anywhere else, and does not say the same thing as the oracle in another place; the god who cures at Epidaurus,[9] and who tells those who come to consult him what their illness is and what remedy they must apply, only cures and expresses the truth of the illness at Epidaurus and nowhere else. A truth, then, which has its geography, and which has its calendar as well, or, at least, its own chronology.

Take another example. In the old Greek, Latin and medieval medicine of crises, to which I will come back, there is always a moment for the truth of the illness to appear. This is precisely the moment of the crisis, and there is no other moment at which the truth can be grasped in this way. In alchemical practice, the truth is not lying there waiting to be grasped by us; it passes, and it passes rapidly, like lightning; it is in any case linked to the opportunity, to the *kairos*, and must be seized.[10]

It is not only a truth with its geography and calendar, but also with its messengers or privileged and exclusive agents. The agents of this discontinuous truth are those who possess the secrets of times and places, those who undergo tests of qualification, those who have uttered the required words or performed ritual actions, and those again whom truth has chosen to sweep down on: prophets, seers, innocents, the blind, the mad, the wise, etcetera. This truth, with its geography, its calendars, and its messengers or privileged agents, is not universal. Which does not mean that it is rare, but that it is a dispersed truth, a truth that occurs as an event.

So you have attested truth, the truth of demonstration, and you have the truth-event. We could call this discontinuous truth the truth-thunderbolt, as opposed to the truth-sky that is universally present behind the clouds. We have, then, two series in the Western history of truth. The series of constant, constituted, demonstrated, discovered truth, and then a different series of the truth which does not belong to the order of what is, but to the order of what happens, a truth, therefore, which is not given in the form of discovery, but in the form of the event, a truth which is not found but aroused and hunted down: production rather than apophantic. It is not a truth that is given through the mediation of instruments, but a truth provoked by rituals, captured by ruses, seized according to occasions. This kind of truth does not call for method, but for strategy. The relationship between this truth-event and the person who is seized by it, who grasps it or is struck by it, is not a relationship of subject to object. Consequently it is not a relationship within knowledge but, rather, a relationship of a shock or clash, like that of a thunderbolt or lightning. It is also a hunting kind of relationship, or, at any rate, a risky, reversible, warlike relationship; it is a relationship of domination and victory, and so not a relationship of knowledge, but one of power.

There are those who are in the habit of writing the history of truth in terms of the forgetting of Being,[11] that is to say, when they assert forgetting as the basic category of the history of truth, these people place themselves straightaway within the privileges of established knowledge, that is to say, something like forgetting can only take place on the ground of the assumed knowledge relationship, laid down once and for all. Consequently, I think they only pursue the history of one of the two series I have tried to point out, the series of apophantic truth, of discovered, established, demonstrated truth, and they place themselves within that series.

What I would like to do, what I have tried to do in the last years, is a history of truth starting with the other series,[12] that is to say, I have tried to single out the technology—today, effectively dismissed, brushed aside and supplanted—of the truth-event, truth-ritual, truth-power relationship, as opposed to the truth-discovery, truth-method, truth-knowledge relationship, as opposed, therefore, to truth that is presupposed and placed within the subject-object relationship.

I would like to emphasize the truth-thunderbolt against the truth-sky, that is to say, on the one hand, to show how this truth-demonstration, broadly identified in its technology with scientific practice, the present day extent, force and power of which there is absolutely no point in denying, derives in reality from the truth-ritual, truth-event, truth-strategy, and how truth-knowledge is basically only a region and an aspect, albeit one that has become superabundant and assumed gigantic dimensions, but still an aspect or a modality of truth as event and of the technology of this truth-event.

Showing that scientific demonstration is basically only a ritual, that the supposedly universal subject of knowledge is really only an individual historically qualified according to certain modalities, and that the discovery of truth is really a certain modality of the production of truth; putting what is given as the truth of observation or demonstration back on the basis of rituals, of the qualifications of the knowing individual, of the truth-event system, is what I would call the archeology of knowledge.[13]

And then there is a further move to be made, which would be to show precisely how, in the course of our history, of our civilization, and in an increasingly accelerated way since the Renaissance, truth-knowledge assumed its present, familiar and observable dimensions; to show how it colonized and took over the truth-event and ended up exercising a relationship of power over it, which may be irreversible, but which for the moment anyway is a dominant and tyrannical power, to show how this technology of demonstrative truth colonized and now exercises a relationship of power over this truth whose technology is linked to the event, to strategy, and to the hunt. We could call this the genealogy of knowledge, the indispensable historical other side to the archeology of knowledge, and which I have tried to show you, very schematically, with some dossiers, not what it might consist of, but how it might be sketched out. Opening up the dossier of judicial practice was an attempt to show how, through judicial practice, politico-juridical rules were gradually formed for establishing the truth in which we saw the technology of the truth-test ebbing away and disappearing with the advent of a certain type of political power and the establishment of the technology of a truth of certified observation, of a truth authenticated by witnesses, etcetera.

What I would now like to do with regard to psychiatry is show how in the nineteenth century this event type of truth is gradually hidden by a different technology of truth, or at least, how, with regard to madness, there was an attempt to cover up this technology of the truth-event with a technology of demonstrative truth, of observation. We could also do this, and in the next years I will try to do it with regard to pedagogy and the dossier on childhood.[14]

It could be said that this is all very well historically, but all the same, there is little now that corresponds to the truth-test-event series in our society; we may be able to find this technology of the truth-event in some old practices—say in oracular, prophetic practices, etcetera—but it is a long time since this game was played and there is no point in returning to it. Actually, I think there really is something else here, and that in actual fact, within our civilization, this truth-event, this technology of the truth-thunderbolt, seems to me to have subsisted for a long time and has considerable historical importance.

First, with regard to the judicial forms I have talked about in previous years and to which I have just referred, a very profound and fundamental transformation is involved. You remember what I said to you about archaic medieval justice, of justice before the twelfth century, more or less: the medieval procedure for discovering the guilty person, or rather, for assigning individual culpability, the procedures broadly placed under the rubric of "the judgment of God," were in no way methods for discovering what really happened. There was absolutely no question of reproducing within "God's judgment" something like the *analogon*, the image itself of what really happened at the level of the criminal action. "God's judgment" and tests of this kind were procedures for governing how to determine the victor in a confrontation between two individuals in dispute.[15] Even confession was not a sign or a method for discovering a sign of culpability in medieval judicial techniques.[16] When the Inquisitors of the Middle Ages tortured someone, they did not appeal to the kind of argument made by present day torturers, that someone's acknowledgement of guilt is the best proof, even better, closer, than that of an eye witness; the torturer of the Middle Ages did not seek to obtain this kind of proof *a fortiori*. In fact, torturing someone in the Middle Ages involved the judge and the person accused or suspected in a real physical struggle—the rules of which, while not rigged, were of course completely unequal and with no reciprocity—to find out whether or not the suspect would stand up to it. When he gave way, this was not so much a demonstrative proof that he was guilty, as quite simply the reality of the fact that he had lost in the game, in the confrontation, and could consequently be sentenced. All this could then be inscribed, secondarily as it were, in a system of significations: God, then, has abandoned him, etcetera. But this was absolutely not the mundane sign of his culpability; it was the final phase, the final episode, the conclusion of a confrontation.[17] And finally to pass from this technique for establishing the truth in the test to the establishment of truth in the certified report, through evidence and demonstration, required the whole process by which penal justice was brought under State control.[18]

We could say the same about alchemy. The basic reason why alchemy has never really been refuted by chemistry, why it cannot figure in the history of science as an error or scientific impasse, is that it does not correspond, and never has corresponded, to the technology of demonstrative truth; from start to finish it corresponded to the technology of the truth-event or of the truth-test.

Very roughly, summarizing its main characteristics, what is alchemical research in fact? First of all it involves the individual's initiation, that is to say, his moral or ascetic qualification; he must prepare himself for the test of truth, not so much by the accumulation of certain contents of knowledge as by the fact that he really has gone through the required ritual.[19] Moreover, in the alchemical process itself, the alchemical *opus* is not the final acquisition of a certain result; the *opus* is the ritual staging of certain events, which, according to a certain margin of luck, chance, or blessing, may include, may possibly include, the truth, which will burst forth or pass by as an opportunity to be grasped in a ritually determined moment that is always enigmatic for the person who brings it about and that this individual will, precisely, have to grasp and understand.[20] Which means, moreover, that alchemical knowledge is always knowledge that is lost and so cannot have the same rules of accumulation as a scientific type of knowledge: alchemical knowledge must always start again from zero, that is to say, every alchemist has to start again the whole cycle of initiations; you are not borne on the shoulders of your predecessors in alchemical knowledge.

The only thing is that sometimes something like an enigmatic and indecipherable secret, which may have been overlooked or cast aside but which actually contains the essential, falls into someone's hands. And this secret, so secret that we do not even know it is a secret unless, precisely, we have undergone the ritual initiations or are prepared, or if the occasion is good, puts us on the track of something which may or may not take place. In any case, the secret will be lost again, or buried in some text or book of magic that chance, like an opportunity, like the Greek *kairos*, will once more put into the hands of someone else, who may or may not be able to recognize it anew.[21]

Good! All this belongs to a technology of truth which has nothing to do with the technology of scientific truth, and in this sense alchemy is not part of the history of science, [not] even as a sketch or possibility. However, this technology of truth-test or truth-event survived for a long time within knowledge that might not be described as scientific, but which was nonetheless very close to science, lived on its borders, and accompanied its birth in the eighteenth century; that is to say, it survived in medicine, at the heart of medical practice.

It was at the heart of medical practice for centuries, roughly from Hippocrates[22] to Sydenham,[23] or even until eighteenth century medicine, that is to say, for 22 centuries.[24] It was not in medical theory, or in what began to take the form of anatomy or physiology in medicine, but in medical practice, in the relationship to the disease established by medicine that for 22 centuries there was something that did not fall within the sphere of demonstrative truth but within the sphere of this technology of truth-test. This is the notion of "crisis," or rather the set of medical practices organized around the notion of crisis.

What in actual fact is the crisis in medical thought since Hippocrates? What I am going to say to you is obviously very schematic since I am going to cover these 22 centuries presumptuously without considering all the modifications, sudden changes, disappearances and reappearances of the notion, etcetera, over this time.

What is the crisis in medical practice prior to pathological anatomy? It is well known that the crisis is the moment at which the evolution of the disease risks being resolved, that is to say, risks the decision of life or death, or also transition to the chronic state.[25] Is it a moment in an evolution? It is not exactly this; the crisis is quite precisely the moment of combat, the moment of the battle, or even the point at which the battle is decided. The battle between Nature and Evil, the body's struggle against the morbific substance,[26] or, as doctors in the eighteenth century will say, the battle between solids and humors.[27] The combat has its definite days, its moments prescribed by the calendar. However, this prescription of the days of the crisis is ambiguous in the sense that the crisis days for a disease actually mark a sort of natural rhythm that is typical of the disease, and of this particular disease. That is to say, every disease has its own rhythm of possible crises; every patient has days when the crisis may be triggered. Hippocrates had already distinguished in this way fevers which have crises on even days from those which have them on odd days; for those with crises on even days, this may be the fourth, sixth, eighth, tenth, fourteenth, twenty-eighth, thirty-fourth, thirty-eighth, fiftieth, or eightieth day.[28] For Hippocrates, and for the Hippocratic type of medicine, this gives a kind of description of the disease—we cannot say a symptomatological description—that characterizes it on the basis of the, possible, necessary crisis day. It is therefore an intrinsic feature of the disease.

But it is also an opportunity to be seized, somewhat like the favorable date in Greek manticism.[29] Just as there were days on which one could not engage the enemy in battle, so there are days when there should not be a crisis; and just as there were bad generals who did not join battle on a propitious day, so there were patients or diseases which produced their crisis on a day that was not propitious, so that on those occasions one had bad crises, that is to say, crises which necessarily led to an unfavorable development, a kind of supplementary complication, but without this meaning that crises occurring at a propitious moment always have favorable outcomes. You can see the role of this crisis, which is both the intrinsic feature and, at the same time, the obligatory opportunity, the ritual rhythm, to which events should conform.

Now when the crisis occurs, the disease breaks out in its truth; that is to say, it is not only a discontinuous moment but also the moment at which the illness, I won't say "reveals" a hidden truth, but appears in its own truth, its intrinsic truth. Before the crisis the disease is one thing or another; it is nothing in truth. The crisis is the reality of the disease becoming truth, as it were. And it is precisely then that the doctor must intervene.

What is the doctor's role in the technique of the crisis? He must consider the crisis as the way, practically the only way, through which he can get a hold on the disease. With its variables of time, intensity, and types of resolution, etcetera, the crisis defines the way in which the doctor must intervene.[30] On the one hand, the doctor must first foresee the crisis, identify when it will occur,[31] wait for the exact day on which it will take place, and then, at that point, engage in battle to defeat the disease,[32] in short, so that nature triumphs over the disease. That is to say, in a sense the doctor's role is to reinforce the energy of nature. But we must be careful when reinforcing nature's energy, because what happens if we reinforce it too much when struggling against the disease? The result is that being, as it were, exhausted, and lacking strength, the disease will not join in the combat and the crisis will not take place, and if the crisis does not take place, then the harmful condition will persist.

So a proper balance must be maintained. Similarly, if we reinforce nature too much, if nature becomes too vigorous and too strong, then the movement by which it tries to expel the disease will be too violent, and there will be the danger of the patient dying from the violence of nature's efforts against the disease. So we must neither weaken the illness too much, which risks avoiding the crisis, as it were, nor reinforce nature too much, because then there is the danger of the crisis being too violent. So you can see that in this technology of the crisis the doctor is much more the manager and arbitrator of the crisis than the agent of a therapeutic intervention.* The doctor must foresee the crisis, know the opposing forces, imagine its outcome, and arrange things so that it occurs at the right time; he must see how and with what force it approaches, and he must introduce only those necessary adjustments to each side of the balance so that the crisis takes its proper course.

And you can see that in its general form the technique of the crisis in Greek medicine is no different from the technique of a judge or arbitrator in a judicial dispute. In this technique of the test you have a sort of model, a juridico-political matrix, which is applied both to the contentious battle in a case of penal law and to medical practice. Moreover, in medical practice there is a sort of supplementary complexity that is found again in judicial practice. This is that, as you can see, the doctor does not cure, and it cannot even be said that he directly confronts the disease, since it is nature that confronts the disease; he foresees the crisis, he gauges the contending forces, and he succeeds if he manages nature's success. And, to come back to this word crisis, which after all means "to judge,"[33] just as the disease comes up for judgment on the day of the crisis, so the doctor, in this role as a kind of arbitrator, is judged in turn by how he presides over the combat, and he may come out as victor or vanquished in relation to the disease.

In relation to the combat of nature and the disease, the doctor's is a second order combat, from which he will come out victor or vanquished in relation to these internal laws, but equally in relation to other doctors. And here again we come back to the juridical model. You know

* The manuscript adds: "more the role of observance of rules than of the observation of phenomena."

that judges could be disqualified when they judged badly, in turn having to undergo a trial from which they will come out either victors or vanquished. And this kind of joust between the adversaries and between the laws of combat and then the judge had a sort of public character. This double combat always had public features. Now medical consultation, as you see it at work from Hippocrates up to Molière's famous doctors—on the meaning and status of which we should nonetheless reflect a little—always involved several people.[34] That is to say, it involved at once a joust of nature against the disease, of the doctor with regard to this struggle of nature against the disease, and of the doctor with other doctors.

They were all present, each confronting the others, each making his own prediction about when the crisis must occur, what its nature would be, and what would be the outcome. However self-justifying it may be, it seems to me that the famous scene Galen describes to explain how he made his fortune in Rome is an entirely typical scene of this kind of enthronement of the doctor. The story recounts how the young Galen, an unknown doctor coming to Rome from Asia Minor, participates in a kind of medical joust around a patient. When the doctors were predicting this or that, Galen says, looking at the ill young man: There will be a crisis shortly; this crisis will be a nosebleed, and he will bleed from the right nostril. This is in fact what happens, and, Galen says, one by one all the doctors around me were quietly overshadowed.[35] The joust was also a joust between the doctors.

The doctor's appropriation of a patient, the recognition of the family doctor, the doctor-patient discourse, are all the effect of a whole series of economic, sociological and epistemological transformations of medicine. However, in this medicine of the test, in which the crisis was the main component, the joust between doctors was as essential as the joust between nature and the disease. So you can see, this technology of truth-test, of truth-event, persists for a long time in medicine, in medical practice, which, once again, like alchemy, was not utterly foreign to the developments of the scientific knowledge which adjoined, cut across, and were tangled up with it.

A word more on this subject. With the example of medicine you can see, of course, that the extension of the other series, of the demonstrative technology of truth, was not brought about at a stroke, like a kind of overall reversal, and it certainly does not take place in the same way in astronomy as in medicine, or in judicial practice the same way as in botany. However, broadly speaking, I think we can say that two processes have supported this transformation in the technology of truth, at least in what concerns empirical knowledge.

I think the transition from a technology of truth-event to truth-demonstration is linked, on the one hand, to the extension of political procedures of the inquiry. The inquiry, the report, the evidence of several people, the cross-checking of information, the circulation of knowledge from the center of power to the points where it ends up and back again, as well as all the agencies of parallel verification, progressively, over a long history, gradually constituted the instrument of the political and economic power of industrial society; hence the refinement, the increasingly fine grid of these techniques of inquiry within the elements where they were usually applied. Broadly speaking, the refinement by which we passed from a basically fiscal kind of inquiry in the Middle Ages—knowing who collects what, who possesses what, so that the necessary deductions are made—to a police kind of investigation into people's behavior, into how they live, think, make love, etcetera, this transition from fiscal inquiry to police investigation, the constitution of a police individuality starting from fiscal individuality, which was the only individuality known by power in the Middle Ages, reveals the tightening of the technique of inquiry in our kind of society.[36]

Moreover, there was not only a local tightening, but also a planetary extension to the entire surface of the globe. There is a double movement of colonization: colonization in depth, which fed on the actions, bodies, and thoughts of individuals, and then colonization at the level of territories and surfaces. We can say that from the end of the Middle Ages we have seen the entire surface of the Earth, down to the finest grain of things, bodies, and actions, subjected to generalized investigation: a sort of grand inquisitorial parasitism. That is to say, at any time, at any place, and with regard to anything in the world, the question of truth can and must be posed. Truth is everywhere and awaits us everywhere, at any place and at any time. This, very schematically, is the great process that led to this move from a technology of the truth-event to a technology of truth-findings.

The other process was a sort of opposite process, [...*] establishing the rarity of this truth of anywhere and anytime. This rarefaction is not brought to bear on the emergence or production of truth however, but precisely on who can discover it. In one sense, this universal truth of anywhere and anytime, which any inquiry can and must track down and discover with regard to no matter what, is accessible to anyone; anyone can have access to it, since it is there, everywhere and all the time. However, the necessary circumstances are still required, and we must acquire the forms of thought and techniques that will give us access to this truth that is everywhere, but always deep down, buried, and difficult to reach.

So we will have, of course, a universal subject of this universal truth, but it will be an abstract subject because, concretely, the universal subject able to grasp this truth is rare, since it must be a subject qualified by procedures of pedagogy and selection. Universities, learned societies, canonical teaching, schools, laboratories, the interplay of specialization and professional qualification, are all ways of organizing the rarity of those who can have access to a truth that science posits as universal. It will be the abstract right of every individual to be a universal subject, if you like, but to be one in fact, concretely, will necessarily entail rare individuals being qualified to perform the function of universal subject. In the history of the West since the eighteenth century, the appearance of philosophers, men of science, intellectuals, professors, laboratories, etcetera, is directly correlated with this extension of the standpoint of scientific truth and corresponds precisely to the rarefaction of those who can know a truth that is now present everywhere and at every moment. Fine. That's the little history I wanted to present. What is its relationship to madness? We're just coming to it.

In the medicine in general that I have been talking about, the notion of crisis disappears at the end of the eighteenth century. It not only

* (Recording:) we could call it

disappears as a notion, after Hoffmann[37] say, but also as an organizing principle of medical technique. Why did it disappear? Well, I think it disappeared for the reasons I have just given in a general schema, that is to say, with regard to disease, as with regard to everything henceforth, there is the organization of a sort of inquisitorial space or grid.[38] The construction of what we can broadly call hospital and medical facilities in Europe in the eighteenth century basically ensures the general surveillance of populations, making it possible, in principle, to investigate the health of every individual.[39] The hospital also makes possible the integration of the living individual's body, and especially his dead body, into the disease.[40] That is to say, at the end of the eighteenth century we will have both a general surveillance of populations and the concrete possibility of establishing a relationship between a disease and a body on which an autopsy has been carried out. The birth of pathological anatomy and, at the same time, the appearance of a statistical medicine, of a medicine of large numbers[41]—both the ascription of precise causality by the projection of the illness on a dead body and the possibility of inspecting a set of populations—provide the two major epistemological tools of nineteenth century medicine. And it is quite clear that henceforth a technology of observation and demonstration will progressively make the technique of crisis unnecessary.

What happens in psychiatry then? Well, I think something very strange takes place. On the one hand, it is clear that the psychiatric hospital, like the hospital of general medicine, cannot but tend to make the crisis disappear. The psychiatric hospital, like any other hospital, is a space of inquiry and inspection, a sort of inquisitorial site, and there is no need at all for that test of truth. I have also tried to show you that not only is there no need for the test of truth, but there is no need for truth at all, whether arrived at by the technique of the test or by that of demonstration. Furthermore, not only is there no need for it, but to tell the truth the crisis as an event in the madman's madness and behavior is ruled out. Why is it ruled out? Essentially for three reasons I think.

First, it is ruled out precisely by the fact that the hospital functions as a disciplinary system, that is to say, as a system subject to rules, expecting a certain order, imposing a certain regime that excludes anything like the raging and raving outburst of the crisis of madness.

Moreover, the main instruction, the main technique of this asylum discipline, is: Don't think about it. Don't think about it; think about something else; read, work, go into the fields, but anyway, don't think about your madness.[42] Cultivate, not your own garden, but the director's. Do woodwork, earn your keep, but don't think about your illness. The disciplinary space of the asylum cannot permit the crisis of madness.

Second, constant recourse to pathological anatomy in asylum practice, from about around 1825, played the role of theoretical rejection of the crisis.[43] Actually, nothing, apart from what took place with general paralysis, permitted the assumption, or anyway the ascription, of a physical cause to mental illness. Now, the practice of autopsy was, at least in a great many hospitals, a sort of regular practice the basic meaning of which was, I think, the following: if there is a truth of madness, it is certainly not in what the mad say; it can only reside in their nerves and their brain. To that extent, the crisis as the moment of truth, as the moment at which the truth of madness burst forth, was ruled out epistemologically by recourse to pathological anatomy, or rather, I think that pathological anatomy was the epistemological cover behind which the existence of the crisis could always be rejected, denied, or suppressed: We can strap you to your armchair, we can refuse to listen to what you say, since we will seek the truth of madness from pathological anatomy, when you are dead.

Finally, the third reason for rejecting the crisis was a process I have not considered until now: the relationship between madness and crime. In fact, from around 1820-1825 we see a very strange process in the courts in which doctors—who were not called on by the prosecutor or by the president of the court, and often not even by lawyers—gave their opinion on a crime and, as it were, tried to claim the crime for mental illness itself.[44] Faced with any crime, the doctors raised the question: Could not this be a sign of illness? And it was in this way that they constructed the very curious notion of monomania which, schematically, means this: when someone commits a crime which has no raison d'être, no justification at the level of his interest, wouldn't the fact alone of committing the crime be the symptom of an illness, the essence of which would basically be the crime itself? Monomania was a sort of single symptom illness with just one symptom occurring only once in the individual's life, but a symptom that was, precisely, the crime?[45]

One wonders why psychiatrists take this interest in crime, and why they insist so strongly and, in a way, so violently on the potential identity of crime and mental illness. There are, of course, a number of reasons, but I think one of them is the attempt to demonstrate not so much that every criminal may be mad, but to demonstrate something that is much more serious, and also much more important for psychiatric power, namely, that every mad person is a possible criminal. The determination to pin madness on a crime, even on every crime, was a way of founding psychiatric power, not in terms of truth, since precisely it is not a question of truth, but in terms of danger: We are here to protect society, since at the heart of every madness there is the possibility of crime. In my view, pinning something like a madness on a crime is, for social reasons of course, a way of getting the individual out of trouble, but, as a general rule, at the level of the general operation of this ascription of madness to crime, there is the psychiatrists' wish to base their practice on something like social defense, since they cannot base it in truth. So, we can say that the effect of the disciplinary system of psychiatry is basically to get rid of the crisis. Not only is it not needed, it is not wanted, since the crisis could be dangerous, since the madman's crisis could well be another person's death. There is no need for it, pathological anatomy dispenses with it, and the regime of order and discipline means that the crisis is not desirable.

However, at the same time as this is taking place, there is a movement in the opposite direction, for the explanation and justification of which there are two reasons. On the one hand, the crisis is needed because, in the end, neither the disciplinary regime, nor the obligatory calm imposed on the mad, nor pathological anatomy, enabled psychiatric knowledge to be founded as truth. So that this knowledge, which I have tried to show you operated as a supplement of power, was for a long time running on empty, and obviously it could not fail to seek to provide itself with a content of truth according to the same norms of the medical technology of the time, that is to say, the technology of reported findings. But since this was not possible, the crisis was resorted to for another, positive reason.

The real point at which psychiatric knowledge is exercised is not initially or essentially what enables the illness to be specified, described, and explained. In other words, whereas the doctor, given his position, is basically obliged to respond to the patient's symptoms and complaints with an activity of specification and characterization—hence the fact that differential diagnosis has been the major medical activity since the nineteenth century—the psychiatrist is not required, or called in at the patient's request, to give the latter's symptoms a status, character, and specification. The psychiatrist is needed at an earlier stage, at a lower level, where it has to be decided whether or not there is an illness. For the psychiatrist it is a matter of answering the question: Is this individual mad or not? The question is put to him by the family in cases of voluntary admission, or by the administration in cases of compulsory admission—although the administration only puts the question on the quiet, since it reserves the right to disregard what the psychiatrist says—but, in any case, the psychiatrist is situated at this level.

Whereas [general] medical knowledge functions at the point of the specification of the illness, at the point of differential diagnosis, medical knowledge in psychiatry functions at the point of the decision between madness or non-madness, the point, if you like, of reality or non-reality, reality or fiction, whether this be fiction on the part of the patient who, for one reason or another, would like to pretend to be mad, or the fiction of the family circle, which imagines, wishes, desires, or imposes the image of madness. This is the point at which the psychiatrist's knowledge, and also his power, functions.[46]

Now what tools does the psychiatrist possess that enable him to function at this level and decide on the reality of madness? It is precisely here that we encounter the paradox of nineteenth century psychiatric knowledge once again. On the one hand, psychiatric knowledge really tried to construct itself on the model of medicine-observation, of inquiry and demonstration; it really tried to constitute a symptomatological type of knowledge for itself; a description of different illnesses was actually constituted, etcetera, but, to tell the truth, this was only the cover and justification for an activity situated elsewhere, and this activity was precisely that of deciding between reality or lie, reality or simulation. The activity of psychiatric knowledge is really situated at the point of simulation, at the point of fiction, not at the point of characterization.

There are, I think, a number of consequences of this. The first is that in order to resolve this problem the psychiatric hospital literally invented a new medical crisis. This was no longer that old crisis of truth played out between the forces of the disease and the forces of nature that was typical of the medical crisis put to work in the eighteenth century, but a crisis that I will call a crisis of reality, which is played out between the mad person and the power that confines him, the doctor's power-knowledge. The doctor must be able to arbitrate on the question of the reality or non-reality of the madness.

So, as you can see, unlike the hospital of general medicine, the psychiatric hospital's function is not to be the place where an "illness" exhibits its specific and differential characteristics in comparison with other illnesses. The psychiatric hospital has a much simpler, more elementary, more fundamental function. Its function is, precisely, to give madness reality, to open up a space of realization for madness. The psychiatric hospital exists so that madness becomes real, whereas the hospital's function *tout court* is both knowing what the illness is and eliminating it. The psychiatric hospital's function, following the psychiatric decision concerning the reality of the madness, is to make it exist as reality.

Here we encounter an institutional type of criticism of the psychiatric hospital, which charges it, precisely, with fabricating the mad out of the people it claims to cure. This institutional type of criticism thus poses the question: What kind of institution could work in such a way that the mad could be cured and not pushed deeper into illness? How could the [asylum] institution work like any hospital?[47] However, in the end I think this criticism is quite inadequate because it lacks the essential. That is to say, it lacks an analysis of the distribution of psychiatric power that makes it possible to show that the fact that the psychiatric hospital is a place for the realization of madness is not an accident or due to a deviation of the institution, but that the very function of psychiatric power is to have before it, and for the patient, a space of realization for the illness (that, when it comes to it, may or may not be in the hospital). We can say then that the function of psychiatric power is to realize madness in an institution where the function of discipline is precisely to get rid of all the violence, crises, and, if necessary, all the symptoms of madness. The real function and effect of the asylum institution in itself, of this institution of discipline—and it is in this respect that my analysis differs from institutional analyses—is to suppress, I do not say madness, but the symptoms of madness, at the same time as the function of psychiatric power, which is exercised within and fixes individuals to the asylum, is to realize madness.

All in all, there is an ideal for this double functioning of psychiatric power, which realizes madness, and of the disciplinary institution, which refuses to listen to madness, which flattens out its symptoms and planes down all its manifestations: this is dementia. What is a demented person? He is someone who is nothing other than the reality of his madness; he is the person in whom the multiplicity of symptoms or, rather, their flattening out, is such that it is no longer possible to ascribe to him a specific symptomatology by which he could be characterized. The demented person is therefore someone who corresponds exactly to the working of the asylum institution, since, by means of discipline, all the symptoms in their specificity have been smoothed out: there are no longer any outward signs, externalizations, or crises. And, at the same time, someone who is demented answers to what psychiatric power wants, since he actually realizes madness as an individual reality within the asylum.

The famous development of dementia, which nineteenth century psychiatrists could observe as a natural phenomenon in madness, is nothing other than the series of intertwined effects of an asylum discipline that smoothes away outward signs and symptoms, and medical power's appeal to the patient to be a madman, to realize madness. The demented person is actually what was fabricated by this double game of power and discipline.

As for the hysterics, those famous, dear hysterics, I would say that they were precisely the front of resistance to this gradient of dementia that involved the double game of psychiatric power and asylum discipline. They were the front of resistance, because, what is a hysteric? A hysteric is someone who is so seduced by the best and most clearly specified symptoms—those, precisely, offered by the organically ill—that he or she adopts them. The hysteric constitutes herself as the blazon of genuine illnesses; she models herself as a body and site bearing genuine symptoms. To the ascription of and propensity towards the subsidence of symptoms in dementia, the hysteric responds with the exacerbation of the most precise and well-determined symptoms; and while doing this, she pursues a game such that when one wants to fix her illness in reality, one can never manage to do so, since, when her symptom should refer to an organic substratum, she shows that there is no substratum, so that she cannot be fixed at the level of the reality of her illness at the very moment she displays the most spectacular symptoms. Hysteria was the effective way of defending oneself from dementia; the only way not to be demented in a nineteenth century hospital was to be a hysteric, that is to say, to counter the pressure that annihilated symptoms, that obliterated them, by building up the visible, plastic edifice of a whole panoply of symptoms, and, by means of simulation, resisting madness being fixed in reality. The hysteric has magnificent symptoms, but at the same time she sidesteps the reality of her illness; she goes against the current of the asylum game and, to that extent, we salute the hysterics as the true militants of antipsychiatry.[48]

1. Discovered in the sixteenth century, the use of ether spread in the nineteenth century in the treatment of neuroses and for screening simulated illnesses, on account of its "stupefying" property. See above, note 18 to lecture of 9th January 1974.
2. Discovered simultaneously in 1831 by Justus Liebig in Germany and by Soubeiran in France, the use of chloroform as an anesthetic began in 1847. See, E. Soubeiran, "Recherches sur quelques combinaisons de chlore" *Annales de chimie et de physique*, vol. XLIII, October 1831, pp. 113-157; H. Bayard, "L'utilisation de l'éther et le diagnostic des maladies mentales"; H. Brochin, "Maladies nerveuses", § "Anesthésiques: éther et chloroforme"; and, Lailler (pharmacist of the Quatre Mares asylum) "Les nouveaux hypnotiques et leur emploi en médecine mentale" *Annales médico-psychologiques*, 7th series, vol. IV, July 1886, pp. 64-90.
3. See above, note 1 to lecture of 19 December 1973.
4. See above, note 2 to lecture of 19 December 1973.
5. J.J. Moreau de Tours discovered the effects of hashish on his journey in the East from 1837 to 1840 and he subsequently devoted his research to it, foreseeing possibilities of experiment to clarify the relations between its effects and dreams and delirium. See, *Du haschich et d'aliénation mentale. Études psychologiques* (Paris: Fortin, 1845).
6. Experiments in "animal magnetism" took place in hospitals under the Restoration. Thus, at the Hôtel Dieu, on 20 October 1820, the head doctor, Henri Marie Husson (1772-1853) invited the baron Dupotet de Sennevoy to make some demonstrations; under the supervision of Joseph Récamier and Alexandre Bertrand, a young woman of 18, Catherine Samson, was given magnetic treatment. See J. Dupotet de Sennevoy (1790-1866), *Exposé des expériences sur le magnétisme animal faites à l'Hôtel Dieu de Paris pendant le cours des mois d'octobre, novembre et décembre 1820* (Paris: Béchet Jeune, 1821). At Salpêtrière, Étienne Georget and Léon Rostan used some of their patients as experimental subjects. Without giving their names, Georget records these experiments in *De la physiologie du système nerveux, et spécialment du cerveux*, vol. I, p. 404. See, L. Rostan, *Du magnétisme animal* (Paris: Rignoux, 1825). See also, A. Gauthier, *Histoire du somnambulisme*, vol. II, p. 324. See below, note 48 to lecture of 30 January 1974.
7. Foucault is alluding to the debate between Socrates and Parmenides on the problem of the things of which there are Ideas. See, Plato, *Parmenides*, 130c-d.
8. From the middle of the eighth century B.C. until the end of the fourth century A.D., Delphi, a town of Phocis at the foot of Parnassus, was a favorite site for Apollo to deliver his oracles through the mouth of the Pythia. See, M. Delcourt, *Les Grands Sanctuaires de la Grèce* (Paris: Presses universitaires de France, 1947) pp. 76-92; M. Delcourt, *L'Oracle de Delphes* (Paris: Payot, 1955); R. Flacelière, *Devins et Oracles grecs* (Paris: Presses universitaires de France, 1972) pp. 49-83; and, G. Roux, *Delphes, son oracle et ses dieux* (Paris: Les Belles Lettres, 1976).
9. Epidaurus, a town of Argolis on the east Peloponnese, was the site of the sanctuary Apollo's son, Asclepius, where divination through dreams was practiced. See, M. Delcourt, *Les Grands Sanctuaires*, pp. 93-113; R. Flacelière, *Devins et Oracles grecs*, pp. 36-37; and, G. Vlastos, "Religion and medicine in the cult of Asclepius: a review article" *Review of Religion*, vol. 13, 1948-1949, pp. 269-290.
10. The notion of *καιρόϛ* (*kairos*) defines the occasion, the opportunity to be seized, and consequently the time of possible action. Hippocrates (460-377 B.C.) devotes a chapter of his *Des Maladies*, I, to this notion, in *Œuvres complètes*, éd. Littré (Paris, J.-B. Baillière, 1849) vol. VI, ch. 5, "Of the opportune and inopportune" pp. 148-151; English translation, "Diseases 1" in *Hippocrates*, vol. V, trans. Paul Potter (Cambridge, Mass.: Harvard University Press, The Loeb Classical Library, 1988). See, P. Joos, "Zufall. Kunst und Natur bei dem Hippokratitkern" *Janus*, no. 46, 1957, pp. 238-252; P. Kucharski, "Sur la notion pythagoricienne de *kairos*" *Revue philosophique de la France et de l'étranger*, vol. CLII, no. 2, 1963, pp. 141-169; and P Chantraine, "καιρόϛ" in *Dictionnaire étymologique de la langue grecque. Histoire des mots* (Paris: Klincksieck, 1970) vol. II, p. 480.
11. Foucault is alluding here to the Heideggerian problematic that, in a discussion with G. Preti, he then associated with that of Husserl in the same reproach of calling into "question all our knowledge and its foundations (...) on the basis of that which is

original (...) at the expense of all articulated historical content," M. Foucault, "Les problèmes de la culture. Un débat Foucault-Preti" (September 1972) *Dits et Écrits*, vol. 2, p. 372. So it is the Heideggerian conception of history that is intended here. See especially, M. Heidegger, (1) *Sein und Zeit* (Halle: Nemeyer, 1927); English translation, *Being and Time*, trans. J. Macquarrie and E. Robinson (Oxford: Blackwells, 1967); (2) *Vom Wesen des Grundes* (Halle: Nemeyer, 1929); English translation, *The Essence of Reasons*, trans. Terrence Malick (Evanstan: Northwestern University Press, 1969); (3) *Vom Wesen der Wahreit* (Frankfurt: Klostermann, 1943); English translation, *The Essence of Truth, on Plato's parable of the cave allegory and Theaetetus*, trans. T. Sadler (London: Continuum, 2002); (4) *Holzwege* (Frankfurt: Klostermann; 1952); English translation, *Off the Beaten Track*, trans. J. Young and K. Haynes (Cambridge: Cambridge University Press, 2002); (5) *Vorträge und Aufsätze* (Pfullingen: Neske, 1954); (6) *Nietzsche*, vol. 2 (Pfullingen: Neske, 1961); English translation, *Nietzsche, vol. 2: The Eternal Recurrence of the Same*, trans. David Farrell Krell (San Francisco: Harper & Row, 1984). On the relations between Foucault and Heidegger, see M. Foucault, (1) *Les Mots et les choses*, ch. 9, "L'Homme et ses doubles" § iv and vi; *The Order of Things*, ch. 9, "Man and his doubles" sections 4 and 6; (2) "L'Homme est-il mort?" (interview with C. Bonnefoy, June 1966) *Dits et Écrits*, vol. 1, p. 542; (3) "Ariane s'est pendue" (April 1969) *Dits et Écrits*, vol. 1, p. 768 and p. 770; (4) "Foucault, le philosophe, est en train de parler. Pensez" (29 May 1973) *Dits et Écrits*, vol. 2, p. 424; (5) "Prisons et asiles dans le mécanisme du pouvoir" (interview with M. D'Eramo, March 1974), *Dits et Écrits*, vol. 2, p. 521; (6) "Structuralisme et poststructuralisme" (interview with G. Raulet, Spring 1983) *Dits et Écrits*, vol. 4, p. 455; English translation, "Structuralism and Post-Structuralism," trans. Jeremy Harding, *Essential Works of Foucault*, 2, p. 456; (7) "Politique et éthique: une interview," *Dits et Écrits*, vol. 4, p. 585; "Politics and Ethics: An Interview" trans. P. Rabinow, *The Foucault Reader*, pp. 373-374; (8) "Le retour de la morale" (interview with G. Barbedette and A. Scala, 29 May 1984) *Dits et Écrits*, vol. 4, p. 703; English translation, "The Return of Morality" trans. Thomas Levin and Isabelle Lorenz, in Michel Foucault, *Politics, Philosophy, Culture. Interviews and Other Writings, 1977-1984*, ed. Lawrence D. Kritzman (New York and London: Routledge, 1988); (9) "Verité, pouvoir et soi" (interview with R. Martin, 25 October 1982) *Dits et Écrits*, vol. 4, p. 780.

12. In the third lecture of the 1970-1971 course, "The Will to Knowledge (*savoir*)," Foucault proposed the "opposite view" of a history of the "will to knowledge (*connaître*)," in which truth has "the immediate, universal and bare form of observation, external to the procedure of judgment," proposing the need to "write a history of the relationships between truth and torture (*supplice*)," in which "truth is not observed but decided in the form of the oath and the invocation prescribed by the ritual of the ordeal." A regime, consequently, in which "truth is not linked to the possible light and gaze brought to bear on things by a subject, but to the obscurity of the future and disturbing event." Other fragments of such a history are put forward in the ninth lecture of the 1971-1972 course, "Penal Theories and Institutions," which deals with the system of proof in procedures of the oath, ordeals, and judicial duel from the tenth to the thirteenth century. Foucault was inspired by M. Detienne, *Les Maîtres de verité dans la Grèce archaïque* (Paris: Maspero, 1967); English translation, *The Masters of Truth in Archaic Greece*, trans. Janet Lloyd (New York: Zone Books, 1999).
13. The thirteenth lecture of the course "Penal Theories and Institutions" dedicated to "the confession, the test" explains the meaning of the detour through what Foucault calls "juridico-political matrices" such as the test, the inquiry, etcetera, and distinguishes three levels of analysis: (a) an "historical description of the sciences," in which "the history of the sciences" consists; (b) an "archeology of knowledge" which takes the relationships of knowledge and power into account; and (c) a "dynastic of knowledge" which, thanks to the freeing of the juridico-political matrices which authorize the archeology, is situated "at the level which combines the most profit, knowledge and power" (course manuscript consulted thanks to the kindness of Daniel Defert). Foucault takes up this distinction between the "archeological" and "dynastic" in an interview with S. Hasumi, September 1972 "De l'archéologie à la dynastique," *Dits et Écrits*, vol. 2, p. 406. On "archeology," see the many definitions given by Foucault: (1) in *Dits et Écrits*, vol. 1: "Michel Foucault, *Les Mots et les*

Choses" pp. 498-499; "Sur les façons d'écrire l'histoire" p. 595; "Réponse à une question" p. 681, and "Michel Foucault explique son dernier livre" pp. 771-772; (2) in *Dits et Écrits*, vol. 2: "La volonté de savoir" p. 242; "La vérité et les formes juridiques" pp. 643-644; English translation, "Truth and Juridical Forms," trans. Robert Hurley, *Essential Works of Foucault, 3*; (3) in *Dits et Écrits*, vol. 3: "Cours du 7 janvier 1976" p. 167; English translation, lecture of 7 January 1976, "*Society Must Be Defended*" ch. 1, pp. 10-11; "Dialogue sur le pouvoir", pp. 468-469; (4) in *Dits et Écrits*, vol. 4: "Entretien avec Michel Foucault" p. 57; "Structuralisme et poststructuralisme" p. 443; English translation, "Structuralism and Post-Structuralism," trans. Jeremy Harding, *Essential Works of Foucault, 2*, pp. 444-445.

14. In fact Foucault will not keep to this program apart from some comments on the role of childhood in the generalization of psychiatric knowledge and power in the 1974-1975 Collège de France lectures of 5, 12, and 19 March: *Les Anormaux*, pp. 217-301; *Abnormal*, pp. 231-321.

15. From the Old English, *ordal*, judgment, the "judgment of God" or "ordeal," means to settle contentious questions with the idea that God intervenes in the case to judge during tests likes those of "fire," the "branding iron," "cold or boiling water," and the "cross," etcetera. See L. Tanon, *Histoire des tribunaux de l'Inquisition en France* (Paris: L. Larose and Forcel, 1893) on the penalties of "fire" (pp. 464-479) and the "cross" (pp. 490-498). As J.-P. Lévy emphasizes in his, *La Hiérarchie des preuves dans le droit savant du Moyen Âge, depuis la renaissance du droit romain jusqu'à la fin du xive siècle* (Paris: Sirey, 1939), in this procedure "the trial is not an investigation with the aim of finding out the truth (...). It is originally a struggle, and later, an appeal to God; the concern with making the truth come out is left up to Him, but the judge does not seek it himself" (p. 163).

    Foucault referred to the question of the ordeal in the third lecture of the 1970-1971 Collège de France lectures, "The Will to Knowledge," in which he noted that in "the treatments to which madness was subjected, we find something like this ordeal test of the truth." The ninth lecture of the 1971-1972 lectures, devoted to accusatory procedure and the system of proof, refers to it (see above note 12). See also, M. Foucault, "La vérité et les formes juridiques"; "Truth and Juridical Forms." See, A. Esmein, *Histoire de la procédure criminelle en France, et spécialement de la procédure inquisitoire depuis le xiiie siècle jusqu'à nos jours* (Paris: Larose et Forcel, 1882) pp. 260-283; E. Vacandard, "L'Église et les ordalies" in *Études de critique et d'histoire religieuse*, vol. I (Paris: V. Lecoffre, 1905) pp. 189-214; G. Glotz, *Études sociales et juridiques sur l'antiquité grecque*, ch. 2, "L'ordalie" (Paris: Hachette, 1906) pp. 69-97; A. Michel, "Ordalies" in, A. Vacant, ed., *Dictionnaire de théologie catholique*, vol. XI (Paris: Letouzey et Ané, 1930) col. 1139-1152; Y. Bongert, *Recherches sur les cours laïques du xe au xiiie siècles* (Paris: A et J. Picard, 1949) pp. 215-228; H. Nottarp, *Gottelsurteilstudien* (Munich: Kosel-Verlag, 1956); and J. Gaudemet, "Les ordalies au Moyen Âge: doctrine, législation et pratique canonique" in *Recueil de la Société Jean Bodin* (Brussels: 1965) vol. XVII, Part 2, *La Preuve*.

16. In the basically accusatory procedures that involved taking God as witness so that he produces the accuracy or retraction of the accusation, confession was not enough to pronounce sentence. See, H.C. Lea, *A History of the Inquisition of the Middle Ages*, vol. 1, pp. 407-408; A. Esmein, *Histoire de la procédure criminelle*, p. 273; and J.-P. Lévy, *La Hiérarchie des preuves*, pp. 19-83. On confession, see *Surveiller et Punir*, pp. 42-45; *Discipline and Punish*, pp. 37-40.

17. Torture, unlike the sovereign means of proof by ordeal—the expression of God's testimony—was a way of provoking judicial confession. The inquisitorial procedure was integrated into canon law in 1232 when Pope Gregory IX called upon the Dominicans to establish a tribunal of Inquisition specifically for the search for and punishment of heretics. Recourse to judicial torture was approved by the bull, *Ad Extirpanda*, of Pope Innocent IV of 15 May 1252, and later, in 1256, by that of Alexander IV, *Ut Negotium Fidei*. Referring to the question of the Inquisition in the third lecture of the 1970-1971 lectures, "The Will to Knowledge," Foucault said that "it is a matter of something other than obtaining a truth, a confession (...). It is a challenge which, within Christian thought and practice, takes up the forms of the ordeal." See *Surveiller et Punir*, pp. 43-47; *Discipline and Punish*, pp. 38-42; "Michel Foucault. Les réponses du philosophe" *Dits et Écrits*, vol. 2, pp. 810-811. See, H.C. Lea, *A History of the Inquisition*, vol. 1, ch. 9, "The Inquisitorial Process," pp. 399-429, and on torture, pp. 417-427; L. Tanon, *Histoire des tribunaux de l'Inquisition*, section III,

"Procédure des tribunaux de l'Inquisition," pp. 326-440; E. Vacandard, *L'Inquisition. Étude historique et critique sur le pouvoir coercitif de l'Église* (Paris: Bloud et Gay, 1907, 3rd ed.) p. 175; H. Leclercq, "Torture" in F. Cabrol, H. Leclercq, H.I. Marrou, eds. *Dictionnaire d'archéologie chrétienne et de liturgie*, vol. XV (Paris: Letouzey et Ané, 1953) col. 2447-2459; P. Fiorelli, *La Tortura giudiziaria nel diritto comune* (Milan: Giuffrè, 1953). On the Inquisition in general, see, J. Guiraud, *Histoire de l'Inquisition au Moyen Âge*, in two volumes (Paris: A. Picard, 1935-1938); and H. Maisonneuve, *Études sur les origines de l'Inquisition* (Paris: J. Vrin, 1960, 2nd ed.).

18. This question was the topic of the third lecture of the 1971-1972 lectures, "Penal Theories and Institutions," devoted to confession, investigation and proof. See the course summary, "Théories et institutions pénales" *Dits et Écrits*, vol. 2, pp. 390-391, English translation "Penal Theories and Institutions" *Essential Works of Foucault*, 1, pp. 18-20.
19. See, M. Eliade, *Forgerons et Alchimistes* (1956) (Paris: Flammarion, 1977 rev. ed.): "No virtue or erudition could do without the initiatory experience which was alone able to bring about the break of level implied in the 'transmutation' " (p. 136) and "Every initiation includes a series of ritual tests which symbolize the neophyte's death and resurrection" (p. 127).
20. As Lucien Braun will recall in a paper on "Paracelse et l'alchimie," "the alchemist's approach must be relentlessly that of a seeker on the look out (...). Paracelsus sees constant parturition in the alchemical process, in which the subsequent moment is always a surprise in relation to the one preceding it" in J.-C. Margolin and S. Matton, eds. *Alchimie et Philosophie à la Renaissance (Actes du colloque international de Tours, 4-7 décembre 1991)* (Paris: Vrin, 1993) p. 210. See also, M. Eliade, pp. 126-129, on the phases of the "*opus alchymicum*."
21. See, W. Ganzenmüller, (1) *Die Alchemie im Mittelalter* (Paderborn: Bonifacius, 1938), French translation by G. Petit-Dutaillis, *L'Alchimie au Moyen Âge* (Paris: Aubier, 1940), and (2) studies collected in *Beiträge zur Geschichte der Technologie und der Alchimie* (Weinheim: Verlag Chemie, 1956); F. Sherwood Taylor, *The Alchemists, Founders of Modern Chemistry* (New York: H. Schuman, 1949); R. Alleau, *Aspects de l'alchimie traditionnelle* (Paris: Éditions de Minuit, 1953); T. Burckhardt, *Alchimie, Sinn und Weltbild* (Olten: Walter Verlag, 1960); M. Caron and S. Hutin, *Les Alchimistes* (Paris: Le Seuil, 1964, 2nd ed.); H. Buntz, E. Ploss, H. Roosen-Runge, and H. Schipperges, *Alchimia: Ideologie und Technologie* (Munich: Heinz Moos Verlag, 1970); B. Husson, *Anthologie de l'alchimie* (Paris: Belfond, 1971); F.A. Yates, *Giordano Bruno and the Hermetic Tradition* (London: Routledge and Kegan Paul, 1964). Foucault broaches the question of alchemy in his third lecture (23 May 1973) on "La vérité et les formes juridiques"; "Truth and Juridical Forms," and in "La maison des fous" *Dits et Écrits*, vol. 2, pp. 693-694.
22. Hippocrates was born in 460 A.D. on the Dorian island of Cos in Asia Minor and died around 375 A.D. at Larissa in Thessaly. His works, written in the Ionian dialect of the learned, constitute the core of what became the Hippocratic corpus. See, Gossen, "Hippocrates" in A.F. Pauly and G. Wissowa, eds., *Realencyclopädie der classischen Altertumswissenschaft*, vol. VIII (Stuttgart: Metzler, 1901) col. 1810-1852; M. Pohlenz, *Hippokrates und die Begründung der wissenschaftlichen Medizin* (Berlin: De Gruyter, 1938); C. Lichtenthaeler, *La Médicine hippocratique* (studies in French and German) in 9 volumes (Geneva: Droz, 1948-1963); L. Edelstein, "Nachträge: Hippokrates," in *Realencyclopädie*, supplement VI, 1953, col. 1290-1345; R. Joly, *Le Niveau de la science hippocratique. Contribution à la psychologie de l'histoire des sciences* (Paris: Les Belles Lettres, 1966); J. Jouanna, *Hippocrate. Pour une archéologie de l'école de Cnide* (Paris: Les Belles Lettres, 1974). The basic edition of the works of Hippocrates is the bilingual Littré edition (see above, note 10). The basic, bilingual, English edition is the Loeb Classical Library edition of *Hippocrates*, in 8 volumes (Cambridge, Mass.: Harvard University Press, 1923-1995).
23. Thomas Sydenham (1624-1689) was an English practitioner known for the changes he introduced into medical knowledge. As Foucault notes in *Histoire de la folie*, pp. 205-207 (omitted from the English translation), he organized knowledge of pathology according to new norms by making a method of observation, taking into account the symptoms described by the patient, against the medical systems, like Galenism or iatrochemistry, which relied on a speculative approach—earning him the name "the English

Hippocrates"—and by developing a "naturalist" description of diseases offering the possibility of reducing clinical cases to morbid "species" defined in a botanical style. He published the results of his observations in his *Observationes medicae circa morborum acutorum historiam et curationem. Methodus curandi febres, propiis observationibus superstructa* (London: Kettilby, 1676); English translation, *Medical Observations Concerning the History and Cur of Acute Diseases*, trans. R.G. Latham, in *The Works of Thomas Sydenham, M.D.*, vol. 1 (London: The Sydenham Society, 1848). See, K. Faber, *Thomas Sydenham, der englische Hippocrates, und die Krankheitsbegriffe der Renaissance* (Munich: Medizinische Wochenschrift, 1932) pp. 29-33; E. Berghoff, *Entwicklungsgeschichte des Krankheitsbegriffes* (Vienna: W. Maudrich, 1947) pp. 68-73; and L.S. King, "Empiricism and rationalism in the works of Thomas Sydenham," *Bulletin of the History of Medicine*, vol. 44, no. 1, 1970, pp. 1-11.

As Foucault recalls in *Histoire de la folie*, pp. 305-308 (*Madness and Civilization*, pp. 146-150) Sydenham was among those who contributed to a preference for an explanation of hysteria in terms of physiological disorders of the nerves, attributed to disorders of the "animal spirits," against the traditional explanation which referred to the uterus and the humoral model of the "vapors": "it is not any corruption of either the semen or the menstrual blood, to which, according to many writers, this disease is to be referred. It is rather the faulty disposition of the animal spiritis" *Dissertatio epistolaris ad G. Cole de observationis nuperis circa curationem variolarum, confuentium, necnon de affectione hysterica* (London: Kettilby, 1682); English translation, "Epistolary Dissertation" trans. R.G. Latham, *The Works of Thomas Sydenham*, vol. 2, 1850, p. 95; French translation in, *Œuvres de médecine pratique*, vol. II, trans. A.F. Jault and J.-B. Baumes (Montpellier: J. Tourel, 1816), p. 85. See, I. Veith, "On hysterical and hypochondriacal affections," *Bulletin of the History of Medicine*, vol. 30, no. 3, 1956, pp. 233-240, and I. Veith, *Hysteria: the History of a Disease* (Chicago: Chicago University Press, 1965). More generally, see, C. Daremberg, *Histoire des sciences médicales, comprenant l'anatomie, la physiologie, la médecine, la chirurgie et les doctrines de pathologie générale*, vol. II (Paris: J.-B. Baillière, 1870), ch. 23, "Sydenham, sa vie, ses doctrines, sa pratique, son influence," pp. 706-734; K. Dewhurst, *Dr Thomas Sydenham (1624-1689): His Life and Original Writings* (London: Wellcome Historical Medical Library, 1966).

24. Foucault bases himself on the work, referred to in the manuscript, of John Barker, *Essai sur la conformité de la médecine des anciens et des modernes, en comparaison entre la pratique d'Hippocrate, Galien, Syndenham et Boerhaave dans les maladies aiguës*, trans. R. Schomberg (Paris: Cavalier, 1749) pp. 75-76: "Of necessity, it is indispensable for the doctor to have a basic knowledge of the doctrine of crises and critical days (...) to be able to discover whether or not the heat of the humors is as it should be, at what moment to expect the crisis, of what kind it will be, and whether or not it will prevail over the disease." See also J.-B. Aymen, *Dissertation [sur] les jours critiques* (Paris: Rault, 1752). The importance of the notion is indicated by the fact that the article "Crise" in the *Encyclopédie ou Dictionnaire raisonné des sciences, des arts et des métiers* of D'Alembert and Diderot was written by a great name in medicine, Théophile Bordeu (1722-1776) and fills 18 folio pages (vol. IV, Lausanne: Société typographique, 1754).
25. The καιρόϛ designates the moment in the evolution of the illness when a decisive change occurs: "There is crisis in diseases when they increase, get weaker, are transformed into another disease or end" Hippocrates, *Affections*, § 8, in *Œuvres complètes*, vol. VI (1847); English translation, *Affections*, in *Hippocrates*, vol. V, trans. Paul Potter (Cambridge, Mass: Harvard University Press, Loeb Classical Library, 1988). See, G. Hamelin, "Crise" in *Dictionnaire encyclopédique des science médicales*, 1st series, vol. XXIII (Paris: Masson/Asselin, 1879) pp. 258-319; P. Chantraine "καιρόϛ" in *Dictionnaire étymologique de la langue grecque*, vol. II, p. 584; L. Bourgey, *Observation et expérience chez les médecins de la Collection Hippocratique* (Paris: Vrin, 1953) pp. 236-247. On the Greek medical terms: N. Van Brock, *Recherches sur le vocabulaire médical du grec ancien. Soins et guérison* (Paris: Klincksieck, 1961). See Foucault, "La maison des fous" *Dits et Écrits*, vol. 2, pp. 693-694.
26. This is more or less the definition put forward by Sydenham in his *Observationes medicae*, Section 1, ch. 1, § 1; *Medical Observations*, p. 29: "(...) a disease (...) is nothing more than an effort of Nature, who strives with might and main to restore the health of the patient by the elimination of the morbific matter."

27. In *Histoire de la folie*, p. 285 and p. 245, *Madness and Civilization*, p. 123 and p. 86, Foucault noted the shift carried out in eighteenth century medicine, when it is "from the body's liquid and solid elements that the secret of disease was sought" rather than from the "animal spirits." Hermann Boerhaave (1668-1738), integrating the contributions of physics, chemistry and the natural sciences, made illness the result of an alteration of the balance of solids and liquids: *Institutiones medicae, in usus annae exercitationis domesticos digestae* (Leyden: Van der Linden, 1708) p. 10, French translation by J.O. de La Mettrie, *Institutions de médecine*, vol. I (Paris: Huart, 1740). See, C. Daremberg, *Histoire des sciences médicales*, vol. II, ch. xxvi, pp. 897-903; L.S. King, *The Background of Hermann Boerhaave's Doctrines (Boerhaave Lecture, September 17th, 1964)* (Leyden: University of Leyden publications, 1965).
    Friedrich Hoffmann (1660-1742), a doctor at Halle, considered diseases to be the result of alterations of the solid and liquid parts of the body and of their functions, and, in accordance with his mechanistic perspective, he gave a major role to modifications of the tonicity of the fibers and of the mechanics of the blood flow: (1) *Fundamenta medicinae ex principiis mechanicis et practicis in usum Philiatrorum succincte proposita ... jam aucta et emendata, et cetera* (Halle: Magdeburgicae, 1703), English translation, *Fundamenta Medicinae*, trans. L.S. King (London/New York: Macdonald/American Elsevier, 1971) p. 10; (2) *Medicina rationalis systemica*, in 2 volumes (Halle: Renyeriana, 1718-1720), French translation by J.-J. Bruhier (Paris: Briasson, 1738). See C. Daremberg, *Histoire*, vol. II, pp. 905-952; K.E. Rothschuh, "Studien zu Friedrich Hoffmann (1660-1742)" *Studhoffs Archiv für Geschichte der Medizin*, vol. 60, 1976, pp. 163-193 and pp. 235-270. On this eighteenth century medicine, see, L.S. King (1) *The Medical World of the Eighteenth Century* (Chicago: University of Chicago Press, 1958), and (2) "Medical theory and practice at the beginning of the eighteenth century," *Bulletin of the History of Medicine*, vol. 46, no. 1, 1972, pp. 1-15.
28. Hippocrates, *Épidémies*, I, 3rd section, § 12 in *Œuvres complètes*, vol. II (1840), pp. 679-681; English translation, *Epidemics*, Book 1, (iii), 26, in G.E.R. Lloyd, ed. *Hippocratic Writings*, trans. J. Chadwick and others (Harmondsworth and New York: Penguin, 1978), p. 101: "Fevers attended by paroxysms at even numbers of days, reach their crisis also in an even number; if the paroxysms are on odd days, so is the crisis. The first period of [fever] in those maladies which reach the crisis in an even number of days is 4, 6, 8, 10, 14, 20, 24, 30, 40, 60, 80 or 120 days. (...). It must be noted that if a crisis occurs on any other day than those mentioned, there will be a relapse and also it may prove a fatal sign. One must pay attention to these days which have been specified in the course of a particular fever and realize that on them a crisis may take place leading to recovery or death, to improvement or to deterioration."
29. On the determination of lucky or ill-fated days for consulting the oracle, see P. Amandry, *La Mantique appollinienne à Delphes. Essai sur le fontionnement de l'oracle* (Paris: E. de Boccard, 1940) ch. vii, "Fréquence des consultations" pp. 81-85. On Greek "manticism" in general, derived from the verb μάντεύεσθαι meaning "to prophecy," to conjecture according to oracles, to act as a seer (μάντις), the basic book, although old, is still that of A. Bouché-Leclercq, *Histoire de la divination dans l'Antiquité*, in 4 volumes (Paris: Leroux, 1879-1882). Also, W.R. Halliday, *Greek Divination: A Study of its Methods and Principles* (London: Macmillan, 1913); J. Defradas, "La divination en Grèce" in A. Caquot and M. Leibovici, eds. *La Divination*, vol. I (Paris: Presses universitaires de France, 1968) pp. 157-195; R. Flacelière, *Devins et Oracles grecs*; and ed. J.-P. Vernant, *Divination et Rationalité* (Paris: Le Seuil, 1974).
30. Hippocrates "considers an important part of the art of medicine" to be the ability "to observe the order of the critical days and to extract the elements of prognosis from it. When we know these things, we know too when and how to give nourishment to the patient" Hippocrates, *Épidémies*, III, 3rd section, § 16, in *Œuvres complètes*, vol. III; English translation, Hippocrates, *Epidemics, 3*, trans. W.H.S. Jones, *Hippocrates*, vol. I, Loeb Classical Library (Cambridge, Mass: Harvard University Press, 1923).
31. Hippocrates, *Pronostic*, §1: "The best doctor seems to me to be one who can know in advance ... He will treat best those diseases whose future course he can foresee with the help of the present condition" *Œuvres complètes*, vol. II, p. 111; *Prognosis* § 1, in *Hippocratic Writings*: "It seems to be highly desirable that a physician should pay much attention to

prognosis. . . . he will be better able to effect a cure if he can foretell, from the present symptoms, the future course of the disease." p. 170.

32. In Hippocrates's own terms, the doctor's task is to "combat (ανταγονισαθαί) each of the accidents through his art." Or again, "if we know the cause of the disease, we will be in a position to administer what is useful to the body, starting from contraries to counter (έκ τού έναντίον έπτάσμένος) the disease" *Des Vents*, I, in *Œuvres complètes*, vol. VI, p. 93 [translation amended by J.L.]; English translation, *Airs*, I, in *Hippocrates*, vol. I, Loeb Classical Library (1923).

33. Taken from juridical language, the term *krisis* means "judgment," "decision," before designating in medicine the crucial moment at which "the disease judges [κρινεταί] for death or life "*Des Affections internes*, 21-220, 9, in *Œuvres complètes*, vol. VII, p. 217; "Internal Affections," trans. Paul Potter, *Hippocrates*, vol. VI, Loeb Classical Library (1988). Or again there is this expression in *Épidémies*, I, 2nd section, § 4: "In some (. . .) the illness is decided by a crisis" in *Œuvres complètes*, vol. II, p. 627; *Epidemics*, Book One, (ii), § 8, p. 92. As for the doctor, he is judged on his sense of opportunity and his interventions; see, *Des maladies*, I, 5. pp. 147-151; *Diseases*, I, trans. Paul Potter, *Hippocrates*, vol. V, Loeb Classical Library (1988).

34. See the medical scenes in the plays by Molière (1622-1673): (1) *L'Amour médecin* (performed on 14 September, 1665), Act II, scene 2, in which four doctors are involved, and scenes 3-4 of the consultation, in *Œuvres complètes*, ed. M. Rat (Paris: Gallimard, 1947) vol. II, pp. 14-25; (2) *Monsieur de Pourceaugnac* (6 October 1669) in Act I, scenes 7-8, of which, two doctors and an apothecary are involved, *Œuvres complètes*, vol. II, pp. 141-120; and (3) *Le Malade imaginaire* (10 February 1673), posthumous work (1682), Act II, scenes 5-6, and Act III, scene 5, *Œuvres complètes*, vol. II , pp. 845-857 and pp. 871-873. See, F. Millepierres, *La Vie quotidienne des médecins au temps de Molière* (Paris: Hachette, 1964).

35. This refers to an episode that took place during Galen's (b. Pergamum 129 A.D.) first stay in Rome from the autumn of 162 until the summer of 166, before coming back to settle there from 169 until his death around 200. See, *De Praecognitione* § 13 in *Opera Omnia*, vol. XIV, ed. and Latin trans. C.G. Kühn (Lipsiae: in officina, C. Cnoblochii, 1827) pp. 666-668; English translation, *On Prognosis: Corpus Medicorum Graecorum*, V, 8, 1, trans. Vivian Hutton (Berlin: Akademie-Verlag, 1979) pp. 135-137. On Galen's relations with the Roman medical world, see J. Walsh, "Galen clashes with the medical sects at Rome (163 A.D.)," *Medical Life*, vol. 35, 1928, pp. 408-444. On his practice, see, J. Ilberg, "Aus Galens Praxis. Ein Kulturbild aus der Kaiserzeit," *Neue Jahrbücher für das klassische Altertum* (Leipzig: Teubner, vol. 15, 1905, pp. 276-312; and, V. Nutton, "The chronology of Galen's early career," *The Classical Quarterly*, vol. 23, 1973, pp. 158-171.

36. This passage echoes a number of treatments by Foucault of "the inquiry": (1) The 1971-1972 lectures at the Collège de France, the first part of which deals with the inquiry and its development in the Middle Ages; see the course summary, "Théories et Institutions pénales" *Dits et Écrits*, vol. 2, pp. 390-391; "Penal Theories and Institutions," trans. Robert Hurley, *Essential Works of Foucault, 1*, pp. 17-19; (2) The Collège de France lectures of 1972-1973, "The Punitive Society," in which, in the lecture of 28 March 1973, Foucault returns to the constitution of an "inquiry knowledge"; (3) The third lecture (23 May 1973) on "La Vérité et les formes juridiques" pp. 581-588; "Truth and Juridical Forms" pp. 44-52. Foucault returns to the process of the colonization of a "truth-test" in the form of the event by a "truth-findings" in the form of a body of knowledge in 1975 in "La Maison des fous" *Dits et Écrits*, vol. 2, pp. 696-697.

37. In the second half of the eighteenth century, since Friedrich Hoffmann, who still believed in the theory of crises, albeit with reservations about the notion of critical days, died in 1742. See, C. Daremberg, *Histoire des sciences médicales*, vol. II, p. 929.

38. This grid, which dates from the organization of administrative health correspondence by the Intendants in order to collect information on epidemics and endemic diseases, found institutional expression with the creation on 29 April 1776, on Turgot's initiative, of the "Société Royale de Médecine" responsible for studying epidemics and epizootic diseases, before disappearing in 1794. See, C. Hannaway, "The Société Royale de Médecine and epidemics in the Ancient Regime," *Bulletin of the History of Medicine*, vol. 46, no. 3, 1972, pp.

257-273. Concerning these inquiries, see, J. Meyer, "Une enquête de l'Académie de médecine sur les épidémies (1774-1794)" *Annales ESC*, 21st year, no. 4, August 1966, pp. 729-749; H. Dupin and L. Massé, "Une enquête épidémiologique à péripéties multiple: l'étude de la pellagre," *Revue d'épidémiologie, médecine sociale et santé publique*, vol. XIX, no. 8, 1971, pp. 743-760; J.-P. Peter, (1) "Une enquête de la Société Royale de Médecine. Malades et maladies à la fin du xviiie siècle," *Annales ESC*, 22nd year, no. 4, July-August 1967, pp. 711-751; (2) "Les mots et les objets de la maladie. Remarques sur les épidémies et la médecine dans la société française de la fin du xviiie siècle," *Revue historique*, no. 499, 1971, pp. 13-38; J.-P. Desaive, P. Goubert, E. Le Roy Ladurie, *Médecins, climats et épidémies à fin du xviiie siècle* (Paris: Mouton, 1972). See also the pages devoted to this in M. Foucault, *Naissance de la clinique*, ch. 2, "Une conscience politique," pp. 21-36; *Birth of the Clinic*, ch. 2, "A Political Consciousness," pp. 22-37.

39. On the development of hospital facilities and the advent of a medical police, see, G. Rosen, (1) "Hospitals, medical care and social policy in the French Revolution," *Bulletin of the History of Medicine*, vol. 30, no. 1, 1956, pp. 124-149, reprinted in G. Rosen, *From Medical Police to Social Medicine: Essays on the History of Health Care* (New York: Science History Publications, 1974) pp. 220-245; (2) *A History of Public Health* (New York: MD Publications, 1958); (3) "Mercantilism and health policy in eighteenth-century French thought," *Medical History*, vol. III, October 1959, pp. 259-277, reprinted in *From Medical Police*, pp. 201-219; M. Joeger, (1) "Les enquêtes hospitalières au xviiie siècle," *Bulletin de la Société française d'histoire des hôpitaux*, no. 31, 1975, pp. 51-60; (2) "La structure hospitalière de la France sous l'Ancien Régime," *Annales ESC*, 32nd year, no. 5, September-October 1977, pp. 1025-1051; M.-J. Imbault-Huart, "L'hôpital, centre d'une nouvelle médecine (1780-1820)," in *Zusammentrang Festschrift für Marilene Putscher*, vol. II (Cologne: Wienand, 1984) pp. 581-603. Foucault takes up this question in a number of places: (1) *Naissance de la clinique*, ch. v, "La leçon des hôpitaux," pp. 63-86; *Birth of the Clinic*, ch. 5, "The lesson of the Hospitals" pp. 64-87; "La politique de la santé au xviiie siècle," in Michel Foucault, Blandine Barret-Kriegel, Anne Thalamy, Francois Beguin, and Bruno Fortier, *Les Machines à guérir. Aux origines de l'hôpital moderne. Dossiers et documents* (Paris: Institut de l'Environnement, 1976) pp. 11-21, reprinted in *Dits et Écrits*, vol. 3, pp. 13-27; English translation, "The politics of health in the eighteenth century," trans. Colin Gordon, *Essential Works of Foucault, 3*, pp. 90-105; (3) he refers to it in his first lecture on the history of medicine in Rio de Janeiro in October 1974: "Crise de la médecine ou crise de l'antimédecine?" *Dits et Écrits*, vol. 3, pp. 50-54, and in the third "L'incorporation de l'hôpital dans la technologie moderne," *Dits et Écrits*, vol. 3, pp. 508-521.

40. See M. Foucault, *Naissance de la clinique*, ch. viii, "Ouvrez quelques cadavres," pp. 125-149; *Birth of the Clinic*, ch. 8, "Open Up a Few Corpses," pp. 124-148. E.H. Ackerknecht, *La Médecine hospitalière à Paris (1794-1848)* pp. 209-214.

41. Foucault takes up this point in his second lecture at Rio de Janeiro, "La naissance de la médecine sociale," *Dits et Écrits*, vol. 3, pp. 212-215; English translation "The Birth of Social Medicine," trans. Robert Hurley, *Essential Works of Foucault, 3*. See G. Rosen, "Problems in the application of statistical knowledge analysis to questions of health (1711-1880)" *Bulletin of the History of Medicine*, vol. 29, no. 1, 1955, pp. 27-45; M. Greenwood, *Medical Statistics from Graunt to Farr* (Cambridge: Cambridge University Press, 1948).

42. Thus, Georget states as "1st principle: never direct the minds of the insane towards their delirium" in chapter 5, "Traitement de la folie," of his work: *De la folie. Considérations sur cette maladie*, p. 280. Leuret states that "one must impose silence on the patient with regard to his delirium, and occupy them with something else" *Du traitement moral de la folie*, p. 120. On this "principle of distraction" see above, note 6 to the lecture of 5 December 1973.

43. Recourse to the research of pathological anatomy was recommended by Jean-Pierre Falret in the introduction (September 1853) to his *Des maladies mentales*, p. v: "Against the doctrines of our teachers, we yielded, like the others, to that anatomical direction of the science that at that time was thought to be the true basis of medicine (...). We quickly convinced ourselves that only pathological anatomy could give the primary cause of the phenomena observed in the insane." Thus, research into pathological anatomy was pursued at Charenton and gave rise to various publications: Jean-Baptiste Delaye (1789-1879), attached to Esquirol's department, defended his thesis on 20 November 1824, *Considération*

sur une espèce de paralysie qui affecte particulièrement les aliénés, Medical Thesis, Paris, No.224 (Paris: Didot, 1824); Louis Florentin Calmeil (1798-1895), intern in the department of Royer-Collard, chief doctor at Charenton from 1805 until his death in 1825, published: *De la paralysie considérée chez les aliénés. Recherches faites dans le service de feu M. Royer-Collard et de M. Esquirol* (Paris: J.-B. Baillière, 1826); Antoine Laurent Jessé Bayle, arrived at the same department in 1817 where he pursued anatomical research resulting in his thesis of 1822: *Recherches sur les maladies mentales. Recherches sur l'arachnitis chronique, la gastrite, la gastro-entérite et la goutte considérées comme causes de l'aliénation mentale*, Medical Thesis, Paris, no. 147 (Paris: Didot, 1822) as well as his work of 1826: *Traité des maladies du cerveau et de ses membranes*. See J.E.D. Esquirol, "Mémoire historique et statistique sur la Maison Royale de Charenton" (1835) in *Des maladies mentales*, vol. II, § "Ouvertures de corps," pp. 698-700. The results of Jean-Pierre Falret's research at Salpêtrière were presented on 6 December 1823 at the Athénée de Médecine: *Inductions tirées de l'ouverture du corps des aliénés pour servir au diagnostic et au traitement des maladies mentales* (Paris: Bibliothèque Médicale, 1824); Étienne Georget presents the results of around 300 *ouvertures des corps* of insane persons at the Salpêtrière hospital in chapter 5, "Recherches cadavériques. Études de l'anatomie pathologique" in his *De la folie*, pp. 423-431. A. [de] Foville pursued anatomical research resulting in his thesis: *Observations cliniques propres à éclairer certaines questions relatives à l'aliénation mentale*, Medical Thesis, Paris, no. 138 (Paris: Didot Jeune, 1824). Félix Voisin undertook anatomical work for his, *Des causes morales et physiques des maladies mentales, et de quelques autres affections telles que l'hystérie, le nymphomanie et le satyriasis*.

44. C.C.H. Marc, for example, took up the case of the wife of a journalist of Sélestat—who, in July 1817, killed her fifteen month old child, and cut off his right thigh, cooked it, and then partly ate it—and analyzed the medico-legal report of Dr. F.D. Reisseisen, "Examen d'un cas extraordinaire d'infanticide" (originally published in German in *Jahrbuch der Staatsartheilkund*, J.H. Kopp, ed., vol. XI, 1817) in his *De la folie considérée dans ses rapports avec les questions médico-judiciaires*, vol. II (Paris: J.-B. Baillière, 1840) pp. 130-146. Étienne Georget, in particular, considers several criminal cases: (1) *Examen médical des procès criminels de Léger, Feldman, Lecouffe, Jean-Pierre, Papavoine, dans lesquels l'aliénation mentale a été alléguée comme moyen de défense, suivi de quelques considérations médico-légales sur la liberté morale* (Paris: Migneret, 1825); (2) *Nouvelles discussions médico-légales sur la folie ou aliénation mentale, suivies de l'examen de plusieurs procès criminels dans lesquels cette maladie a été alléguée comme moyen de défense* (Paris: Migneret, 1826). On these medical strategies we can turn to, R. Castel, "Les médecins et les juges," in Michel Foucault, ed. *Moi, Pierre Rivière, ayant égorgé ma mère, ma sœur et mon frère. Un cas de parricide au xixe siècle* (Paris: Gallimard, 1973) pp. 315-331; English translation, "The Doctors and Judges," *I, Pierre Rivière, having slaughtered my mother, my sister and my brother . . .*, trans. F. Jellinek (New York: Pantheon, 1975 and Harmondsworth: Penguin, 1984) pp. 250-268. P. Devernoix, *Les Aliénés et l'expertise médico-légale. Du pouvoir discrétionnaire des juges en matière criminelle, et des inconvénients qui en résultent* (Toulouse: C. Dirion, 1905). Michel Foucault returns to these cases in his course, *Les Anormaux*, lectures of 29 January and 5 February 1975, pp. 94-100 and pp. 101-126; *Abnormal*, pp. 102-104 and 109-134.

45. In a note to chapter 4, "De l'impulsion insolite à une action déterminée," section III of J. Hoffbauer's treatise, *Médecine légale relative aux aliénés et aux sourds-muets, ou les lois appliquées aux désordres de l'intelligence*, trans. A.M. Chambeyron, with notes by Itard and Esquirol (Paris: J.-B. Baillière, 1827), Esquirol gives the following definition of monomania: "There is a kind of homicidal monomania in which one can observe no intellectual or moral disorder; the murderer is driven by an irresistible power, by a force he cannot overcome, by a blind impulse, by a thoughtless determination, without interest, without motive, without distraction, to an atrocious action" (reprinted in *Des maladies mentales*, vol. II, p. 804). On the history of the concept, see, R. Fontanille, *Aliénation mentale et Criminialité (Historique, expertise médico-légale)* (Grenoble: Allier Frères, 1902); P. Dubuisson and A. Vigouroux, *Responsibilité pénale et Folie. Étude médico-légale* (Paris: Alcan, 1911); and A. Fontana, "Les intermittences de la raison," in *Moi, Pierre Rivière . . .*, pp. 333-350; "The Intermittences of Rationality," *I, Pierre Rivière, . . .*, pp. 269-288.

46. Thus, C.C. Marc states that "one of the most serious and delicate functions that can be devolved on the expert in forensic medicine is that of determining whether the mental

alienation is real or feigned" in "Matériaux pour l'histoire médico-légale de l'aliénation mentale," *Annales d'hygiène publique et de médecine légale*, vol. II, 2nd part (Paris: Gabon, 1829) p. 353.

47. Foucault is alluding here to the movements of institutional criticism which developed after the 2nd World War and which denounced an asylum, the medicalized heir to the "hôpitaux généraux" of the "great confinement," which had become a pathogenic institution through the conditions of life it provided for the patients; see the Report presented by Lucien Bonnafé, Louis Le Guillant and Henri Mignont, "Problèmes posés par la chronicité sur le plan des institutions psychiatriques," in *XIIe congrès de Psychiatrie et de Neurologie de langue française*, Marseilles, 7-12 September 1964 (Paris: Masson, 1964). The question then was one of knowing whether "the aim pursued by the institution (...) truly conforms to the aim that we can agree to formulate as: psychiatric therapy" (L. Bonnafé, "Le milieu hospitalier vu du point de vue thérapeutique, ou théorie et pratique de l'hôpital psychiatrique," *La Raison*, no. 17, 1958, p. 26) and it was a matter of promoting "the use of the hospital milieu itself as treatment and social readaptation" (ibid. p. 8). The following articles contain detailed bibliographies on the problem: G. Daumezon, P. Paumelle, F. Tosquellès, "Organisation thérapeutique de l'hôpital psychiatrique. I: Le fonctionnement thérapeutique," in *Encylopédie médico-chirurgicale. Psychiatrie*, vol. I, February 1955, 37-930, A-10, pp. 1-8; G. Daumezon and L. Bonnafé, "Perspectives de réforme psychiatrique en France depuis la Libération." See also, below, "Course context."

48. This qualification of "militants of antipsychiatry" derives from the definition Foucault put forward in his contribution, "Histoire de la folie et antipsychiatrie," during the Montreal colloquium organized by H.F. Ellenberger in May 1973, "Faut-il interner le psychiatres?": "I call antipsychiatry everything which challenges and calls into question the role of a psychiatrist formerly called upon to produce the truth of the illness in the hospital space." Hysterics are the "militants" of this in that, providing their crises on demand, they gave birth to "the suspicion that the great master of madness, the person who made it appear and disappear, Charcot, was the person who did not produce the truth of the illness, but rather its artifice" (typed manuscript, pp. 12-13). See also, below, "Course summary." In this Foucault was inspired by the analyses T. Szasz devoted to Charcot in the first chapter of *The Myth of Mental Illness: Foundations of a Theory of Personal Conduct* (New York: Harper and Row, 1974) ch. 1, "Charcot and the problem of hysteria"; French translation *Le Mythe de la maladie mentale*, trans. D. Berger (Paris: Payot, 1975). This is confirmed by an interview on this text: "there is a chapter which seems to me exemplary: hysteria is taken apart as a product of psychiatric power, but also as the counter-attack on it and the trap into which it falls" "Sorcellerie et folie" *Dits et Écrits*, vol. 3, p. 91. Foucault saw in "the explosions of hysteria which broke out in psychiatric hospitals in the second half of the nineteenth century (...) an after-effect of the exercise of psychiatric power" "Les rapports de pouvoir passent à l'intérieur du corps" ibid. p. 231.

eleven

30 January 1974

*The problem of diagnosis in medicine and psychiatry. ~ The place of the body in psychiatric nosology: the model of general paralysis. ~ The fate of the notion of crisis in medicine and psychiatry. ~ The test of reality in psychiatry and its forms: 1. Psychiatric questioning (*l'interrogatoire*) and confession. The ritual of clinical presentation. Note on "pathological heredity" and degeneration. ~ 2. Drugs. Moreau de Tours and hashish. Madness and dreams. ~ 3. Magnetism and hypnosis. The discovery of the "neurological body."*

I HAVE TRIED TO show you how and why the medical crisis, which as well as being a theoretical notion was above all a practical instrument in medicine, disappeared at the end of the eighteenth and the beginning of the nineteenth century, basically because the appearance of pathological anatomy made it possible to bring to light the reality of the disease in a localized lesion within the organism and identifiable in the body. Then, on the other hand, starting with these different lesions that individualized diseases, this same pathological anatomy made it possible to constitute clusters of signs from which the differential diagnosis of diseases could be established. You can see that under these conditions—ascription of the disease to the body and the possibility of a differential diagnosis—the crisis, as the test in which disease produced its own truth, became pointless. In the realm of psychiatry the situation is completely different, for two reasons.

The first is that in the psychiatric order, the problem is not fundamentally, not at all in fact, one of differential diagnosis. Of course, at a certain level in psychiatric practice, diagnosis does appear to develop as the differential diagnosis of one illness as distinct from another; mania or melancholy, hysteria or schizophrenia, etcetera. But in truth, I think all this is only a superficial and secondary activity in relation to the real question posed in every diagnosis of madness, which is not whether it is this or that form of madness, but whether it is or is not madness. I think the position of psychiatry is very different from that of medicine in this respect. You will say that the prior question of whether or not one is dealing with an illness is also necessary in medicine; however, truly, it is both a relatively simple and, at bottom, marginal question; it is almost only in cases of dissimulation or hypochondriacal delirium that the problem of "illness or not" can really be posed seriously. In the domain of mental illness, however, the only real question is posed in the form of yes or no. That is to say, the differential field within which the diagnosis of madness is practiced is not constituted by the range of nosographic species, but simply by marking the difference between what is madness and what is not: the diagnosis of madness is carried out in this binary domain, in this strictly dual field. So I would say that, except as a second order and, as it were, superfluous justification, psychiatry does not require differential diagnosis. Psychiatric diagnosis does not involve a differential diagnosis but, if you like, a decision, or an absolute diagnosis. Psychiatry functions, then, in terms of the model of an absolute, and not a differential, diagnosis.

Second, psychiatry as it is being established in the nineteenth century again contrasts with medicine in that it is clearly a medicine in which the body is absent. However, we must be clear here, because it is absolutely certain that, on the one hand, from the beginnings of the development of nineteenth century psychiatry, there was a search for organic correlations, the domain of lesion, the type of organ that might be involved in an illness like madness. There was the search for this, and in some cases it was found; in 1822-1826 it was Bayle's definition of general paralysis, and meningeal lesions as after-effects of syphilis.[1] This is true, and we can say that the body was no more absent from the psychiatric order than it was from standard medicine. And yet there was an essential difference: the problem to be resolved in psychiatric activity was not so much, or was not primarily, whether a particular form of behavior, a way of speaking, a type of illusion, or a category of hallucination, were due to this or that form of lesion, but whether or not saying such things, conducting oneself in such a way, hearing such voices, and suchlike, belonged to madness. And the best proof that this was the fundamental question is that in 1826 Bayle recognized that in general paralysis, which was one of the major forms in which it was thought there was an assignable relationship between mental illness and the organism, there were three major types of syndromes: the motor syndrome of progressive paralysis; second, the psychiatric syndrome of madness; and third, the terminal condition of dementia.[2] Now, forty years later, Baillarger said: Everything that Bayle said is more or less true, but there is a fundamental error nonetheless, which is that there is no madness at all in general paralysis, only an intrication of paralysis and dementia.[3]

So, I think we can say that the liquidation of the medical crisis was acceptable to medicine thanks to pathological anatomy, but was not possible in the psychiatric domain due to absolute diagnosis and the absence of the body.* The problem psychiatry faces becomes precisely that of constituting, of establishing, the kind of test, or series of tests, that will enable it to meet this requirement of absolute diagnosis, that is to say, the kind of test that will accord reality or unreality to what is taken to be madness, to inscribe it within the field of reality or disqualify it as unreal.

In other words, we can say that the classical notion of crisis in medicine, the classical practice of the medical crisis as it was put to work for over two thousand years, basically had two nineteenth century descendants. On the one hand, through pathological anatomy, procedures of verification, in the form of the objective report and demonstration, were substituted for the classical medical crisis and its test: this was the medical offspring. The psychiatric offspring of the classical crisis was different. Since there was no field within which psychiatry could ascertain

* The manuscript clarifies: "This therefore implies a completely specific procedure for establishing the illness."

the truth, it had to establish and substitute something for the old classical medical crisis which was, like the old medical crisis, a test, but a test of reality rather than a test of truth. Put differently, the test of truth splits into techniques for ascertaining the truth on one side: this is standard medicine; [and, on the other], a test of reality: this is what happens in psychiatry.

To summarize, and to start studying this system, this game, this panoply of tests of reality, I think we can say the following: In psychiatry, the essential moment that punctuates, organizes, and at the same time distributes this field of disciplinary power I have been speaking about, is this test of reality, which has a double meaning.

On the one hand, it involves making the reasons given for a requested confinement, or for possible psychiatric intervention, exist as illness, or possibly non-illness. The psychiatric test is then what I will call the test of administrative-medical reduplication: Can what has motivated the request be retranscribed in terms of symptoms and illness? The first function of the psychiatric test is to retranscribe the request as illness, to make the grounds for the request exist as symptoms of illness.

The second function is correlative to this and in a way is much more important. The test involves making the power of intervention and the disciplinary power of the psychiatrist exist as medical knowledge. I have tried to show you how this power operated within a disciplinary field, which had a medical stamp of course, but which lacked real medical content. Well, this disciplinary power must now be made to function as medical power, and the psychiatric test will be, on the one hand, what constitutes the request for confinement as illness, and, on the other, what makes the person given powers of decision in confinement function as a doctor.

In organic medicine, the doctor vaguely formulates the following demand: Show me your symptoms and I will tell you what your illness is. In the psychiatric test, the psychiatrist's demand is much weightier, much more surcharged, and is: With what you are, with your life, with the grounds for people's complaints, [. . .*], with what you do, and what you say, provide me with some symptoms, not so that I know what your illness is, but so that I can stand before you as a doctor.

---

* (On the recording, repetition of:) with what you are

That is to say, the psychiatric test is a double test for the official establishment of an individual's life as a tissue of pathological symptoms, as well as the constant official establishment of the psychiatrist as a doctor, or of the supreme disciplinary authority as a medical authority. Consequently, we can say that the psychiatric test is an endless test of admittance into the hospital. Why is it that one cannot leave the asylum? One cannot leave the asylum, not because the exit is far away, but because the entrance is too near. One never stops entering the asylum, and every encounter, every confrontation between the doctor and the patient begins again and indefinitely repeats this founding, initial act by which madness will exist as reality and the psychiatrist will exist as doctor.

Consequently you can see how there is a very curious and complex game into which all the real games of the asylum and of the history of psychiatry and madness in the nineteenth century throw themselves. If you consider things at the level of the disciplinary functioning of the asylum, (which I analyzed in the previous sessions), then at this level there is a formidable medical surplus-power because the doctor and the disciplinary system ultimately form a single body; the hospital itself is the doctor's body. However, on the other side, there is a prodigious surplus-power of the patient, since it is the patient, in terms, precisely, of the way in which he undergoes and comes out from the psychiatric test, who will or will not establish the psychiatrist as doctor, who will either refer him back to his pure and simple disciplinary role or allow him to play his doctor's role—and you understand through what opening.

You can see how the phenomena I will try to explain to you next week, the phenomena of hysteria and the game between Charcot and the hysterics, will be able to rush in here. The hysteric is precisely someone who says: It is thanks to me, but thanks only to me, that what you do to me—confine me, prescribe me drugs, and so on—really is a medical act, and I crown you doctor to the extent that I provide you with symptoms. Underneath the doctor's surplus power is the patient's surplus power.

⚜

There is, then, [a] general framework of the psychiatric test which, as I told you last week, took, I think, three principal forms in the first sixty years of the nineteenth century. There are, then, three techniques for this test of the realization of the illness that invests the psychiatrist with the status of doctor and makes the demand for psychiatry function as symptom: first, psychiatric questioning (*l'interrogatoire*); second, drugs; and third, hypnosis.

First, the technique of questioning in the broad sense. Let's say: questioning, anamnesis, confession, etcetera. To what does questioning correspond? How exactly is it practiced? I have already pointed out the disciplinary aspect of questioning, insofar as it involves pinning the individual to his identity, obliging him to recognize himself in his past, in certain events of his life.[4] But this is only a minor, superficial function of questioning. There are, I think, others, which are so many processes of realizing madness. And I think questioning realizes madness in four ways, or by four processes.

First, classical psychiatric questioning, as you see it at work from around 1820 to 1830, always includes what we can call the search for a medical history. What is this search for a medical history? It is asking the patient what different illnesses his ancestors or collaterals may have had. This search is very paradoxical because, until the end of the nineteenth century at least, it is completely anarchical and collates everything that comes up that might have been illness in the patient's ancestors and collaterals. And it is a very curious search because at the time I am considering, that is to say, at the time of its appearance around 1830 to 1840, there is neither the notion of pathological heredity,[5] nor even of degeneration, which is formulated much later around 1855 to 1860.[6]

That is to say, we should be surprised by the sheer extent of the research undertaken in this examination of the medical history of all the patient's ancestors and collaterals, of all the sorts of illnesses from which they may have suffered, and we should also be surprised by its early appearance and persistence still today. What basically was involved when a mental patient was asked about the illnesses in his family, and when it was carefully noted down if his father had died of apoplexy, if his mother suffered from rheumatism, if his uncle had been an idiot child, and so on? What was going on? Of course, it extended the search for certain signs, prodromes, etcetera, to a multi-individual scale, but

I think it was above all and essentially a way of making up for the lack of pathological anatomy, for that absence of the body or distance from the body I have spoken to you about. Insofar as one cannot and does not know how to find any organic substratum of the illness in the patient, one looks for pathological events at the level of the patient's family which are such that, whatever their nature, they will refer to the communication, and consequently existence, of a pathological material substratum. Heredity is a way of giving body to the illness at the very moment that this illness cannot be situated at the level of the individual body; so one invents, one cuts out a sort of huge fantastical body of the family affected by a mass of illnesses: organic and non-organic diseases, constitutional and accidental diseases, it doesn't matter, since if they are transmitted then they have a material support, and as long as one gets back to the material support in this way then one has the organic substratum of madness, but an organic substratum that is not the individual substratum of pathological anatomy. It is a sort of meta-organic substratum, but one which constitutes the true body of the illness. The sick body in the questioning of madness, the sick body one palpates, touches, percusses, sounds and in which one wants to try to find pathological signs, is in reality the body of the entire family; it is, rather, the body constituted by the family and family heredity. Trying to trace heredity therefore means substituting a different body and correlative material for the body of pathological anatomy; it constitutes a meta-individual *analogon* of the doctors' organism. I think this is the first aspect of medical questioning: the search for a medical history.

Second, there is the search for prodromes, signs of predisposition, an individual medical history. What are the phases through which the approach of madness is indicated before it really exists as madness? And this is another very constant aspect of psychiatric questioning: Recount your childhood memories. Tell me what happened. Give me some information about your life. Tell me what happened to you when you were ill? In fact this assumes that madness as illness always precedes itself; elements of a medical history must be found even in cases of illnesses marked by their sudden onset.

In general medicine, elements of a previous history, events indicating the onset of the illness, are discovered so as to be able to distinguish this or that type of illness, to find out whether it is a case of a progressive or a chronic illness, for example. The search for a medical history is quite different in the psychiatric domain. Looking for these individual medical histories basically means trying to show that madness existed before being constituted as illness, and, at the same time, that these signs are not yet the madness itself, but the conditions of possibility of madness. So signs must be found that are not exactly pathological—since that would mean they are signs of the illness, real elements of the illness, and not just prodromes—but which must be something different from the internal signs of the illness while at the same time having a certain relationship with the illness so that they can be given as prodromes, warning signs, marks of a predisposition to an illness—both internal and external to the illness.[7] That is to say, basically, setting madness in the individual context of what we can call abnormality.[8]

Abnormality is the individual condition of possibility of madness; it is what must be established in order to show that what one is treating, that what one is dealing with, and what precisely one wants to show are symptoms of madness, is really of a pathological order. For the different elements constituting the object or motive for the demand for confinement to be transformed into pathological symptoms, these elements must be set within this general web of abnormality.

I refer you, for example, to the Pierre Rivière dossier for some of the details on this.[9] When the doctors tried to determine whether or not Pierre Rivière was mentally ill, whether or not he was suffering from something that one hardly dared call "monomania"—at this time monomania had been defined by Esquirol as an illness that suddenly exploded and was characterized precisely by its suddenness and by its main symptom being the sudden appearance of a criminal form of conduct[10]—their problem was how this criminal conduct could be proven to be mad? It had to be set in a field of abnormalities constituted by a number of elements. A child cutting off the heads of cabbages while imagining himself at the head of an army destroying his enemies, for example, or crucifying a frog,[11] formed a horizon of abnormalities within which the conduct in question could then be realized as madness. So, the second operation of questioning is the constitution of a horizon of abnormalities.

The third role of questioning is to organize what could be called the junction or chiasmus between responsibility and subjectivity. My impression is that at the bottom of every psychiatric interview there is always a sort of transaction taking the following form. The psychiatrist says to the person before him: Well, here we are, you are here either of your own free will or at the behest of someone else, but you have come here because people are uneasy and complain about you; you say certain things, you have done certain things, you behave in a certain way. I am not in any way questioning you about the truth of these facts and I do not want to know the truth or falsity of the reproaches made against you, or even of the malaise you feel—I am not an investigating magistrate—however, I am prepared to relieve you of legal or moral responsibility for what you have done or for what happens to you, or for the feelings you experience, on the one condition that you subjectively accept the reality of all this, on condition that you give all these facts back to me as subjective symptoms of your existence, of your consciousness. I want to find all these elements again in your account and confessions, more or less transformed, no matter, as elements of your suffering, as the force of a monstrous desire, as the signs of an irrepressible impulse, in short, as symptoms. I really want to remove the weight of your legal and moral responsibility from the reasons for you being here, but I will only perform this subtraction, I will only lift these reasons from your head on condition, precisely, that you give them to me, in one form or another, as symptoms. Give me some symptoms; I will remove the fault.

I think this kind of deal, played out at the heart of psychiatric questioning, means that questioning essentially always bears in fact on the reasons why the individual finds himself before the psychiatrist. The psychiatric interview must question the reasons for the individual finding himself before the psychiatrist—no matter whether these are linked to voluntary conduct or given by other people—and retransform these reasons into symptoms.

The fourth function of psychiatric questioning is what I will call the organization of the central confession. That is to say, basically psychiatric questioning always has a certain end, and what's more always breaks off at a certain point. This end, this point on the horizon for psychiatric questioning, would be the heart of the madness, its core, a kind of focal point in the realm of madness corresponding to the center of a pathological lesion.* And this center of madness that questioning seeks to realize, to effectuate, is the extreme, indisputable form of the madness. The subject being questioned must not only be got to recognize the existence of this delirious center, he really must actualize it within the interview.

This actualization can be obtained in two ways. Either it can be obtained in the form of confession, of the confession ritually obtained within the questioning: "Yes, I hear voices! Yes, I have hallucinations!";[12] "Yes, I think I'm Napoleon!";[13] "Yes, I rave!" This is the end to which psychiatric questioning must lead. Or, if not actualization in confession, through pinning down the symptom in the first person, the crisis itself must be actualized in the questioning; arousing the hallucination or provoking the hysterical crisis. In short, whether in the form of confession or in the form of actualization of the central symptom, the subject must be forced into a sort of tight corner, a point of extreme contraction at which he is constrained to say "I am mad" and really play out his madness. At that point, pinned in that extreme corner of the interrogation, he can no longer escape his own symptoms; he can no longer thread his way between them. He is constrained to say: Really, I am someone for whom the psychiatric hospital was built, I am someone for whom a doctor was needed, I am sick and, since I am sick, it is clear that you, whose major function is to confine me, are a doctor. And there we arrive at the essential point of the double establishment of the confined individual as sick and of the confining individual as doctor and psychiatrist.

One extracts an extreme confession, basically on the assumption and with the claim that if one avows the madness, one gets rid of it. In the technique of psychiatric questioning the double analogy with both religious confession and medical crisis comes into play: religious confession helps the pardon; expectoration and excretion bring out the morbific substance in the medical crisis. At the point of their convergence or, if you like, in a kind of oscillation between the confession, which brings

* The manuscript adds: "A bit like the family taking the place of the somatic substratum for madness."

about pardon, and the expectoration, which drives out the disease, the extreme confession of madness is—the psychiatrists of that time, and no doubt many others still today, assure us—ultimately the basis on which the individual will be able to free himself from his madness. "I will free you from your madness on condition that you confess to me your madness," that is to say: "Give me the reasons why I confine you; really give me the reasons why I deprive you of your freedom, and, at that point, I will free you from your madness. The action by which you will be cured of your madness is also that by which I will assure myself that what I do really is a medical act." Such is the entanglement between the doctor's power and the extortion of confession in the patient, which constitutes, I think, the absolutely central point of the technique of psychiatric questioning.

I think this questioning, the principal moments of which I have tried to indicate, can be deciphered at three levels. Let's leave the first, the disciplinary level about which I have already spoken;[14] the other two levels are, I think, essential. The first level involves constituting a medical *mimesis* in psychiatric questioning, the *analogon* of a medical schema given by pathological anatomy: first, psychiatric questioning constitutes a body through the system of ascriptions of heredity, it gives body to an illness which did not have one; second, around this illness, and in order to pick it out as illness, it constitutes a field of abnormalities; third, it fabricates symptoms from a demand for confinement; and finally, fourth, it isolates, delimits, and defines a pathological source that it shows and actualizes in the confession or in the realization of this major and nuclear symptom.

So questioning in nineteenth century psychiatry is a certain way of reconstituting exactly those elements that characterize the activity of differential diagnosis in organic medicine. It is a way of reconstituting, alongside and parallel to organic medicine, something that functions in the same way, but in the order of *mimesis* and *analogon*. The other strata in the interview is the level at which, through the play of sleights of hand, exchanges, promises, gifts and counter-gifts between psychiatrist and patient there is the triple realization of conduct as madness, of madness as illness, and finally, of the mad person's guardian as doctor.

You can see that under these conditions the kind of questioning involving these elements is the completely renovated ritual of absolute diagnosis. What is the psychiatrist's activity in a model hospital of the nineteenth century? You know that there are two and only two. First, the visit; second, questioning. The visit is the action by which the doctor brings about the daily mutation of discipline into therapy by passing through the different departments of his hospital: I will pass through the entire asylum machinery, I will see all the mechanisms of the disciplinary system in order to transform them, simply by my presence, into a therapeutic apparatus (*appareil*).[15]

The second activity, questioning, is precisely this: Give me some symptoms, make some symptoms from your life for me, and you will make me a doctor.

The two rites, of the visit and questioning, are, as you can see, the elements by which the disciplinary field I have spoken about functions. You also see why this great rite of questioning needs to be reinvigorated from time to time. Just as alongside Low Mass there is solemn High Mass, so the clinical presentation to students is to private questioning of the patient what the sung Mass is to Low Mass. And why is it that psychiatry is thrown so soon, so quickly, into this *Missa sollemnis*, into this rite of almost public presentation, of anyway the clinical presentation of patients to students? I have already said why in a couple of words,[16] but I think you now find here the possibility of grasping a different level of the working of this clinical presentation.

Given the characteristic double absence of the body and the cure in psychiatric practice, how could one bring about the real investiture of the doctor as a real doctor, and how could the processes of the transmutation of the demand for confinement into symptoms, of life events into abnormalities, and of heredity into a body, etcetera, be really effectuated if, in addition to the daily working of the asylum, there were not this kind of rite solemnly marking what happens in psychiatric questioning? Well, precisely, a space is organized in which the alienist is marked out as doctor solely by the fact that there are students around him as spectators and listeners. So the medical character of his role will in no way be actualized by the success of his cure, by his discovery of the true etiology, since, precisely, it is not a question of this. The medical character of his role and the processes of transmutation I have talked about are possible inasmuch as the doctor is surrounded by the chorus and body of the students. Since the patient's body is lacking, it really will be necessary for there to be this kind of institutional corporeality which will be the crown of students around the master, listening to the patient's answers. As soon as this listening is coded in this way and institutionalized as students listening to what the psychiatrist says as master, and as master of medical knowledge, from that point on, all the processes I have talked about really will play their part, with a renewed intensity and vigor, in this medical transmutation of madness into illness, of the demand for confinement into symptom, and so on.

In other words, I think the professorial dimension of speech, which, in the doctor's case, is merely additive, if you like, a way of increasing his prestige and making what he says a little more true, is much more essential and much more inherent in the case of the psychiatrist; the professorial dimension of the psychiatrist's words is constitutive of his medical power. In order for this speech really to carry out the medical transmutations I have spoken about, it must, from time to time at least, be ritually and institutionally marked as professorial by the rite of the clinical presentation of the patient to students.

That's what I wanted to say to you about questioning. Obviously all this needs to be refined inasmuch as the forms of questioning have varied. In someone like Leuret it takes much more subtle forms. Leuret invented questioning by silence, for example, in which one says nothing to the patient, waits for him to speak, and lets him say what he wants, because, according to Leuret, this is the only way, or at any rate the best way to arrive at precisely that focal confession of madness.[17] Again in Leuret, there is the kind of game in which another demand is recognized behind a symptom, and this is what the questioning must analyze. Anyway, all of these are supplementary with regard to the central rite of psychiatric questioning.

Alongside questioning and, to tell the truth, here again in a secondary form, but with much more of a future than Leuret's techniques, there are the two other major agents of medicalization, of the realization of madness as illness: drugs and hypnosis.

Drugs first. Here again, I have drawn your attention to the disciplinary use of certain drugs, which goes back to the eighteenth century: laudanum,[18] opiates, and so forth.[19] At the end of the eighteenth century you see the new phenomenon of the medico-legal use of drugs. At the end of the eighteenth century, an Italian doctor had the idea of using massive doses of opium in order to determine whether a subject really is or is not a mental patient, of using opium as an authority for deciding between madness and its simulation.[20]

This was the start, and then we find, we can say for the first eighty years of the nineteenth century, an enormous use of drugs in psychiatric hospitals, the main ones being opium, amyl nitrate,[21] chloroform,[22] and ether:[23] in 1864 an important text by Morel appeared in the *Archives générales de médecine* on etherisation of patients in psychiatric hospitals.[24] However, I think the [major] episode in all this was obviously the book *Du haschisch et de l'aliénation mentale*, and the practice, of Moreau de Tours in 1845.[25] In his book on hashish, which I think was very important historically, Moreau de Tours recounts that he has "himself"—and we will see [the meaning]* of this "himself"—tested hashish, and that, after having taken a fairly considerable amount of it in jam, he was able to pick out a number of phases in hashish intoxication, which were the following: first, "feeling of well-being"; second, "excitement, dissociation of ideas"; third, "errors of time and space"; fourth, "development of sensibility, both visual and auditory: exaggeration of sensations when listening to music, etcetera"; fifth, "fixed ideas, delirious convictions"; sixth, alteration or, as he says, "lesion of the affections," exaggeration of fears, excitability, and amorous passion, etcetera; seventh, "irresistible drives"; eighth and last, "illusions, hallucinations."[26] I think there are a number of reasons for considering Moreau de Tours's experiment and the use he made of it.

First—and I won't be able to give you an explanation, or even an analysis, here—is the fact that, in this experiment, Moreau de Tours immediately, straightaway [. . .†] refers the drug's effects to the processes of mental illness.‡ When he describes the different stages I have just mentioned, from the second stage, the feeling of well-being having passed—and yet we will see that he succeeds in recuperating it—we are very

* (Recording:) the importance
† (On the recording, repeat of:) immediately
‡ Section in the manuscript entitled: "Idea that the phenomena deriving from the absorption of hashish are identical to those of madness."

quickly in the realm of mental illness: dissociation of ideas, errors of time and space, etcetera. I think this psychiatric appropriation of the effects of the drug within the system of mental illness raises an important problem, but to tell the truth I think it should be analyzed within a history of drugs rather than within a history of mental illness. Anyway, with regard to the history of mental illness, according to Moreau de Tours this use of the drug, and the immediate assimilation of the effects of the drug and symptoms of mental illness, provide the doctor with a possible reproduction of madness, a reproduction which is both artificial, since intoxication is needed to produce the phenomena, and natural, because none of the symptoms he lists are foreign, either in their content or successive sequence, to the course of madness as a spontaneous and natural illness. So, we have an induced but authentic reproduction of the illness. This is in 1845 when a series of works of experimental physiology are under way. This is the Claude Bernard of madness; it is the liver's glycogenic function transposed by Moreau de Tours.[27]

Another important thing is that we not only have the idea, and so the instrument it seems, of a concerted, intentional experiment on madness, but in addition we have this idea that the different phenomena typical of hashish intoxication constitute a natural, necessary succession, a spontaneous sequence, a homogeneous series. That is to say, since these phenomena and those of madness are homogeneous, we arrive at the idea that the different symptoms of madness, which nosographers might distribute on this or that level, or attribute to this or that form of illness, basically all belong to the same series. Whereas Pinel's, and especially Esquirol's type of psychiatry tried to see what faculty was injured in this or that mental illness,[28] here we have instead the idea that there is basically only one madness that evolves throughout the individual's life, which may, of course, be halted, blocked, and fixed at a particular stage, just like hashish intoxication, but which in any case is the same madness found everywhere and throughout its evolution. So, hashish will enable the psychiatrist to discover what he had sought for so long, that is to say, precisely the kind of single "core" from which all the symptoms of madness can spread. Through the hashish experiment we will obtain this center, the famous center that pathological-anatomists had the opportunity to grasp and fix in a point of the body, since we will have the nucleus itself from which all madness unfurls. And this fundamental nucleus that Moreau de Tours thought he had found is what, in 1845, he called the "original intellectual modification"[29] and that, in 1869, he will call "the primordial modification."[30] This is how he describes this original modification: "Every form, every accident of delirium or madness strictly speaking—fixed ideas, hallucinations, irresistibility of drives [you see these are all the symptoms we come across in hashish intoxication; M.F.]—owe their origin to an original intellectual modification, always identical to itself, which is evidently the essential condition of their existence. This is maniacal excitation."[31] This expression is not quite right, for it is a matter of a "simple and complex state of, at one and the same time, vagueness, uncertainty, oscillation and mobility of ideas, which are often expressed in a profound incoherence. It is a disaggregation, a veritable dissolution of the intellectual composite that we call the moral faculties."[32]

So, the major symptom, or rather, the very center from which the different symptoms of madness spread out, is located thanks to hashish. Through hashish we can then reproduce, reconstitute, and truly actualize that essential "core" of all madness. But you can see, and this is what is important, that we reproduce this essential "core" through hashish, and in whom do we reproduce it? In anyone and, as it happens, in the doctor. That is to say, the hashish experiment gives the doctor the possibility of communicating directly with madness through something other than the external observation of visible symptoms; it will be possible to communicate with madness through the doctor's subjective experience of the effects of hashish intoxication. For the famous organic body that the pathological anatomists have before them, and which the alienist lacked, for that body, ground of evidence, and level of experimental verification the psychiatrist lacked, the psychiatrist could substitute his own experience. Hence it becomes possible to pin the psychiatrist's experience on to the mad person's experience and so gain access to something like the zero point between moral psychology and pathological psychology. And, especially for the psychiatrist, in the name of his normality and of his experiences as a normal, but intoxicated psychiatrist, it becomes possible to see, express, and lay down the law to madness.

Prior to the Moreau de Tours's experiment it was, of course, the psychiatrist who, as a normal individual, laid down the law to madness, but he did so in the form of exclusion: You are mad because you do not think like me; I recognize you are mad insofar as what you do is impenetrable to the reasons valid for me. It was as a normal individual that the psychiatrist had dictated the law to the mad in the form of this exclusion, of this alternative. Now however, with the hashish experiment, the psychiatrist will be able to say: I know the law of your madness, I recognize it precisely because I can reconstitute it in myself; under the condition of modifications like hashish intoxication, I can follow and reconstitute the typical thread of events and processes of madness in myself. I can understand what happens; I can grasp and reconstitute the authentic and autonomous movement of your madness and consequently grasp it from within.

And this is how that famous and absolutely novel grasp of madness by psychiatry in the form of understanding was founded. The relationship of interiority established by the psychiatrist through hashish will enable him to say: This is madness, for, as a normal individual, I myself can really understand the movement by which this phenomenon occurs. We find the original source here of understanding as the normal psychiatrist's law on the intrinsic movement of madness. Whereas previously madness was precisely what could not be reconstituted by normal thought, it is now what must be reconstituted by and on the basis of the psychiatrist's understanding. Consequently, this internal grasp gives additional power.

But what is this primordial "core" that the psychiatrist can reconstitute by means of hashish and which is therefore not madness—since hashish is not madness—but which is nonetheless madness—since we find it again in madness in the pure and spontaneous state? What is this primordial core, homogeneous with madness,* which however is not madness, and which is found in both the psychiatrist and the mad person? Of course, Moreau de Tours names this element. You know it already: it is the dream. The hashish experience opens up the dream as the mechanism that can be found in the normal individual and that will

* The manuscript adds: "so as to be both the basis and model."

serve precisely as the principle of intelligibility of madness. "It seems that man has been granted two modes of moral existence, two lives. The first arises from our relations with the external world, with the great whole that we call the universe; it is common to us and to beings like us. The second is only the reflection of the first, only feeds, as it were, on material provided by the first, but is nevertheless perfectly distinct from it. Sleep is like a barrier set up between the two, the physiological point where external life ends and internal life begins."[33]

What is madness exactly? Well, madness, like hashish intoxication, is that particular state of our nervous system in which the barriers of sleep or the barriers of wakefulness, or the double barrier constituted by sleep and wakefulness, are broken or, at any rate, breached at a number of places. The irruption of dream mechanisms in the waking state will induce madness if the mechanism is, as it were, endogenous, and it will induce the hallucinatory experience of someone who is intoxicated if the breach is induced by the absorption of a foreign body. The dream is therefore fixed as the law common to normal life and pathological life; it is the point from which the psychiatrist's understanding will be able to impose its law on the phenomena of madness.

Of course, the expression, "the mad are waking dreamers,"[34] is not new; you find it already clearly [stated]* in Esquirol;[35] and after all there is a whole psychiatric tradition in which we find this expression.[36] However, what I think is absolutely new and crucial in Moreau de Tours and his book on hashish is not just a comparison between madness and the dream, but a principle of analysis.[37] Furthermore, when Esquirol and all the psychiatrists who said at this time, or even before, "the mad are dreamers," the analogy was between the phenomena of madness and dreaming, whereas Moreau de Tours establishes a relationship between the phenomena of dreaming and, at one and the same time, the phenomena of normal wakefulness and the phenomena of madness.[38] It is the dream's position between wakefulness and madness that Moreau de Tours pointed out and established, and it is this that makes him the absolutely founding point in the history of psychiatry and the history of

* (Recording:) formulated

psychoanalysis. In other words, the founding point was not Descartes, who said that the dream goes beyond madness and includes it,[39] but Moreau de Tours, who put the dream in a position such that it envelops madness, includes it, and enables it to be understood. And following Moreau de Tours, the psychiatrist says, and the psychoanalyst basically never stops repeating: I can well understand what madness is, because I can dream. With my dream, and with what I can grasp of my dream, I will end up understanding what is going on in someone who is mad. This is in Moreau de Tours and his book on hashish.

So, the drug is the dream injected into the waking state; it is wakefulness intoxicated, as it were, by the dream. It is the real effectuation of madness. Hence the idea that by giving hashish to a patient who is already ill, one will quite simply exaggerate his madness. That is to say, giving hashish to a normal individual will make him mad, but giving hashish to a patient will make his madness more visible; it will hasten its progress. That is how Moreau de Tours introduced therapy with hashish into his services. As he says himself, he began with a mistake: he gave hashish to some melancholics, thinking that the "maniacal excitation," that kind of agitation that is at one and the same time the primordial fact of madness and the characteristic of the dream, would compensate for the sad, frozen and immobile features of the melancholics; his idea was to compensate for melancholic fixity with the maniacal agitation of hashish.[40] He very quickly saw that it did not work, and then he had the idea of reactualizing the old technique of the medical crisis.

He said to himself: since mania consists in a kind of excitation, and since in the classical medical tradition, still found in Pinel moreover,[41] the crisis is precisely the point at which the phenomena of a disease become speeded up and intensified, let's make the maniacs a bit more maniacal; give them some hashish, and thanks to that we will cure them.[42] In the manuals of this time we find a considerable number of cures, but obviously with no analysis of possible cases of the recurrence of illness, since it was understood that, once established, a cure was a cure, even if it was called into question some days later.

You can see that alongside questioning, and having nothing to do with questioning, there is a kind of reconstitution of precisely those mechanisms we saw coming into play in questioning. Hashish is a sort of automatic questioning, and if the doctor loses power, inasmuch as he allows the drug to act, the patient finds himself caught in the automatism of the drug and cannot oppose his power to the doctor's, and what the doctor may lose as power he regains through having an internal understanding of madness.

The third system of tests in the psychiatric practice of the first two-thirds of the nineteenth century is magnetism and hypnosis. To start with magnetism was basically used as a sort of displacement of the crisis. In magnetic practice at the end of the eighteenth century, the magnetizer was basically someone who imposed his will on the magnetized, and so when psychiatrists had the idea of using magnetism within psychiatric hospitals—around 1820 to 1825 at Salpêtrière—it was precisely to reinforce further the effect of power that the doctor wanted to attach to himself.[43] But there was something more: the effect of the use of magnetism at the end of the eighteenth and the beginning of the nineteenth century, was to give doctors a hold, and a total, absolute hold, over the patient, but it was also to give the patient a supplementary lucidity, what mesmerists called "intuitiveness," a supplementary "intuitiveness" thanks to which the subject will be able to know his own body, his own illness, and, possibly the illness of others.[44] At the end of the eighteenth century, magnetism was basically a way of entrusting the patient himself with what had been the doctor's task in the classical crisis. In the classical crisis, it was the doctor who had to foresee what the illness was, to divine in what it consisted, and to adjust it in the course of the crisis.[45] Now, within the magnetism practiced by orthodox mesmerists, the patient is put in a state in which he can really know the nature, process and term of his illness.[46]

So, in the experiments conducted at Salpêtrière from 1820-1825, we find the first tests of this type of magnetism. A male or female patient is put to sleep and asked what their illness is, how long they have been affected by it, for what reasons and how must they get over it? There is a whole series of reports of this.

Here is a case of mesmerism from around 1825-1826. A patient is presented to the magnetizer who asks him: "Who put you to sleep?—It was you.—Why did you vomit yesterday?—Because they gave me cold bouillon.—At what time did you vomit?—At four-o-clock.—Did you eat afterwards?—Yes, monsieur, and I did not vomit what I had eaten.—What accident made you ill for the first time?—Because I was cold.—Was it a long time ago?—One year ago.—Didn't you have a fall?—Yes monsieur.—In this fall, did you fall on your stomach?—No, I fell backwards, etcetera."[47] Medical diagnosis is carried out therefore in the opening, as it were, contrived by magnetic practice.

And this is how one of the most serious alienists of the time, Georget, magnetized two patients, one of whom was called "Pétronille" and the other "Braguette."[48] Questioned by Georget under magnetism, Pétronille said: "What made me ill was that I fell in the water, and if you want to cure me you too must throw me in the water."[49] Georget does this, but the cure does not take place because actually the patient had made it clear that she had fallen in the Ourcq canal, and Georget had simply made her fall in a pool.[50] Pétronille was really demanding the repetition of the trauma. Afterwards she was thought to be a simulator and Georget the innocent and naive victim of her maneuvers, but this is not important, I just wanted to stress the above to show you how magnetism in this period, that is to say, still around 1825, functioned as a supplement, an extension of the classical crisis: knowing, testing the illness in its truth.

In actual fact, the real insertion of magnetism and hypnosis into psychiatric practice takes place much later, after Braid, that is to say, after the appearance of *Neurhypnology, or the Rationale of Nervous Sleep* in 1843,[51] and especially, in France, after the introduction of Braid's practices, around Broca in 1858-1859.[52]

Why was Braidism accepted, whereas the old mesmerism was abandoned around 1830?[53] If it was abandoned it was precisely because the magnetizers naively wanted to entrust patients, and their "lucidity," with the medical power and knowledge which, in the actual working of the institution, could only fall to the doctor; hence the barrier erected by the Académie de médecine and by doctors against the first practices of hypnosis. On the other hand, from the 1860s, Braidism was accepted and penetrated asylum and psychiatric practice quite easily. Why? On the one hand, of course, because Braidism, let's just say hypnosis, abandons the old theory of the material basis of magnetism.[54] That is to say, in Braid's definition of hypnotism, all its effects are due solely to the doctor's will. That is to say, only the doctor's assertion, only his prestige, only the power he exercises over the patient without any intermediary, without any material basis or the passage of fluid, will succeed in producing the specific effects of hypnosis.

The second reason is that Braidism deprived the patient of the ability to produce the medical truth that he was still being asked to provide in 1825 or 1830. In Braidism, hypnosis constitutes the element within which medical knowledge can be deployed. What seduced the doctors and got them to accept what they rejected in 1830 is that, thanks to Braid's technique, one could completely neutralize the patient's will, as it were, and leave the field absolutely open to the doctor's pure will. What officially reinstalled hypnosis in France was the operation performed by Broca (Broca's performance of a surgical operation on someone in a hypnotic state).[55] At that point, in fact, hypnosis appeared as the opening through which medical power-knowledge was able to force its way in and take hold of the patient.

This neutralization of the patient by hypnosis, the fact that the hypnotized patient is no longer required to know his illness but is given instead the task of being like a neutral surface on which the doctor's will is registered, will be very important because it will enable hypnotic action to be defined. This is what was done by Braid, and after Braid, especially in France, by someone whose books bore the name Philips, but whose real name was Durand de Gros, who had emigrated in 1852 and then returned to France after some years, living and publishing under the name of Philips. Around 1860 to 1864, Philips defined the processes and different phases of hypnotic action.[56] He shows how hypnosis is important first of all because it has a disciplinary effect; it is, precisely, sedative, just like questioning, drugs. I won't return to this. But above all, the subject's state when he has begun to be hypnotized—what Philips calls "the hypotaxic state"[57]—enables the doctor to get the patient to do what he wants. First of all it allows him to direct behavior; by giving the patient an order he will be able to prevent him from conducting himself in this or that way, or he will be able to constrain him to do something. So, there is the possibility of what Durand de Gros calls "orthopedics": "Braidism," he says, "gives us the basis for an intellectual and moral orthopedics which one day will surely be introduced into educational and penitentiary establishments."[58] So, hypnosis makes it possible to fashion, to train behavior.

It also makes possible a nullification of symptoms. With hypnosis one must be able to prevent the appearance of a symptom; Durand de Gros claims that the shaking of chorea can be completely quashed by giving an order to the patient.[59]

Finally, third, the hypnotist can get a hold on the patient's body at the level of the analysis and modification of functions: he can produce a muscular contraction or paralysis; he can excite or nullify sensibility on the body's surface; he can weaken or arouse the intellectual or moral faculties; he can even modify automatic functions like circulation and breathing.[60]

So, in the hypnosis that is now accepted, you see the patient's famous body, previously absent from psychiatric practice, being defined, or appearing rather. Hypnosis will enable action on the body, not just at the disciplinary level of manifest behavior, but also at the level of muscles, nerves, and basic functions. Hypnosis is consequently a new, much more sophisticated and intensive way than questioning for the psychiatrist to obtain a real hold on the patient's body; or rather, it is the first time that the patient's body is finally available to the psychiatrist in, as it were, its functional detail. Psychiatric power will finally get a hold on the body that had eluded it since it became known that pathological anatomy could never account for the functioning and mechanisms of madness.*

So, with these different instruments, these different techniques for realizing the illness, I think we have the elements from which the great central episode in the history of nineteenth century psychiatry and madness will develop. There are, then, three instruments: questioning, hypnosis, and drugs. Questioning, hypnosis and drugs are really three

---

* The manuscript adds: "With hypnosis we have then a type of test of the illness—which draws close to drugs through the effect of discipline and through the effect of the reproduction of the pathological reality.

- but it is distinct from and, in a sense, privileged with regard to drugs,
- because it is entirely suited to the doctor's will: doing what one wants with the patient.
- because it allows, or at least one expects from it, nullification of the symptoms, one by one, and because it makes possible a direct hold on the body."

ways of actually realizing the illness, but, of course, in questioning, this realization only takes place in language and has above all the double defect of, firstly, not putting the psychiatrist in internal communication with the mechanisms of madness other than through the game of questions and answers, and, secondly, not giving a hold on the detail of the patient's body.

With drugs, rather, there is the possibility of this internal hold, this kind of supplement of power given to the psychiatrist by the fact that he thinks he can understand the phenomena of madness; an internal hold therefore. And hypnosis will be the instrument by which the psychiatrist will get a hold on the very functioning of the patient's body.

You see that we have here the elements from which it will be possible to constitute, or rather, the elements which are in place and which, quite suddenly, around 1860 to 1880, will assume extreme importance and intensity when, precisely within classical organic medicine, a new definition, or rather, a new reality of the body will appear, that is to say, when a body is discovered which is not just a body with organs and tissues, but a body with functions, performances, and behavior—in short, when, around Duchenne de Boulogne, between 1850 and 1860, the neurological body is discovered.[61]

At this point, by connecting up through the techniques of hypnosis and drugs with this new body discovered by medicine, it will finally be possible to try to inscribe the mechanisms of madness in a system of differential knowledge, in a medicine basically founded on pathological anatomy or pathological physiology; the major phenomenon will now be this inscription, this attempt to inscribe madness within a general medical symptomatology, which the absence of the body and of differential diagnosis had always marginalized. The failure of this attempt by Charcot, the fact that the neurological body, like the body of pathological anatomy, will elude the psychiatrist, will leave psychiatric power with the three instruments of power established in the first half of the nineteenth century. That is to say, after the disappearance of the great neurological hope, we will find again only the three elements: questioning—language—hypnosis, and drugs, that is to say, the three elements with which psychiatric power, within or outside the asylum space, still operates today.

---

1. In fact, it was not until 1879 that the works of Alfred Fournier (1832-1914) revealed general paralysis as a frequent complication of tertiary syphilis: see his *Syphilis du cerveau* (Paris: Masson, 1879). Before being accepted, this relationship gave rise to many debates at the Société médico-psychologique, from April to June 1879 and from February to November 1898. On 27 March 1893, Le Filliatre, in a communication, "Des antécédents syphilitiques chez quelques paralytiques généraux," presented syphilis as "a major predisposing cause," and met with hardly any opposition; see, *Annales médico-psychologiques*, 7th series, vol. XVII, July 1893, p. 436. As the general secretary of the Société médico-psychologiques later recalled, "in 1893, the exclusive partisans of the specific origin of general praralysis were still rare among us" A. Ritti, "Histoire des travaux de la Société médico-psychologiques (1852-1902)" *Annales médico-psychologiques*, 8th series, vol. XVI, July 1902, p. 58. Its specific etiology will only become imperative in 1913 with the discovery by Noguchi and Moore of pale treponema in the brains of general paralytics.
2. A.L.J. Bayle, *Traité des maladies du cerveau et de ses membranes*, pp. 536-537: "Among the many symptoms with which this ailment is accompanied, we can reduce to two those which basically serve to characterize it (...): 1. derangement of the intellectual faculties, or delirium; 2. incomplete paralysis. 1. Delirium: Mental alienation (...), partial to start with and consisting in a sort of monomania with enfeeblement of the faculties, then becomes general and maniacal with over-excitement (...); it then degenerates into a condition of dementia (...); 2. Paralysis: The paralysis which, together with delirium, establishes the diagnosis of chronic meningitis, is a diminution and an enfeeblement which, very slightly at first, and confined to a single organ, increases progressively and gradually extends to a greater number of parts, and ends by invading the entire locomotive system, in such a way that the name which seems the most suitable to us (...) is that of *general and incomplete paralysis*." See above, note 17 to the lecture of 12 December 1973, and see also J. Christian and A. Ritti, "Paralysie générale," in *Dictionnaire encyclopédique des sciences médicales*, 2nd series, vol. XX (Paris: Masson/Asselin, 1884).
3. Jules Baillarger (1809-1890) states that "it is impossible to go along with Bayle in considering madness as a constant and essential symptom of general paralysis. There are therefore no grounds for accepting the two orders of symptoms essential for the characterization of general paralysis: the symptoms of dementia and paralysis" in the Appendix to Doumic's French translation of the 2nd, revised and expanded edition of Wilhelm Griesinger's *Die Pathologie und Therapie de psychischen Krakheiten* (*Traité des maladies mentales. Pathologie et thérapeutique*), preceded by a work on general paralysis by Dr. Baillarger: *Des symptômes de la paralysie générale et des rapports de cette maladie avec la folie* (Paris: A. Delahaye, 1865) p. 612. Baillarger returns to this problem on several occasions: (1) "Des rapports de la paralysie générale e dal folie" *Annales médico-psychologiques*, 2nd series, vol. V, January 1853, pp. 158-166; (2) "De la folie avec prédominance du délire des grandeurs dans ses rapports avec la paralysie générale," ibid. 4th series, vol. VIII, July 1866, pp. 1-20. In his article on the theory of general paralysis, (3) "De la folie paralytique et de la démence paralytique considérées comme deux maladies distinctes," he reasserts that 'general paralysis' must be *completely separated from madness* and considered as a special independent disease" ibid. 6th series, vol. IX, January 1883, p. 28, author's emphasis.
4. See above, Lecture of 19 December 1973, pp. 158-162.
5. Actually, heredity was already invoked as one of the causes of madness. P. Pinel, in the 2nd edition of his *Traité* asserted that it would be difficult "to deny any hereditary transmission of mania when we note everywhere and in several successive generations some members of certain families affected by this illness" *Traité médico-philosophique*, 1809 edition. Esquirol states that "heredity is the most common predisposing cause of madness" *Des maladies mentales*, vol. I, p. 64; *Mental Maladies*, p. 49. However, heredity is not treated separately as a distinct subject until the work of C. Michéa, *De l'influence de l'hérédité dans la production des maladies nerveuses* (a work awarded a prize by the Académie de médecine on 20 December 1843) and the article by J. Baillarger, "Recherches statistique sur l'hérédité de la folie" (note read to the Académie de médecine, 2 April 1844) in which he was able to state (*ab initio*) that: "Everyone agrees about the influence of heredity in the production of madness" *Annales médico-psychologiques*, vol. III, May 1844, p. 328. The notion of "pathological

heredity" is specified between 1850 and 1850 by the works of Jacques Moreau de Tours, who introduced the idea of a transmission of the pathological in different forms, or "dissimilar heredity," thereby opening up the possibility for most forms of insanity to enter the hereditary framework. See his (1) "De la prédisposition héréditaire aux affections cérébrales. Existe-t-il des signes particuliers auxquels on puisse reconnaître cette prédisposition?" report to the Académie des sciences, 15 December 1851, *Annales médico-psychologiques*, 2nd series, vol. IV, January 1852, pp. 119-129; July 1852, pp. 447-455; and (2) *La Psychologie morbide dans ses rapports avec la philosophie de l'histoire, ou De l'influence des névropathies sur le dynamisme intellectuel* (Paris: Masson, 1859). The high point of hereditarianism is reached in 1885 and 1886 with the last debates of the Société médico-psychologique on the signs of hereditary madness (see below, note 7). See J. Déjerine, *L'Hérédité dans les maladies du système nerveux*; A. Voisin, "Hérédité" in *Nouveau Dictionnaire de médecine et de chirurgie pratiques*, vol. XVII (Paris: J.-B. Baillière, 1873). Foucault returns to the question on 19 March 1975, is his lectures *Les Anormaux*, pp. 296-300; *Abnormal*, pp. 313-318.

6. See above, note 71 to lecture of 16 January 1974, and *Les Anormaux*, lectures of 5 February, p. 110, and 19 March 1975, pp. 297-300; *Abnormal*, p. 119 and pp. 314-318.
7. See the report of Moreau de Tours on the question of prognostic signs of madness: "De la prédisposition héréditaire aux affections cérébrales," and his "Mémoire sur les prodromes de la folie" (read to the Académie de médecine, 22 April 1851). In 1868, Morel's intern, Georges Doutrebente, received the Prix Esquirol for his "Étude généalogique sur les aliénés héréditaires" devoted to "moral, physical and intellectual signs which enable the immediate diagnosis of a morbid hereditary influence in individuals predisposed to or affected by mental alienation" *Annales médico-psychologiques*, 5th series, vol. II, September 1869, p. 197. From 30 March 1885 to 26 July 1886, the Société médico-psychologique devoted ten sessions, spread over more than a year, to the question of the "intellectual and moral signs of hereditary madness."
8. On the formation of the notion of abnormality, see the lectures of 22 January 1975 and 19 March 1975 in *Les anormaux*, pp. 53-56 and pp. 293-298; *Abnormal*, pp. 57-60 and pp. 310-315.
9. *Moi, Pierre Rivière; I, Pierre Rivière.*
10. On the notion of "homicidal monomania" see above, the lecture of 23 January 1974, note 45, pp. 263-264.
11. "Particulars and explanation of the occurrence on June 3 in Aunay at the village of la Faucterie written by the author of this deed" *Moi, Pierre Rivière*, p. 124 and p. 127; *I, Pierre Rivière*, p. 101 and p. 104.
12. This refers to the questioning of A., 42 years old, admitted to Bicêtre on 18 June 1839 suffering from auditory and visual hallucinations, and for erotic and ambitious ideas. See, F. Leuret, *Du traitement moral de la folie*, "Hallucinés," Observation 1, pp. 199-200.
13. Reference to the cure of M. Dupré. See ibid. pp. 441-442 and above, lecture of 9 January 1974.
14. See above, lecture 19 December 1973, pp. 161-162.
15. On the visit, see J.-P. Falret, *De l'enseignement clinique des maladies mentales*, pp. 105-109.
16. See above, lecture of 9 January 1974, pp. 186-188.
17. To illustrate the interview by silence, the manuscript refers to Example XLV of Griesinger's *Traité*, p. 392; *Mental Pathology and Therapeutics*, pp. 334-335: "I would have said that she was listening (...) I walked a hundred paces without saying a word, and without appearing to fix my attention on her (...). I stopped again, and regarded her attentively, without seeming to be the least curious (...). We continued looking at each other in this way for nearly half an hour, when she murmured some words which I did not comprehend. I gave her my notebook, on which she wrote (...)." See also, J.-P. Falret, *Leçons cliniques de médecine mentale*, p. 22: "Instead of sharpening the madman's cunning in eluding an authority that bothers him, show (...) neglect; remove from his mind any idea (...) of a desire to penetrate his thoughts, and then you may be sure, seeing that you are not concerned to control everything in him, he will be without defiance, he will show himself as he is, and you will be able to study him more easily and with greater success."
18. See above, lecture of 19 December 1973, note 2.

19. See above, lecture of 19 December 1973, note 1.
20. This was Monteggia, the surgeon for the Milan prisons, who, suspecting a criminal of feigning madness, administered repeated strong doses of opium, so that he felt so tired "by the action of the opium, that fearing death, he considered continued pretence pointless." "Folie soupçonée d'être feinte, observée par le professeur Monteggia" trans. C.C.H. Marc in "Matériaux pour l'histoire médico-légale de l'aliénation mentale," *Annales d'hygiène publique et de médecine légale*, vol. II, Part 2, 1829, p. 375. See also, C.C.H. Marc, *De la folie considérée dans ses rapports avec les questions médico-judiciaires*, vol. I, p. 498, and A. Laurent, *Étude médico-légale sur la simulation de la folie*, p. 239.
21. Discovered in 1844 by Antoine Jérôme Balard (1802-1876) for the treatment of angina chest pains, amyl nitrate found material for therapeutic experimentation in epilepsy and hysteria. See A. Dechambre, "Nitrite d'amyle" in *Dictionnaire encyclopédique des sciences médicales*, 2nd series, vol. XIII (Paris: Masson/Asselin, 1879) pp. 262-269.
22. See above, note 2 to lecture of 23 January 1974.
23. See above, note 18 to lecture of 9 January 1974.
24. B.A. Morel recommended the use of etherisation as "the most innocent and speedy way to reach knowledge of the truth" "De l'étherisation dans la folie du point du vue du diagnostique et de la médecine légale," p. 135.
25. J.J. Moreau du Tours, *Du haschisch et de l'aliénation mentale.*
26. The rubrics given correspond to the titles of sections 2 to 8 of chapter 1, "Phénomènes psychologiques," ibid. pp. 51-181.
27. Foucault is referring to the work of Claude Bernard (1813-1878) which, begun in 1843, led him to the liver's glycogenic function, the object of his doctoral thesis in natural science, defended 17 March 1853: *Recherches sur une nouvelle fonction du foie, considéré comme organe producteur de matière sucrée chez l'homme et les animaux* (Paris: J.-B. Baillière, 1853). The history of the stages of his discovery appears in his *Introduction à l'étude de la médecine expérimentale* (Paris: J.-B. Baillière, 1865) pp. 286-289 and pp. 318-320; English translation, Claude Bernard, *Experimental Medicine*, trans. Henry Copley Greene (New Brunswick and London: Transaction Publishers, 1999) pp. 163-167 and pp. 181-183.
28. See above, note 12 to lecture of 5 December 1973.
29. J.J. Moreau de Tours, *Du haschisch*, p. 36.
30. J.J. Moreau de Tours, *Traité pratique de la folie névropathique (vulgo hystérique)* (Paris: J.-B. Baillière, 1869) pages iv, xiv, xvii, and xix.
31. J.J. Moreau de Tours, *Du haschisch*, pp. 35-36.
32. Ibid. p. 36.
33. Ibid. pp. 41-42, and, by the same author, "De l'identité de l'état de rêve et de la folie," *Annales médico-psychologiques*, 3rd series, vol. I, July 1855, pp. 361-408.
34. As Foucault recalls in *Histoire de la folie*, the idea of an analogy between the mechanisms which produce dreams and madness develops from the seventeenth century; see *Histoire de la folie*, Part II, ch. 2, "La transcendance du délire," pp. 256-261; *Madness and Civilization*, ch. 4, "Passion and Delirium," pp. 101-107. To the texts to which he refers there we can add a letter from Spinoza to Pierre Balling in which he evokes a type of dream which, depending on the body and the movement of its humors, is analogous to what we see in those suffering from delirium, (Letter to Pierre Balling, 20 July 1664, in *Œuvres*, vol. IV, trans. and notes by C. Appuhn [Paris: Garnier-Flammarion, 1966] p. 172), as well as Kant's famous expression: "The madman is also a waking dreamer/*Der Verrückte ist also ein Traumer im Wachen*" in *Essai sur les maladies de la tête*, trans. J.-P. Lefevre, in *Évolution psychiatrique* (Toulouse: Privat, 1971) p. 222. See also I. Kant, *Anthropologie in pragmatischer Hinsicht aßgefasst von Immanuel Kant* (Königsberg: Friedrich Nicolovius, 1798); French translation, *Anthropologie du point de vue pragmatique*, trans. Michel Foucault (Paris: Vrin, 1964); English translation, *Anthropology from a Pragmatic Point of View*, trans. Mary J. Gregor (The Hague: Martinus Nijhoff, 1974) Part I, § 53, p. 89: "The man who (. . .) is abandoned to a play of thought in which he sees, conducts and judges himself, [is] not in a world in common with others, but in his own world (as in dreaming)."
35. J.E.D. Esquirol, (1) "Délire" in *Dictionnaire des sciences médicales*, vol. VIII (1814) p. 252: "Delirium like dreams only works on objects which appear to our senses in a healthy state and while we are awake (. . .). Then we could distance ourselves from them or draw near

to them; in sleep and delirium we do not enjoy that faculty"; reprinted in *Des maladies mentales*, vol. I; (2) "Hallucinations" in *Dictionnaire des sciences médicales*, vol. XX (Paris: C.L.F. Panckoucke, 1817) p. 67: "The person who is delirious, the person who dreams (...) is abandoned to his hallucinations, to his dreams (...); he dreams completely awake"; reprinted in *Des maladies mentales*, vol. I, p. 292; and (3) in his "Des illusions chez les aliénés (Erreurs des sens)," reprinted in *Des maladies mentales*, vol. I; "Illusions of the insane" in *Mental Maladies*, Esquirol writes that those "hallucinating are dreamers wide awake."

36. On this psychiatric tradition we can refer to the following: A. Maury, (1) "Nouvelles observations sur les analogies des phènomènes du rêve et de l'aliénation mentale," paper given to the Société médico-psychologique, 25 October 1852, *Annales médico-psychologiques*, 2nd series, vol. V, July 1853, pp. 404-421; (2) "De certains faits observés dans le rêves et dans l'état intermédiare entre le sommeil et la veille," in which Maury, placing himself in this tradition, proposes that "the man who falls under the sway of a dream truly represents man affected by mental alienation" *Annales médico-psychologiques*, 3rd series, vol. III, April 1857, pp. 157-176, passage quoted p. 168; and (3) *Le Sommeil et les Rêves. Études psychologiques sur ces phènomènes et les divers états qui s'y attachent* (Paris: Didier, 1861), especially ch. 5, "Des analogies de l'hallucination et du rêve," pp. 80-100, and ch. 6, "Des analogies du rêve et de l'aliénation mentale" pp. 101-148; S. Freud, *Die Traumdeutung* (1901) chs. 1 and 8, in *GW*, vols. II-III (Frankfurt: S. Fischer Verlag, 1942) pp. 1-99 and pp. 627-642; French translation, *L'Interprétation des rêves*, trans. D. Berger (Paris: Presses universitaires de France, 1967) pp. 11-89 and pp. 529-551; English translation, "The Interpretation of Dreams" in *Standard Edition*, translation under general editorship of James Strachey (1953-1974) vol. 4, pp. 1-95 and vol. 5, pp. 626-628; H. Ey, (1) "Brèves remarques historiques sur les rapports des états psychopathiques avec le rêve et les états intermédiaires au sommeil et à la veille," *Annales médico-psychologiques*, 14th series, vol. II, June 1934; (2) *Études psychiatriques*, vol. I: *Historique, Méthodologie, Psychopathologie générale*, Part 2: "Le 'rêve, fait primordial' de la psychopathologie. Historique et position du problème" et "Bibliographie" (Paris: Desclée de Brouwer, 1962, 2nd revised and expanded ed.), pp. 218-228 and p. 282; (3) "La dissolution de la conscience dans le sommeil et le rêve et ses rapports avec la psychopathologie," *Évolution psychiatrique*, vol. XXXV, no. 1, 1970, pp. 1-37. See also the pages Foucault devotes to the question in *Histoire de la folie*, pp. 256-261; *Madness and Civilization*, pp. 101-107.

37. Which is what J. Baillarger finds in the discussion of the summary of the work of J.J. Moreau de Tours by Dr. Bousquet: "Du délire au point de vue pathologique et anatomo-pathologique," paper read to the Académie impériale de médecine, 8 May 1855, *Annales médico-psychologiques*, 3rd series, vol. I, July 1855, pp. 448-455. Replying to criticisms of Bousquet, he notes that "what is important to get accepted is not the identity of the organic state in the two cases, but only the extreme analogy, from the psychological point of view, presented by the sleeping state and the mad state, and the precious things we can learn from this comparative study" ibid. p. 465. Moreau de Tours, for his part, referring to the "organic conditions" of sleep, and the "fundamental phenomena of delirium," proposes that "to grasp, study, and understand well a set of phenomena as complex as that of intellectual disorders, we must... group these phenomena according to the analogies, the more or less numerous affinities that they present" *Du hashish*, p. 44.

38. Moreau de Tours, ibid. Part II, § 1: "Généralités physiologiques," pp. 32-47.

39. An allusion to the privilege that, according to J. Derrida, Descartes accords to the dream over madness in the "First meditation: Some things that one can put in doubt," *Méditations touchant la première philosophie* (1641), in *Œuvres et Lettres*, pp. 268-269; English translation, "Meditations on First Philosophy" trans. John Cottingham, in *The Philosophical Writings of Descartes*, vol. II, pp. 13-14; See Foucault's commentaries in *Histoire de la folie*, Part I, ch. 2, pp. 56-59 (omitted from the English translation of *Madness and Civilization* except for one short paragraph, p. 38) and "Mon corps, ce papier, ce feu" in, *Dits et Écrits*, vol. 2, pp. 245-268; English translation, "My Body, This Paper, This Fire" trans. Geoff Bennington, in *Essential Works of Foucault*, 2, pp. 393-417.

40. J.J. Moreau de Tours, *Du haschisch*, Part III: "Thérapeutique," p. 402: "One of the effects of hashish that I was most struck by (...) is that sort of maniacal excitation always

accompanied by a sense of cheerfulness and happiness (...). I saw in this an effective means for combating the fixed ideas of melancholics (...). Was I mistaken in my conjectures? I am led to think so."

41. Ibid. p. 405: "Pinel, and with him all doctors of the insane, saw mental alienation decided by bouts of agitation." An allusion to the accounts of cures obtained following a "critical attack (*accès critique*)" that Pinel reports in his *Traité médico-philosophique*, section I, § xiii: "Reasons which lead considering most bouts of mania as the healthy and favorable reaction to the cure" pp. 37-41; *A Treatise on Insanity*, pp. 39-43. See also the article by Landré-Beauvais (Pinel's assistant at Salpêtrière) "Crisis" in *Dictionnaire des sciences médicales*, vol. VII (Paris: C.L.F. Panckoucke, 1813) pp. 370-392.
42. J.J. Moreau de Tours, *Du haschisch*: "A precise indication emerged that could be formulated in this way: to preserve his primary acuity in the delirium tending to the chronic state, or to call back this acuity, to revive it when it threatens to become extinguished. The extract of Indian hemp was, of all the medicaments known, the most eminently suited for fulfilling this indication."
43. See above, note 21 to lecture of 12 December 1973.
44. P. Foissac, *Mémoire sur le magnétisme animal, adressé à messieurs les membres de l'Académie royale de médecine* (Paris: Didot Jeune, 1825) p. 6: "When they have fallen into a deep sleep, the magnetized display the phenomena of a new life (...). The sphere of consciousness grows, and already that faculty appears that is so precious that the first magnetizers will call 'intuitive' or 'lucidity' (...). With it, the somnambulists (...) recognize the illness from which they suffer, the near and distant causes of these illnesses, their seat, their prognosis and their appropriate treatment (...). By placing a hand successively on the head, chest, and abdomen of someone unknown, the somnambulists also discover their illnesses, the pains and various alterations that they occasion; in addition they indicate whether cure is possible, easy or difficult, near at hand or far off, and what means must be used to achieve the result."
45. See above, notes 28 and 33 the lecture of 23 January 1974.
46. Thus the magnetic cure carried out on 4 May 1784 by Armand Marc Jacques de Chastenet, marquis of Puységur (1751-1825), on Victor Race, a peasant attached to his property at Buzancy (Soissonnais): asleep, the latter answered questions, gave an opinion of his state, indicated a course of therapy, and gave a prognosis with the date of his return to health, which will be confirmed. And on Charles François Amé, aged 14, who when put in a magnetic sleep announced the duration and intensity of his future crises. See, A.M.J. Chastenet de Puységur, (1) *Mémoires pour servir à l'histoire et à l'établissement du magnétisme animal*, vol. I, (Paris: 1784) pp. 199-211 and pp. 96-97; (2) *Détail des cures opérées à Buzancy, près de Soissons, par le magnétisme animal*, a short anonymous work published by Puységur (Soissons: 1784); (3) see also the account of the cure of the young Hébert, preceded by a plea in favor of magnetism: *Appel aux savans observateurs du dix-neuvième siècle de la décision portée par leurs prédécesseurs contre le magnétisme animal, et fin du traitement du jeune Hébert* (Paris: Dentu, 1813). On the history of magnetic cures one can consult: S. Mialle, *Exposé par ordre alphabétique des cures opérées en France par le magnétisme animal depuis Mesmer jusqu'à nos jours (1774-1826)* (Paris: Dentu, 1826). See also, H.F. Ellenberger, "Mesmer and Puységur: from magnetism to hypnotism," *Psychoanalytic Review*, vol. 52, no. 2 (1965).
47. This is taken from the eighth session conducted on 2 November 1820 by the Baron Jules Dupotet de Sennevoy in the service of Dr. Husson, head doctor at the Hôtel Dieu, on Catherine Samson, aged 18: see, *Exposé des expériences publiques sur le magnétisme animal faites à l'Hôtel-Dieu de Paris, pendant le cours des mois d'octobre, novembre et décembre 1820* (Paris: Béchet Jeune, 3rd edition, 1826) p. 24.
48. In 1816, Étienne Jean Georget entered Esquirol's department at Salpêtrière. On 8 February 1820 he defended his thesis, "Dissertation sur les causes de la folie," then published the work on which his reputation is based: *De la folie. Considérations sur cette maladie*. In 1821, with Léon Rostan, he turned two patients into experimental subjects, Pétronille and Manoury, the widow Brouillard, called Braguette (see above, note 43).
49. "Pétronille... asks Georget to throw her in the water while she is having her period" C. Burdin and F. Dubois (known as Dubois d'Amiens), *Histoire académique du magnétisme animal* (Paris: J.-B. Baillière, 1841) p. 262.

50. Ibid. pp. 262-263: "Pétronille's instructions had not been carried out meticulously; Pétronille had said that she had to be plunged in the Ourcq canal, since it was in this canal that she had fallen and contracted her illness: *similia similibus*; such had to be the end of the story."
51. James Braid (1795-1860), Scottish surgeon, converted to magnetism as a result of demonstrations of "mesmerism" at Manchester in November 1841 by Charles Lafontaine, a disciple of the marquis de Puységur, and popularized his practice under the term "hypnotism." See, J. Braid, *Neurhypnology, or the Rationale of Nervous Sleep Considered in relation with Animal Magnetism. Illustrated by Numerous Cases of its Successful Application in the Relief and Cure of Diseases* (London: John Churchill, 1843); French translation, with a preface by E. Brown-Séquard, *Neurhypnologie, ou Traité du sommeil nerveux considéré dans ses rapports avec le magnétisme animal, et relatant de nombreux succès dans ses applications au traitement des maladies*, trans. G. Simon (Paris: A. Delahaye, 1883).
52. See below, note 55.
53. During the Restoration, the increasing potential of magnetism was seen as a threat by institutional medicine. The confrontation corresponds to the setting up of official commissions: the first, appointed on 28 February 1826, started work in January 1827 and delivered its conclusions on 28 June 1831, which, being deemed too favorable, were not published by the Académie de médecine. A second, unfavorable, was voted on 5 September 1837. The death warrant for magnetism was signed on 15 June 1842 with the decision of the Académie to no longer concern itself with the question. See, L. Peisse, "Des sciences occultes au xixe siècle. Le magnétisme animal," *Revue des deux mondes*, vol. I, March 1842, pp. 693-723.
54. Whereas mesmerism proposed to "demonstrate that the heavenly bodies act on our earth and that our human bodies are equally subject to the same dynamic action" (A. Mesmer, *Dissertatio physico-medica de planetarum influxu* [Vienna: Chelem: 1766] p. 32), and that the action of the magnetizer consists in canalizing this fluid on the patient, James Braid invoked a subjective action founded on the physiology of the brain: see, *The Power of the Mind over the Body: An Experimental Enquirey into the Nature and Cause of the Phenomena Attributed by Baron Reichenbach and Others to a New Imponderable* (London: John Churchill, 1846), for which he was hailed by, among others, the doctor Edgar Bérillon: "It is to Braid that honor is due for having definitively introduced the study of induced sleep into the scientific domain," and for having rendered "a great service to science by giving to the whole of his research the generic name of hypnotism" *Histoire de l'hypnotisme expérimental* (Paris: Delahaye, 1902) p. 5.
55. Foucault refers here to the operation performed by E.F. Follin and Paul Broca (to whom the works of Braid became known through a Bordeaux surgeon, Paul Azam) on a 40 year old woman on 4 December 1859 at the Necker hospital. The operation was the subject of a report to the Académie des sciences presented by A.A.L.M. Velpeau on 7 December 1859: "Note sur une nouvelle méthode anesthésique," *Comptes rendus hebdomadaires des séances de l'Académie des sciences*, vol. 49 (Paris: Mallet-Buchelier, 1859) pp. 902-911.
56. Joseph Pierre Durand, known as Durand de Gros (1826-1900), was an exile in England where he discovered Braidism, and then in the United States. He returned to France where he published under the pseudonym of Joseph Philips, *Électrodynamisme vital, ou les Relations physiologiques de l'esprit et de la matière, démontrées par des expériences entièrement nouvelles* (Paris: J.-B. Baillière, 1855), and then, *Cours théorique et pratique de braidisme, ou Hypnotisme nerveux considéré dans ses rapports avec la psychologiie, la physiologie et la pathologie, et dans ses applications à la médecine, à la chirurgie, à la physiologie expérimentale, à la médecine légale et à l'éducation* (Paris: J.-B. Baillière, 1860).
57. Durand de Gros defines "the hypotaxic state" as "a preparatory modification of vitality, a modification which usually remains latent and the whole effect of which is to incline the organization to undergo the determinant and specific action constituting the second stage" *Cours théorique et pratique*, p. 29.
58. Ibid. p. 112.
59. Ibid. Chorea is a nervous disorder characterized by sweeping and jerky involuntary movements, with a gesticulatory appearance.

60. Ibid. p. 87: "Braidism is a process by which we seek to determine certain physiological changes in man with the aim of fulfilling certain indications for medical or surgical treatment, or in order to facilitate the experimental studies of biology."
61. Between 1850 and 1860, under the impulse of Guillaume Benjamin Amand Duchenne de Boulogne (1806-1875), the nosology of functional disorders of motivity was redefined and enriched by two new groups of affections. On the one hand, "progressive muscular atrophy," studied from 1849, and the "muscular atrophies with myopathic origin," in 1853: (1) *La Paralysie atrophique de l'enfance* (Paris: 1855). On the other hand, "progressive locomotor atrophy," known up until then as *tabes dorsalis*: (2) "De l'ataxie locomotrice progressive. Recherches sur une maladie caracterisée spécialement par des troubles généraux de coordination des mouvements," *Archives générales de médecine*, 5th series, vol. 12, December 1858, pp. 641-652; vol. 13, January 1859, pp. 5-23; February 1859, pp. 158-164; April 1859, pp. 417-432. In 1860 he described (3) the "paralysie glosso-labio-laryngée," ibid. 5th series, vol. 16, 1860, pp. 283-296 and pp. 431-445. On Duchenne de Boulogne, see P. Guilly, *Duchenne de Boulogne* (Paris: Baillière, 1936). On the constitution of the neurological field, see W. Riese, *A History of Neurology* (New York: MD Publications, 1959), and F.H. Garrison, *History of Neurology*, edition revised and expanded by Laurence McHenry (Springfield, Ill.: C.C. Thomas, 1969).

twelve

6 FEBRUARY 1974

The emergence of the neurological body: Broca and Duchenne de Boulogne. ~ Illnesses of differential diagnosis and illnesses of absolute diagnosis. ~ The model of "general paralysis" and the neuroses. ~ The battle of hysteria: 1. The organization of a "symptomatological scenario." ~ 2. The maneuver of the "functional mannequin" and hypnosis. The question of simulation. ~ 3. Neurosis and trauma. The irruption of the sexual body.

LAST WEEK I SAID that one of the important events in the history of the consolidation of psychiatric power was, in my view, the appearance of what I called the "neurological body."* What should we understand by "neurological body"? I would like to begin with this today.

Of course, the neurological body is still, always, the body of pathological-anatomical localization. There is no opposition between the neurological body and the body of pathological anatomy; the second is part of the first; it is, if you like, a derivative or expansion of it. And the best proof of this is that in one of his courses, in 1879, Charcot said that the constitution, progress, and, in his view, the culmination of neurology, was the triumph of the "spirit of localization."[1] Except that what I think is important is that the procedures for matching up anatomical localization and clinical observation in the case of neurology are not at all the same as in the case of ordinary general medicine. It seems to me

* The manuscript adds: "From 1850 to 1870, emergence of a new body."

that neurology, clinical neurology, involves a quite different deployment of the body in the field of medical practice. My impression is that the encounter of the patient-body and the doctor-body in neurology takes place in terms of a very different arrangement from that in general medicine. And it is the setting up of this new apparatus that seems to me to be the important episode, which is why I would like to try to identify the new apparatus set up by and through the constitution of a neuropathology or neurological clinical medicine.

What is this apparatus, and in what does it consist? How is the sick body* captured in clinical neurology? Its capture takes place, I think, very differently from the way the body was captured at the time of the formation of pathological anatomy, more or less between Bichat[2] and Laënnec.[3] I will give you an example straightaway by taking a text that is not by Charcot himself, but which is found in the Charcot archives at Salpêtrière and was quite certainly written by one of his students—clearly we don't know which one. It is an observation of a patient. This is how the patient is described: the patient's symptom was something very simple, the drooping of the left eyelid, called *ptosis*. So, the student takes the following notes for Charcot for him then to use for a lecture—I am not giving you the description of the whole of the patient's face, but just a quite small excerpt.

"If we tell him to open his eyelids, he raises the right one normally, the left one however, does not noticeably move, no more than the eyebrow, so that the superciliary asymmetry becomes more marked. In this movement (...) the skin of the forehead wrinkles transversally on the right side, while it remains almost smooth on the left. At rest, the skin of the forehead is wrinkled neither on the right nor the left (...)."

"Two more points should be noted: a small dimple, quite visible under a certain angle of light, eight millimeters above the left eyelid and about two centimeters to the left of the median line of the forehead; and a little projection within the dimple which seems due to the contraction of the eyelid muscle. These two points are very noticeable in comparison with the normal state of the right side."[4]

* The manuscript clarifies: "body whose surface is the bearer of plastic values."

You have here a type of description which is, I think, really quite different from what is found in the anatomical-pathological procedure, in anatomical-pathological observation.[5] In a sense, this sort of description takes us back to a sort of surface, almost impressionistic gaze, such as could be found in eighteenth century medicine, when the patient's complexion, color, red cheeks and bloodshot eyes, etcetera, were important elements for clinical diagnosis.[6] Pathological anatomy—Bichat, Laënnec, if you like—infinitely reduced this impressionistic description of the surface and codified what were ultimately a quite limited number of surface signs intended to identify what was essential according to a well-established clinical code, this being, precisely, the lesion, which then, thanks either to a surgical operation or, especially, the autopsy, was described by the anatomical pathologist with almost as many details as, if not more than, the description I have just read to you. In other words, anatomical-pathology brought its minutely detailed description to bear on the deep and injured organ, the surface only being questioned through a grid of ultimately simple and limited signs.

Here, rather, as you can see, you have the striking reemergence of surface values within medical discourse and knowledge. It is this surface that must be covered in all its hollows and bumps, and practically by looking only, by looking only that far. In fact, and no doubt even more than this clinical re-validation of the almost impressionistic values of the surface, what is important and, I think, decisive, in this new clinical capture of the neurological patient, and in the correlative constitution of a neurological body before this gaze and apparatus of capture, is that the neurological examination is basically looking for "responses."

What I mean is that in the pathological anatomy of Bichat-Laënnec one can, of course, identify the signs straightaway, at the first glance; one can also obtain them from a stimulation: one taps, one listens, etcetera. That is to say, what is sought in classical pathological anatomy is essentially the system of stimulation-effect: one sounds the chest and listens to the noise;[7] one asks the patient to cough and listens to its harshness; one palpates and sees if there is any heat. So: stimulation-effect.

In the case of the neurological examination being constituted in the mid-nineteenth century, the main part of the signs, in short what makes a sign a sign, is not so much that it is [deciphered as] a more or less mechanical effect, like the noise following percussion in classical pathological anatomy, but that a sign is [deciphered] as a response. I think the substitution of the schema of stimulus-response for the schema of stimulus-effect, and the organization of a whole battery of stimuli-responses, is crucial.

We have a number of examples of this staging of a battery of stimuli-responses. At the strictly elementary level, there was the founding discovery of neuropathology in Duchenne de Boulogne's research into what he called "localized Faradization," when, by moistening two electrodes, he succeeded in getting a single muscular response, or, rather, the response of a single muscle to electrification of the surface of the skin; by moistening the surface of the skin he succeeded in limiting the effect of the charge and obtained a single response of a single muscle: this was the founding discovery of everything here.[8] Then, starting from this, there were the studies of reflexes and then, especially, the study of complex behavior involving either a gearing of diverse automatisms or a prior learning, and it is there that we find, more or less, the two great domains in which the capture, the apparatuses of neurological capture, were completely established. This was Broca's study of aphasia,[9] the study of walking, and notably Duchenne de Boulogne's study of tabetics.[10]

Taking the second example, Duchenne produced a description of the walking of tabetics that is presented precisely in terms of stimulus-response or, rather, in terms of behavior and the sequence of episodes of behavior that constitute the action of walking. Duchenne's problem was to distinguish the disorder of balance found in tabetics, that is to say, at a certain stage and in a certain form of general paralysis, from the vertigo of alcoholic intoxication or even of certain cerebellar disorders. In 1864, in a fundamental article, Duchenne managed to give a differential description of the gait of tabetics and the rocking of vertigo.[11] In the case of vertigo, the subject gives way to wide swaying, whereas in the subject suffering from tabes the rocking movements are "short," "they are abrupt"—Duchenne de Boulogne says that the subject has the bearing of a tightrope walker without his balancing pole, cautiously advancing one step at a time while trying to restore his balance.[12] In the case of vertigo, there is no muscular contraction, but a general weakening of the musculature and tone instead, whereas [...*] the tabetic is always holding himself back, and if we observe what happens at the level of his calves and legs, we see, even before he loses his balance, even before he is aware of losing his balance, some small, brief spasms which flicker across the musculature of his legs, and then, gradually, these contractions become more significant, until they become voluntary when the subject becomes aware that he is losing his balance.[13] This is completely different, therefore, from the collapse in vertigo. In vertigo, the subject zigzags; that it to say, going from one point to another, he cannot keep to a straight line. The tabetic however, goes completely straight ahead; it is just his body that wobbles around this straight line.[14] And finally, in drunkenness, there is the internal sensation of vertigo, whereas the tabetic has the impression that it is not his body that lacks balance at all, but only his legs, locally as it were.[15] These are the principal themes, more or less, of Duchenne de Boulogne's analysis of the tabetic's gait.

Now, in this kind of analysis—and the same would be true for Broca's analyses of aphasia roughly at the same time, between 1859 and 1865—what is achieved by seeking to obtain a system of signs of responses that show dysfunctions, rather than a system of signs of effects that would reveal the presence of lesions at a given point? What we obtain, of course, is the possibility of distinguishing and analyzing what neurologists called, and still call today, synergies, that is to say, the different correlations existing between this or that muscle: What are the different muscles that must be used in order to get such and such a response? What happens when it is precisely just one of them that is put out of play? So, we get a study of synergies.

Secondly, and I think this is the important thing, it becomes possible to set out the phenomena analyzed in different levels according to an axis of the voluntary and the automatic. That is to say, on the basis of this analysis of behavior, of responses to different stimuli, we can see the functional difference, the difference of neurological and muscular implementation, between simple reflex behavior, automatic behavior, spontaneous voluntary behavior, and, finally, spontaneous behavior produced

* (On the recording, repetition of:) rather

by an order coming from outside. All of this hierarchy in the bodily implementation of the voluntary and the involuntary, of the automatic and the spontaneous, of what is required by an order or what is spontaneously linked together within behavior, will make possible—and this is the essential point—a clinical analysis, an analysis in terms of physical ascription, of the individual's intentional attitude.

Consequently, a capture of the subject's attitude, of the subject's consciousness, of the will itself within his body, becomes possible. Neuropathology showed the will invested in the body, the effects of the will or the degrees of will legible in the organization of responses to stimuli. You are familiar with all the analyses Broca initiated on the different levels of the performance of aphasics, according to whether it is a matter of simple mumblings, of swear words uttered automatically, of phrases triggered spontaneously in a certain situation, or of phrases which must be repeated in a certain order and on a certain injunction.[16] All of these clinical differences of performance between different levels of behavior make possible the clinical analysis of the individual at the level of his intention, at the very level of that much vaunted will that I have tried to show you was the great correlate of discipline. It was the will, in fact, on which and to which disciplinary power had to be applied; it really was the vis-à-vis of disciplinary power, but then it was only accessible through the system of reward and punishment. Neuropathology now provides the clinical instrument by which it is thought the individual can be captured at the level of this will itself.

Let's consider things a bit differently and bit more precisely. We could say that, in one respect, with the neurological examination medicine will lose power in comparison with classical anatomical-pathology. That is to say, in the anatomical-pathology constituted by Laënnec, Bichat, and others, ultimately very little was demanded from the individual: he was asked to lie down, bend his leg, cough, breathe deeply, and so on. Consequently there was a minimum of injunctions on the doctor's part, and minimum dependence on the patient's will. On the other hand, with neuropathology, the doctor's understanding of his patient will have to pass through the latter's will, or at any rate through his cooperation. He will not just say: "Lie down! Cough!", but will have to say to him: "Walk! Put out your leg! Hold out your hand! Speak! Read this sentence! Try to write this!" and so on. In short, we now have a technique of examination reliant on instruction and injunction. Consequently, since instruction and injunction necessarily have to pass through the patient's will, the latter will be at the very heart of the examination and, to that extent, the doctor's authority will be at the very heart of this neurological apparatus. The doctor will give orders, he will try to impose his will, and the patient, after all, may always feign inability or unwillingness. That is to say, one really will depend on the patient's will. However, the clinical possibility of identifying voluntary and involuntary, automatic and spontaneous behavior, the possibility of clinically deciphering the levels of will in behavior that I was just telling you about, will enable one to see whether the patient really responds as he is told to, the quality and nature of his responses, and the extent to which his responses have or have not been faked by the will which comes into play; and here the doctor will recapture the power he lost by giving instructions. For example, after Broca, neurologists could easily distinguish voluntary mutism from an aphasia like anarthria: in the case of anarthria, the impossibility of speaking is always accompanied by a series of background sounds, of automatisms which accompany the attempt to speak; it is also always accompanied by correlative motor disorders, and it is also accompanied by expressive deficiencies in gestures and written expression, etcetera.[17] Someone who refuses to speak, and furthermore a hysteric who does not speak, is someone who has gestures, can write, understands, and has none of the accompanying supplementary disorders typical of anarthria.

So you can see that the individual's will can be captured at the level of his real behavior, at the level, rather, of the clinical observation of his behavior. Consequently, if it is true that, on the one hand, the game of instruction typical of the neurological examination makes the possibility of examination depend on the patient's will to a certain extent, on the other hand, with clinical observation, with the clinical decipherment now available, the patient can be circumvented and short-circuited.

To summarize this in a few words, let's say that a new clinical medical apparatus is put in place that is different in its nature, equipment, and effects from what we can call the Bichat-Laënnec clinical apparatus, as well as from the psychiatric apparatus. In organic medicine, the patient was given a minimum of injunctions like "Lie down! Cough!" and the rest was given over entirely to the doctor's examination carried out through the interplay of stimuli and effects. I have tried to show you that the essential component of capture in psychiatry was questioning, which is the substitute for the examination techniques of organic medicine. Questioning depends, of course, on the subject's will, and for the psychiatrist the answers are not a test of truth or the possibility of a differential decipherment of the disease, but merely a test of reality; questioning simply corresponds to the question: "Is he mad?"

So, neurology is neither an examination in the sense of pathological-anatomy, nor questioning; it is a new apparatus which replaces questioning with injunctions, and which through these injunctions seeks to get responses, but responses which are not the subject's verbal responses, as in questioning, but the responses of the subject's body; responses which can be clinically deciphered at the level of the body and which one can consequently submit to a differential examination without fear of being duped by the subject who responds. We can now differentiate between someone who does not want to speak and someone suffering from aphasia, that is to say, we can now establish a differential diagnosis within forms of behavior for which this was hitherto not possible and which were previously questioned in terms of an absolute diagnosis. The test of reality is no longer necessary: clinical neurology, in a certain domain at least, will enable differential diagnosis to get a hold, like organic medicine, but on the basis of a completely different apparatus. Broadly speaking, the neurologist says: Obey my orders, but keep quiet, and your body will answer for you by giving responses that, because I am a doctor, I alone will be able to decipher and analyze in terms of truth.

"Obey my orders, keep quiet, and your body will respond": you see that it is precisely here that the hysterical crisis will quite naturally rush in. Hysteria will enter into this apparatus. I am not talking about the appearance of hysteria: in my view the question of the historical existence of hysteria is a futile question. I mean that the emergence of hysteria within the medical field, the possibility of making it an illness, and its medical manipulation are only possible when this new clinical apparatus, the origin of which is neurological and not psychiatric, was established; or when this new trap was set.

"Obey, keep quiet, your body will speak." So, you want my body to speak! My body will speak, and I really promise you that there will be much more truth than you can imagine in the answers it will give you. Not, certainly, that my body knows more about it than you, but because there is something in your injunctions that you do not formulate but which I can clearly hear; a certain silent injunction to which my body will respond.* And it is this, the effect of your silent injunctions, that you will call "hysteria in its nature." This, more or less, is the hysteric's discourse rushing in to the trap I have just described.

Fine. So, what takes place once this trap, this new apparatus of capture has been set?

Broadly speaking, I think we could say that until then, in medicine, until the existence of neurology and the clinical apparatus specific to neurology, there were two great domains of illnesses: mental illnesses and the others, the true illnesses. I do not think it is enough to say that mental illnesses and all the others are opposed to each other as illnesses of the mind on the one hand, and illness of the body on the other. This would not be correct, first of all because for many psychiatrists, from 1820 to 1870-1880, illnesses of the mind are just illnesses of the body with the characteristic of having psychical symptoms or syndromes. Then, it was absolutely accepted in this period that the so-called convulsive illnesses—medically, clinically, no effective difference was made between epilepsy and the others[18]—were illnesses of the mind. So I do not think that the mind/body opposition, organic illnesses/psychical illnesses, is the real distinction that divided medicine between 1820 and 1880, whatever the theoretical discussions were, and even because of the theoretical discussions on the organic basis of illness.[19] Actually, I think that the only true difference is the one I talked about last week. That is to say, there were certain illnesses which could be evaluated in terms of differential diagnosis—and these were the good, solid illnesses with which genuine and serious doctors concern themselves—and then the illnesses on which the latter could get no hold, and which could only be

* The manuscript adds: "I will hear what you do not say, and I will obey, providing you with symptoms the truth of which you will have to recognize, since they will respond, without your knowing, to your unspoken injunctions."

recognized by a test of reality—and these were the so-called mental illnesses, those to which there was only a binary response: "He really is mad" or "He is not mad."

I think this is the real division of medical practice and knowledge in the first two thirds of the nineteenth century: between illnesses integrated within a differential diagnosis and illnesses falling solely under an absolute diagnosis. Between these two categories of illnesses there were obviously a number of intermediaries, of which there were basically two that I think are important. There was the good intermediary, the good illness, which was of course general paralysis. This was an epistemologically good illness and, consequently, it was morally good to the extent that, on the one hand, it included psychological syndromes—delirium according to Bayle,[20] and then dementia according to Baillarger[21]—and motor syndromes: trembling of the tongue, progressive paralysis of the muscles, etcetera. There are the two syndromes, and in terms of pathological-anatomy both of them refer to an encephalic lesion. A good illness, consequently, exactly intermediary between those illnesses of the test of reality, which were, if you like, the so-called mental illnesses, and then the illnesses differentially allocated and referring to pathological anatomy.[22] General paralysis was an absolutely good illness, better, more complete, and giving a stronger foundation to all these phenomena in that it was not yet known that general paralysis had a syphilitic origin.[23] Consequently, one had all the epistemological benefits and none of the moral inconveniences.

On the other hand, still intermediary between illness of differential diagnosis and illness of absolute diagnosis, there was a completely different, bad and swampy region, which was at that time called "the neuroses."[24] What did the word "neurosis" mean around the 1840s? The word covered illnesses with all the motor or sensory components—"disorders of relational functions" as it was said—but without any pathological-anatomical lesion which would allow an etiology to be established. So, of course, these illnesses of "disorders of the relational functions" without ascribable anatomical correlates, covered convulsions, epilepsy, hysteria, hypochondria, and so forth.

Now these were bad illnesses for two reasons. They were epistemologically bad because in these illnesses there was a kind of symptomatic confusion or irregularity. In the domain of convulsions, for example, one could not make a division between the different types because, precisely, the neuropathological apparatus did not enable one to make a precise analysis of different forms of behavior. Faced with a convulsion, one said: "This is a convulsion"; one could not make those firm bodily interpretations that I was talking about a moment ago, and, consequently, one was faced with a "region" of confusion and irregularity. In the first number of the *Annales médico-psychologiques*, in 1843, the editors said: We must concern ourselves with madness; we should also concern ourselves with the neuroses, but it is so difficult, "because these disorders are fleeting, varied, protean, exceptional, difficult to analyze and understand, we banish them from observation and dismiss them as we reject troublesome memories."[25]

Epistemologically bad, these disorders were also morally bad due to the ease with which they could be simulated and the fact that, in addition to this possibility, there was a constant sexual component of behavior. Thus, Jules Falret, in an article which was reprinted in 1890 in his *Études cliniques*, said: "The life of hysterics is just a constant lie; they put on airs of pity and devotion and succeed in passing themselves off as saints, while they secretly abandon themselves to the most shameful actions, while at home with their husband and children they make the most violent scenes in which they say coarse and sometimes obscene things."[26]

The emergence of the neurological body, or rather, of the system constituted by neurology's clinical apparatus of capture and the correlative neurological body, will make it possible to remove the disqualification, this double epistemological and moral disqualification, to which the neuroses were subject until the 1870s. It will be possible to remove this disqualification to the extent that it will finally be possible to place these illnesses called "neuroses," that is to say, illnesses with sensory and motor components, not exactly in the domain of neurological illnesses strictly speaking, but very close by, not so much through their causes, but basically because of their forms. That is to say, thanks to the clinical apparatus of neurology, the blade of differential diagnosis will now be able to separate neurological illnesses, such as disorders due to a cerebellar tumor, for example, from hysterical convulsions and trembling.

This famous differential diagnosis, which one had never been able to apply to madness, which never really managed to get a grip on the mental illnesses, this differential diagnosis that one could never insert between an ordinary illness and madness, because madness, above all and essentially, fell under an absolute diagnosis, this differential diagnosis then, through the apparatus I have tried to describe, can now be inserted between neurological disorders with ascribable anatomical lesions, and those disorders called "neuroses." So that what was, morally and epistemologically, the last category in the domain of mental illness—the neuroses—will suddenly be promoted to the closest proximity to genuine and serious illnesses by this new instrument of neurological analysis, of clinical neurology. That is to say, through the use of differential diagnosis the previously discredited zone of the neuroses will receive pathological consecration.

In a book—what's more, not a very good book—which a contemporary neurologist called Guillain devoted to Charcot, his predecessor, the author says, with a kind of radiant joy: "Charcot all the same rescued hysteria from the psychiatrists," which is to say that he really brought it into the domain of the medicine of differential diagnosis, which is the only medicine.[27] Basically, I think Freud thought the same when he put Charcot alongside Pinel and said: Pinel freed the mad from their chains, that is to say, he brought about their recognition as patients. Well, in a way, Charcot too made it possible for hysterics to be seen as ill: he pathologized them.[28]

If we situate Charcot's operation in this way then I think we can see how what I will call "the great maneuvers of hysteria" unfolded at Salpêtrière, and how they were constituted. I will not try to analyze this in terms of the history of hysterics any more than in terms of psychiatric knowledge of hysterics, but rather in terms of battle, confrontation, reciprocal encirclement, of the laying of mirror traps, of investment and counter-investment, of struggles for control between doctors and hysterics.* I do not think that there was exactly an epidemic of hysteria; I think hysteria

* The manuscript adds: "of deals also, of tacit pacts."

was the set of phenomena, and phenomena of struggle, which occurred within as well as outside of the asylum, around this new medical apparatus of clinical neurology; and it was the maelstrom of this battle which in fact summoned around hysterical symptoms all those people who actually joined in the battle. Rather than an epidemic, there was a maelstrom, a kind of hysterical vortex within psychiatric power and its disciplinary system. So how was this played out? I think we can pick out certain maneuvers in this struggle between neurology and the hysteric.

The first maneuver is what could be called the organization of the symptomatological scenario. I think we can schematize things in the following way: for hysteria to be put on the same level as an organic illness, for it to be a genuine illness falling under a differential diagnosis, that is to say, for the doctor to be a true doctor, the hysteric must present a stable symptomatology. Consequently, the doctor's consecration as a neurologist, unlike the psychiatrist, necessarily implies an injunction given to the patient on the quiet: "Give me some symptoms, but give me some stable, coded, regular symptoms"—something that the psychiatrist was already saying—and this regularity and stability had to have two forms. First, consistent symptoms which should be permanently legible on the patient whenever the neurological examination takes place: No more of those illnesses that appear and disappear, the only symptoms of which are the flash of a gesture or the return of fits; we want stable symptoms, and in this way we will find them whenever we ask for them. This was how what Charcot and his successors called the "stigmata" of hysteria were defined. "Stigmata" are phenomena found in every hysteric, even when not suffering an attack:[29] contraction of the visual field,[30] simple or double hemianaesthesia,[31] pharyngal anesthesia, contracture caused by a circular bond around a joint.[32] Moreover Charcot said: All these stigmata are typical of hysteria; they are constants in hysteria, but, despite their constancy, I have to acknowledge that it quite often happens that we do not find them all, or even, in extreme cases, we do not find any.[33] But the epistemological requirement was there, the injunction was there, and I would point out that all of these wonderful stigmata were clearly responses to instructions: instructions to move, to feel a rubbing or contact on the body.

And then, second, the attacks (*crises*) themselves had to be ordered and regular, and so develop according to a very typical scenario sufficiently close to an existing illness, to an existing neurological illness, so that it crosses the line of differential diagnosis, and yet nonetheless sufficiently different for the diagnosis to be made; hence the codification of the hysterical attack (*crise*) on the model of epilepsy.[34] In this way the huge domain of what before Charcot was called "hystero-epilepsy," the "convulsions," is divided in two.[35] You had two illnesses, one which included the famous elements of the epileptic fit, that is to say, tonic phase, clonic phase, and period of stupor; and the other, which had to have tonic and clonic phases like epilepsy, with certain minor signs, differences in the phases, and then some elements absolutely specific to hysteria: the phase of illogical, that is to say, disordered movements; then the phase of passionate postures, that is to say, expressive movements, movements meaning something, a phase that was also called "plastic," inasmuch as it reproduced and expressed emotions like lustfulness, terror, etcetera; and finally, the phase of delirium, which was also found in epilepsy moreover. And there you have the two great classical pictures of the hysteria/epilepsy opposition.[36]

You can see that there is a double game in this maneuver. On the one hand, in appealing to these supposedly constant stigmata of hysteria, and in appealing to regular attacks, the doctor thereby gets rid of his own stigmata, that is to say, the fact that he is only a psychiatrist and obliged to demand at every moment, in each of his questionings: "Are you mad? Show me your madness! Actualize your madness." In appealing to the hysteric's stigmata and the regularity of her attacks, the doctor asks her to give him the possibility of performing a strictly medical act, that is to say, a differential diagnosis. However, at the same time—and this is the advantage for the hysteric and why she will give a positive response to the psychiatrist's demand—the hysteric will thereby escape medical extra-territoriality or, more simply, she will escape asylum territoriality. That is to say, as soon as she has been able to provide her symptoms, which, through their constancy and regularity, allow the neurologist to make a differential diagnosis, the hysteric will cease to be a mad person in the asylum; she will acquire citizenship within a hospital worthy of the name, that is to say, of a hospital which will no longer be entitled to the mere status of an asylum. The hysteric acquires the right to be ill and not mad thanks to the constancy and regularity of her symptoms.

Now what is the basis of this right acquired by the hysteric? It is founded on the situation in which the doctor ultimately finds himself dependent upon her. Because if the hysteric were to refuse to give her symptoms, then straightaway the doctor could no longer be a neurologist in relation to her; he would be consigned to the status of psychiatrist and to the obligation of making an absolute diagnosis and answering the inescapable question: "Are you or are you not mad?" Consequently, to function as a neurologist the doctor depends on the hysteric actually providing him with regular symptoms. To that extent, what the psychiatrist is offered not only ensures his own status as a neurologist, but also ensures the patient's hold over the doctor, since the patient gains a hold over him by providing him with symptoms, since she thereby sanctions his status as doctor, and no longer as psychiatrist.

You can understand the pleasure the hysterics will invest in the supplement of power they are given when they are asked for regular symptoms; and we can see why they never hesitated to provide all the symptoms one wanted, and even more than one wanted, since, the more they provided the more their surplus-power was thereby asserted in relation to the doctor. And we have evidence that they provided a plentiful supply of symptoms, since one of Charcot's patients—and it is one example taken from many—who was at la Salpêtrière for thirty-four years, regularly provided the same stigmata for fifteen years: a "complete left hemianaesthesia."[37] So one got what one wanted from the point of view of duration; one also got what one wanted from the point of view of quantity, since one of Charcot's patients had 4506 attacks in thirteen days and, not content with this, some months later, she had 17,083 attacks in fourteen days.[38]

The second maneuver is the one I will call the maneuver of the "functional mannequin."[39] It is triggered by the first maneuver inasmuch as the doctor, in calling for this proliferation of symptoms—since his status and power depend on it—finds himself both confirmed, and then losing out. Actually, this plethora, these 17,083 attacks in fourteen days, is clearly much more than he can control and more than his little neurological clinical apparatus (*appareil*) can record. So the doctor must provide himself with the possibility, obviously not of controlling this overabundance of hysterical symptomatology but, at any rate—a bit like Duchenne de Boulogne whose problem was: "how to limit electrical stimulation so that it only acts on one muscle"—of giving himself the kind of instrument that will enable him to trigger typically and exclusively hysterical phenomena, but without getting this torrent of thousands of attacks in such a short time.

In answer to the objective of arousing these phenomena on demand, when one wants them, showing that they [are] all pathological, naturally pathological, to get round as it were the maneuver of exaggeration, the hysteric's exaggerated generosity, and succeed in bypassing this plethora, two techniques were established.

First, the technique of hypnosis and suggestion, that is to say: putting the subject in a situation such that, on a precise order, one will be able to get a perfectly isolated hysterical symptom: paralysis of a muscle, inability to speak, trembling, etcetera. In short, hypnosis is used for precisely this purpose, placing the patient in a situation such that he will have exactly the symptom one wants, when one wants it, and nothing else. Charcot did not use hypnosis to multiply hysterical phenomena; it was, like Duchenne's localized electrification, a way of limiting the phenomena of hysteria and of being able to trigger them exactly at will.[40] Now, as soon as we have triggered at will one and only one hysterical symptom, by means of hypnosis, do we not come up against a difficulty: If I induced it, if I said to a hypnotized patient, "you cannot walk," and he became paralyzed, "you cannot speak," and he became aphasic, is this really an illness? Is it not merely the effect in the patient's body of what has been forced on him? So if hypnosis is a good technique for isolating hysterical phenomena, it is also dangerous since it risks being only the effect of an instruction given: the effect, and not the response.

Consequently, precisely when and insofar as doctors put hypnosis to work, they are obliged to find some kind of correlative outside hypnosis to guarantee the natural character of hypnotically induced phenomena. Patients must be found outside all asylum culture and medical power, and so, of course, outside all hypnosis and suggestion, who display exactly the disorders that are observable on demand, under hypnosis, in hospitalized patients. In other words, a natural hysteria, without hospital, doctor, and hypnosis, is needed. In fact, it turned out that Charcot had these patients to hand, patients whose role, faced with hypnosis, was to naturalize, as it were, the effects of hypnotic intervention.

He had them, and this requires a very short reference to a completely different history that connects up with the history of hysteria in a way that is very curious, but not without important historical effects. In 1872 Charcot takes over the hysteria-epilepsy department,[41] and he begins hypnosis in 1878.[42] This is the time of accidents at work and on the railway, of accident and health insurance systems.[43] Not that accidents at work date from that time, but it is at this time that an absolutely new category of patients is making its appearance within medical practice—but whom, sadly, historians of medicine rarely mention—that is, patients who are neither paying nor receiving aid. In other words, in the medicine of the eighteenth and the beginning of the nineteenth century, there were basically only two categories of patient: those who were paying and those who were receiving aid at the hospital. Now a new category of patient appeared, the insured patient, who is neither entirely paying, nor entirely supported by aid.[44] The appearance together of the insured patient and the neurological body, arising from completely different elements, is probably one of the important phenomena of the history of hysteria. What actually took place was that, from the end of the eighteenth century, precisely to the extent that it wanted to profit from a maximized health, society was gradually led to perfect a whole series of techniques of supervision, close control, cover, and insurance also, of illness and accidents.

However, precisely to the extent that society was obliged to divide up, control, and supervise health and to insure against accidents and illnesses in order to extract maximum profit from bodies, at the point when these techniques were established, and by the same process, illness became something profitable for the person who was ill. In the eighteenth century, the only profit a patient receiving aid could draw from his illness was to stay a bit longer in hospital, and this minor problem is frequently encountered in the history of hospital institutions in the eighteenth century. With the tight control dating from the nineteenth century, and with this general cover of phenomena of illness by both medicine and insurance, illness itself, as such, can become a source of profit for the subject and, at any rate, a way of benefiting from this general system.

Illness becomes profitable precisely when it raises a problem at the general level of the profits of society. Illness is consequently intertwined with the whole economic problem of profit.

As a result, we see the appearance of new patients, that is to say, insured patients with what are called post-traumatic disorders such as paralysis, anesthesia, spasms, pains, convulsions, etcetera, without any assignable anatomical basis. And the problem at this time, still in terms of profit, is whether they should be considered as patients, and so covered by insurance, or as malingerers (*simulateurs*).[45] There is a huge literature on the results of railroad accidents—and also on accidents at work, but to a lesser degree and a bit later, almost at the end of the century—which covers, I think, an enormous problem that in a way supported the development of neurological techniques, of the techniques of examination I have been talking about.[46]

The insured patient, who joins up with the neurological body, who is the bearer of a neurological body that can be captured by the clinical apparatus of neuropathology, is the other figure facing the hysteric, precisely the person one is looking for, so that one can be played off against the other. On one side are these patients who are not yet hospitalized, not yet medicalized, and who are not therefore under hypnosis, under medical power, and who display certain natural phenomena if they are not stimulated. And then, on the other side, are the hysterics within the hospital system, under medical power, on whom artificial illnesses have been imposed by means of hypnosis. So, when compared with the trauma, the hysteric will make it possible to recognize whether or not the traumatized person is a simulator, a malingerer. There are two possibilities in fact: either the traumatized person displays the same symptoms as the hysteric—obviously I am talking about someone traumatized who has no trace of a lesion—and, as a result, we can say: "he has the same illness as the hysteric," since the first maneuver consisted in showing that the hysteric was ill, and so the hysteric will authenticate the traumatized person's illness; or the traumatized person will not have the same illness, will not display the same symptoms as the hysteric, and as a result will fall outside the field of pathology and one will be able to ascribe his symptoms to simulation.

On the other hand, with regard to hysteria, comparison will lead to the following result: if someone who is not hypnotized can be found with symptoms similar to those obtained in a hysteric by means of hypnosis, then this really will be the sign that the hypnotic phenomena obtained in hysterics are indeed natural phenomena. So, the hysteric is naturalized by means of the traumatized person, and the traumatized person's possible simulation is revealed by means of the hysteric.

Hence Charcot's grand stagecraft. It is often said that this consisted in getting a hysteric and saying to his students: "See what illness she is affected by," and, effectively, dictating symptoms to the patient. This is true, it corresponds to the first maneuver I was telling you about, but I think the major and most subtle and perverse of Charcot's maneuvers, was precisely displaying these two figures together. When traumatized people from outside the hospital appeared at his private office—the victims of different kinds of accidents with no visible traces of lesions and suffering from paralysis, coxalgia, anesthesia—Charcot called for a hysteric, hypnotized him and said: "You can no longer walk," and looked to see whether the hysteric's paralysis really was similar to that of the person traumatized. A famous case of this kind was one of post-traumatic coxalgia in a railroad employee. Charcot was almost sure that the coxalgia was not caused by a lesion; he had a feeling however that it was not a pure and simple simulation. He called for two hysterics, hypnotized them, and gave them instructions through which he managed to reconstitute the employee's coxalgia on the kind of functional mannequin that the hysteric had become, and so the coxalgia had to be considered hysterical.[47]

Everyone benefits. In the first place, the insurance companies, of course, and the people who had to pay, and, also the patient to a certain extent, since, if he is not a simulator, a malingerer, Charcot said, we cannot deny him something, albeit, obviously, not of the same order as if he had a real injury. So the cake was cut in two. However, clearly this is not the important problem: the doctor also benefits since, thanks to the use of the hysteric as a functional mannequin, the doctor could make a differential diagnosis that will now be brought to bear on the simulator. One will now be able to master the famous panic dread of the simulator that so obsessed doctors in the first half of the nineteenth century, since one will have these hysterics who, traitors to their own lie, as it were, will make it possible to denounce the lie of others, and, as a result, the doctor will finally have the upper hand over simulation.[48]

Finally, of course, the hysterics benefit, since if they serve as functional mannequins in this way, authenticating the functional or, as it was said at this time, "dynamic" illness without lesion, if the hysteric is there to authenticate this illness, then she inevitably escapes all suspicion of simulation, since she is the basis on which the simulation of others can be denounced. As a result, it is once again thanks to the hysteric that the doctor will be able to ensure his power; if he escapes the simulator's trap it is because he has the hysteric who makes possible the double, organic/dynamic/simulation, differential diagnosis. And consequently, the hysteric has the upper hand over the doctor a second time, since by obeying the instructions he gives her under hypnosis, she gets to be the authority of verification, as it were, the authority adjudicating truth between illness and lie. The second triumph of the hysteric. You understand that here too the hysterics do not hesitate to reconstitute, on demand, the coxalgia and anesthesia, etcetera that they are asked for under hypnosis.

Hence the third maneuver of redistribution around the trauma. At the end of the second maneuver, the doctor is therefore once again newly dependent on the hysteric, because if the disorders reproduced on order by the hysteric, and so generously, so profusely, with such obedience and, at the same time, with such a thirst for power, will not this be proof after all that it is all fabricated, as Bernheim was already beginning to say?[49] In the end, is not the appearance of this great hysterical symptomatology at la Salpêtrière all due to the set of medical powers being exercised within the hospital?

If the doctor is not to be entirely dependent on this hysterical behavior which could well be said to be fabricated, if he is to renew his power over all this phenomena and take it back under his control, he will have to include within a strict pathological schema both the fact that someone can be hypnotized and the fact that he reproduces pathological types of phenomena under hypnosis, and, at the same time, that those well-known functional disorders, which Charcot had shown were so close to hysterical phenomena, can be placed in this pathological framework. A pathological framework is needed which simultaneously envelops hypnosis, the hysterical symptoms produced under hypnosis, and the event which brings about the functional disorders of patients who are not hypnotized. Since the body cannot speak because there is no lesion, this search for a pathological framework leads Charcot to look for an assignable cause. One will have to look at the etiological level for something on which to pin all these phenomena and thereby attach them to a rigorous pathology, that is to say, what one will have to discover is an event.

This was how Charcot developed the concept of trauma.[50]

What is a trauma for Charcot? It is something—a violent event, a blow, a fall, a fear, a spectacle, etcetera—which provokes a sort of discrete, localized hypnotic state, but which sometimes lasts for a long time, so that, following the trauma, a certain idea enters the individual's head, inscribes itself in his cortex, and acts like a sort of permanent injunction.

An example of a trauma: a child is knocked down by a vehicle; he faints. In the moment before fainting he has the feeling that the wheels of the vehicle run over his body. He comes to and, after a time, realizes that he is paralyzed; and if he is paralyzed it is because he thinks the wheels ran over his body.[51] Now this belief is inscribed and continues to function within a set of micro-hypnotic states, within a localized hypnotic state concerning this belief. What provokes paralysis of the legs is, as it were, this idea that has become a hypnotic injunction.[52] We see here how the notion of trauma, which will be so important in the future, is established and, at the same time, the link between this notion and the old conception of delirium. Since if he is paralyzed, it is because he believes that the wheels of the van ran over him—you can see how this is linked with the old conception of madness always concealing a delirium.[53] So, a trauma is something that provokes a localized and permanent hypnotic state on just this point.

As for hypnotism, what is it? Well, it will also be a trauma, but in the form of a complete, brief, transitory shock, which will be suspended solely by the doctor's will, but which will envelop the individual's general behavior, so that within this state of hypnosis, which is a sort of generalized and provisional trauma, the doctor's will, his words, will be able to implant ideas and images in the subject which thus have the same role, the same function, and the same effect of injunction as the injunction I was talking about with regard to natural, non-hypnotic traumas. Thus, between hysterical phenomena produced under hypnosis and hysterical phenomena following an event, there is a convergence which points towards this fundamental notion of trauma. Trauma is what provokes hypnosis, and hypnosis is a sort of general reactivation of the trauma through the doctor's will.

Hence the need in Charcot's practice to go in search of the trauma itself.

That is to say, to be sure that the hysteric really is a hysteric and that all her symptoms, whether under hypnosis or outside of hypnosis, really are pathological, one will have to discover the etiology, to find the trauma, the kind of invisible and pathological lesion which makes all of this a well and truly morbid whole.* Hence the necessity for hysterics, whether or not they are under hypnosis, to recount their childhood, their life, so as to find again that kind of fundamental and essential event that will persist and is always present in the hysterical syndrome, and of which the latter is in some way the permanent actualization.[54]†

However—and here we find the hysteric again and her counter-maneuver—what will the patients do with this injunction to find the trauma that persists in the symptom? Into the breach opened by this injunction they will push their life, their real, everyday life, that is to say, their sexual life. It is precisely this sexual life that they will recount, that they will connect up with the hospital and endlessly reactualize in the hospital. Unfortunately, we cannot trust Charcot's text for proof of this counter-investment of the search for the trauma by the story of sexual life, because Charcot does not talk about it. However, when we look at his students' observations, we see what is involved throughout these anamneses, what was at stake, what was talked about, and also what was really involved in the famous attacks with a pseudo-epileptic form. I will take just one example, a case recorded by Bourneville.

This is how the patient recounted her life. From age six to thirteen she was a boarder in a religious convent "at La Ferté-sous-Jouarre where she enjoyed a degree of freedom, wandered in the countryside, willingly let herself be kissed for sweets." This is the protocol produced by one of Charcot's students on the basis of the patient's own accounts. "She often

---

* The manuscript clarifies: "Hence the double search: (a) for the nervous diathesis which causes susceptibility to trauma; search for heredity. And then (b) for the trauma itself."

† The manuscript adds: "Hence the violence of the opposition to Bernheim: if everyone could be hypnotized the edifice would collapse."

visited the wife of a workman, Jules, a painter. The latter was in the habit of getting drunk, and when this happened there were violent arguments in the household; he beat his wife, dragged her or tied her up by the hair. Louise [the patient; M.F.] sometimes witnessed these scenes. One day, Jules would have tried to kiss her, even rape her, which gave her a great fright. During the holidays [she was aged between six and thirteen years; M.F.], she came to Paris and spent the days with her brother, Antonio, one year younger than her, who seems to have been very precocious and taught her many things she should not have known. He mocked her naivety, which led her to accept the explanation he gave to her of, amongst other things, how children are made. During the holidays, in the house where her parents were in service, she had the opportunity to see a Mr. C [the master of the house; M.F.], who was her mother's lover. Her mother obliged Louise to kiss this man and wanted her to call him her father. On her permanent return to Paris, Louise was placed [after her period of boarding, so she was 13; M.F.] in C's home on the pretext of learning to sing and sew, etcetera. She slept in a little isolated room. C, whose relationship with his wife was a bit strained, took advantage of her absences to try to have relations with Louise, aged thirteen and a half. The first time, he failed; he wanted her to go to bed in front of him. A second attempt ended in some incomplete approaches, due to her resistance. A third time, C, after dangling all sorts of promises before her eyes, fine gowns, etcetera, seeing that she did not want to give in, threatened her with a razor; taking advantage of her fear, he got her to drink a liqueur, undressed her, threw her down on his bed, and had full sexual intercourse with her. The following day Louise was suffering, etcetera."[55]

The lives of hysterics recounted by Charcot's patients are in fact often of this order and level. And, if we look at the observations taken for Charcot by his students, what really happened in those famous attacks that Charcot said were strangely similar to epileptic fits and very difficult to distinguish from epileptic fits if you were not a good neurologist?

At the level of the discourse, this is what Louise said: "Tell me! . . . You must tell me! Peasant! You must be vile. So you believe this boy more than me . . . I swear to you that this boy has never laid a hand on me . . . I did not respond to his caresses, we were in a field . . . I assure you that I did not want it... Call them (Commanding physiognomy). Well? (She suddenly looks to her right)... But that is not what you said to him!... Antonio, you must repeat what he told you... that he touched me... But I did not want. Antonio, you are lying!... It is true, he had a snake in his pants, he wanted to put it in my belly, but he did not even find me... let's finish with it... We were on a bench... You kissed me more than once, I did not kiss you; I am a lunatic... Antonio, you are laughing..."[56]

Discourses like this take place in the period called delirious, the last period of Charcot's analysis. And if we go back to the "plastic" phase of "passionate poses," this is the form they take in another patient: "Celina M is attentive, sees someone, motions with her head for him to come to her, opens her arms, brings them together as if she was embracing the imaginary being. Her physiognomy expresses discontent to start with, disappointment, then, in a sudden change, happiness. At this point we see some movements of the stomach; her legs bend, M falls back on her bed and makes new clonic movements. With a rapid movement she moves her body to the right side of the bed, her head resting on the pillow; her face is flushed, her body partly rolls over on itself, her right cheek lying on the pillow, her face looking to the right, the patient presents her buttocks, which are raised, the lower limbs being bent. After some moments, while maintaining this lubricious position, M makes some movements with her pelvis. She then stands up and has some major clonic movements. Finally, she grimaces, cries, seems deeply frustrated. She sits down again, looks to the left, signals with her head and right hand. She witnesses varied scenes, seeming, by the play of her physiognomy, to experience pleasant and painful sensations alternately. Suddenly, she puts her body back in the middle of the bed, raises it slightly and, with her right hand, makes the gestures of the *mea culpa*, followed by contortions and grimaces. Then she lets out some sharp cries: 'Oh! là! là!' smiles, looks around with a lubricious air, sits down, seems to see Ernest and says: 'Well come on then! Come on!' "[57]

So, at the level of the daily observations of patients by Charcot's students, this is the real content of these attacks.

Now I think this is where the hysterics, for the third time, take back power over the psychiatrist, for these discourses, scenes, and postures, which Charcot codified under the term "pseudo-epilepsy" or "major hysterical attack," analogous to but different from epilepsy, all of this real content that we see in everyday observations, could not in fact be admitted by Charcot. Not for reasons of morality or prudishness, if you like, but he quite simply could not accept it. If you recall, I spoke to you about neurosis as it existed and was discredited around the 1840s, as it was again in Charcot's time by Jules Falret. Why was it discredited?[58] It was discredited both because it was simulation—and Charcot tried to get round this objection—and because it was sexual, because it included a number of lubricious elements. If one really wanted to succeed in demonstrating that hysteria was a genuine illness, if one absolutely wanted to make it work within the system of differential diagnosis, if one did not want its status as illness to be challenged, then it had to be entirely shorn of that disqualifying element which was as harmful as simulation, namely lubricity or sexuality.* Therefore it really was necessary that it did not arise, or was not said.

Now, he could not prevent it from occurring, since it was he, Charcot, who was calling for symptoms, for attacks. And, in fact, the patients provided many attacks, the surface symptomatology and general scenario of which conformed to the rules laid down by Charcot. But under the cover of this scenario, as it were, they crammed in all their individual life, sexuality, and memories; they reactualized their sexuality, and at the very heart of the hospital, with the interns or doctors. Consequently, since Charcot could not prevent this from happening, there was only one thing he could do, which was not to say it, or rather, to say the opposite. In fact, you can read this in Charcot, which is paradoxical when you know the observations on which it is based. He said: "For my own part, I am far from thinking that lubricity is always at work in hysteria; I am even convinced of the contrary."[59]

And you recall the episode that takes place one evening in the winter of 1885-1886, while Freud was training with Charcot and, invited to Charcot's house, was amazed to hear Charcot say in an aside to someone: "Oh! hysteria, everyone knows full well that it is a matter of sexuality." And Freud comments saying: "When I heard this I was really surprised

* The manuscript adds: "If it was let back in, then the whole edifice of pathologization constructed in competition with the hysterics was going to collapse."

and said to myself: 'But if he knows, why doesn't he say so?' "[60] If he did not say so, it was, I think, for these reasons. Only, one might wonder how Freud, who spent six months at la Salpêtrière, and who therefore was present every day at the scenes of which I have given you [two] examples, did not speak of it either with regard to his stay at la Salpêtrière, and one might wonder how the discovery of sexuality in hysteria only emerged for him some years later.[61] Charcot's only possibility was quite precisely not to see and not to speak.

For amusement, I will quote this little episode I found in the Charcot archives; it is a student's note, that what's more is without irony: "M. Charcot sends for Geneviève, suffering from hysterical spasms. She is on a stretcher; the interns, the senior doctors have previously hypnotized her. She undergoes her major hysterical attack. Charcot, following his usual technique, shows how hypnosis can not only provoke, induce hysterical phenomena, but can also stop them; he takes his baton, resting it on the patient's belly, precisely on the ovaries, and the attack is in fact suspended. Charcot removes his baton; the attack begins again; tonic period, clonic period, delirium and, at the moment of delirium, Geneviève cries out: 'Camille! Camille! Kiss me! Give me your cock.' Professor Charcot has Geneviève taken away; her delirium continues."[62]

It seems to me that this kind of bacchanal, this sexual pantomime, is not the as yet undeciphered residue of the hysterical syndrome. My impression is that this sexual bacchanal should be taken as the counter-maneuver by which the hysterics responded to the ascription of trauma: You want to find the cause of my symptoms, the cause that will enable you to pathologize them and enable you to function as a doctor; you want this trauma, well, you will get all my life, and you won't be able to avoid hearing me recount my life and, at the same time, seeing me mime my life anew and endlessly reactualize it in my attacks!

So this sexuality is not an indecipherable remainder but the hysteric's victory cry, the last maneuver by which they finally get the better of the neurologists and silence them: If you want symptoms too, something functional; if you want to make your hypnosis natural and each of your injunctions to cause the kind of symptoms you can take as natural; if you want to use me to denounce the simulators, well then, you really will have to hear what I want to say and see what I want to do! And Charcot, who saw everything, who, in the low slanting daylight, saw even the smallest dimples and the smallest bumps on a paralytic's face,[63] was indeed obliged to turn his admirable eyes away when the patient was saying all that she had to say.

At the end of this kind of great battle between the neurologist and the hysteric, around the clinical apparatus of neuropathology, a new body appears beneath the apparently captured neurological body,* beneath the body that the neurologist hoped and believed he had really captured in truth. This new body is no longer the neurological body; it is the sexual body. It is the hysteric who imposes this new personage on neurologists and doctors, which is no longer the pathological-anatomical body of Laënnec and Bichat, the disciplinary body of psychiatry, or the neurological body of Duchenne de Boulogne or Charcot, but the sexual body, confronted with which henceforth only two attitudes were possible.

Either there is the attitude of Charcot's successor, Babinski, which consists in a retrospective devaluation of hysteria, which, since it has these connotations, will no longer be an illness.[64] Or there is a new attempt to circumvent the maneuver of hysterical encirclement, so as to give a medical meaning to this new course that loomed up on all sides around the neurological body fabricated by the doctors. This new investment will be the medical, psychiatric, and psychoanalytic take over of sexuality.

By breaking down the door of the asylum, by ceasing to be mad so as to become patients, by finally getting through to a true doctor, that is to say, the neurologist, and by providing him with genuine functional symptoms, the hysterics, to their greater pleasure, but doubtless to our greater misfortune, gave rise to a medicine of sexuality.

---

* Manuscript variant: "and by which one wanted to judge madness, to question it in truth . . ."

1. "If I have succeeded in putting the works relating to the morbid anatomy of the nervous centers in their true light, you will not have failed to recognize the main tendency which becomes more pronounced in all these works. All seem, in some way, dominated by what we could call the spirit of localization, which is in fact only an offshoot of the spirit of analysis" J.-M. Charcot, "Faculté de Médecine de Paris: Anatomo-pathologie du système nerveux," *Progrès médical*, 7th year, no. 14, 5 April 1879, p. 161.
2. On Bichat, see above note 38 to the lecture of 9 January 1974.
3. On Laënnec, see ibid. From 1803, Laënnec gave a private course of pathological anatomy, which he wanted to make into a separate discipline. He put forward an anatomical-pathological classification of organic affections derived from, but more complete than that of Bichat; see, "Anatomie pathologique," in *Dictionnaire des sciences médicales*, vol. II (Paris: C.L.F. Panckoucke, 1812) pp. 46-61. See the chapter Foucault devotes to pathological anatomy, "L'invisible visible" in *Naissance de la clinique*, pp. 151-176; *The Birth of the Clinic*, ch. 9, "The Visible Invisible" pp. 149-173.
4. This is the observation of I.N., eighteen years old, suffering from *ptosis* of the left eyelid, presented at the consultation of 18 February 1891. See J.-M. Charcot, *Clinique des maladies du système nerveux (1889-1891)*, Lectures edited by G. Guinon, Lecture of 24 February 1891 (recorded by A. Souques), vol. I (Paris: Aux bureaux du Progrès médical/Vve Babé, 1892) p. 332.
5. On the "anatomical-clinical gaze" see *Naissance de la clinique*, ch. 8, "Ouvrez quelques cadavres," pp. 136-142, and ch. 9, "L'invisible visible," pp. 164-172; *The Birth of the Clinic*, ch. 8, "Open Up a Few Corpses," pp. 124-148, and ch. 9, "The Visible Invisible," pp. 149-173.
6. Ibid., ch. 6, "Des signes et des cas"; ibid., ch. 6, "Signs and Cases."
7. Foucault is referring to the clinical mode of examination by "percussion" for which Jean Nicolas Corvisart (1755-1821) became the advocate after translating and annotating the work of the Viennese Leopold Auenbrugger (1722-1809): *Inventum novum ex percussione thoracis humani ut signo abstrusos interni pectoris morbos detegendi* (Vindobonae: Typis Joannis Thomas Trattner, 1761; French translation, *Nouvelle méthode pour reconnaître les maladies internes de la poitrine par la percussion de cette cavité*, trans. and commentary J.N. Corvisart (Paris: Migneret, 1808)). In September 1816 Laënnec perfected the stethoscope at the Necker hospital; see R.T.H. Laënnec, *De l'auscultation médiate*; *A Treatise on Mediate Auscultation.*
8. As a result of numerous works, including those of the physiologist François Magendie (1783-1855) in 1826, which resorted to electrical stimulation in order to study the mechanisms of nervous excitation and muscular contraction, G.B.A. Duchenne de Boulogne used "Faradization" to explore the excitability of muscles and nerves and to establish the diagnosis and treatment of their affections. He set out the results in a first paper presented in 1847 to the Académie des sciences: (1) "De l'art de limiter l'action électrique dans les organes, nouvelle méthode d'électrisation appelée 'électrisation localisée,' " republished in *Archives générales de médecine*, July and August 1850, and February and March 1851. In 1850 he set out in a second report a method of "galvanization" using continuous currents with the aim of studying muscular functions and providing the means for "a differential diagnosis of paralyses": (2) *Application de la galvanisation localisée à l'étude des fonctions musculaires* (Paris: J.-B. Baillière, 1851). All these works were brought together in one work: (3) *De l'électrisation localisée et de son application à la physiologie, à la pathologie et à la thérapeutique* (Paris: J.-B. Baillière, 1855). See also above, note 61 to lecture of 30 January 1974, and R.A. Adams, "A. Duchenne" in W. Haymaker and F. Schiller, eds. *The Founders of Neurology*, vol. 2 (Springfield, Ill.: C.C. Thomas, 1970) pp. 430-435.
9. Pierre Paul Broca (1824-1880), surgeon at Bicêtre, presented a note to the Paris Société d'Anthropologie on 18 April 1861: (1) "Remarques sur le siège de la faculté du langage articulé, suivies d'une observation d'aphémie (perte de la parole)" concerning a patient, Leborgne, hospitalized at Bicêtre for twenty-one years, who had recently lost the use of speech and could now only pronounce the syllable "tan" repeated twice. Transferred into Broca's department on 11 April 1861, where he died on 17 April, his autopsy revealed a center of softening of the foot of the third left frontal convolution, to which Broca

attributed the loss of articulated speech; see *Bulletin de la Société d'Anthropologie de Paris*, 1st series, vol. II, August 1861, pp. 330-357, republished in H. Hécaen and J. Dubois, *La Naissance de la neurophysiologie du langage, 1826-1865* (Paris: Flammarion, 1969) pp. 61-91. Between 1861 and 1865, further observations confirmed to Broca the role of the third left convolution: see (2) "Localisation des fonctions cérébrales. Siège du lanage articulé," *Bulletin de la Société d'Anthropologie de Paris*, 1st series, vol. IV, 1863, pp. 200-204, and (3) "Sur le siège de la faculté du langage articulé," ibid. 1st series, vol. VI, 1865, pp. 377-393, republished in H. Hécaen and J. Dubois, *La Naissance de la neurophysiologie du langage*, pp. 108-123.

10. To Duchenne de Boulogne we owe the description of "progressive locomotor ataxia" or *tabes dorsalis*, of syphilitic origin, characterized by lack of motor coordination and usually accompanied by abolition of the reflexes and deep sensibility: see, "De l'ataxie locomotrice progressive," republished in *De l'ataxie locomotrice progressive* (Paris: Rignoux, 1859).
11. G.B.A. Duchenne, *Diagnostic différentiel des affections cérébelleuses et de l'ataxie locomotrice progressive* (extract from *La Gazette hebdomadaire de médecine et de chirurgie*, 1864) (Paris: Martinet, 1864).
12. Ibid. p. 5: "When the man begins to feel the effects of alcoholic intoxication, his body, in the upright position, sways in every direction (...). In subjects struck by locomotor ataxia, the body's oscillations, in an upright position, have a very different character; they are abrupt, shorter and more rapid, whereas those of drunkenness resemble a sort of swaying. I have already compared the upright ataxic to a dancer who wants to keep his balance on a taut wire." See G.B.A. Duchenne, *De l'ataxie locomotrice progressive*, p. 78: "To a certain extent the patient can be compared to an individual who is trying with difficulty to keep his balance on a stretched wire without a balancing pole."
13. G.B.A. Duchenne, *Diagnostic différentiel des affections cérébelleuses*, pp. 5-6.
14. Ibid. p. 6: "The man who is drunk (...) walks making alternative curves to the left and right, or zigzags, and cannot go straight ahead (...). The ataxic (...) usually walks straight ahead unsteadily, but without making curves or zigzags like the drunken man."
15. Ibid. p. 7: "I asked them if, standing upright or walking (...) they did not feel the head heavy or turn, as when one has drunk too much wine or spirits. They answered that their head was completely free, and that *they only lacked balance in the legs*" (author's emphasis).
16. Foucault is referring to the analyses put forward by Broca in his 1861 article: "Remarques sur le siège de la faculté du langage articulé," in which he proposed the term "aphémie" (see above, note 9) to designate this loss of the "faculty of articulating words" in H. Hécaen and J. Dubois, *La Naissance de la neurophysiologie du langage*, p. 63.
17. Anarthria is a motor aphasia linked to an affection of the Broca area, situated on the external face of the dominant cerebral hemisphere, at the lower part of the third frontal convolution. Characterized by disorders of the articulation of speech, without lesions of the phonatory organs, it was described by Pierre Marie (1853-1940) in "De l'aphasie (cécité verbale, surdité verbale, aphasie motrice, agraphie)," *Revue du médecine*, vol. III, 1883, pp. 693-702.
18. As testifies the use of the term "hystero-epilepsy" to designate a hybrid form (composed of hysteria and epilepsy) marked by convulsive crises, as states J.-B. Lodoïs Briffaut: "We see the hysteric becoming epileptic, remaining both the one and the other, which constitutes hystero-epilepsy, or epilepsy increasingly dominating, and suppressing, as it were, the original hysteria" *Rapports de l'hystérie et de l'épilepsie*, Medical Thesis, Paris, no.146 (Paris: 1851) p. 24. See E.J. Georget—according to whom hysteria is a convulsive nervous disorder that forms a continuum with epilepsy—the article "Hystérie," in *Dictionnaire de médecine*, vol. 11 (Paris: Béchet Jeune, 1824) pp. 526-551. On the confusion of epilepsy with other "convulsive disorders," see O. Temkin, *The Falling Sickness: A Story of Epilepsy from the Greeks to the Beginnings of Modern Neurology* (Baltimore, Md.: The Johns Hopkins Press, [1945] 1971, 2nd revised edition) pp. 351-359.
19. Foucault takes two dates as reference points:
(i) 1820, the year in which the debate on the causes of madness begins on the occasion of Étienne Georget's defence of his thesis, 8 February 1820: "Dissertation sur les causes de la folie" (see above, note 18 to lecture of 12 December 1973). Published in January 1843 by J. Baillarger, L. Cerise and F. Longet, the *Annales médico-psychologiques. Journal de*

l'anatomie, de la physiologie et de la pathologie du système nerveux, specifically intended to gather all the documents concerning the relationships between the physical and the moral, mental pathology, legal medicine of the insane, and clinical neuroses (Paris, Fortin and Masson), was the site for an almost permanent debate on the organic and moral causes of madness, with a significant moment in the 1840s which saw conflict with the supporters of organicism, such as (a) L. Rostan, author of *Exposition des principes de l'organcisme, précédée de reflexions sur l'incrédulité en matière de médecine* (Paris: Asselin, 1846); (b) A. [de] Foville, author, with J.-B. Delaye, of a paper for the Prix Esquirol in 1821, "Sur les causes de la folie et leur mode d'action, suivies de recherches sur la nature et le siège spécial de cette maladie," *Nouveau Journal de médecine*, vol. XII, October 1821, pp. 110 *sq.*; as well as G. Ferrus, and L. Calmeil; [c] J.J. Moreau de Tours, who on 9 June 1830, defended a thesis entitled: *De l'influence du physique, relativement au désordre des facultés intellectuelles, et en particulier dans cette variété de délire désignée par M. Esquirol sous le nom de Monomanie*, Paris Medical Thesis, no. 127 (Paris: Didot, 1830) taking up the terms "organicism," and "organicist" as a banner—and the partisans of the pscyhological school, who preferred to be called "dualists": P.-N. Gerdy, Frédéric Dubois d'Amiens (1799-1873), C. Michéa, Louis François Émile Renaudin (1808-1865). As well as (d) J. B. Parchappe de Vinay, author of an article entitled precisely "De la prédominance des causes morales dans la génération de la folie," *Annales médico-psychologiques*, vol. II, November 1843, pp. 358-371. And [e] L.F. Lélut, who criticizes the use of pathological anatomy in mental medicine in his *Inductions sur la valeur des altérations de l'encéphale dans le délire aigu et dans la folie* (Paris: Trinquart, 1836).

(ii) 1880, when a third organicist wave spreads out with the works of Magnan and Charcot, who, thinking they have mastered the physiopathology of the brain, think the time has arrived for definitive conclusions.

20. On Bayle's conception, see above, note 17 to the lecture of 12 December 1973, and note 2 to the lecture of 9 January 1974.
21. Against Bayle, who admitted "three orders of essential symptoms belonging to madness, dementia and paralysis," Baillarger maintained that "the essential symptoms of this illness, those without which it never exists, are of two orders: those constituted by phenomena of paralysis and the others by phenomena of dementia," and delirium, when it exists, only "constitutes a completely accessory symptom." J. Baillarger, "Des symptômes de la paralysie générale et des rapports de cette maladie avec la folie," Appendix to the translations of W. Griesinger's *Traité*, p. 614 and p. 612.
22. "Good illness" or, as Foucault said, " 'good form'. The major structure which governs all perception of madness is exactly represented in the analysis of the psychiatric symptoms of nervous syphilis" *Histoire de la folie*, p. 542 (omitted from the English translation). Already, in 1955, Henri Ey saw a "prototype" in it having exercised "an invincible power of attraction on psychiatrists" ("Histoire de la psychiatrie" in *Encyclopédie médico-chirurgicale. Psychiatrie*, vol. I, 1955, p. 7). This stems from the fact that, just as clinical anatomy is constituted, A.L.J. Bayle isolates an entity in psychiatry corresponding to the medical model (see above, note 17 to the lecture of 12 December 1973): it has a definable cause from the angle of pathological anatomy, it presents a specific symptomatology, and it has an evolution defined by three periods leading to motor impotence and dementia. On the history of the problem, see J. Baillarger, "De la découverte de la paralysie générale et des doctrines émises par les premiers auteurs," *Annales médico-psychologiques*, 3rd series, vol. V, October 1859, 1st part, pp. 509-526, and 3rd series, vol. VI, January 1860, 2nd part, pp. 1-14.
23. See above, note 1 to the lecture of 30 January 1974.
24. In the 1840s, the basic definition of the neuroses had hardly changed from when the Scottish doctor William Cullen introduced the term in his *Apparatus ad nosologium methodicam, seu Synopsis nosologiae methodicae*, before it being laid down with the appearance of *First Lines of the Practice of Physic*, in 4 volumes (Edinburgh: Elliot, 1777) vol. 3, p. 122: "In this place I propose to comprehend, under the title NEUROSES, all those preternatural affections of the sense or motion which are without pyrexia [fever; J.L.], as a part of the primary disease; and all those which do not depend upon a topical affection of the organs, but upon a more general affection of the nervous system, and of those powers of the system

upon which the sense and motion more especially depend"; French translation *Éléments de médecine pratique*, trans, with notes from the 4th edition, M. Bosquillon (Paris: Barois et Méqiugnon, 1785) vol. II, p. 185. Thus, in 1843, under the rubric "Neuroses," the Introduction to the *Annales médico-psychologiques*, vol. I, January 1843, pp. xxiii-xxiv, states: "NEUROSES: We see disturbance of the functions of relational life predominating here, as in the different forms of mental alienation. This disorder appears in a thousand ways in hypochondria, hysteria, catalepsy, epilepsy, somnambulism, neuralgia, hystericism, etcetera (...). Intermediary in some way between disorders of nutritional life and mental illnesses, they seem to share two natures. Here a functional disorder of organic life commands the attack, there an intellectual disorder dominates the paroxysms." See, (a) A. [de] Foville, entry for "Neuroses" in *Dictionnaire de médecine et de chirurgie pratiques*, vol. XII (Paris: Gabon, 1834), pp. 55-57; (b) E. Monneret and L. Fleury, entry for "Neuroses" in *Compendium de médecine pratique*, vol. VI (Paris: Béchet, 1845) p. 209; (c) E. Littré and C. Robin, *Dictionnaire de médecine, de chirurgie, de pharmacie, des sciences accessoires et de l'art vétérinaire* (Paris: 1855): "NEUROSIS: generic name for illnesses whose seat one assumes is in the nervous system and which consist in a functional disorder without perceptible lesion in the structure of the parts or material agent able to produce it"; and (d) J.-M. Bruttin, *Différents Théories sur l'hystérie dans la première moitié du XIXe siècle* (Zurich: Juris, 1969).

25. "Introduction" to the *Annales médico-psychologiques*, vol. I, January 1843, p. xxv.
26. Jules Falret, "La folie raisonnante ou folie morale" read at the Société médico-psychologique on 8 January 1866, *Annales médico-pschologiques*, 4th series, vol. VII, May 1866: "Another principal fact, basically typical of hysterics, is the spirit of duplicity and lies. These patients (...) have no greater pleasure than deceiving and leading the people with whom they have relations into error. Hysterics, who exaggerate their convulsive movements (which are often partly simulated), equally misrepresent and exaggerate all the movements of their soul (...). In short, the life of hysterics is just a constant lie (...)"; reprinted in *Études cliniques sur les maladies mentales et nerveuses* (Paris: J.-B. Baillière, 1889), Study II, p. 502.
27. It was Jules Déjerine who expressed himself in this way in his "Leçon inaugurale à la clinique des maladies du système nerveux" on 31 March 1911, *La Presse médicale*, 1st April, 1911, pp. 253-258: "Through his studies on hysteria, Charcot rescued a domain from the psychiatrists that the latter vainly tried to regain. Certainly his doctrine of hysteria has not remained wholly intact. But even if Charcot had only the merit of making doctors understand that, beyond material lesions, the problems posed by certain psychical disorders offered their activity a considerable field, for this we would owe him all our gratitude." Quoted in G. Guillain, *J.-M. Charcot (1825-1893): sa vie, son œuvre* (Paris: Masson, 1955) p. 143. An illustration of this will be the transfer of paternity rights over hysteria to neurologists in medical encyclopedias and dictionaries.
28. Foucault is referring here to the obituary notice Freud wrote in August 1893 and published in the *Wiener medizinische Wochenschrift*, vol. 43, no. 37, 1893, pp. 1513-1520: "In the hall in which he gave his lectures there hung a picture which showed 'citizen' Pinel having the chains taken off the poor madmen in the Salpêtrière." S. Freud, "Charcot" *GW*, vol. I, 1952, p. 28; English translation, "Charcot" in *Standard Edition*, vol. 3, p. 18; French translation, "Charcot" trans. J. Altounian and others in S. Freud, *Résultats, Idées, Problèmes*, vol. I, 1890-1920 (Paris: Presses universitaires de France, 1984) p. 68.
29. J.-M. Charcot, *Leçons sur les maladies du système nerveux*, vol. 1, Lecture 11: "De l'hyperesthésie ovarienne," pp. 320-345; English translation, *Clinical Lectures on Diseases of the Nervous System*, trans. George Sigerson (London: New Sydenham Society, 1877) vol. 1, Lecture 11: "Ovarian hyperaesthesia" pp. 262-282: "most of the accidents which persist, in a more or less permanent manner, in the intervals between the convulsive fits of hysterical patients, and which almost always enable us, on account of the characteristics they present, to recognise the great neurosis for what it really is, even in the absence of convulsions" p. 262. Thus "*Hemianaesthesia, paralysis, contracture, fixed painful points* occupying different parts of the body," p. 262.
30. J.-M. Charcot, *Leçons*, vol. 1, Appendice V: "Des troubles de la vision chez les hystériques," pp. 427-434. (This appendix is omitted from the English translation.)

31. *Leçons*, vol. 1, Lecture 10: "De l'héminesthésie hystérique" pp. 300-319; *Clinical Lectures*, vol. 1, "Hysterical hemianaesthesia" pp. 246-261.
32. Ibid. Lecture 12: "De la contracture hystérique" pp. 347-366; "Hysterical contracture" pp. 283-299; *Leçons sur les maladies*, vol. 3, Lecture 7: "Deux cas de contracture hystérique d'origine traumatique" pp. 97-107, and Lecture 8, (*continued*), pp. 109-123; *Clinical Lectures*, vol. 3, Lectures 7 and 8, "Two cases of hysterical contracture of traumatic origin" pp. 84-106.
33. Thus, in the Policlinique of 21 February 1888, "Hysteria in young boys," Charcot acknowledged: "It is very strange that in particularly mental forms the stigmata do not appear." *Leçons du mardi à la Salpêtrière. Policlinique 1887-1888*, vol. 1, p. 208: "All these stigmata (...) are constants in hysteria, but despite their constancy, I have to acknowledge that it quite often happens that we do not find them all, or even, when it comes to it, any."
34. Sketched out from 1872 in the *Leçons* (vol. 1, Lecture 13: "De l'hystéro-épilepsie" pp. 373-374, and Appendice 6: "Description de la grande attaque hystérique" pp. 435-448; *Clinical lectures*, vol. 1, Lecture 13, "Hystero-epilepsy" pp. 302-307, [the appendix is omitted from the English translation]), it was codified in 1878 when Charcot reduced it to a "a very simple formula": "All these apparently disordered and variable phenomena... follow a rule of development. The complete attack is made up of four periods: 1. Epileptoid period. It may and usually does resemble the genuine epileptic attack (...). There are grounds for dividing this epileptic period into three phases: a) tonic phase (...); b) clonic phase. Limbs and the whole body are shaken by brief and rapid oscillations (...) which end in big generalized jolts (...); c) phase of resolution (...). 2. Period of contortions and large movements (...). 3. Period of passionate poses. Hallucination clearly governs this third period. The patient herself comes on the stage and through the expressive and animated gesticulations to which she abandons herself (...) it is easy to follow all the episodes of the drama at which she thinks she is present and in which she often plays the leading role (...). 4. Terminal period. Finally the patient returns to the real world." P. Richer's record of "Description de la grande attaque hystérique. Hospice de la Salpêtrière," *Progrès médical*, 7th year, no. 2, 11 January 1879, pp. 17-18.
35. While the term "hystero-epilepsy" (see above, note 19) covered, as Charcot recalls, "a combination of the two neuroses, varying in proportions in different cases," constituting "a mixed form, a kind of hybrid composed half of hysteria and half of epilepsy," Charcot means to distinguish between epilepsy and hystero-epilepsy as pathologically distinct entities, which could not come together to form "a *hybrid*" illness. He also distinguishes a "hystero-epilepsy with distinct crises," in which epilepsy is the primary disease on which hysteria becomes grafted, and a "hysteria, with mixed attacks," in which the epileptic form of convulsion only appears as "an accessory element": "in these cases, hysteria is solely and always present, taking on it the semblance of epilepsy" *Leçons*, vol. 1, Lecture 13: "De l' hystéro-épilepsie" pp. 368-369; *Clinical Lectures*, vol. 1, Lecture 13: "Hystero-epilepsy" pp. 301-302. So the term "hystero-epilepsy" designates no more than the final degree of hysteria taken to its extreme development, or *major hysteria*. He will later reject the term itself: "My respect for tradition previously led me to retain this denomination hystero-epilepsy; but I confess to you that it bothers me a great deal, for it is absurd. There is not the least relationship between epilepsy and hystero-epilepsy, even with mixed attacks" *Leçons du mardi*, Lesson XVIII, 19 March 1889, pp. 424-425. Foucault returns to the question in *Les Anormaux*, lecture of 26 February 1975, p. 167; *Abnormal*, p. 224. See also, C. Féré, "Notes pour servir à l'histoire de l'hystéro-épilepsie," *Archives de neurologie*, vol. III, 1882, pp. 160-175 and pp. 281-309.
36. On this differential picture, see the lecture, "Caractères différentiels entre l'épilepsie et l'hystéro-épilepsie," summarized in *Progrès médical*, 2nd year, no. 2, 10 January 1874, pp. 18-19, and, *Leçons*, vol. 1, Lecture 13; *Clinical Lectures*, vol. 1, Lecture 13.
37. *Leçons*, vol. 3, Lecture 18: "À propos de six cas d'hystérie chez l'homme" pp. 260-261; *Clinical Lectures*, vol. 3, Lecture 18: "Concerning six cases of hysteria in the male,": "a woman named Aurel -, now 62 years of age (...) left hemianaesthesia, complete (...) which (...) still exists to-day, that is to say, after the long period of thirty-four years! This patient has been under our observation for fifteen years and the hemianaesthesia has never ceased (...) to be present" pp. 226-227.

38. The case was that of Habill, who, "had two series of attacks in December 1885: the first, which lasted 13 days in which 4506 attacks were counted, and the other, which lasted 14 days, in which 17,083 attacks were counted" *Leçons du mardi*, vol.. II, Leçon IV, Policlinique du mardi 13 November 1888: Attaque de sommeil hystérique, p. 68.
39. Reference to the artificial reproduction of hysterical manifestations under hypnosis, with regard to which Charcot stated: "Then it is truly that we see before us the *human machine* in all its simplicity, dreamt of by De la Mettrie" *Leçons*, vol. III, p. 337; *Clinical Lectures*, vol. 3, Lecture 21: "On two cases of hysterical brachial monoplegia in the male of traumatic origin.—Hystero-traumatic monoplegia (continuation)" p. 290. See Julien Offray de La Mettrie (1709-1751), *L'Homme machine* (Paris: 1747); English translation, *Machine Man and Other Writings*, trans. Ann Thomson (Cambridge: Cambridge University Press, 1996).
40. Charcot, *Leçons du mardi*, vol. I, Policlinique du mardi 24 January 1888: "Paralysies hystéro-traumatiques développées par suggestion," pp. 135-136: "This paralysis (...) could be reproduced artificially in certain circumstances, which is the wonderful thing about it and ideal in pathological physiology. To be able to reproduce a pathological state is perfection, because it seems that we hold the theory when we have in our hands the means to reproduce the morbid phenomena." See, ibid. Policlinique of Tuesday 1st May 1888: "Production artificielle de parlaysie dans l'état hypnotique: procédés de guérison de ces paralysies expérimentales" (in a hypnotisable hystero-epileptic) pp. 373-385.
41. In 1870, owing to renovations to the Sainte-Laure building, in which the insane, epileptics and hysterics in Louis Delasiauve's department were hospitalized, the administration put the insane and reputedly insane epileptics in Baillarger's department, and opened a department for the other epileptics and hysterics: the "section of simple epileptics," which was entrusted to Charcot in 1872. See the "Leçon d'ouverture" of the chair of the clinic of illnesses of the nervous system, in *Leçons*, vol. III, pp. 2-3; *Clinical Lectures*, vol. 3, "Introductory" pp. 2-3.
42. J.-M. Charcot, "Métallothérapie et hypnotisme. Électrothérapie," in *Œuvres complètes*, vol. IX (Paris: Lecrosnier & Babé, 1890) p. 297: "The research undertaken at the hospital of la Salpêtrière by M. Charcot and, under his direction, by several of his students, date from 1878." Charcot set out his first results in "Leçons sur le grand hypnotisme chez les hystériques." At the Académie des sciences on 13 February 1882 he gave a paper that proposed a description in neurological terms and sought to give hypnosis a scientific status: "Physiologie pathologique. Sur les divers états nerveux déterminés par l'hypnotisation chez les hystériques," *Comptes rendus hebdomadaires des séances de l'Académie des sciences*, vol. 94, no. 1, 13 February 1882 (Paris: Gauthier-Villars, 1882) pp. 403-405. See, A.R. Owen, *Hysteria, Hypnosis and Healing: the Work of J.-M. Charcot* (London: D. Dobson, 1971).
43. In the 1860s problems arose linked to series of industrial and railway accidents: problems of expertise, indemnities, and the determination of employment disability. With regard to industrial accidents, La Sécurité Générale, supported by the Crédit Industriel et Commercial, was created by decree on 14 November 1865. The law of 11 July 1868 recommended the creation of two national funds for insurance in cases of death and accidents arising from industrial and agricultural work; it was spelled out by the decree of 10 August 1868. In May 1880, a draft bill on "responsibility for the accidents suffered by workers in their work" was put forward by Martin Nadaud; it was not until 9 April 1898 that the law on accidents at work was passed. See (a) G. Hamon, *Histoire générale de l'assurance en France et à l'étranger* (Paris: A. Giard and F. Brière, 1897); (b) V. Senés, *Les Origines des compagnies d'assurance* (Paris: L. Dulac, 1900); (c) J.-P. Richard, *Histoire des institutions d'assurance en France* (Paris: Éd. de l'Argus, 1956); (d) H. Hatzfeld, *Du paupérisme à la Sécurité sociale, 1850-1940* (Paris: 1971). Foucault returns to the question in October 1974: see, "Crise de la médecine ou crise de l'antimédecine," *Dits et Écrits*, vol. 3, p. 54.
44. In January and February 1867, Henri Legrand du Saulle (1830-1886) devoted a series of lectures to the question published in his *Étude médico-légale sur les assurances sur la vie* (Paris: Savy, 1868).
45. Thus, Cl. Guillemaud deals with the question of screening for simulation in his work, *Des accidents de chemin de fer et de leurs conséquences médico-judiciaires* (Paris: 1851) pp. 40-41. A. Souques devotes his thesis to the question of simulation: *Contribution à l'étude des syndromes hystériques "simulateurs" des maladies organiques de la moelle épinière*, Medical Thesis, Paris,

no.158 (Paris: Lecrosnier & Babé, 1891). See also above, note 20 to lecture of 12 December 1973, and note 20 to lecture of 30 January 1974.

46. See above p. 184 *sq* and p. 234 *sq*. In the second half of the nineteenth century there is a growing literature on the results of these accidents: [A] Anglo-Saxon, which attributes them to an inflammation either of the spine ("Railway Spine") or the brain ("Railway Brain"). See (a) J.E. Erichsen, *On Railway and Other Injuries of the Nervous System* (Philadelphia: H.C. Lea, 1867), and *On Concussion of the Spine, Nervous Shock, and Other Obscure Injuries of the Nervous System* (New York: Wood, 1875); (b) H.W. Page, *Injuries of the Spine and Spinal Cord without Apparent Mechanical Lesion and Nervous Shock in their Surgical and Medico-legal Aspects* (London: J. Churchill, 1883), and his book, a dedicated copy of which he sent to Charcot, *Railway Injuries with Special Reference to those of the Back and Nervous System in their Medico-legal and Clinical Aspects* (London: Griffin and Co., 1891). [B] German, which considers the results to be a specific "traumatic neurosis." See, (a) H. Oppenheim and R. Thomsen, "Über das Vorkommen und die Bedeutung der sensorishcen Anästhesie bei Erkrankungen des zentralen Nerven-systems" *Archiv für Psychiatrie* (Berlin, 1884) vol. 15, pp. 559-583 and pp. 663-680; (b) H. Oppenheim, *Die traumatischen Neurosen (...)* (Berlin: Hirschwald, 1889). Charcot devotes an 1877 lecture to the question: "De l'influence des lésions traumatiques sur le développement des phénomènes d'hysérie locale" (lecture given at la Salpêtrière, December 1877), *Progrès médical*, 6th year, no. 18, 4 May 1878, pp. 335-338. Not accepting the existence of a specific clinical entity and arguing for the possibility of reproducing paralyses under hypnosis similar to traumatic paralyses, Charcot defined a variety of hysteria: "traumatic hysteria." Between 1878 and 1893 he published twenty cases of paralysis due to accidents at work or railway accidents: (1) *Leçons*, vol. III, Lecture 18 (in which he criticizes the German conception) p. 258; Lecture 22: "Sur deux cas de monoplégie brachiale hystérique chez l'homme," pp. 354-356; Lecture 23: "Sur deux cas de coxalgie hystérique chez l'homme," pp. 370-385; Lecture 24 (pp. 386-398 in which draws an analogy between the English "nervous shock" and the hypnotic state produced by suggestion), and Appendix 1, pp. 458-462; English translation, *Clinical Lectures*, vol. 3: Lecture 18, "Concerning six cases of hysteria in the male," pp. 224-225; Lecture 22, "On two cases of hysterical brachial monoplegia in the male (*continued*)"; Lecture 24, "On a case of hysterical hip disease in a man resulting from injury"; and Appendix 1, "Two additional cases of hystero-traumatic paralysis in men"; (2) *Leçons du mardi*, vol. II, Policlinique of Tuesday 4 December 1888, Lecture 7, pp. 131-139, Appendix 1: "Hystérie et névrose traumatique. Collision des trains et hystérie consécutive," pp. 527-535; (3) *Clinique des maladies du système nerveux*, vol. 1, Lecture 3, 13 November 1889, pp. 61-64; (4) J.-M. Charcot and P. Marie, "Hysteria, mainly hystero-epilepsy"—which opposes the German conception of a specific "traumatic neurosis"—in, D. Hack Tuke, *Dictionary of Psychological Medicine*, vol. 1 (London: J. & A. Churchill, 1892) pp. 639-640. See also, (a) Ch. Vibert, *La Névrose traumatique. Étude médico-légale sur les blessures produites par les accidents de chemin de fer et les traumatismes analogues* (Paris: J.-B. Baillière, 1893); (b) E. Fischer-Homberger, "Railway-Spine und traumatische Neurose. Seele und Rückenmark," *Gesnerus*, vol. 27, 1970, pp. 96-111, and since then we have his book *Die Traumatische Neurose. Vom somatischen zum sozialen Leiden* (Berne: Hans Huber, 1975).

47. *Leçons*, vol. III, Lecture 24, "Sur un cas de coxalgie hystérique de cause traumatique chez l'homme" (from Dr. P. Marie) pp. 391-392; *Clinical Lectures*, vol. 3, Lecture 24: "On a case of hysterical hip disease in a man, resulting from injury" pp. 333-334. To demonstrate that Ch., a sawyer, the victim of an accident at work, was suffering from hysterical coxalgia, without organic lesion, Charcot reproduced the coxalgia in two patients placed in a "hypnotic state."

48. On simulation, see above, note 45. There are references to this literature in: (a) A. Laurent, *Étude médico-légale sur la simulation de la folie*; (b) E. Boisseau, article, "Maladies simulées," in *Dictionnaire encyclopédique des sciences médicales*, 2nd series, vol. IV (Paris: Masson/Asselin, 1876) pp. 266-281; (c) G. Tourdes, article, "Simulation." Charcot takes up the question on several occasions: (1) *Leçons du mardi*, vol. I, Policlinique of Tuesday 20 March 1888: "Ataxie locomotrice. Forme anormale," pp. 281-284; (2) *Leçons*, vol. I, Lecture 9, "De l'ischurie hystérique" § "Simulation" pp. 281-283, *Clinical lectures*, vol. 1,

Lecture 9: "Hysterical ischuria" pp. 230-232; vol. III, "Leçon d'ouverture de la chaire de la clinique des maladies du système nerveux" § VII, "Simulation" pp. 17-22; vol. 3, Lecture 1: "Introductory—§ Simulation," and Lecture 26, "Cas de mutisme hystérique chez l'homme. Les simulations" p. 422; "A case of hysterical mutism in a man—§ Malingerers."

49. From the 1880s, Hippolyte Bernheim (1840-1919), professor of the Faculty and president of the Nancy Société médicale, criticized Charcot's experiments: *De la suggestion dans l'état hypnotique et dans l'état de veille* (Paris: Doin, 1884). He makes the criticism clearer in *Hypnotisme, Suggestion, Psychothérapie. Études nouvelles* (Paris: Doin, 1891) p. 172: "One would not believe how many neuropaths and hysterics we are liable to produce by unconscious suggestion: we create neuralgia, hysterogenic zones (...); we externalize our conceptions on the patient; we fabricate an observation with the preconceived ideas we have in our mind." Already, in an article that appeared in *Le Temps*, 29 January 1891, he declared: "I believe that the attack of grand hysteria that la Salpêtrière gives us as classical, unfolding in clear and precise phases (...) is an hysteria of culture." Refusing moreover to confine hypnotism in the pathological register, he asserts that "what we call hypnotism is nothing other than the activation of a normal property of the brain, suggestibility, that is to say the capacity to be influenced by an accepted idea and to seek its realization." On the Charcot-Bernheim debate, see Hillman, "A scientific study of hystery" *Bulletin of the History of Medicine*, vol. 29, no. 2, 1955, pp. 163-182.

50. The notion of "trauma," understood first of all as a "mechanical action" liable to trigger hysterical accidents, was established from 1877. See, *Leçons*, vol. I, Appendix VII, "De l'influence des lésions traumatique sur le dévelopment des phénomènes d'hystérie locale" (December 1877) pp. 446-457 [the Appendix does not appear in the English translation, *Clinical Lectures*]. From 1885 the notion is deepened in the sense of taking a mechanism of "traumatic suggestion" into account; see, ibid. vol. III, Lectures, 20, 21 and 22, "Sur deux cas de monoplégie brachiale hystérique, de cause traumatique chez l'homme" (with a section devoted to "Hypnotism and nervous shock"); *Clinical Lectures*, vol. III, Lectures 20, 21 and 22, "On a case of hysterical hip disease in a man, resulting from injury."

51. This is the case of Le Logeais, a messenger of 29 years, knocked down on 21 October 1885 by a horse-drawn van. After being hospitalized twice, at Beaujon and the Hôtel-Dieu, he was admitted into Charcot's department on 21 March 1886, with paralysis and anesthesia of the limbs; see, *Leçons*, vol. III, Appendix I, "Cas de paralysie hystéro-traumatique survenue à la suite d'un accident de voiture" (Observation recorded by M. Berbèz) pp. 541-559; *Clinical Lectures*, vol. 3, Appendix 1: "A case of hystero-traumatic paraplegia supervening on a street accident." The accident "gave rise to the conviction in Le Log-'s mind that the wheels of the van which knocked him over 'passed over the body,' as he puts it. Nevertheless, this conviction, which has even appeared to him in his dreams, is completely erroneous" p. 386.

52. Ibid. pp. 553-554; ibid. p. 385: "in the very fact of local shock, and particularly in the sensory and motor phenomena attached thereto, must be sought the point of departure of the suggestion. The sensation of heaviness or even absence of the limb struck, and, again, the paralysis which is never wanting, in some degree at any rate, will give rise quite naturally, as it were, to the idea of motor weakness of the limb. And this idea, by reason of the somnambulic mental condition, comes to acquire, after a period of incubation, a considerable development, and is finally able to become realised objectively in the form of a complete paralysis" p. 385.

53. A conception illustrated by the remarks of Esquirol's article "Manie," in *Dictionnaire des sciences médicales*, vol. XXX (Paris: C.L.F. Panckoucke, 1818) p. 454: "The actions to which the insane abandon themselves are always the result of the delirium"; or of E.J. Georget, *De la folie. Considérations sur cette maladie*, p. 75: "There is no madness without delirium"; or again of F.E. Fodéré, *Traité de médecine légale et d'hygiène publique*, vol. I (Paris: Mame, 1813) p. 184.

54. On the story of childhood, see the case of Augustine, in *Iconographie photographique de la Salpêtrière*, published by D.M. Bourneville, Delahaye and Regnard, vol. II (Paris: Delahaye, 1878) p. 167.

55. The case is that of Louise Augustine, who entered Charcot's department at the age of fifteen and a half. See, *Leçons*, vol. I, Part Two: "Hystéro-epilepsie," Observation 2,

pp. 125-126 ["Observation 2," and the case history quoted at length by Foucault to which this refers, cannot be found in the English translation, *Clinical Lectures*. The same is true for the cases cited in the following notes 56 and 57. See Foucault's comments on the publication of Charcot's lectures in M. Foucault, *The History of Sexuality. Volume 1: An Introduction*, p. 56 and note; G.B.].

56. This concerns the scene during which she calls on a friend, Emile, to exonerate her, before her brother, of the latter's charges. See ibid. p. 149 [See previous note; G.B.].
57. The case of Celina, who entered Charcot's department in 1870: ibid. p. 132 [see note 55; G.B.].
58. See above, note 26. See also, Jules Falret, "Responsabilitié légale des aliénés," §"Hystérie" (1876) in *Les Aliénés et les Asiles d'aliénés*, p. 189: "These patients often present disorders of a more or pronounced character which give them a particular style and which has been designated under the generic term of hysterical character. They are fantasists, inclined to lies and invention; they are romancers, loving domination and capricious."
59. *Leçons*, vol. I, Lecture 10, "De l'hémianesthésie hystérique," p. 301; *Clinical Lectures*, vol. 1, Lecture 10, "Hysterical hemianaethesia," p. 247. Charcot makes the remark with reference to Paul Briquet's *Traité clinique et thérapeutique de l'hystérie* (Paris: H.-B. Baillière, 1859).
60. It was at "one of Charcot's evening receptions" that Freud overheard a discussion between Charcot and Paul Brouardel, professor of legal medicine. With reference to a patient, Charcot said "'*Mais, dans ces pareils c'est toujours la chose génitale, toujours ... toujours ... toujours*' ['But in this sort of case it's always a genital thing—always, always, always': words left in French in the English *Standard Edition*] (...). I know that for a moment I was almost paralysed with amazement and said to myself: 'Well, but if he knows that, why does he never say so?'" "On the History of the Psycho-Analytic Movement," *Standard Edition*, vol. 14 (1957) p. 14; *Zur Geschichte der psychoanalytischen Bewegung* (1914) in *GW*, vol. X (1946) p. 51.
61. Freud's stay in Charcot's department from 30 October 1885 to 28 February 1886 was thanks to a bursary. See S. Freud, "Bericht über meine mit Universitäts-Jubiläums Reisestipendium unternommene Studenreise nach Paris und Berlin" (1886), in J. and R. Gicklhorn, *Sigmund Freuds akademische Laufbahn, im Lichte der Dokumente von J. and R. Gicklhorn* (Vienna: Urban & Schwarzenberg, 1960) pp. 82-89; English translation, "Report on my Studies in Paris and Berlin," *Standard Edition*, vol. 1 (1966). The first texts in which Freud envisaged a sexual etiology of the neuroses concerned neurasthenia and anxiety neuroses: see *La Naissance de la psychanalyse*, Manuscript A, 1892, pp. 59-60, and Manuscript B, 8 February 1893, pp. 61-65; English translation, "Extracts from the Fliess Papers" Drafts A and B, *Standard Edition*, vol. 1 (1966) pp. 177-178 and pp. 179-184. He extends this hypothesis to the psychoneuroses in 1894: see, *Die Abwehr-Neuropsychosen*, in *GW*, vol. I; "The Neuro-Psychoses of Defence" *Standard Edition*, vol. 3 (1962). See also the article which recapitulates the problem: "Die Sexualität in der Ätiologie der Neurosen" (1898), in *GW*, vol. I, pp. 489-516; "Sexuality in the Aetiology of the Neuroses" *Standard Edition*, vol. 3 (1962).
62. The case concerns the "period of erotic delirium" of Geneviève, who was born at Loudon on 2 January 1843 and entered Charcot's department in 1872 as a "simple epileptic." See *Iconographie photographique de la Salpêtrière*, vol. I, p. 70: "The observer, still not accustomed to these scenes, was quite astounded seeing the hideous contortions of her face, that expression of extreme lubricity ... speaking to one of the assistants, she suddenly leaned towards him, saying: 'Kiss me! (...). Give me (...).'" The observation is quoted by Foucault in *La Volonté de savoir*, p. 75, n. 1; *The History of Sexuality. 1. An Introduction*, p. 56, n. 1.
63. See above, note 4.
64. Joseph François Félix Babinski (1857-1932), after having been senior doctor in Charcot's department from 1885 to 1887, and following the latter's death, in a communication to the Paris Société de Neurologie on 7 November 1901, distanced himself from his conceptions by proposing to replace the term "hysteria" with that of "pithiatism" (from πείθειν, to persuade), in order to designate a class of morbid phenomena resulting from suggestion and curable by suggestion, thus dissociating hysteria from hypnotism: "the greek words *peithō* [πειθώ] and *iatos* [ἰατος] signify, the first 'persuasion' and the second 'curable,' the

neologism 'pithiatism' could very well designate the psychical state displayed by disorders curable by persuasion and replace advantageously the word 'hysteria'." "Définition de l'hystérie," *Revue neurologique*, 1901, no. 9, p. 1090; reprinted in *Œuvres scientifique*, Part 9: "Hystérie-Pithiatisme" (Paris: Masson, 1934) p. 464. Babinski developed his conception between 1906 and 1909: (1) "Ma conception de l'hystérie et de l'hypnotisme (Pithiatisme)" lecture at the Société de l'Internat of Paris hospitals, 28 June 1906, in ibid. pp. 465-485; (2) "Démembrement de l'hystérie traditionnelle. Pithiatisme" *La Semaine médicale*, 6 January 1909, pp. 66-67, where he states: "We no longer see those major attacks with the four famous periods, those great hypnotic states characterized by lethargy, catalepsy, and somnambulism. Students and young doctors who read the description of these disorders in the books of the period get the impression that it is a matter of paleo-pathology" (republished in *Œuvres scientifiques*, p. 500).

COURSE SUMMARY*

FOR A LONG TIME, medicine, psychiatry, penal justice, and criminology remained, and to a large extent remain still today, on the borders of a manifestation of truth in accordance with the norms of knowledge and of a production of truth in the form of the test, the latter always tending to hide behind and get its justification from the former. The current crisis of these "disciplines" does not merely call into question their limits or uncertainties within the field of knowledge, it calls into question knowledge itself, the form of knowledge, the "subject-object" norm; it puts in question the relationships between our society's economic and political structures and knowledge (not in its true or false contents, but in its power-knowledge functions). It is, then, a historico-political crisis.

Take, first of all, the example of medicine, along with the space connected to it, the hospital. Even quite late the hospital was still an ambiguous place, both a place for finding a hidden truth through observation and a place of testing for a truth to be produced.

In the hospital there is a direct action on the disease: the hospital does not only enable disease to reveal its truth to the doctor's gaze, it produces that truth. The hospital is a birthplace of the true disease. It was assumed, in fact, that left at liberty—in his "milieu," his family and his social circle, with his regimen, habits, prejudices, and illusions—the sick person would be affected by a complex, confused, and tangled disease, a sort of unnatural disease that was both the mixture of several diseases and the obstacle preventing the true disease from appearing in its authentic nature. In removing that parasitic vegetation, those aberrant

* Published in the *Annuaire du Collège de France, 75e année. Histoire des systèmes de pensée, année 1973-1974, (1974)*, pp. 293-300, and in *Dits et écrits*, 1954-1988, vol. 2 (Paris: Gallimard, 1994), pp. 674-685. An earlier translation of this summary appears in M. Foucault, *The Essential Works of Michel Foucault, 1954-1984, Vol. 1: Ethics: subjectivity and truth*, ed. Paul Rabinow, trans. Robert Hurley and others (New York: New Press, 1997) pp. 39-50.

forms, the role of the hospital, therefore, was not only to make the disease visible just as it is, but also finally to produce it in its hitherto enclosed and fettered truth. Its distinctive nature, its essential characteristics, and its specific development would finally be able to become reality through the effect of hospitalization.

The eighteenth century hospital was supposed to create the conditions for the truth of the disease to manifest itself. It was therefore a place of observation and demonstration, but also of purification and testing. It was a sort of complex equipment for both revealing and really producing the disease: both a botanical site for the contemplation of species, and a still alchemical site for the elaboration of pathological substances.

This dual function continued to be taken on for a long time by the great hospital structures established in the nineteenth century. For a century (1760-1860), the theory and practice of hospitalization, and, in a general way, the conception of disease, were dominated by this ambiguity: as a reception structure for the disease, should the hospital be a space of knowledge or a place of testing?

Hence a series of problems pervaded the thought and practice of doctors. Here are a few:

1. Therapy consists in suppressing the illness, in reducing it to nonexistence; however, for therapy to be rational and grounded in truth, should it not allow the disease to develop? When should one intervene, and in what way? Should one intervene at all? Should one act so that the disease develops or so that it stops, so as to alleviate it or so as to lead it to its term?
2. There are diseases and modifications of diseases, pure and impure, simple and complex diseases. In the end, is there not just one disease, of which all the others are more or less distantly derived forms, or should we assume the existence of irreducible categories? (The debate between Broussais and his opponents concerning the notion of irritation. The problem of essential fevers.)
3. What is a normal disease? What is a disease that follows its course? Is it a disease that leads to death, or a disease that is cured spontaneously after completing its evolution? It was in these terms that Bichat wondered about the position of disease between life and death.

We know that Pasteurian biology brought a prodigious simplification to all these problems. By determining the agent of the sickness and identifying it as a specific organism, it enabled the hospital to become a place of observation, diagnosis, and clinical and experimental identification, but also one of immediate intervention and counter-attack against the microbial invasion.

As for the testing function, we see that it may disappear. The place where the disease will be produced is the laboratory, in the test tube; however, the disease is not realized in a crisis there; its process is reduced to a magnified mechanism; it is reduced to a verifiable and controllable phenomenon. For the disease, the hospital milieu no longer has to be the site that favors a decisive event; it simply makes possible a reduction, a transfer, a magnification, an observation; the test (*épreuve*) is transformed into proof (*preuve*) within the technical structure of the laboratory and in the doctor's description.

If we wanted to produce an "ethno-epistemology" of the medical personality, we would have to say that the Pasteurian revolution deprived him of his doubtless age-old role in the ritual production and testing of the disease. The disappearance of this role was no doubt dramatized by the fact that Pasteur did not merely show that the doctor did not have to be the producer of the disease "in its truth," but that, due to his ignorance of the truth, he had on thousands of occasions made himself the propagator and reproducer of disease: the hospital doctor going from bed to bed was one of the major agents of contagion. Pasteur inflicted a formidable narcissistic wound on doctors, for which they took a long time to forgive him: the hands that the doctor had to run over the patient's body, palpate it, and examine it, those hands that had to discover the disease, bring it to light and display it, Pasteur designated as carriers of disease. Until then, the role of the hospital space and of the doctor's knowledge was to produce the "critical" truth of the disease; and now the doctor's body and the crowded hospital appeared as the producers of the disease's reality.

Disinfection of the doctor and the hospital gave them a new innocence from which they have drawn new powers and a new status in men's imagination. But that is another story.

These few remarks may help us to understand the position of the madman and the psychiatrist in the asylum space.

There is no doubt a historical correlation between the fact that madness was not systematically interned before the eighteenth century, and the fact that it was essentially considered a form of error or illusion. At the start of the Classical age, madness was still seen as belonging to the chimeras of the world; it could live amongst them and had to be separated from them only when it took extreme or dangerous forms. Under these conditions, we can understand why the artificial space of the hospital could not be the privileged place where madness could and had to manifest itself. The first of the recognized therapeutic sites was nature, since it was the visible form of truth; it had the power to dispel error and make chimeras vanish. The prescriptions given by doctors were therefore likely to be traveling, resting, walking, retirement, a break with the artificial and vain world of the town. Esquirol will recall this again when he was drawing up the plans of a psychiatric hospital and recommended that each courtyard open out wide onto the view of a garden. The other therapeutic site put to use was nature reversed, the theater: the comedy of the patient's own madness was acted out and staged for him, given a fictitious reality for a moment; by means of stage props and costumes it was treated as if it was true, but in such a way that the error, caught in this trap, would finally become strikingly apparent in its victim's own eyes. This technique also had not completely disappeared in the nineteenth century; Esquirol, for example, recommended staging proceedings against melancholics in order to stimulate their energy and taste for combat.

The practice of internment at the beginning of the nineteenth century coincides with the moment when madness is perceived less in terms of error than in relation to regular and normal conduct; when it no longer appears as disturbed judgment but as disorder in ways of acting, willing, experiencing passions, taking decisions and being free; in short, when it is no longer situated on the line of truth-error-consciousness, but on that of passion-will-freedom; the moment of Hoffbauer and Esquirol. "There are insane people (*aliénés*) whose delirium is scarcely visible; there is not one whose passions, whose moral affections are not disordered, perverted, or destroyed (. . .) Weakening of the delirium is a sure sign of recovery only when the insane (*les aliénés*) return to their first affections."[1] What actually is the process of recovery? Is it the movement by which error vanishes and truth becomes clear again? No, it is "the return of moral affections within their proper bounds, the desire to see one's friends and children again, the tears of sensitivity, the need to open one's heart, to be back in the bosom of one's family, to resume one's routine."[2]

What, then, might the asylum's role be in this movement back toward regular behavior? First of all, of course, it will have the function that hospitals were given at the end of the eighteenth century: to make discovery of the truth of the mental illness possible, excluding everything in the patient's milieu that may conceal it, muddle it, give it aberrant forms, as well as sustain it and stimulate it. But even more than a site of revelation, the hospital for which Esquirol provided the model is a site of confrontation; within it, madness, the disturbed will and perverted passion, must come up against a sound will and orthodox passions. Their head-on encounter, their inevitable and in fact desirable clash, will produce two effects: the unhealthy will, which could very well remain elusive if not expressed in any delirium, will bring its illness out into the open through its resistance to the doctor's healthy will, and, on the other hand, if conducted well, the ensuing struggle should lead to victory for the healthy will and to the submission, the renunciation, of the disturbed will. There is, then, a process of opposition, struggle and domination. "A disruptive method must be applied, using the spasm to break the spasm (...) The whole character of some patients must be subjugated, their rage subdued and their pride broken, while others must be stimulated and encouraged."[3]

This is how the very strange function of the nineteenth century psychiatric hospital is established: a diagnostic and classificatory site, a botanical rectangle in which the species of disease are distributed in courtyards whose layout brings to mind a vast kitchen garden, but also an enclosed space for a confrontation, the site of a duel, an institutional field in which victory and submission are at stake. The great asylum doctor—whether Leuret, Charcot, or Kraepelin—is both he who can state the truth of the illness through the knowledge he has of it, and he who can produce the illness in its truth and subjugate it in reality through the power his will exerts on the patient. All the techniques or procedures put to work in the nineteenth century asylum—isolation, public or private cross-examination, treatments-punishments like the shower, moral talks (encouragements or reproofs), strict discipline, obligatory work, rewards, preferential relationships between the doctor and some of his patients, relationships of vassalage, possession, domesticity and sometimes servitude, binding the patient to the doctor—the function of all of this was to make the medical figure the "master of madness": the person who makes it appear in its truth (when it is hidden, when it remains buried and silent) and the person who dominates it, pacifies it, and gradually makes it disappear after having artfully unleashed it.

Let us say, then, schematically, that the "truth-producing" function of the disease continues to diminish in the Pasteurian hospital; the doctor as producer of truth disappears in a structure of knowledge. In the hospital of Esquirol or Charcot, however, the "truth-production" function hypertrophies, redoubles around the figure of the doctor. And this takes place in a process in which what is at stake is the doctor's surplus-power. Charcot, the miracle worker of hysteria, is doubtless the most highly symbolic figure of this type of operation.

Now this redoubling takes place at a time when medical power is guaranteed and justified by the prerogatives of knowledge: the doctor is competent, he knows the diseases and the patients, he possesses a scientific knowledge which is of the same type as that of the chemist or the biologist, and this is now what justifies his interventions and decisions. The power that the asylum gives to the psychiatrist will therefore have to be justified (and at the same time masked as primordial surplus-power) by producing phenomena that can be integrated within medical science. We can see why the technique of hypnosis and suggestion, the problem of simulation, and the diagnostic distinction between organic disease and psychological disease, were at the heart of psychiatric theory and practice for so many years (from 1860 to 1890 at least). The point of perfection, of a too miraculous perfection, was reached when, at the request of medical power-knowledge, Charcot's patients began to reproduce a symptomatology whose norm was epilepsy, that is to say, a symptomatology that could be deciphered, known and recognized in terms of an organic disease.

This is a critical moment when the two functions of the asylum (testing and production of truth, on the one hand; observation and knowledge of phenomena, on the other) are redistributed and exactly superimposed on one another. The doctor's power now enables him to produce the reality of a mental illness the distinctive feature of which is its reproduction of phenomena fully accessible to knowledge. The hysteric was the perfect patient, since she provided material to be known: she herself retranscribed the effects of medical power in forms that the doctor could describe in terms of a scientifically acceptable discourse. As for the power relationship that made this whole operation possible, how could its determining role have been detected when—supreme virtue of hysteria, unequalled docility, veritable epistemological sanctity—the patients took it upon themselves and assumed responsibility for it: the power relationship appeared in the symptomatology as morbid suggestibility. Everything was henceforth set out in the clarity of knowledge purified of all power, between the knowing subject and the object known.

⚜

A hypothesis: the crisis becomes apparent, and the still barely delineated age of antipsychiatry begins, with the suspicion, and soon after the certainty, that Charcot actually produced the hysterical fit he described. This gives us the rough equivalent of Pasteur's discovery that the doctor was transmitting the diseases he was supposed to be combating.

At any rate, it seems that the major tremors that have shaken psychiatry since the end of the nineteenth century have all basically called the doctor's power into question; his power and its effect on the patient, more than his knowledge and the truth he told regarding the illness. More precisely, let us say that, from Bernheim to Laing or Basaglia, what was at stake was how the doctor's power was involved in the truth of what he said and, conversely, how this truth could be fabricated and compromised by his power. Cooper has said: "At the heart of our problem is violence";[4] and Basaglia: "The typical feature of these institutions (school, factory, hospital) is a clear-cut separation between those who hold power and those who do not."[5] All the great reforms, not just of psychiatric practice but also of psychiatric thought, revolve around this power relation: they are so many attempts to shift it, conceal it, eliminate it, or nullify it. Fundamentally, the whole of modern psychiatry is permeated by antipsychiatry, if by that we understand everything that calls into question the role of the psychiatrist previously given responsibility for producing the truth of illness within the hospital space.

We could, then, speak of antipsychiatries that have permeated the history of modern psychiatry. But perhaps it is more worthwhile to distinguish carefully between two processes that are quite distinct from the historical, epistemological and political point of view.

To start with there was the movement for "depsychiatrization." It appears immediately after Charcot. It involves not so much invalidating the doctor's power as shifting it in the name of a more exact knowledge, giving it a different point of application and new measures. Depsychiatrizing mental medicine so as to restore to its proper effectiveness a medical power that Charcot's imprudence (or ignorance) had led to produce illnesses improperly, and so false illnesses.

1. A first form of depsychiatrization begins with Babinski, in whom it finds its critical hero. Instead of seeking to produce the truth of the illness theatrically, it is more worthwhile to seek to reduce it to its strict reality, which perhaps is often only its susceptibility to letting itself be theatricalized: pithiatism. Henceforth, not only will the doctor's relation of domination over the patient not lose any of its rigor, but this rigor will focus on the reduction of the illness to its strict minimum: the necessary and sufficient signs for it to be diagnosed as a mental illness, and the indispensable techniques for ensuring the disappearance of these symptoms.

This involves, as it were, "Pasteurizing" the psychiatric hospital so as to obtain the same effect of simplification in the asylum that Pasteur had imposed on hospitals: directly linking diagnosis with therapy, knowledge of the nature of the illness with suppression of its symptoms. The moment of testing, the moment when the illness appears in its truth and arrives at its completion, no longer has to figure in the medical process. The hospital can become a silent place in which the form of medical power is maintained in its strictest aspect, but without having to encounter or confront madness itself. Let us call this "aseptic" and "asymptomatic" form of depsychiatrization "psychiatry of zero production." Psychosurgery and pharmacological psychiatry are its two most notable forms.

2. Another form of depsychiatrization is exactly the opposite of the preceding one. It involves making the production of madness in its truth as intense as possible, but in such a way that the relationships of power between doctor and patient are invested exactly in this production, that they remain appropriate for it, do not let themselves be outflanked by it, and keep it under control. The first condition for this maintenance of "depsychiatrized" medical power is its disconnection from all the specific effects of the asylum. Above all, to avoid the trap into which Charcot's thaumaturgy fell, one must prevent hospital discipline from making a mockery of medical authority and, in this place of collusions and obscure collective knowledge, ensure that the doctor's sovereign science is not caught up in mechanisms that it may have unwittingly produced. Hence, the rule of private consultation; the rule of a free contract between doctor and patient; the rule of the limitation of all the effects of the relationship to the level of discourse alone ("I ask just one thing of you, which is to speak, but to say really everything that crosses your mind"); the rule of discursive freedom ("you will no longer be able to boast of deceiving your doctor, since you will no longer be answering his questions; you will say what comes into your mind, without you even having to ask me what I think about it, and, if you want to deceive me by breaking this rule, I won't really be fooled; you will be the one caught in the trap, since you will have disrupted the production of truth and added further sessions to those you owe me"); and the rule of the couch that grants reality only to the effects produced in that privileged place and during that particular hour in which the doctor's power is exercised—a power that cannot be caught in any counter-effect, since it has withdrawn entirely into silence and invisibility.

Psychoanalysis can be read historically as the other major form of depsychiatrization prompted by the Charcot trauma: withdrawal outside the space of the asylum in order to get rid of the paradoxical effects of psychiatric surplus-power; but reconstitution of a truth-producing medical power in a space arranged so that that production of truth is always exactly adapted to that power. The notion of transference as the process essential to the cure is a way of thinking this perfect adaptation conceptually in the form of knowledge; the payment of money, the monetary counterpart of the transference, is a way of guaranteeing it in reality: a way of preventing the production of truth from becoming a counter-power that traps, nullifies and overturns the doctor's power.

These two major forms of depsychiatrization—both of which retain and preserve power, one because it invalidates the production of truth, the other because it tries to make the production of truth and medical power perfectly adapted to each other—are opposed by antipsychiatry. Instead of a withdrawal outside the space of the asylum, antipsychiatry involves its systematic destruction through work inside; and it involves transferring to the patient himself the power to produce his madness and the truth of his madness, instead of seeking to reduce it to zero. I think this enables us to understand what is at stake in antipsychiatry, which is not at all the truth value of psychiatry in terms of knowledge (of diagnostic accuracy or therapeutic effectiveness).

The struggle with, in, and against the institution is at the heart of antipsychiatry. When the great asylum structures were established at the beginning of the nineteenth century, they were justified by a marvelous harmony between the requirements of public order—which demanded protection from the disorder of the mad—and the needs of therapy—which demanded isolation of the patients.[6] Esquirol gave five main reasons to justify isolating the mad:

1. to ensure their personal safety and the safety of their families;
2. to free them from outside influences;
3. to overcome their personal resistances;
4. to subject them to a medical regimen;
5. to impose new intellectual and moral habits on them.

Clearly, it is always a question of power: mastering the madman's power; neutralizing external powers that may be exerted on him; establishing a power of therapy and training (*dressage*)—an "orthopedics"—over him. Now it is in fact the institution as site, form of distribution, and mechanism of these power relationships that antipsychiatry attacks. Beneath the justifications for confinement that, in a purified site, would make it possible to observe what is the case and where, when, and how one should intervene, antipsychiatry brings out the relationships of domination peculiar to the institutional relationship: "The doctor's pure power," says Basaglia, observing the effects of Esquirol's prescriptions in the twentieth century, "increases as vertiginously as the patient's power diminishes; the latter, simply by virtue of being confined, becomes a citizen without rights, handed over to the arbitrariness of the doctor and nurses, who can do with him what they like without any possibility of appeal."[7] It seems to me that we could situate the different forms of antipsychiatry in terms of their strategies with regard to these games of institutional power: escaping them in the form of a contract freely entered into by the two parties (Szasz[8]); creation of a privileged site where they must be suspended or rooted out if they are reconstituted (Kingsley Hall[9]); identify them one by one and gradually destroy them within a classic type of institution (Cooper at Villa 21[10]); link them up to other power relations outside the asylum that may have brought about an individual's segregation as a mental patient (Gorizia[11]). Power relations were the *a priori* of psychiatric practice: they conditioned how the asylum institution functioned, they determined the distribution of relationships between individuals within it, and they governed the forms of medical intervention. The typical reversal of antipsychiatry consists in placing them, rather, at the center of the problematic field and questioning them in a fundamental way.

Now, what these power relations involved first and foremost was the absolute right of nonmadness over madness. A right translated into terms of expertise being brought to bear on ignorance, of good sense (access to reality) correcting errors (illusions, hallucinations, fantasies), and of normality being imposed on disorder and deviation. This triple power constituted madness as a possible object of knowledge for a medical science, constituted it as illness, at the very moment that the "subject" affected by this illness was disqualified as mad—that is to say, stripped of all power and knowledge with regard to his illness: "We know enough about your suffering and its peculiarity (of which you have no idea) to recognize that it is an illness, we know this illness sufficiently for us to know that you cannot exercise any right over it and with regard to it. Our science enables us to call your madness illness, and that being the case, we doctors are qualified to intervene and diagnose a madness in you that prevents you from being a patient like other patients: hence you will be a mental patient." This interplay of a power relationship that gives rise to a knowledge, which in turn founds the rights of this power, is the characteristic feature of "classical" psychiatry. It is this circle that antipsychiatry undertakes to unravel: giving the individual the task and right of taking his madness to the limit, of taking it right to the end, in an experience to which others may contribute, but never in the name of a power conferred on them by their reason or normality; detaching behavior, suffering, and desire from the medical status given to them, freeing them from a diagnosis and symptomatology that had the value not just of classification, but of decision and decree; invalidating, finally, the great retranscription of madness as mental illness that was begun in the seventeenth and completed in the nineteenth century.

Demedicalization of madness is correlative with this fundamental questioning of power in antipsychiatric practice. This enables us to take the measure of the latter's opposition to "depsychiatrization," which seemed to be the characteristic feature of both psychoanalysis and psychopharmacology, both of which stemmed rather from an overmedicalization of madness. Straightaway the problem opens up of the possibility of freeing madness from that singular form of power-knowledge (*pouvoir-savoir*) that is knowledge (*connaissance*). Is it possible for the production of the truth of madness to be carried out in forms other than those of the knowledge relation? It will be said that this is a fictitious problem, a question that arises only in utopia. Actually, it is posed concretely every day with regard to the role of the doctor—of the statutory subject of knowledge—in the depsychiatrization project.

The seminar was devoted alternately to two subjects: the history of the hospital institution and of hospital architecture in the eighteenth century; and the study of medico-legal expertise in psychiatric questions since 1820.

1. J.E.D. Esquirol, *De la folie* (1816), §1, "Symptômes de la folie," in *Des maladies mentales considérées sous les rapports médical, hygiénique et médico-legal*, 2 volumes (Paris: Baillière, 1838), vol. 1, p. 16 (republished, Paris: Frénésie, 1989, in the series "Les Introuvables de la psychiatrie"); English translation, *Mental Maladies. A Treatise on Insanity*, trans. E.K. Hunt (Philadelphia: Lea and Blanchard, 1845) p. 27.
2. Ibid.
3. Esquirol, *De la folie*, § 5: "Traitement de la folie," pp. 132-133; *Mental Maladies*, p. 79.
4. D. Cooper, *Psychiatry and Antipsychiatry* (London: Tavistock, 1967), p. 14; French translation, *Psychiatrie et Antipsychiatrie*, trans. M. Braudeau (Paris: Éd. du Seuil, 1970), p. 33.
5. F. Basaglia, ed. *L'Istituzione negata. Rapporto da un ospedale psichiatrico* (Turin: Nuovo politecnico, 1968); French translation, *Les Institutions de la violence*, in F. Basaglia, ed., *L'Institution en négation. Rapport sur l'hôpital psychiatrique de Gorizia*, trans. L. Bonalumi (Paris: Éd. du Seuil, 1970), p. 105.
6. On this subject, see R. Castel, *Le Psychanalysme* (Paris: Maspero, 1973), pp. 150-153.
7. F. Basaglia, *L'institution en négation*, p. 111.
8. Thomas Stephen Szasz, is an American psychiatrist and psychoanalyst, born in Budapest in 1920. Professor of psychiatry at the University of Syracuse (New York), he was the only American psychiatrist to join the "antipsychiatric" movement that developed in the 1960s. His work carries out a critique of psychiatric institutions on the basis of a liberal and humanist conception of the subject and human rights. See his collection of articles, *Ideology and Insanity* (London: Calder & Boyars, 1970); French translation, *Idéologie et Folie. Essais sur la négation des valeurs humanistes dans la psychiatrie d'aujourd'hui*, trans. P. Sullivan (Paris: P.U.F., 1976), and *The Myth of Mental Illness* (New York: Harper & Row, 1961); French translation, *Le Mythe de la maladie mentale*, trans. D. Berger (Paris: Payot, 1975).
9. Kingsley Hall is one of three reception centers created in the 1960s. Situated in a working class area of London's East End, it is known through the account given by Mary Barnes, who spent five years there, and her therapist, Joe Berke, in their book, *Two Accounts of a Journey Through Madness* (London: MacGibbon and Kee, 1971); French translation, *Mary Barnes, un voyage autour de la folie*, trans. M. Davidovici (Paris: Seuil, 1973).
10. The experiment at Villa 21, which began in January 1962 in a psychiatric hospital in North West London, inaugurated the series of antipsychiatric community experiments, one of the best known of which is Kingsley Hall. David Cooper, its director until 1966, provides an account in *Psychiatry and Antipsychiatry*.
11. An Italian public psychiatric hospital in northern Trieste. In 1963 Franco Basaglia and his team began to undertake its institutional transformation. *L'institution en négation* provides an account of this anti-institutional struggle that became an example. Basaglia gave up the direction of Gorizia in 1968 in order to pursue his experiment in Trieste.

Course Context

Jacques Lagrange

THE LECTURES DEVOTED TO "Psychiatric Power," delivered between 7 November 1973 and 6 February 1974, have a paradoxical relationship to earlier works. There is continuity to the extent that, as Michel Foucault himself notes, they take off at the "the point reached by my earlier work, *Histoire de la folie*, or, at any rate, the point where it broke off" (lecture of 7 November 1973). In fact, *Histoire de la folie* had opened a space for future research that would have reconstructed "the constitutive but historically mobile ground that made possible the development of concepts from Esquirol and Broussais up to Janet and Freud."[1] This is confirmed by an (unpublished) interview with Colin Gordon and Paul Patton of 3 April 1978: "When I wrote *Histoire de la folie* I had in mind that it would be the first chapter, or the beginning, of a study that would continue up to the present."

But there is also discontinuity, as is evident from statements that are careful to mark shifts and, in his own words, "see what I had done from a new vantage point and in a clearer light."[2] The first works were interested in "mental illness" rather than "mental medicine,"[3] and in the Preface to the first edition, *Histoire de la folie* is presented as a "history not of psychiatry, but of madness itself, in its vivacity, before all capture by knowledge."[4] What's more, if the lectures take up the analysis at the point it left off in *Histoire de la folie*, they shift the stake and change both the terrain on which it is set out and the conceptual tools it puts to work. Hence, the question arises of what made these shifts possible and necessary? This involves understanding the production of this series of lectures, not only in the conceptual dynamic that leads them to give an important and strategic place to power and its apparatuses (*dispositifs*), but also in the field of problems that psychiatry had to confront in the 1970s that brought the question of power to the fore.

1. The Stake of the Course

The first lecture envisioned taking as a starting point the present situation of psychiatry in the light of the contribution of antipsychiatry to a reorientation of questions around the "power relations" that "conditioned how the asylum institution functioned" and "governed the forms of medical intervention,"[5] and proceeding to a retrospective analysis, starting from the present, of the historical formation of this apparatus of power. This is what gives this way of writing the history of psychiatry its specificity.[6] In contrast to approaches engaged in reconstructing the evolution of concepts and doctrines, or in analyzing the working of institutions in which psychiatry produces its effects, this way of analyzing the history of the psychiatric apparatus seeks to reveal its lines of force or fragility, its points of resistance or possible attack. Thus, it is no longer a question, as it was in the first writings, of putting psychiatry on trial and accusing it of concealing the real conditions of mental pathology behind nosological abstractions and a causal way of thinking.[7] Neither is it a question, as in *Histoire de la folie*, of understanding why, at a certain point in the history of our relationships with the mad, the latter were placed in specific, supposedly curative institutions. Henceforth, history is used to bring to light obscure relations of continuity which connect our present apparatuses to old bases linked to a given system of power, with the aim of isolating objectives of struggle: "In the domain of psychiatry," Foucault stated in May 1973, "it seems to me interesting to know how psychiatric knowledge, the psychiatric institution, was installed at the beginning of the nineteenth century (...) if we wish today to struggle against all the instances of normalization."[8]

Hence the originality of the course's problematic. For if at times there was a clear suspicion that the light of medical truth was supported by the shadow of force relations appearing in forms of authority and domination,[9] this was not accompanied by an analysis of the extraordinarily meticulous and skillfully hierarchized power of the asylum. Concerning power, Foucault later recognized: "I'm perfectly aware that I scarcely ever used the word and never had such a field of analyses at my disposal."[10]

What brought the problem of psychiatric power to the fore no doubt involved the conjunction of two elements: one specific to the conceptual dynamic of Foucault's research, and the other arising from the conjuncture of the 1970s.

This conjunction involves the shift carried out by Foucault that led him to replace references to institutional "violence" and modes of "domination" by what, in the 1971-1972 Collège de France lectures, "Penal Theories and Institutions," he will call "the basic forms of 'power-knowledge.' "[11] This reorientation is no doubt linked to the interest in medico-legal expertise—the subject matter of his seminar—which confronted him with the need to consider how and why a discourse that claimed to be scientific, but which was also questionable, brought with it effects of power in penal practice. This interest was strengthened by cases that had caused quite a stir: those of Denise Labbé and Jacques Algarron in 1955, or of Georges Rapin in 1960—referred to in the lecture of 8 January 1975 in his lectures on "Les Anormaux."[12] His attention to problems of the prison also convinced him that the problem of power should be approached "in terms of technology, in terms of tactics and strategy."[13] But, at the same time, the conjuncture must also have ensured that it was no longer a question of the theoretical justification of psychiatry, as it was in the fifties when, Foucault recalls, "one of the great problems that arose was that of the political status of science and the ideological functions it could serve,"[14] but suddenly revealed this elementary rock: power. Who has power? Over whom is it wielded? With regard to what is it exercised? How does it function? Of what use is it? What is its place amongst other powers?[15]

Certainly, the first response to the crisis of psychiatry in the post-war period was at least as much political as medical. Thus, the "*désaliéniste*" movement initiated by the communist psychiatrist Lucien Bonnafé, who set himself the goal of "opening our eyes to that alienated-alienating system established, with the assistance of the science of 'alienation' (...) in an order modeled on the principles and habits of a social order that excludes what disturbs it."[16]

But these denunciations of a psychiatry (*aliénisme*) accused of complicity with procedures of discrimination and exclusion do not succeed in formulating the question of psychiatric "power" as such. There are several reasons for this.

First of all, because the legacy of the war raised the question of not so much psychiatric power as of "the destitution of psychiatry."[17] Then, as Foucault notes, because "those psychiatrists in France who, for political reasons, would have been in a position to question the psychiatric apparatus (...) found themselves blocked by a political situation in which, basically, one did not want the question to be raised at all, because of what was taking place in the Soviet Union."[18] Finally, criticism may well have questioned the means available to psychiatric practice, or denounced the contradiction between what the psychiatric institution claims to do and what it really does, but it was still expressed in terms of the institutional project and its own criteria, proposing new, more supple modalities of intervention, further removed from the "medical" model, and appealing to a "different psychiatry," to use the terms of Lucien Bonnafé and Tony Laîne.[19] And if this questioning of psychiatric practices did not open up the question of "psychiatric power," it is no doubt because the struggles taken up could not get beyond the framework of psychiatric corporatism and defense of the medical corps of psychiatric hospitals, as Foucault emphasizes: "Because of the position of psychiatrists, most of whom were state employees, many were brought to question psychiatry from a defensive trade-union angle. Thus, those individuals who, by virtue of their abilities, their interests, and their openness to so many things, would have been able to address the problems of psychiatry, were led into impasses."[20] As a result of this, the problem of power could only find expression in a derivative mode: the trade-union struggle of the medical corps of psychiatric hospitals. As Foucault notes, psychiatrists "could struggle against medicine and the administration without being able to free themselves from either one or the other."[21]

It needed the intervention of events from outside, therefore, for psychiatry to be posed the question of its "power." This was a new political activism that, after '68, challenged a doctor's power to decide on a person's mental state, and proposed giving space for a different mode of reception of madness freed from psychiatric structures and ideology. Thus we see the development of local and dispersed sectional struggles in which Foucault saw "the insurrection of subjugated knowledge," that is to say, of forms of knowledge usually dismissed as poorly developed theoretically and of a lower status. There was, for example, the struggle of young psychiatrists whose less pronounced corporatist concerns allowed them to take a more political position that, on the model of GIP (Groupe Information Prisons), led to the creation of GIA (Groupe Information Asiles) in 1972, which was soon taken over by the "psychiatrized" themselves to denounce the scandals of arbitrary confinement. New alliances were forged with the "psychiatrized" that gave rise to the journal *Psychiatrisés en lutte* and the chance for the voices of mental health workers and patients to be heard.[22] As a counterpoint to the Congress of Psychiatry and Neurology on the theme of the *Formation et rôle de l'infirmier en psychiatrie* (Auxerre, September 1974), a movement developed that was run by nurses who were anxious to free themselves from a medical supervision that they accused of hiding their practice and knowledge, and who sought to reintegrate into their work social and political elements marginalized by "establishment" psychiatry. In this way the Association for the study and creation of the White Book of psychiatric institutions (AERLIP) was born, and the report of its counter-congress, *Des infirmiers psychiatriques prennent la parole.*[23] Seeing reference to "specialized competence" as conferring social legitimacy on the psychiatrist's "power," some so-called "anti-psychiatric" tendencies undertook to break with all the ways of taking care of patients that reduce the complexity of their situation to a technical problem to be dealt with by competent specialists. This view inspired the title of a work by Roger Gentis: *Psychiatry must be practiced/dismantled by everyone.*[24]

Learning from these movements, in June 1973 Foucault could say: "the importance of anti-psychiatry is that it challenges the doctor's power to decide on an individual's state of mental health."[25]

2. The Register of the Course

Fixing for oneself a "historico-political" stake involving the analysis of the conditions of formation of psychiatric knowledge and practice so as to define "strategies of struggle" calls for a shift of the points of problematization. It is difficult, in fact, to undertake such an analysis as long as the historical order is relativized by reference to some constitutive "ground," or, as in *Maladie mentale et Psychologie*, by reference to the original experience of a "true man."[26] Also, whereas in *Histoire de la folie* "the fine rectitude that leads rational thought to the analysis of madness as mental illness" is reinterpreted "in a vertical dimension,"[27] the lectures abandon this imaginary of depth so as to keep to the reality of surface effects. The lectures thus seek to grasp the discursive practices of psychiatry at their point of formation: an "apparatus (*dispositif*)" of power bringing together heterogeneous elements like discourses, modes of treatment, administrative measures and laws, regulatory arrangements, architectural plans, and so forth.[28] This involves a problem of "proximity," therefore, rather than one of "foundation." Hence a style of analysis according to a principle of "dispersion," one that multiplies knowledges and practices in order to bring out their components, reconstruct their associated spaces, and establish connections, thereby giving a "shape" to the documentary mass brought under analysis.

3. Conceptual Tools

Taking up the work begun by *Histoire de la folie* on a fresh basis requires a change of conceptual tools. First of all, reference to an "apparatus of power" replaces the reference to forms of "representation" to which, on Foucault's own admission, *Histoire de la folie* was still attached. Thus, the lectures replace a style of analysis that put a kind of "core of representations"[29] at its center—the image constructed of madness, the dread it provoked, a madness that portrayed "the *déjà-là* of death,"[30] etcetera—with reference to an "apparatus of power" that at a given moment has a dominant strategic function.

Second, recourse to the notion of "violence," which underlay analyses of the modes of treatment presented in the second and third parts of the work, has to be abandoned. In fact, the connotations of this notion make it particularly unsuitable for the analysis of the power relations and tactics that permeate psychiatric practice. Suggesting the idea of immediate coercion, of the irregular, unreflected exercise of power, it cannot reconstruct the idea of a calculated and meticulous exercise of power put to work in the asylum, and for which "violence" represents only a limit figure. Moreover, this notion, which makes power an agency for solely negative effects—exclusion, repression, interdiction—fails to take into account the productivity of psychiatric power and its capacity to produce discourses, forms of knowledge, and induce pleasure, etcetera. In short, bringing with it the idea of an unbalanced relation of force that makes it impossible for the other person to do anything other than what he is forced to do, this notion is hardly suited for reconstructing the complexity of games of power like the "great maneuvers" of the hysterics faced with medical power at Salpêtriere.[31]

Finally, the asylum "institution" is no longer to be taken as the essential reference, but analysis moves to its "outside" so as to resituate its constitution and operations within a technology of power typical of society. Hence the distance taken from *Histoire de la folie*, which, in Foucault's own words, claimed to be a "history of the psychiatric institution" and linked the formation of psychiatric knowledge to a process of the "institutionalization" of mental medicine.[32]

This is what gives this course its originality in comparison with all the critical tendencies that developed after the war, and which have in common that they take the asylum "institution" as their target, either in order to reform it, or to sublimate it, or to deny its legitimacy.

3.1. *Reforming the asylum institution.* Previously thought of as inseparably both a milieu for treatment and a space of segregation, shortly after the war there is a movement that accuses psychiatry (*aliénisme*) of complicity with practices of discrimination and exclusion, and that aims to free psychiatric intervention from the straitjacket of the asylum structure and its "stagnation" in order to make it an "activity entirely directed by a therapeutic perspective".[33] This is why Lucian Bonnafé calls his criticism "post-Esquirolism," demonstrating his concern to transform an inherited milieu of segregation into a real therapeutic instrument, by referring to "the mutation accomplished in the fundamental idea of the institution of treatment (. . .) formulated in 1822 with Esquirol's well-known clarity: 'In the hands of a skilled doctor, a lunatic asylum is an instrument of cure, it is the most powerful therapeutic agent against mental illnesses'."[34]

However, by asserting "the unity and indivisibility of prevention, prophylaxis, cure and post-cure,"[35] this movement at the same time increasingly took its distance from an asylum institution, constituted by the law of 30 June 1838 as the quasi-exclusive site of psychiatric intervention, in order to make it no more than one element among others in an apparatus directly linked to the community.[36] However, what represents an *aggiornamento* of psychiatry does not break with the latter's stakes: the constitution of "pathological" social behavior as an object of medical intervention and the assembly of apparatuses for deploying a therapeutic activity. So, although this movement may well identify the contradictions between what the institution claims to do and what it really does, it does not succeed in addressing the question of "psychiatric power," since the criticism is formulated in terms of the institutional project and of its own criteria.

3.2. *Sublimating the institution.* Whereas supporters of the first kind of "institutional psychotherapy" submitted to the existence of the establishments to which they were appointed, trying to use them as best they could on the therapeutic level, those of the second kind of "institutional psychotherapy" engaged in a radical modification of the therapeutic institution on the basis of a supposed discontinuity between psychiatry and psychoanalysis. Taking place on a completely different scene, involving a completely different type of relationship between patient and therapist, and organizing a different mode and formation of discourse, psychoanalysis appeared as a permanent resource with regard to the problems posed by asylum life, making it possible to readapt the structures of care. It is as if the institution is "sublimated" from within through a sort of collectivization of analytic concepts: transferences become "institutional"[37] and fantasies become "collective." The "political" criticism of psychiatry is then expressed in the name of the logic of the unconscious, and sources of resistance to the truth of desire, the hierarchical structures of institutions, and the socio-cultural representations of mental illness in which both therapists and patients are caught, are all equally denounced. Just as the hospital of Saint-Alban (Lozère) had been the reference point of the first "institutional psychotherapy," the La Borde clinic at Cour-Cheverny (Loir-et-Cher), opened in April 1953 by Jean Oury and Félix Guattari, represented the model realization of analytic "institutional psychotherapy" and its main center of diffusion.[38]

In a perspective focused on the institution's "interior," it was difficult to get back to what, outside the institution, determines its organization and role. So much so that the correlation of psychiatry with the public domain as organized by the law, which means that the psychiatrist takes on certain functions insofar as he exercises a public mandate, was dissolved in the field of discourses and the imaginary. Thus Tosquellès could say that "the problematic of power as it functions within treatment groups ends up, of itself, being expressed in the field of speech, usually as an imaginary projection in the collective discourse woven in the group in question."[39]

The corresponding Italian version—although Franco Basaglia (1924-1980) challenged the "anti-psychiatry" label[40]—criticized the asylum apparatus from a political point of view as the privileged site of the contradictions of capitalist society. Born in the very specific context of the law of 14 February 1904, which essentially gave the police and magistrates responsibility for aid to mental patients, and within the framework of Basaglia's experience of the deplorable conditions of the hospitalization of patients in 1961, when he took over direction of the psychiatric hospital at Gorizia, near Trieste, the Italian current was situated in a decidedly revolutionary perspective.[41] The Italians rejected the idea of a possible restructuring of the asylum, whether in the form of division into "sectors" or in that of "therapeutic communities," which they suspected of reviving the old apparatus of social control in a tolerant form;[42] they turned to practices based on a break with all the institutional mechanisms that could reproduce the separation and sequestration of the social life of those who have dealings with psychiatry: "Our action," Basaglia declared, "can only be continued in a negative dimension that, in itself, is a destruction and overcoming that, going beyond the coercive-carceral system of psychiatric institutions (. . .) moves onto the terrain of violence and exclusion inherent in the socio-political system."[43] With the aim of working towards the de-institutionalization of responsibility for patients, the Italian movement opted for an opening towards non-professionals and an alliance with political and trade-union forces of the left, which resulted in the constitution of *Psichiatrica Democratica* in 1974.

However, it was the English current, coming out of the work of David Cooper (1931-1989), Aaron Esterson and Ronald Laing (1927-1989) on schizophrenics and their family circle, which had the greatest impact in France.[44] In the sixties this movement developed a radical critique of psychiatry and its institutional and symbolic violence, accepting Cooper's label of "anti-psychiatry."[45] This violence was not only the physical violence of the constraints of confinement, but also the violence exercised by the analytic rationality that, through its nosological categorization, passes off as "mental illness"—which is subject to a specialized competence and calls for the establishment of a relationship of tutelage—the way in which a subject tries to respond to the oppression of which he has been the victim since birth and which is continued through various institutions delegated by society: family, school, work, etcetera. It is because of the "violence" of the psychiatric institution towards this "experience"—which the subject should take to its extreme limits if he would be "transformed" by it, in a process that Laing describes, in evangelical terms, as "conversion," or *metanoia*—that its space should be de-medicalized and removed from the relations of power deployed within it. "Instead of the mental hospital, a sort of re-servicing factory for human breakdowns, we need a place where people who have travelled further and, consequently, may be more lost than psychiatrists and other sane people, can find their way *further* into inner space and time, and back again."[46] From this came the constitution of the *Philadelphia Association*, in April 1965, by Cooper, Esterson, and Laing, with the aim of "organising places to welcome people who are suffering from or have suffered from mental illnesses," and to "change the way in which the facts of 'mental health' and 'mental illness' are considered."[47]

Now, whereas these post-War critical currents focus on the psychiatric institution as the point of problematization, the lectures shift the site by adopting the principle that "before tackling institutions, we have to deal with the relations of force in these tactical dispositions that permeate institutions."[48] Actually, the notion of the institution harbors a number of inadequacies and "dangers" to which Foucault returns on a number of occasions. First of all, approaching the problem of psychiatry through this notion amounts to starting with given, pre-constituted objects—the group and its functional regularities, the individual who is a member of the group, etcetera—when it would be more appropriate to analyze the procedures of its constitution at the level of dispositions of power and the processes of individualization they involve. Then again, by focusing on an institutional microcosm, one runs the risk of separating it from the strategies in which it is formed and in which it produces its effects, consequently "throwing in," as the lectures say, "all the psychological or sociological discourses." The problematic of the lectures can be compared, for example, with that of Erving Goffman's *Asylums*, to which Foucault pays tribute on a number of occasions.[49] Certainly, one merit of the book is to make it possible to escape from medical rationalizations by "de-specifying" the psychiatric institution, so to speak, by placing it within a range of different structures—school, prison, etcetera—through the perspective of the notion of *total institutions* [English in original; G.B.] which typify establishments specialized in supervising individuals and controlling their mode of life. But this quasi-ethnographic approach to the asylum institution has its limits. Taking the latter as, in effect, an autonomous "totality," so as simply to situate it in a range of other institutions, it fails to show that the asylum is a response to an evolving historical problematic. Consequently, the nature of the break constitutive of the asylum site can only be thought in a static way, through binary oppositions like inside/outside, being confined/leaving, etcetera, which mark the barriers "to social intercourse with the outside and to departure that" total institutions often build "right into the physical plant, such as locked doors, high walls, barbed wire, cliffs, water, forests, or moors."[50] If, for this image of a "shut up" space, we substitute the idea of "an enclosed space for a confrontation, the site of a duel, an institutional field in which victory and submission are at stake,"[51] then the asylum break acquires a new dimension. This "enclosed" milieu then appears for what it really is: a milieu actively cut out, that is to say, captured from old forms of custody through historical processes that make the mad person emerge as someone who is differentiated less by reference to the family than within a technico-administrative field. This is emphasized in the lecture of 5 December 1973: "The mad individual now emerges (...) as a danger for society, and no longer as someone who may jeopardize the rights, wealth, and privileges of a family." At the same time, the central place of the psychiatrist, emphasized by Goffman, takes on another dimension; the psychiatrist is not distinguished from the madman by the fact that he is free, but by the fact that he intervenes as an ambassador of the external world, charged with imposing the norms of society within the asylum. He is "someone who must give reality that constraining force by which it will be able to take over the madness, completely penetrate it, and make it disappear as madness."[52]

Whereas the problem for Goffman is the problem posed by the institution itself and its functioning, the problem to which the lectures are devoted is that of how a certain technique, connected to social and political structures, authorizes "the rationalization of the management of the individual."[53]

From this derives the particular style of an archeology of the psychiatric institution, which, from George III to Charcot, multiplies wonderful panoptic "scenes" that reveal the operations and procedures making up this "microphysics" of power, and break up what solidity the asylum institution had. As the manuscript for the lecture of 14 November 1973 makes clear, by "scene" we should understand, "not a theatrical episode, but a ritual, a strategy, a battle"; scenes which, inserted in the work of the analysis like fragments of mirror, bring together, in a glance, the theoretical implications that the argument will develop.

Approaching the apparatus of psychiatry in this way, by reference to mechanisms of power, weakens the foundation on the basis of which psychiatry deployed its theoretical and practical conquests: a requirement of specificity. In fact, from its constitution as a "special medicine" endowed with "special establishments," "specialized" doctors, the psychiatrists, and "special" legislation, the law of 30 June 1838, up until the attempts at transforming its institutional structures just after the war, this idea of a "specificity" of mental medicine constitutes a main theme around which, we can say, the best part of the profession has rallied.[54]

4. Points of Problematization

The analysis of the psychiatric apparatus is structured around three axes: that of power, insofar as the psychiatrist is established as a subject acting on others; the axis of truth, insofar as the insane individual is constituted as an object of knowledge; and the axis of subjectivation, since the subject has to make the norms imposed on him his own.

4.1. *Power.* Defined in the seventies with the problematic of knowledge-power, this axis shifts previous questionings. Basically, the first texts, in fact, addressed to psychiatry the question: "What you say is true? Give me the grounds of your truth!" Henceforth the question, the demand is: "Give us the grounds of your power! By what right do you exercise it? In whose name? To what advantage?" "Power" therefore, and no longer "violence" as in the previous works. As a result, there is a change in the paradigmatic figure around which the criticism of the Anglo-Saxon "anti-psychiatrists" was ordered, and which put the question of the "violence" exercised by society in general and psychiatry in particular at its core:[55] the schizophrenic.[56]

However, when we approach the psychiatric apparatus by reference to the mechanisms of power that organize it, it is the hysteric who, by laying the "trap" of the lie for a doctor like Charcot armed with the highest medical knowledge, paradigmatically portrays the militant underside of psychiatric power.[57] This is why, in Foucault's view, the hysteric deserves the title of the first "militant of anti-psychiatry," as he puts it in the lecture of 23 January 1974, since, by her "maneuvers," she challenges the doctor's role of "responsibility for producing the truth of illness within the hospital space."[58] Foucault can also declare in his contribution to a colloquium organized by Henri Ellenberger in May 1973: "The age of anti-psychiatry began when one suspected, and then, soon afterwards, was sure, that Charcot, the great master of madness, the person who made it appear and disappear, was not the person who produced the truth of the illness, but the one who fabricated its artifice."[59]

Now, this power to which the lectures are devoted has a double characteristic. In the final instance its point of application is bodies: their distribution in the asylum space, their ways of behaving, their needs, their pleasures; in short, it is a power "commanded by all the dispositions of a kind of microphysics of bodies." Moreover, the relations of power installed between the psychiatrist and his patient are fundamentally unstable, constituted by struggles and confrontations in which points of resistance are present at every moment. This is the case with these "counter maneuvers" by which the hysterics shake Charcot's power, escaping the categorizations to which he wanted to assign them, thereby giving a new impetus to the apparatus of medical power-knowledge on the basis of these resistances, to the point that, Foucault says, "a crisis" is opened up "that had to lead to anti-psychiatry."[60]

4.2. *Knowledge and truth.* As the lecture of 5 December 1973 recalls, "as a disciplinary system, the asylum is also a site for the formation of a certain type of discourse of truth." Hence the analyses of the ways in which apparatuses of power and games of truth are articulated. This is the case for the "proto-psychiatric" modality, in which a game is organized around the delirious conviction, within the regime of a "test" in which the doctor is posed as the ambiguous master of reality and truth, or, on the other hand, a game in which the question of truth no longer arises in the confrontation of doctor and patient, since it is now only posed within psychiatric power established as medical science. In this mode of analysis we can see that truth is called upon less as an intrinsic property of statements than at the level of its functionality, through the legitimation it provides for the discourses and practices on the basis of which psychiatric power organizes its exercise, and by the mode of exclusion it authorizes.

4.3. *Subjection* (assujettissement). The therapist who approaches the individual to be treated from the outside, at the same time as he resorts to procedures that enable him to extract from this individual his inner subjectivity—questioning, anamnesis, etcetera—puts the subject in the position of having to interiorize the orders and norms imposed on him. In the lecture of 21 November 1973, the problem is also broached from the angle of the modes of subjection that make the subject appear as a complex and variable "function" of regimes of truth and discursive practices.

However, these lectures, which sought to give a sequel, on new bases, to *Histoire de la folie*, will remain without future. For, in these years, circumstances are such as to give preference to participation in effective action, instead of, as Foucault says, the "scribbling of books." Thus, from 1972 he recognized that "writing today a sequel to my *Histoire de la folie*, which would continue up to the present, is for me without interest. On the other hand, a concrete political action in favor of prisoners seems to me to be highly meaningful."[61] However, at the same time, Foucault was preparing *Discipline and Punish. Birth of the Prison.*

1. Michel Foucault, *Histoire de la folie à l'âge classique* (Paris: Gallimard, 2nd edition, 1972) p. 541. This is omitted from the abridged English translation: Michel Foucault, *Madness and Civilization. A History of Insanity in the Age of Reason*, trans. Richard Howard (New York: Random House, 1965 and London: Tavistock, 1967).
2. Michel Foucault, "Usage des plaisirs et techniques de soi," in *Dits et Écrits, 1954-1988*, ed. D. Defert and F. Ewald, with the collaboration of J. Lagrange (Paris: Gallimard, 1994) vol. 4, p. 545; English translation, "Introduction," *The Use of Pleasure. The History of Sexuality, vol. 2*, trans. Robert Hurley (New York: Pantheon Books, 1985) p. 11.
3. Michel Foucault, *Maladie mentale et Personnalité* (Paris: Presses universitaires de France, 1954) and the modified version of this, *Maladie mentale et Psychologie* (Paris: Presses universitaires de France, 1962); English translation, *Mental Illness and Psychology*, trans. Alan Sheridan (New York: Harper and Row, 1976).
4. Michel Foucault, "Préface" to *Folie et Déraison. Histoire de la folie à l'âge classique* (Paris: Plon, 1961) p. vii (omitted from the French 1972 edition and from the English translation); reprinted in *Dits et Écrits*, vol. 1, p. 192.
5. "Course summary," above, p. 345.
6. That is, its specificity in relation to both earlier and later studies of the history of psychiatry. See in particular, E.H. Ackerknecht, *A Short History of Psychiatry* (New York: Hafner, 1968).
7. Thus, Foucault's "Introduction" to L. Binswanger, *Le Rêve et l'Existence*, trans. J. Verdeaux (Paris: Desclée de Brouwer, 1954) denounces the tendency of psychiatrists to consider "the illness as an 'objective process,' and the patient as an inert thing in which the process takes place" p. 104. Reprinted in *Dits et Écrits*, vol. 1, p. 109; English translation, "Dream, Imagination and Existence. An Introduction to Ludwig Binswanger's *Dream and Existence*" trans. Forrest Williams, in M. Foucault and Ludwig Binswanger, *Dream and Existence*, trans. Forrest Williams and Jacob Needleman, ed. Keith Hoeller, Special Issue from *Review of Existential Psychology and Psychiatry*, vol. XIX, no. 1, 1984-85, p. 66.
8. "La vérité et les formes juridiques" *Dits et Écrits*, vol. 2, p. 644; English translation, "Truth and Juridical Forms" trans. Robert Hurley, *The Essential Works of Michel Foucault 1954-1984, Vol. 3: Power*, ed. James D. Faubion, trans. Robert Hurley and others (New York: The New Press, 2000). See also the interview with Foucault on Radio-France, 8 October 1972, "Punir ou guérir": "I think this historical analysis is politically important inasmuch as it is necessary to locate exactly what one is struggling against."
9. "If the medical personage could isolate madness, it was not because he knew it, but because he mastered it; and what for positivism would be an image of objectivity was only the other side of this domination" *Histoire de la folie*, p. 525; *Madness and Civilization*, p. 272.
10. "Entretien avec Michel Foucault" *Dits et Écrits*, vol. 3, p. 146; English translation, "Truth and Power" trans. Colin Gordon, *Essential Works of Foucault, 3*, p. 117.
11. "Théories et institutions pénales" *Dits et Écrits*, vol. 2, p. 390; English translation, "Penal Theories and Institutions" trans. Robert Hurley, *The Essential Works of Michel Foucault, 1954-1984, vol. 1: Ethics: subjectivity and truth*, ed. Paul Rabinow, trans. Robert Hurley and others (New York: The New Press, 1997) p. 17.
12. Michel Foucault, *Les Anormaux. Cours au Collège de France, 1974-1975*, ed. V. Marchetti and A. Saomoni (Paris: Gallimard/Seuil, 1999) pp. 16-20 and pp. 143-144; English translation, *Abnormal. Lectures at the Collège de France* 1974-1975, ed. Valerio Marchetti and Antonella Salomoni, English series ed. Arnold I. Davidson, trans. Graham Burchell (New York: Picador, 2003) pp. 16-21 and pp. 154-156.
13. "Les rapports de pouvoir passent à l'intérieur des corps" *Dits et Écrits*, vol. 3, p. 229.
14. "Entretien avec Michel Foucault" p. 140; "Truth and Power" p. 111.
15. See above, "Course Summary."
16. L. Bonnafé, "Sources du désaliénisme" in *Désaliéner? Folie(s) et Société(s)* (Toulouse: Presses universitaires du Mirail/Privat, 1991) p. 221.
17. *Esprit*, 20th year, December 1952, "Misère de la psychiatrie. La vie asilaire. Attitudes de la société (Textes de malades, de médecins, d'un infirmier, dénoncant la vie asilaire chronicisante, la surpopulation, le règlement modèle de 1838)." Foucault refers to this "remarkable number of *Esprit*" in *Maladie mentale et Personnalité*, p. 109, n. 1.

18. An allusion to the cases of arbitrary confinement, the most famous cases of which are those of General Grigorenko, arrested in February 1964 under the charge of anti-Soviet activities and confined in the Serbski Institute in Moscow, and Vladimir Borissov, confined in the special psychiatric hospital of Leningrad—for the liberation of whom a campaign was led by Victor Fainberg, supported by some intellectuals including David Cooper and Michel Foucault. See, "Enfermement, psychiatrie, prison" *Dits et Écrits*, vol. 3, pp. 332-360. There was also the confinement of the dissident Wladimir Boukovski in autumn 1971. See W. Boukovski, *Une nouvelle maladie mentale en URSS: l'opposition* (Paris: Le Seuil, 1971).
19. T. Laîne, "Une psychiatrie différente pour le malaise à vivre," *La Nouvelle Critique*, no. 59, December 1972; reprinted in the Éditions de la Nouvelle Critique, April 1973, pp. 23-36.
20. "Entretien avec Michel Foucault (*Conversazione con Michel Foucault*)" *Dits et Écrits*, vol. 4, p. 61; English translation, "Interview with Michel Foucault" trans. Robert Hurley, *Essential Works of Foucault*, 3, p. 260 [English translation slightly amended; G.B.].
21. "Michel Foucault. Les réponses du philosophe" *Dits et Écrits*, vol. 2, p. 813.
22. In April 1970 a journal of the extreme left had already appeared which sought to struggle against "class psychiatry," *Cahiers pour la folie*, a special issue of which, *Clés pour Henri Colin*, June 1973, was devoted to the security unit for difficult patients of the Villejuif psychiatric hospital. The journal *Marge* devoted its April-May 1970 issue to this "*rottenness of psychiatry*." In November 1973 a pamphlet appeared entitled: *Psychiatrie: la peur change de camp*, and in December 1973 number 0 of *Psychiatrie et Lutte de classe* appeared which put itself forward as "a site of theoretical development for the formation of slogans promoting a revolutionary consciousness of 'social' workers in connection with the battle of the working class" (p. 1). On the role of the "young psychiatrists" see "Entretien avec Michel Foucault" *Dits et Écrits*, vol. 4, p. 60; "Interview with Michel Foucault," *Essential Works of Foucault*, 3, pp. 259-260.
23. *Des infirmiers psychiatriques prennent la parole* (Paris: Capédith, 1974).
24. M. Burton and R. Gentis, *La psychiatrie doit être faite/défaite par tous* (Paris: Maspero, 1973).
25. "Le monde est un grand asile" *Dits et Écrits*, vol. 2, p. 433.
26. *Maladie mentale et Psychologie*, p. 2; *Mental Illness and Psychology*, p. 2.
27. *Histoire de la folie*, p. 40 (omitted from the English translation).
28. "Le jeu de Michel Foucault" *Dits et Écrits*, vol. 3, p. 299; abridged English translation "The Confession of the Flesh," trans. Colin Gordon, in M. Foucault, *Power/Knowledge. Selected Interviews and Other Writings 1972-1977*, ed. Colin Gordon, trans. Colin Gordon and others (Brighton: Harvester Press, 1980) p. 194. In an unpublished interview with Paul Patton and Colin Gordon of 3 April 1978, Foucault says: "What I study is an architecture."
29. See above, lecture of 7 November 1973, pp. 14-15.
30. *Histoire de la folie*, p. 26; *Madness and Civilization*, p. 16.
31. See above, lecture of 6 February 1974, p. 308, where Foucault marks the difference between his problematic and that of the Anglo-Saxon and Italian anti- psychiatry movements that, taking as their target the "violence" exercised by society in general and psychiatry in particular, model themselves on the paradigmatic figure of the "schizophrenic" who, refusing to constitute an alienated "false self" subservient to social demands, tears off the masks of this everyday violence, and thanks to which, as R.D. Laing says, "the light began to break through the cracks in our all-too-closed minds"; R.D. Laing, *The Politics of Experience and the Bird of Paradise* (Harmondsworth: Penguin, 1967) p. 107; French translation, *La Politique de l'expérience. Essai sur l'aliénation et l'Oiseau de Paradis*, trans. Cl. Elsen (Paris: Stock, 1969), p. 89. See the works of David Cooper: (1) *Psychiatry and Antipsychiatry* (London: Tavistock Publications, 1967); French translation, *Psychiatrie et Anti-psychiatrie*, trans. M. Braudeau (Paris: Le Seuil, 1970); (2) with R.D. Laing, *Reason and Violence* (London: Tavistock Publications, 1964); French translation, *Raison et Violence. Dix ans de la philosophie de Sartre (1950-1960)*, trans. J.-P. Cottereau, Avant-propos by J.-P. Sartre (Paris: Payot, 1972). See also F. Basaglia and others, "L'Istituzione negata. Rapporto da un ospedale psichiatrico," in *Nuovo Politecnico*, vol. 19, Turin, 1968; French translation, F. Basaglia, ed., *L'Institution en négation. Rapport su l'hôpital psychiatrique de Gorizia*, trans. I. Bonalumi (Paris: Le Seuil, 1970).
32. "Pouvoir et savoir" *Dits et Écrits*, vol. 3, p. 414.
33. L. Bonnafé, "Le milieu hospitalier au point de vue psychothérapique, ou Théorie et pratique de l'hôpital psychiatrique," *La Raison*, no. 17, 1958, p. 7.

34. L. Bonnafé, "De la doctrine post-esquirolienne. I. Problèmes généraux," *Information psychiatrique*, vol. 1, no. 4, April 1960, p. 423. The reference is to J.E.D. Esquirol, "Mémoires, statistiques et hygiéniques sur la folie. Préambule," in *Des maladies mentales, considérées sous les rapports médical, hygiénique et médico-légal* (Paris: J.-B. Baillière, 1838), vol. 2, p. 398.
35. L. Bonnafé, "Conclusions des journées psychiatriques de mars 1945," *Information psychiatrique*, 22nd year, no. 2, October 1945, p. 19.
36. L. Bonnafé, "De la doctrine post-esquirolienne, II. Examples appliqués," *Information psychiatrique*, vol. 1, no. 5, May 1960, p. 580: "The pivot of the service is no longer the asylum, but the town, at the heart of the territory in which the psychiatrist's function is exercised, extended to the protection of mental health."
37. [a] H. Torrubia, "Analyse et interprétation du transfert en thérapeutique institutionelle," *Revue de psychothérapie institutionelle*, vol. 1, 1965, pp. 83-90. [b] J. Oury, [i] "Dialectique du fantasme, du transfert et du passage à l'acte dans la psychothérapie institutionelle," *Cercle d'études psychiatriques* (Paris: Laboratoire Specia, 1968); [ii] "Psychothérapie institutionelle: transfert et espace du dire" *Information psychiatrique*, vol. 59, no. 3, March 1983, pp. 413-423. [c] J. Ayme, Ph. Rappard, H. Torrubia, "Thérapeutique institutionelle," *Encyclopédie médico-psychiatrique. Psychiatrie*, vol. 3, October 1964, col. 37-930, G. 10, pp. 1-12.
38. On the La Borde clinic, see the special issue of the review *Recherches*, no. 21, March-April 1976: *Histoires de La Borde. Dix ans de psychothérapie institutionelle à la clinique de Cour-Cheverny*, complement, p. 19.
39. F. Tosquellès, "La problématique du pouvoir dans les collectifs de soins psychiatriques," *La Nef*, 28th year, no. 42, January-March, 1971: *L'Antipsychiatrie*, p. 98.
40. He stated this in an intervention at the University of Vincennes on 5 February 1971: "Personally, I do not accept the label anti-psychiatrist." (Personal notes; J.L.)
41. On the Italian movement, see: [a] F. Basaglia, [i] ed., *Che cos'è la psichiatria?* (Turin: Einaudi, 1973); French translation, *Qu'est-ce qu la psychiatrie?* trans. R. Maggiori (Paris: Presses universitaires de France, 1977); [ii] "L'Istituzione negata. Rapporto da un ospedale psichiatrico"; *L'Institution en négation. Rapport su l'hôpital psychiatrique de Gorizia*; [iii] "Le rapport de Trieste," in *Pratiques de la folie. Pratiques et folie* (Paris: Éd. Solin, 1981) pp. 5-70. On this current, see also: [b] G. Jervis, "Il Mito dell'Antipsichiatria," *Quaderni Piacentini*, no. 60-61, October 1976; French translation, *Le Mythe de l'antipsychiatrie*," trans. B. de Fréminville (Paris: Éd. Solin, 1977). [c] R. Castel, "Le ville natale de 'Marco Cavallo,' emblème de l'antipsychiatrie," *Critique*, no. 435-436, August-September 1983, pp. 628-636. More generally, on anti-psychiatry movements in Europe, see [d] *Réseau. Alternative à la psychiatrie. Collectif international* (Paris: Union générale d'Édition, 1977).
42. F. Basaglia, "L'assistance psychiatrique comme problème anti-institutionnel: une expérience italienne," *Information psychiatrique*, vol. 47, no. 2, February 1971: "The tolerant institution, the other face of the violent institution, continues to perform its original function without changing its strategic and structural meaning, or the games of power on which it is based."
43. F. Basaglia, "Les institutions de la violence," in *L'institution en négation*, p. 137.
44. The works of English anti-psychiatry began to be translated and known in France following a colloquium organized in 1967 in Paris by the Fédération des groupes d'Études et de Recherches institutionnelles (FGERI), to which Cooper and Laing were invited. See [a] R. Castel, *La Gestion des risques. De l'antipsychiatrie à l'après-psychanalyse*, 1 § "Grandeurs et servitudes contestaires" (Paris: Éd. de Minuit, 1981) pp. 19-33. [b] J. Postel and D.F. Allen, "History and anti-psychiatry in France" in M. Micale and R. Porter, eds. *Discovering the History of Psychiatry* (Oxford: Oxford University Press, 1994) pp. 384-414. [c] *Recherches* special issue *Enfance aliénée*, vol. 2, December 1968 in which there are contributions from D. Cooper, "Aliénation mentale et aliénation sociale" pp. 48-50, and R. Laing, "Metanoia. Some experiences at Kingsley Hall" pp. 51-57.
45. "A more radical questioning led some of us to put forward conceptions and procedures that seem to be absolutely opposed to traditional conceptions and procedures, and which can in fact be considered as the germ of an anti-psychiatry" David Cooper, *Psychiatrie et Antipsychiatrie*, p. 9. (This passage does not appear in the original English, *Psychiatry and Anti-Psychiatry*.)

46. R.D. Laing, *The Politics of Experience*, pp. 105-6; *La politique de l'expérience*, p. 88.
47. Report on the activity of the *Philadelphia Association* (1965-1967), quoted in the article by G. Baillon, "Introduction à l'antipsychiatrie," *La Nef*, 28th year, no. 42, January-May 1971: *L'Anti-Psychiatrie*, p. 23. This is why, in his contribution, "Histoire de la folie et antipsychiatrie," to the colloquium at Montreal organized by H. Ellenberger on 9 May 1973: "Faut-il interner les psychiatres?"—to which he refers in "Michel Foucault: An Interview by Stephen Riggins" *Essential Works of Foucault, vol. 1*, pp. 131-132; French translation, "Une interview de Michel Foucault par Stephen Riggins" trans. F. Durand-Bogaert, *Dits et Écrits*, vol. 4, pp. 536-537—he could say: "In the form of anti-psychiatry practiced by Laing and Cooper, it is a question of the de-medicalization of the space in which madness is produced. Consequently, it is an anti-psychiatry in which the power relationship is reduced to zero. This de-medicalization implies not only an institutional reorganization of psychiatric establishments; it is undoubtedly more than a simple epistemological break; the question should perhaps be posed more in terms of an ethnological break than of a political revolution. Maybe it is not just our economic system, or even our present form of rationalism, but the whole of our immense social rationality as it has been woven historically since the Greeks that refuses today to recognize, at the very heart of our society, an experience of madness that may be a test of truth not under the control of medical power" (typescript p. 19).
48. See above, lecture of 7 November 1973, pp. 15-16.
49. E. Goffman, *Asylums: Essays on the Social Situation of Mental Patients and Other Inmates* (New York: Doubleday, 1961); French translation, *Asiles: Études sur la condition sociale des malades mentaux et autres reclus*, trans. L. and Cl. Laîné, with Preface by R. Castel (Paris: Éd. de Minuit, 1968). See M. Foucault [i] "La vérité et les formes juridiques"; pp. 611-612; "Truth and Juridical Forms" pp. 75-76. [ii] "Foucault Examines Reason in Service of State Power" an interview with M. Dillon in *Campus Report*, 12th Year, no. 6, October 1979, pp. 5-6; French translation, "Foucault étudie la raison d'État" trans. F. Durand-Bogaert, *Dits et Écrits*, vol. 3, pp. 802-803. [iii] "Foucault Examines Reason in Service of State Power" *The Three Penny Review*, 1st Year, no. 1, 1980, pp. 4-5; French translation, "*Foucault Étudie la raison d'État*" trans. F. Durand-Bogaert, *Dits et Écrits*, vol. 4, p. 38 (this is a modified version of the previous reference), and [iv] "Space, Knowledge, and Power" an interview with P. Rabinow, in *Essential Works of Foucault, 3*, pp. 356-357; French translation, "Espace, savoir et pouvoir" trans. F. Durand-Bogaert, *Dits et Écrits*, vol. 4, p. 277.
50. E. Goffman, *Asylums*, p. 4.
51. See above, "Course summary," p. 339.
52. See above, lecture of 12 December 1973, p. 132.
53. "Foucault Examines Reason in Service of State Power," pp. 4-5; "*Foucault Étudie la raison d'État*," p. 38.
54. The battle of Henri Ey (1900-1977) to maintain the "specificity" of psychiatry against psychoanalysis and against biological and socio-political temptations, testifies to this, as does the appearance of a collection edited by F. Caroli entitled, precisely, *Spécificité de la psychiatrie* (Paris: Masson, 1980).
55. David Cooper, *Psychiatry and Anti-Psychiatry*: "In so far as psychiatry represents the interests or pretended interests of the sane ones, we may discover that, in fact, violence in psychiatry is pre-eminently the violence *of* psychiatry" p. 14.
56. See above, note 31.
57. See above, lecture of 6 February 1974, p. 304 *sq*.
58. See above, "Course summary" p. 342.
59. "Histoire de la folie et antipsychiatrie" (typescript) p. 12. Summarized with some changes in the "Course summary."
60. Ibid.
61. "Le grand enfermement" *Dits et Écrits*, vol. 2, p. 301.

Index of Names

Index of Notions

Index Of Places

www.ingramcontent.com/pod-product-compliance
Lightning Source LLC
LaVergne TN
LVHW090433230725
816804LV00022B/838
9780312203313